Place-names of Scotland

Place-names of Scotland

Iain Taylor

BIRLINN

Tha an leabhar seo mar chuimhneachan air mo phàrantan,
William John Taylor agus Isobel Stewart à Eilginn

This book is in memory of my parents,
William John Taylor and Isobel Stewart from Elgin

First published in 2011 by
Birlinn Limited
West Newington House
10 Newington Road
Edinburgh
EH9 1QS

www.birlinn.co.uk

ISBN: 978 1 78027 005 0

British Library Cataloguing-in-Publication Data
A catalogue record for this book is available from the British
Library

Typeset by Brinnoven, Livingston
Printed and bound by Clays Ltd, St Ives plc

Contents

Preface

Place-names are a constant source of debate. Who was *Edwin* whose name is said to live on in that of Edinburgh? Are the *drum* and *chapel* still to be found in Drumchapel? Which *king* had a *seat* at Kingseat in Perthshire? This book aims to address these and similar questions, but in the field of Scottish place-names the answers are not always what might be expected at first sight.

In their current form or forms and in their own right, place-names convey meaning whether we seek to analyse their component parts or not. As it stands, *Elgin* (or *Eilginn* in Gaelic), for instance, means the main town in Moray situated on the River Lossie, located between Lossiemouth and Rothes, and between Lhanbryde and Alves. As a word capable of analysis, *Elgin* breaks down into the element *Eilg*, from a root suggesting 'noble' and possibly a poetic term for Ireland, and a possible diminutive ending *-in*. Thus *Elgin* is shown to be a commemorative name rather than one descriptive of its location or founder. The various Elgins throughout the world do not *per se* mean 'little Ireland', but rather suggest that their founders came from Moray and wished to remember Elgin. It may be the case that many of Scotland's Norse names in particular commemorate places in Norway rather than describe the new settlements in the new country.

The creation of names in one language superimposed upon those preceding ones have helped obscure the origin of many names and cause uncertainty and misunderstanding. Conversely, the settling in Scotland by different groups and cultures over the centuries has given the country's place-names a richness, variety and complexity absent in countries such as Iceland and Denmark where the bulk of names stem from one language only. It is beyond the scope of this book to delve into the minutiae of Scottish history, but the peoples and influences with an effect on place-names are outlined in the Introduction. Additionally, this book concentrates on names created in Gaelic or possessing a Gaelic form, as hitherto it has not been possible to find the Gaelic names or forms of places in one accessible volume.

In order to save space in the gazetteer sections, this book lists the most common generic elements from the languages in which place-names were created. In the gazetteer section, each entry takes the following format. The current English name of a place is given in bold type followed in brackets by the name of the county or island in which it is located. If the place has a current or attested Gaelic name, that is then given in plain type. This is followed by the derivation of the name in quotation marks, followed by any other relevant comments, with cross-references to other names shown in bold. Where a place-name in English form, such as *Balmore*, has an obviously Gaelic source, in this case *Baile Mór*, but where that Gaelic original is not in current usage nor found in literary sources, this is shown in the explanatory text rather than in the first line of the entry. Generally, the language(s) from which the place-names are derived are stated in the explanatory text, but where no language is given, it should be assumed that the name was created in Gaelic. In some cases a place-name is explained with reference to another name, as in *Strath of Pitcalnie*, where readers should refer back to *Pitcalnie* for the derivation of that name. Finally, although for the last twenty or more years Gaelic spelling has used only a grave accent to mark long vowels, this book also uses the acute accent as an indication of pronunciation.

Some points on terminology need to be clarified. A name such as *Balmaha* is termed an 'English form' rather an 'English name' because although *Balmaha* is used in English to identify the village on the eastern banks of Loch Lomond, it was created originally in Gaelic and the village is known as *Baile Mo Thatha* in that language. Likewise, *Siabost* is termed a 'Gaelic form' rather than a 'Gaelic name' because although *Siabost* is used in Gaelic to refer to the township on the West Side of Lewis between Barvas and Carloway, it is a Norse name, from *Sjábólsta∂r*. The English form of that name is *Shawbost* which came into English via the Gaelic sound system, as did all Nordic names outside the south-west and Orkney, Shetland and north-east Caithness.

A number of maps are to be found towards the end of the book, showing the distribution of peoples and of important place-name elements.

This is not an academic treatise on Scotland's place-names, which lies more within the remit of the School of Scottish Studies and the recently formed Scottish Place-Name Society. Rather, this is an attempt to present in accessible format a list of names of the larger settlements, islands, areas, rivers, lochs and mountains. The best sources in print, dealing with place-names at a national and local level, are given in the bibliography. In certain instances it has not been possible to work out what a name means. This is either because the sources themselves are unclear or because it is beyond the linguistic ability of the compiler.

Despite the existence of excellent publications on place-names, there is still a need for study and dissemination of information, and the foundation of a state-funded Place-names Commission along the lines of that in Norway or Ireland would be a welcome development.

Tha mi fada an comain a h-uile duine, nach gabh ainmeachadh an seo, a thug cuideachadh dhomh le bhith a' trusadh ainmean às na sgìrean aca fhèin. Cha phàigh taing sibh.

Introduction

The place-names of Scotland can be categorised in a number of ways, but for the purposes of this Introduction they will be grouped according to the language or languages in which they were created. This immediately introduces a historical element in that the various languages of Scotland, although co-existing in different areas at different periods, appeared and disappeared at different times.

With some exceptions, all of Scotland's place-names fall into one of two linguistic groupings, Celtic and Germanic, both of which are branches of the Indo-European language family. The Celtic languages themselves form two groups, Goidelic or Q-Celtic (comprising modern Scottish Gaelic, Irish and Manx) and Brythonic or P-Celtic (comprising modern Welsh, Cornish and Breton, as well as Pictish). The Germanic languages in which place-names in Scotland were created are English (originally Anglian) and Norse (including Danish).

The oldest names are those of major rivers in particular, as well as those of some islands, which have similarities to names in mainland Europe. These rivers were named by people or peoples who lived in what is now Scotland before the Picts or Britons settled here. The Romans were aware of the names of several of the tribes, and these are to be found on Map 1. W J Watson discusses these tribes, their names and their areas in *History of the Celtic Placenames of Scotland*.

Prior to the arrival of the Scots and Angles, the area north of what is now the Central Belt formed the territories of the Northern and Southern Picts, speaking P-Celtic with elements such as *aber* in common with the Brythonic language of the Britons to the south. The Pictish territories are shown on Map 2. The distinguishing feature of the place-names of Pictland is the element *pett* which means a 'share or portion of land', cognate with Welsh *peth* and Gaelic *cuid*. Although *pett* has lasted until the present in anglicised place-names as 'Pit-', the gaelicised forms of most such place-names have replaced *pett* with Gaelic *baile*, 'settlement, farm, village', although certain names in Gaelic have retained *pett* in the form 'Peit'. In addition, the specifiying element in most 'Pit-' names is from Gaelic, as in 'Pittyvaich'. This suggests that Gaelic used *pett* as a generic term over a long period until it ceased to carry any lexical meaning at which time it was replaced with *baile*.

Contemporary with the Picts of the north were the Brythonic speaking Britons south of the Forth-Clyde line in their territories of Strathclyde, Gododdin and Rheged, also shown on Map 2. Although their territories were in the main south of the Forth and Clyde, the capital of Strathclyde was at Dumbarton. Because of the similarity between certain Gaelic and Brythonic elements, such as Gaelic *dùn* and Brythonic *din*, 'fort', or Gaelic *eaglais* and Brythonic *eglwys*, 'church', a degree of uncertainty exists in stating definitively on linguistic grounds alone in which language certain place-names were created. Brythonic place-names share certain elements in common with Pictish names, but some, such as 'Penpont', would be comprehensible to speakers of modern Welsh.

It is reckoned that the Gaelic speaking Scots were settled in Dal Riada in Argyll by around 450 AD, having come from the territory of Dal Riada in northern Ireland. The Scots had early contact with the Picts as recorded in Columba's visit to the northern Pictish capital at Inverness in the 6th century AD. The Angles meanwhile had founded their territory of Bernicia centred on Bamburgh in Northumberland around 550 AD, and soon began an expansion which would bring them into conflict and contact with the equally expansionist Scots. The Scots had entered early into Pictish territory and by 840 the kingdoms of the two peoples had united under the king of the Scots. By 945 the Scots had acquired the Brythonic territory of Strathclyde, and within thirty years, Lothian. At the battle of Carham in 1006, the defeat of the Angles put a temporary stop to their expansion, and by around 1050 Gaelic was at its peak and spoken over the territory of what is now mainland Scotland, with the exception of the extreme south-east and north-east.

Prior to this, the Angles had been spreading throughout the southern part of the country, gaining Rheged through marriage by around 635 and capturing the fort of Din Eidyn (now Dùn Éideann or Edinburgh) around five years later. Their expansion northwards was halted by the Picts at the battle of Nechtansmere in 685, but by the middle of the next century the Angles had control of Kyle. In the north and west the Norse had attacked Iona by around 790 and

Dumbarton by 870, and had established their territories in the west and north.

The Kingdom of the Scots remained in Gaelic speaking hands until the marriage of Malcolm Canmore and Margaret in the 11th century, after which time the gradual decline of Gaelic hegemony began. The settling of fertile, low-lying lands and the setting up of burghs by speakers of English introduced that language to areas previously Gaelic speaking only.

The more recent linguistic history of Scotland is fairly well known as is the uneasy coexistence between Gaelic and English, and the entrenchment of Gaelic within the Highlands and Islands to the north and Galloway and Carrick to the south. By the beginning of the 20th century Gaelic was indigenous only in parts of the counties of Argyll, Bute, Dunbarton, Stirling, Perth, Aberdeen, Banff, Moray, Nairn, Inverness, Ross, Sutherland and Caithness. One hundred years later, with the exception of Gaelic speakers in mainland cities and towns, the language was continuing to be used by and regenerated at community level only in the northern Hebrides.

Because of the long-term coexistence of several languages in different parts of the country, a large proportion of place-names consists of elements from more than one of these languages. The linguistic combinations most frequently found in these hybrids are Gaelic/Norse, Gaelic/Pictish, Gaelic/English, Gaelic/Brythonic, English/Brythonic and English/Norse, as well as three-way combinations such as Gaelic/Norse/English. In the most intensively English part of the country, in the south-east, a common pattern of place-name is that of a Gaelic or Norse personal name attached to English *tún*. Similarly, in the north-east, Gaelic personal names can be found attached to Pictish *pett* and in the north, English personal names can be found in combination with Gaelic *baile*.

A fairly unknown set of combinations came about, particularly in the South-west, in which Gaelic replaced English, leading to established English names such as *Mellington, Swinton* and *Meibothel* (now *Maybole*) being adopted by the Gaelic speaking population who added Gaelic affixes to these, resulting in *Dalmellington, Dalswinton, Meibothelbeg* and *Meibothelmore*. Gradually, English re-replaced Gaelic, but the hybrids such as *Dalmellington* and *Dalswinton* remained.

Another commonly encountered pattern charts the replacement of one language by another, and perhaps by another again, in which the generic of the first language, having lost lexical meaning to the speakers of the second language, is repeated with the same generic in the new language, as in *Knockhill* in Fife. When Fife was Gaelic speaking, the hill in question would have been named simply *Cnoc*, 'hill' or *An Cnoc*, 'the hill'. As Gaelic died out and was replaced by English, this would have changed to *Knock* to fit in with the sound system of English, and would eventually have ceased to connote a hill. However, because the place known by the name of *Knock* was a hill, English speakers came to define it as *Knock Hill*, gradually becoming *Knockhill*.

The change from Norse to Gaelic and then to English can be seen in *Ardtornish Point* in Argyll. This name was originally coined by Norse speakers as *Thorirnes*, 'Thorir's headland'. As Gaelic replaced Norse, this became *Tòirinis* and ceased to have any lexical meaning. Gaelic speakers in turn added their word for a headland, *àird*, and the name became *Àird Tòirinis*, which meant nothing to English speakers other than being a name which they pronounced as *Ardtornish*. They in turn recognised the place as a headland and added their generic, *point*, to explain it and give *Ardtornish Point*, a name which now contains three languages' generic terms for a headland. This name neatly shows how one language's generic can become another's specifier. To Norse speakers, the generic was *nes*, 'headland', and the specifier *Thorir*. Gaelic speakers did not recognise *nes* as a generic and used the entire *Thorirnes* as a specifier, adding their own generic *àird*. Then English speakers, failing to perceive *àird* as a generic in *Àird Tòirinis* or *Ardtornish*, added their own generic *point*. If English were to be replaced by another language in the future, this might in turn add its own generic to the by then meaningless *Ardtornishpoint*.

As well as place-names constructed through different languages, there can be problems in interpreting place-names from a single language due to elements or personal names which are no longer in use, and as a result of change and corruption through the passage of time. This latter point is particularly relevant when considering the place-names of marginal areas in which one language is being replaced by another, as in Braemar and Upper Banffshire in the 19th century. It is not enough to rely on current pronunciation and interpretation which may be flawed or influenced by the incoming language, although if the inhabitants of a particular area call a place by a particular name, then that name is as valid as the official or written one.

Watson is a valuable source of information on the names of Gaelic saints and of rivers, and on the subject of rivers should be read in conjunction with W F H Nicolaisen's *Scottish Placenames*. Much interesting and valuable work has been carried out in particular by Professor G Barrow, Simon Taylor, Richard Cox and Rob Ó Maolalaigh, and some of the latter's findings can be found in the *The Uses of Place-Names*, edited by Simon Taylor. These newest works raise many questions which are outwith the scope of this book.

Gaelic Pronunciation

This brief guide to pronunciation gives approximate equivalents in standard Scottish English (except where otherwise indicated) for the letters and combinations of letters found in Gaelic. The Gaelic alphabet contains 18 letters (a, b, c, d, e, f, g, h, i, l, m, n, o, p, r, s, t, u) but since the language has many more sounds than that, accent marks are used to indicate long vowels, *h* is added after most consonants to change their sound, and when consonants are combined with *i* or *e*, they become palatalised, as indicated below.

Vowels	*Approximate Sound*	*English Example*
a *or* ai	*short* a	c**a**t
à *or* ài	*long* ah	f**a**ther
ao *or* aoi	*between* ay *and* oo	-
ea *or* ei	*short* e *or* ay	**e**gg *or* t**a**ke
èi	*long* e	*French* S**è**vres
éi	*long* ay	d**ay**s
eò *or* eòi	yaw	**ya**wn
eu	*short* ee-u	*Italian* F**ia**t
i *or* io	*short* i *or* ee	**i**n *or* k**ee**p
ì *or* ìo	*long* ee	f**ie**nd
ia	*short* ee-u	*Italian* F**ia**t
iu	*short* yoo	**you**th
iù	*long* yoo	(to) **u**se
o *or* oi	*short* aw *or* oa	t**o**p *or* c**oa**t
ò *or* òi	*long* aw	**awe**
ó *or* ói	*long* oa	m**o**wer
u *or* ui	*short* oo	br**oo**d
ù *or* ùi	*long* oo	br**ew**ed

Consonants	Approximate Sound	English Example
b	b	**b**ig
b (+ e/i)	b + y	**B**ute
bh	v	**v**ery
bh (+ e/i)	v + y	**v**iew
c	k	**c**at
c (+ e/i)	k + y	**k**ilt
ch	kh	lo**ch**
ch (+ e/i)	ch + y	*German* i**ch**
cn	kr	**cr**ock
d	d	**d**o
d (+ e/i)	j	**j**ig
dh	gh	*voiced equivalent of* kh
dh (+ e/i)	y	**y**es
f	f	**f**ig
f (+ e/i)	f + y	**f**ew
fh	*silent*	-
g	g	**g**o
g (+ e/i)	g	a**g**ue
gh	gh	*voiced equivalent of* kh
gh (+ e/i)	y	**y**es
h	h	**h**at
l	l	*American* **l**ook
l (+ e/i)	l + y	**l**ure
m	m	**m**ore
m (+ e/i)	m + y	**m**ew
mh	v	**v**at
mh (+ e/i)	v + y	**v**iew
n	n	**n**ot
n (+e/i)	n + y	**n**ew

p	p	**p**at
p (+ e/i)	p + y	**p**ew
ph	f	**f**our
ph (+ e/i)	f + y	**f**ew
r	r	**r**ock
r (+ e/i)	th	**th**is
rt	rsht	ha**rsh t**one
s	s	**s**ift
s (+ e/i)	sh	**sh**ift
sh	h	**h**at
sh (+ e/i)	h + y	**h**ew
t	t	**t**ug
t (+ e/i)	ch	**ch**ew
th	h	**h**at
th (+ e/i)	h + y	**h**ew

Since the issue of *Gaelic Orthographic Conventions* by the Scottish Examinations Board in 1981, revised in 2005 and 2009 by the Scottish Qualifications Authority, the acute accent mark found in *á*, *é* and *ó* has been replaced by the grave accent mark as in *à*, *è* and *ò*. This is merely a spelling convention and does not affect pronunciation. This book, however, uses the acute accent throughout as an indication of the pronunciation of names, but it should be borne in mind that the acute is obsolete and that words spelled here such as *Leódhas*, *Géirinis* and *Am Baile Mór* have the everyday spelling *Leòdhas*, *Gèirinis* and *Am Baile Mòr*.

Common Generic Elements

The generic element in a name is a general term, for example, in a name such as *Newtown*, the generic is *town* because that is the element describing the type of place under discussion, while *New* specifies the type of *town*. One might find that in the vicinity of Newtown there might be an *Oldtown*, in which *Old* is the specifier, distinguishing this *town* from *Newtown* and all other *towns*.

This section lists alphabetically the most common generic elements found in Scottish place-names. They are listed according to the form in which they are found in current English and Gaelic place-names and not in their form in the original language. For example, Norse *vík* appears under *-aig*, *-bhaig*, *-vaig* and *-wick* (its realisations in current English and Gaelic forms) rather than under the original Norse *vík*. In addition, it is worth noting that in Gaelic names consisting only of a generic (or a generic with an adjective), the definite article is generally used, as in *Am Baile Mór*, 'the big settlement', rather than simply *Baile Mór*, 'big settlement'. In English it is unusual to use the definite article in such instances, so that *Newtown* is used rather than *The Newtown*, but some names such as *The Level* and *The Green* do exist in English.

It should be remembered that not every name ending in *-a* is from Norse *á* or *øy*, and that the list of generics is a general guide only which should help with the derivations in the gazetteer sections.

The lists are in the following format; firstly the generic element is given followed by the word from which it comes in the original language; in brackets is an explanation of the term in English; finally there comes an example of a place-name including the generic. The following abbreviations are used: B for Brythonic, E for English or Anglian, G for Gaelic, N for Norse including Danish, and P for Pictish.

-a	N *á* (river) or	Grìota; Greet**a**
	N *øy* (island)	Diùra; Jur**a**
aber-	B *aber* (river mouth)	**Aber**deen
ach-	G *achadh* (field)	**Ach**nahannet

-aidh	G a locative or dative ending (place of)	Balg**aidh**
-aigh	N *øy* (island)	Barr**aigh**
aird	G *àird* (point)	**Aird** of Sleat
-al	N *fjall* (mountain) or	Lang**al**
	N *vøllr* (field)	Man**al**
ald-	G *allt* (stream)	**Ald**ivalloch
-am	N *holmr* (islet)	Grian**am**
ard	G *àird* (point)	**Ard**kinglas
as	N *áss* (ridge)	Bri**as**cleit
auch-	G *achadh* (field)	**Auch**indachy
auchter-	G *uachdar* (upland)	**Auchter**arder
auld-	G *allt* (stream)	**Auld**earn
ault-	G *allt* (stream)	**Ault**more
-ay	N *øy* (island)	Scalp**ay**
bac	N *bakki* (bank)	Am **Bac**
back	N *bakki* (bank)	**Back**ies
bad-	G *bad* (copse; spot)	**Bad**ralloch
bal-	G *baile* (farm; settlement; town)	**Bal**maha
bar-	G *bàrr* (hill, summit)	**Bar**caldine
beck	E *beck* (stream) or	Water**beck**
	N *bekkr* (stream)	**Beck**rivik
bel-	G *baile* (farm; settlement; town)	**Bel**helvie
ben	G *beinn* (mountain)	**Ben** Nevis
-bhagh	N *vágr* (narrow bay)	Steòrna**bhagh**
-bhaig	N *vík* (bay)	Tarsga**bhaig**
-bhal	N *fjall* (mountain)	Snaoisea**bhal**
-bhat	N *vatn* (water)	Loch
		Langa**bhat**
-bhig	N *vík* (bay)	Bréi**bhig**
-bie	N *byr* (farm)	Hum**bie**
blà-	N *blá* (blue)	**Blà**bheinn
blair	G *blàr* (field; moor; plain)	**Blair**gowrie
bo-	G *both* (hut)	**Bo**henie
bog-	G *bog* (bog; soft)	**Bog**buie
-bol	N *bólstaðr* (farm) or	Circea**bol**
	E *bótl* (dwelling)	May**bole**
bor-	N *borg* (fort; castle)	**Bor**rodale
-bost	N *bólstaðr* (farm)	Sia**bost**
bow	G *bogha* or N *bóða* (submerged rock)	**Bow**more

bràc-	N *brekka* (slope)	**Bràc**adal
brae	E *bra* (brae) or	Burn**brae**
	G *bràigh* (upper part)	**Brae**more
breck-	N *brekka* (slope)	Ard **Breck**nish
brig	N *bekkr* (stream) or	Staoini**brig**
	E *brycg* (bridge)	**Brig** O'Turk
bun-	G *bun* (bottom; river mouth)	**Bun**ree
burgh	E *burh* (farm; fort, town)	Edin**burgh**
burn	E *burna* (stream)	Whit**burn**
-bus	N *bólstaðr* (farm)	Cionna**bus**
-by	N *byr* (farm)	New**by**
cairn-	G *càrn* (cairn; hill)	**Cairn**baan
cambus-	G *camas* (inlet; river bend)	**Cambus**lang
camus-	G *camas* (inlet; river bend)	**Camus**cross
car-	B *caer* (fort) or	**Car**luke
	G *cathair* (fort)	**Car**tomy
carden	P *carden* (thicket; copse)	**Carden**den
circ-	N *kirkja* (church)	**Circ**ebost
clachan	G *clachan* (churchyard; village with a church)	**Clachan** Sands
-cleit	N *klettr* (rock; hill)	Brias**cleit**
-clete	N *klettr* (rock; hill)	Mala**clete**
clun(e)-	G *cluain* (meadow)	**Clun**y
coul	G *cùl* (back) or	**Coul**in
	G *cùil* (secluded spot)	**Coul**hill
craig	G *creag* (rock)	**Craig**entinny
-cro	N *kró* (small enclosure)	Lini**cro**
-cuidh	N *kví* (cattle pen)	Liana**cuidh**
cul-	G *cùl* (back) or	**Cul**duthel
	G *cùil* (secluded spot)	**Cul**eave
-dal	E *dale* (valley) or	Esk**dale**
	N *dalr* (valley)	Glen
		Hinnis**dal**
dal-	G *dail* (haugh)	**Dal**marnock
dean	E *denu* (valley)	**Dean**s
del-	G *dail* (haugh)	**Del**nashaugh
-den	E *denu* (valley)	Carden**den**
doch-	G *dabhach* (davoch)	**Doch**four
druim-	G *druim* (ridge)	An **Druim**

		Mór
drum-	G *druim* (ridge)	**Drum**chapel
dum-	G *dùn* (hill; fort; hillfort)	**Dum**barton
dun-	G *dùn* (hill; fort; hillfort)	**Dun**staffnage
eccle(s)-	B *eglwys* or	**Eccle**fechan
	G *eaglais* (church)	**Eccles**machan
edin-	G *aodann* (hill face)	**Edin**bane
fetter-	G *fothair* (shelving or terraced slope)	**Fetter**cairn
fors	N *forss* (waterfall)	**Fors**inard
-four	G *pòr* (pasture)	Trian**four**
free	G *frìth* (deer forest)	**Free**vater
garr-	N *garðr* (enclosure; dyke)	**Garr**abost
-garry	N *gerði* (pasture land)	Osmi**garry**
gart-	G *gart/gort* (enclosed field)	**Gart**more
gask	G *gasg* (projecting tail or strip of land)	Ger**gask**
gate	E *geatu* (road)	**Gate**house
-gearraidh	N *gerði* (pasture land)	Mùi**gearraidh**
geo	N *gjá* (steep sea inlet)	**Geo**crab
-gil(l)	N *gil* (gully; ravine)	Tràili**gil**
glas	G *glas* (stream)	**Glas**nakille
glen	G *gleann* (valley)	**Glen**elg
-go	N *gjá* (steep sea inlet)	Papi**goe**
-gow	B *cau* (hollow)	Glas**gow**
-gro	N *gróf* (river pit)	Sgealas**gro**
ha-	E *haga* (hedge)	**Ha**wick
-hall	N *halh* (haugh)	Fox**hall**
-ham(e)	E *hám* (homestead)	Nor**ham**
holm	N *holmr* (holm; islet) or	**Holm**isdale
	E *hám* (homestead)	Leit**holm**
hope	N *hóp* (bay)	St Margaret's **Hope**
hùs-	N *hús* (house)	**Hùs**abost
-ie	G a locative or dative ending (place of)	Cairn**ie**
inch-	G *innis* (meadow; island)	**Inch**ree
-ingham	E *-ingaham* (homestead of the people of -)	Twyn**ingham**
-ington	E *-ingatun* (farm of the people of -)	Shear**ington**
inver-	G *inbhir* (river mouth)	**Inver**ness
ken-	G *ceann* (end; head)	**Ken**nacraig

kil-	G *cill* (cell; church)	**Kil**marnock
killie-	G *coille* (wood)	**Killie**crankie
kin-	G *ceann* (end; head)	**Kin**dallachan
kirk	N *kirkja* (church)	**Kirk**patrick
knock-	G *cnoc* (hill)	**Knock**vologan
kyle	G *caol* (strait) or	**Kyle**akin
	G *coille* (wood)	Balna**kyle**
lag-	G *lag* (hollow)	**Lag**avulin
law	E *hláw* (hill)	Gate**law**bridge
leck-	G *leac* (slab; flagstone)	**Leck**melm
letter-	G *leitir* (gentle slope)	**Letter**fearn
lì	N *hlið* (slope)	**Lì**
lin-	B *llyn* or	**Lin**lithgow
	G *linn* (pool; pond; firth)	**Linn** O'Dee
loch	G *loch* (loch; firth; sea loch)	**Loch** Ness
logie	G *lagaidh* (place with a hollow)	**Logie** Easter
lon	G *lòn* (wet meadow)	**Lon**more
mon-	G *monadh* (hill; moor; upland) or	**Mon**crieff
	G *mòine* (peat; peat moss)	**Mon**organ
mull	G *maol* (rounded headland or hill)	**Mull** of Kintyre
muir	E *mór* (moor)	**Muir** of Ord
-ness	E *naes* (headland)	Black**ness**
	N *nes* (headland)	**Ness**
-nis	N *nes* (headland)	Stoca**inis**
-nish	N *nes* (headland)	Ardtor**nish**
òb	N *hóp* (bay)	An t-**Òb**an
obar-	B *aber* (river mouth)	**Obar** Pheallaidh
-ort	N *fjorðr* (firth; sea loch)	Loch Eise**ort**
os	N *óss* (river mouth)	**Àros**
pen-	B *pen* (end; head)	**Pen**pont
	G *peighinn* (pennyland)	**Pen**ifiler
pit-	P *pett* (share; lands)	**Pit**caple
pol-	G *poll* (pool; mud)	**Pol**bain
-pol	N *bólstaðr* (farm)	Crosa**pol**
quie	N *kví* (cattle pen)	Lini**quie**
rath-	G *ràth* (circular fort)	**Rath**illet
rhu-	G *rubha* (headland)	**Rhu**nahaorine

ros-	G *ros* (headland; wood) or	**Ros**yth
	N *hross* (horse)	**Ros**inish
-said	N *saetr* (sheiling)	Liana**said**
-seadar	N *setr* (dwelling) or *saetr* (sheiling)	Grimi**seadar**
sgeir	N *sker* (skerry)	Heill**sgeir**
-sgo	N *skogr* (small wood)	Bircea**sgo**
-shader	N *setr* (dwelling) or *saetr* (sheiling)	Flas**hader**
-shaw	E *sceaga* (wood)	Cobbin**shaw**
-side	N *saetr* (sheiling)	Lin**side**
-sker	N *sker* (skerry)	Has**ker**
slock-	G *sloc* (hollow; pit)	**Slock**avullin
sròm	N *straumr* (current; stream)	An **Sròm** Dearg
-sta	N *staðir* (dwelling place; farm)	Tol**sta**
stac	N *stakk* (pillar; rock)	**Stac** Pollaidh
-stane	E *stán* (stone) or -'*s tún* (-s farm)	Brun**stane**
-stead	E *stede* (place)	New**stead**
stein	N *stein* (stone)	**Stein**nis
strath-	G *srath* (wide valley)	**Strath**more
strome	N *straumr* (current; stream)	**Strome**ferry
stron(e)	G *sròn* (nose-shaped headland)	**Strone**ba
tam-	G *tom* (hillock)	**Tam**dhu
tilly-	G *tulach* (green hill; long low ridge)	**Tilly**fourie
tir-	G *tìr* (land)	**Tir**oran
tom-	G *tom* (hillock)	**Tom**doun
-ton	E *tún* (farm)	Rober**ton**
tor-	G *tòrr* (hill)	**Tor**more
tot-	N *toft* (house site)	**Tot**aig
tra-	B *tref* (settlement)	**Tra**quair
tulloch-	G *tulach* (green hill; long low ridge)	**Tulloch**beg
tully-	G *tulach* (green hill; long low ridge)	**Tully**belton
-vaig	N *vík* (bay)	Toka**vaig**
val	N *fjall* (mountain)	Blashi**val**
-vat	N *vatn* (loch; water)	**Vat**ersay
-wall	N *vollr* (field)	Ding**wall**
-way	N *vágr* (narrow bay)	Carlo**way**
-wick	E *wíc* (village) or	Ber**wick**
	N *vík* (bay)	Ler**wick**
-warth	E *worð* (enclosure)	Pol**warth**

Settlements and Areas

A'Chleit (Argyll), A' Chleit. 'The cliff or rock', from Norse.

Abban (Inverness), An t-Àban. 'The backwater or small stream'.

Abbey St Bathans (Berwick). The abbey of St Baoithean or Bathan'. The surname 'MacGylboythin', from *MacGilleBhaoithein*, 'son of the devotee of Baoithean', appeared in Dumfries in the 13th century, but has since died out.

Abbotsinch (Renfrew). 'The abbot's meadow', from English/Gaelic, on lands once belonging to Paisley Abbey.

Aberarder (Inverness), Obar Àrdair. 'The mouth of the Arder'.

Aberargie (Perth), Obar Fhargaidh. 'The mouth of the angry river', from *fearg*, 'anger'.

Aberbothrie (Perth). 'The mouth of the deaf stream', from *bodhar*, 'deaf', suggesting a silent stream.

Abercairney (Perth). 'The mouth of the Cairney', a river name from *càrnach*, meaning 'stony'.

Aberchalder (Inverness), Obar Chaladair. 'The mouth of the hard water', from *caled* and *dobhar*. Easter Aberchalder was formerly known as *A' Cheann Mhór*, 'the big end'.

Aberchirder (Banff). 'The mouth of the dark water', from *ciar* and *dobhar*. Locally this is known as 'Foggieloan'.

Abercorn (West Lothian). 'Horn-shaped river mouth', cognate with *còrn*, 'horn'. It was known to Bede as 'Aebbercurnig', and is of Brythonic origin.

Abercrombie (Fife), Obar Chromb-aidh. 'Bent river mouth', from *crom*.

Aberdalgie (Perth), Obar Dheilgidh. 'The mouth of the thorny stream'.

Aberdeen, Obar Dheathain. 'The mouth of the Don', a river named after a deity. Aberdeenshire is *Siorrachd Obar Dheathain*.

Aberdour (Fife), Obar Dobhair. 'The mouth of the water'.

Aberfeldy (Perth), Obar Pheallaidh. 'The mouth of the Peallaidh'. *Peallaidh*, which comes from *peallach*, 'shaggy', was an *ùraisg* or water sprite said to live in this stream. The town is mentioned in the saying, *Trì iongantasan na h-Alba: drochaid Obar Pheallaidh, tobraichean Ghlinn Iucha is cluig Pheairt*, 'The three wonders of Scotland: Aberfeldy bridge, the wells of Linlithgow and the bells of Perth'.

Aberfoyle (Perth), Obar Phuill. 'The mouth of the sluggish stream'. *Poll* was borrowed as 'pow' into Scottish English. The market at Aberfoyle was known as *Féill Barachan*, from *Féill Bhearchain*, 'St Barchan's fair'.

Abergairn (Aberdeen), Obar Gharthain. 'The mouth of the Gairn', a noisy river, the name of which comes from *goir*, 'call'.

Abergeldie (Aberdeen), Obar Gheallaidh. 'The mouth of the bright river'.

Aberlady (East Lothian). 'Rotten river mouth', from *lobh*, 'rot'.

Aberlednock (Perth), Obar Liadnaig. 'The mouth of the Lednock', an obscure name.

Aberlemno (Angus), Obar Leamhnach. 'The mouth of the elm stream'.

Aberlour (Banff), Obar Lobhair. 'The mouth of the noisy or talkative stream'. Aberlour Church and Parish respectively are *Cill Drostain* and *Sgìre Dhrostain*, 'the church and parish of St Drostan'. *See* **Charleston of Aberlour**.

Abernethy (Inverness, Perth), Obar Neithich. 'The mouth of the Nethy', a river name suggesting cleanliness.

Aberscross (Sutherland), Abarsgaig. 'Muddy strip of land'.

Abersky (Inverness), Abairsgigh. 'Muddy place'.

Abertarff (Inverness), Obar Thairbh. 'The mouth of the bull river'.

Aberuchill (Perth), Obar Rùchaill. Although local Gaelic speakers understood this to mean 'mouth of the red flood', from *Obar Ruadh Thuil*, evidence points to this name containing *coille*, 'wood', similar to **Orchill**.

Aberuthven (Perth), Obar Ruadhainn. 'The river mouth at the red-brown place'.

Abigil (Sutherland), Àbaigil. 'River-farm gully', from Norse.

Aboyne (Aberdeen), A-bèidh. These Gaelic and English forms are unclear. The fair held here was known as *Fèill Mhìcheil*, 'St Michael's Fair'.

Abriachan (Inverness), Obar Itheachan. This name was originally *Obar Bhritheachan*, 'mouth of the hill river'. *Bodaich Obar Bhritheachan*, 'the old men of Abriachan', were apparently notable in the area. The area known as 'Cords of Abriachan' are *Na Cordachan*, referring to a series of narrow fields. The church at Abriachan is *Cill Fhìonain*, 'St Finnan's church'.

Acairseid Mhor (Eriskay, Raasay), An Acarsaid Mhór. 'The big anchorage'.

Acha (Argyll, Coll), An t-Achadh. 'The field'.

Achachoish (Argyll), Achadh a' Chòis or Achadh a' Chòthais. 'The field at the cave or lair'.

Achachonleich (Inverness), Achadh a' Chonalaich. This may mean 'the stubble field' or 'the field at the place of the whirlpool'.

Achachork (Skye), Achadh a' Choirce. 'Oat field'.

Achadaphris (Argyll), Achadh Dà Phris. 'The field with two bushes'.

Achadesdal (Ross), Acha Deuthasdal. 'The field at Desdal', the latter part of which is a Norse valley name with an unclear first element. Gairloch Hotel was originally known as *Taigh-òsta Acha Deuthasdal*.

Achadunan (Argyll), Achadh an Dùnain. 'The field at the small hill(fort)'.

Achag (Arran), Achag. This appears to be 'small field', and is also known as 'Upper Corrie' in English.

Achagallon (Argyll, Arran), Achadh Ghallain. 'The field with a standing stone'. People from Achagallon in Arran were known as *feannagan*, 'crows'.

Achallater (Perth), Achadh Chaladair or Ach Chaladair. 'The field of the Calder'. *See* **Aberchalder**.

Achaloist (Mull), An t-Achadh Loisgte. 'The burnt field'.

Achalone (Caithness). 'The field by the pool', from *Achadh an Lòin*.

Achamore (Coll, Gigha, Nairn), An t-Achadh Mór. 'The big field'.

Achanalt (Ross), Acha nan Allt. 'The field of the streams'. However, a number of names which seem to contain genitive plural article *nan* may originally have contained *n*, indicating the genitive without the article. Such names include 'Cumbernauld', 'Lochnaw' and 'Palnure'.

Achanamara (Argyll), Achadh na Mara. 'The field by the sea'.

Achandunie (Ross), Achadh an Dùnaidh. 'The field at the hill(fort) place'.

Achanruie (Perth), Achadh an Ruighe. 'The field on the slope'.

Achaphubuil (Argyll), Achadh a' Phùbaill. 'The field of the tent or pavilion'.

Achara (Arran), Acha-Rà. 'The field

at the circular fort', from an older form, *Achadh an Ràtha*. Local people were nicknamed *meanbh-chuileagan*, 'midges'.

Acharacle (Argyll), Àth Tharracail. 'Torcuil's ford'.

Acharanny (Arran), Achadh an Rainich. 'The bracken field'. A more appropriate Gaelic spelling might be *Achadh an Rainigh*, showing more accurately the form of the genitive singular once standard but more recently restricted to some southern dialects.

Acharn (Argyll, Perth), Àth a' Chàirn. 'The ford by the cairn'.

Achateny (Argyll), Ach an Teine. 'The field of the fire'.

Achavaich (Sutherland), Achadh a' Bhàthaich. 'The field with the byre'.

Achavandra (Sutherland), Achadh Anndra. 'Andrew's field'.

Achavanich (Caithness). 'The monk's field', from *Achadh a' Mhanaich*.

Achavarasdal (Caithness). This Gaelic/Norse name may be 'the field at Barr's valley', from *Achadh Bhàrrasdail* and, if so, this second part may be also found in 'Barrisdale', but an alternative derivation could refer to an enclosure for horses, also from Norse.

Achavoulin (Arran). Achadh a' Mhuilinn. 'The field of the mill', also known in English as Millfield.

Achavraie (Argyll), Achadh a' Bhràighe; (Ross), Achd a' Bhràighe. 'The field on the upper land'. The Gaelic form of the Ross name shows *achd* in place of *achadh* which is a fairly common occurrence in that area.

Achbreck (Banff). 'Speckled field', from *Achadh Breac*.

Achdalieu (Argyll), Achadh Do Liubha. 'Do Liubha's field', in memory of a saint.

Achduart (Ross), Achadh Dhubhaird. 'The field at the black headland'.

Acheilidh (Sutherland), Ach Choillidh. 'Field at the wood place'.

Achenbrain (Ayr). *See* **Auchenbrain**.

Acheninver (Ross), Achd an Inbhir. 'The field at the river mouth'.

Achentoul (Perth, Sutherland), Achadh an t-Sabhail. 'The field with the barn'.

Achfary (Sutherland), Achadh Taigh Phairidh. 'The field at Para's house'.

Achgarve (Ross), An t-Acha Garbh. 'The rough field'. Local people were nicknamed *sgairbh*, 'cormorants'.

Achgobhal (Perth), Ach a' Ghobhail. 'The field at the fork'.

Achiltibuie (Ross), Achd Ille Bhuidhe. 'The field of the yellow haired boy'. This name sometimes appears as *Àicheallaidh Buidhe*, 'yellow Achilty', by analogy with Achilty in Easter Ross.

Achilty (Ross), Àicheallaidh. This name is not clear, but may be associated with Celtic *uxellos*, 'high', the origin of the name *Ochil*.

Achimenach (Caithness). 'Middle field', from *Achadh Meadhanach*.

Achinahuagh (Sutherland), Achadh na h-Uamha. 'The field at the cave'.

Achindarroch (Inverness), Achadh nan Darach. 'Field of the oaks'.

Achinduin (Lismore), Achadh an Dùin. 'The field by the hill(fort)'.

Achingall (East Lothian). 'The field of the non-Gaels', from *Achadh nan Gall*.

Achininver (Sutherland), Achadh an Inbhir. 'The field by the river mouth'.

Achintee (Ross), Achadh an t-Suidhe. 'The field of the seat', situated near the hill called *Meall an t-Suidhe*, 'lump of the seat'.

Achintore (Inverness), Achadh an Todhair. 'The bleaching field'. The stream running through Achintore is *Allt nan Dathadairean*, 'stream of the dyers', or 'Ashburn' in English.

Achintraid (Ross), Achadh na Tràghad. 'The field at the beach'.

Achlean (Inverness), An t-Achadh Leathann. 'The wide field'.

Achlochan (Ross), Achd an Lochain. 'The field by the small loch'.

Achlunachan (Perth, Ross), Achadh Ghlùineachain or Achadh Lùinneachain. This may be 'the field of jointed grass'.

Achlusa (Skye), Achadh Lusa. 'The field at the bright river', from Gaelic/Norse.

Achmelvich (Sutherland), Achadh Mhealbhaich. 'The field of Melvich'.

Achmore (Lewis), An t-Acha Mór; (Perth), An t-Achadh Mór; (Ross), Acha Mór. 'The big field'. Achmore and Lochganvich are the only inland settlements in Lewis, and a person not up to their job is said to be *seòladair an Acha Mhóir*, 'an Achmore sailor'. In Lewis, this place was known simply as *An t-Ach*, 'the field'.

Achnaba (Argyll), Achadh na Bà. 'The field of the cow'.

Achnacairn (Argyll), Achadh nan Càrn. 'The field of the cairns'.

Achnacarnan (Argyll), Achadh nan Càrnan. 'The field by the small cairns'.

Achnacarnin (Sutherland), Achadh nan Càrnan. *See* **Achnacarnan**.

Achnacarry (Inverness), Achadh na Cairidh. 'The field by the weir'.

Achnaclerach (Ross), Achadh nan Cléireach. 'The field of the clerics'.

Achnacloich (Argyll, Nairn, Skye), Achadh na Cloiche. 'The field of the stone'.

Achnacloigh (Argyll), Achadh na Cloiche. *See* **Achnacloich**.

Achnacree (Argyll), Achadh na Crithe. 'The field at the shaking place'. Achnacreebeag is *Achadh na Crithe Beag*, 'small Achnacree'.

Achnacroish (Lismore), Achadh na Croise. 'The field of the cross'.

Achnafauld (Perth), Achadh na Follt. The defining element in this field name is unclear.

Achnafearn (Inverness), Achadh na Feàrna. 'The field of the alder'.

Achnagairn (Inverness), Achadh nan

Càrn. 'The field of the cairns', from an older *Achadh na gCàrn*.

Achnagarron (Ross), Achadh nan Gearran. 'The field of the geldings'.

Achnagart (Ross), Ach nan Gart. 'The field of the enclosures'.

Achnagonalin (Moray), Achadh nan Coitheanalan. 'The field of the assemblies or congregations', from older *Achadh na gCoitheanalan*.

Achnagullan (Sutherland), Achadh nan Cuilean. 'The field of the whelps', from an older *Achadh na gCuilean*.

Achnaha (Argyll), Achadh na h-Àtha. 'The field by the kiln or stable'.

Achnahaird (Ross), Achadh na h-Àirde. 'The field by the headland'.

Achnahannet (several), Achadh na h-Annaid. 'The field of the mother church'.

Achnahinich (Ross), Achadh na h-Ìnich. 'The field at the nail place'.

Achnairn (Sutherland), Achadh an Fheàrna. 'The field of the alder'.

Achnaluachrach (Sutherland), Achadh na Luachrach. 'The field with the rushes'.

Achnanconeran (Inverness), Achadh nan Conbhairean. This may be 'the field at the confluences'.

Achnasaul (Inverness), Achadh nan Sabhal. 'The field with the barns'.

Achnasheen (Ross), Acha na Sìne. 'The field of the stormy weather'.

Achnashellach (Ross), Acha nan Seileach. 'The field of the willows'.

Achnatra (Argyll), Achadh na Tràgha. 'The field by the beach'.

Achnebron (Ayr), Achadh na Bràthann. 'The field of the quern'. *See* **Mauchline**.

Achnegie (Ross), Achadh an Fhiodhaich. 'The field at the wooded place'.

Achness (Sutherland), Achadh an Easa. 'The field at the waterfall or stream'.

Achosnich (Argyll, Sutherland), Ach Osnaich. This appears to be 'the field of sighing', but may have contained a different second element which gradually changed.

Achpopuli (Inverness), Achadh Poible. 'The field of the herding hut'.

Achranich (Argyll), Achadh an Rainich. 'The field with the bracken'.

Achray (Perth), Àth Chrathaidh. 'Shaking ford'.

Achreisgill (Sutherland), Achadh Rìdhisgil. 'The field of Reisgill'.

Achriabhach (Inverness), An t-Achadh Riabhach. 'The brindled field'.

Achrimsdale (Sutherland), Achadh Rumasdail. 'The field of Rimsdale'.

Achtar (Perth), Achadh Teàrra. 'Pitch field'.

Achtemarack (Inverness), Ach t-Seamraig. 'Clover field'.

Achterblair (Inverness), Ochdamh a' Bhlàir. 'The octave of the moor', an octave being the eighth part of a davoch.

Achtercairn (Ross), Achd a' Chàirn. 'The field at the cairn'.

Achtoty (Sutherland), Achadh Toitidh. 'The field of smoke or fumigation'.

Achtriochtan (Argyll), Achadh Triachatain. The second element in this field name is unclear.

Adabrock (Lewis), Adabrog. This Norse fort name contains an unclear first element. Adabrock consists of *Adabrog Àrd* and *Adabrog Ìosal*, 'high Adabrock' and 'low Adabrock' respectively.

Advie (Moray), Àbhaidh. This name may contain *magh*, 'plain'.

Affleck (Aberdeen), Achadh Leac. 'Slab field'.

Ahmore (North Uist), An Àth Mhór. 'The big ford'.

Aigas (Inverness), Àigeis. This is unclear, but might be 'edge ridge' from Norse or 'place of the gap' from Gaelic.

Aignish (Lewis), Aiginis. 'Edge point', from Norse.

Ailsa Craig (Ayr), Creag Ealasaid. Although this is said to be 'craig of

the rocky place', also known simply as *A' Chreag*, 'the rock', the 'Ailsa' part of the name is from *Alfsigrsøy*, 'Alfsigr's island'. This rock has been known by a variety of other names, including *Creag Alasdair*, *Ealasaid a' Chuain*, 'Ealasaid of the Ocean', *Alasan* and 'Paddy's Milestone'. The names *Alasdair* and *Ealasaid* appear to have been used due to their vague similarity in sound to *Alfsigr*.

Airbow (Fife). 'High point of cattle', from *Àird Bó*.

Aird (Benbecula, Inverness, Lewis, Ross), An Àird. 'The headland'. However, the Inverness name means 'the prominent hill', and has the extended name of *Àird Mhic Shimidh*, 'Lord Lovat's Aird'. This Aird appears in a number of sayings such as, *Buntàta pronn is uachdar leotha, biadh bodaich na h-Àirde*, 'Mashed potatoes and cream, the food of the old men of the Aird', and *Is mór stàth na h-Àirde do Mhac Shimidh*, 'Lord Lovat benefits greatly from the Aird'. The nicknames given to the people of various places in the Aird are recounted in another saying, *Fithich dhubha Mhilifiach, piatan Cnoc Bhàin, faoileagan a' Chluain, ruadh-chearcan Baile an Todhair, cabair fhada a' Chonfhadhaich, gearran beaga Baile a' Chonais*, 'Black ravens from Milifiach, pet lambs from Knockbain, gulls from Clune, red hens from Balintore, long poles from Convinth, little hares from Balconish'. Aird in Wester Ross is also known by the full name of *An Àird Druiseach*, 'the brambly headland'.

Aird Brenish (Lewis), Àird Bhréinis. 'The headland of Brenish'.

Aird Dell (Lewis), Àird Dhail. 'The headland of Dell'.

Aird Dhubh (Ross), An Àird Dhubh. 'The black headland'.

Aird Donald (Wigtown). 'Donald's headland', from *Àird Dhòmhnaill*.

Aird of Sleat (Skye), Àird Shléite or An Àird. 'The headland of Sleat' or 'the headland'. Local people are nicknamed *faoileagan*, 'gulls'. *See* **Sleat**.

Airdrie (Lanark); (Nairn), An Àrd Ruigh. 'The high slope'.

Aird Tong (Lewis), Àird Thunga. 'The headland of Tong'.

Aird Uig (Lewis), Àird Ùig. 'The headland of Uig'.

Airidhantuim (Lewis), Àirigh an Tuim. 'The sheiling by the hillock'.

Airlie (Angus), Iarlaidh. This may be 'earl's place'.

Airntully (Perth). 'The point at the green hill', from *Àird an Tulaich*.

Airor (Inverness), Eàrar. This may be 'sand spit' or 'beach', from Norse.

Airyolland (Wigtown). This may be 'St Fillan's sheiling', from *Àirigh Fhaolain*.

Aithmuir (Perth). 'Big ford', from *Àth Mór*.

Aitnoch (Moray), Aitneach. 'Juniper place'.

Alavig (Harris), Àlabhaig. This may be either 'eel bay' or 'deep river bay', from Norse.

Alcaig (Ross), Alcaig. 'Auk bay', from Norse.

Aldandulish (Perth), Allt an Dùghlais. 'The stream of the black water'.

Aldbar (Angus). This may be 'top stream', from *Allt Bàrr*.

Aldclune (Perth), Allt Cluaine. 'Meadow stream'.

Aldie (Ross), Alltaidh. 'Stream place'.

Aldivalloch (Banff), Allt a' Bhealaich. 'The stream at the pass'.

Aldour (Perth), Allt Dobhair. 'Water stream'.

Aldourie (Inverness), Allt Dobhraig. 'Dobhrag stream', *dobhrag* being a diminutive of *dobhar*, 'water'.

Alford (Aberdeen), Àthfort. This name may contain the Gaelic and English words for 'ford'.

Aline (Lewis), Àth an Linne or Àth Linne. 'The ford by the pool'.

Alladale (Inverness), Aladal. This is Norse 'Ali's valley' or 'eel valley'.

Allan (Fife); (Ross), Alan Mhór. The name in Fife derives from *Eilean*, representing a meadow, while the Ross name is 'big Allan'.

Allanbank (Ross), An Réim. The English name refers to this place's riverside location while the Gaelic name is 'the course'.

Allanfearn (Inverness), An t-Àilean Feàrna. 'The alder meadow'.

Allangrange (Ross), Alan. The English name is 'the barn on the Allan', while the Gaelic name is that of the river.

Allanmore (Aberdeen, Inverness), An t-Àilean Mór. 'The large meadow'.

Allanquoich (Aberdeen), Àilean Choich. 'The meadow in the hollow'. An over-correct Gaelic form, *Àilean na Cuaiche*, which has the same meaning, is common.

Allargue (Aberdeen), Àth Làirig. 'Ford of the pass'.

Allasdale (Barra), Athalasdal. This may be 'Ali's valley', from Norse.

Alligin (Ross), Àiliginn. This, first attached to a stream, is said to mean 'jewel', from *àilleag*, but the 'l' sound of the name refutes this. Wester Alligin (marked 'Alligin Shuas' on maps) is Bràighe Àiliginn, 'upper Alligin', or simply *am Bràighe*, 'the upper part'. Brybeg or Upper Alligin is *Am Bràighe Beag*, 'the small upper part', and Easter or Inver Alligin is *Inbhir Àiliginn*. Local people are *saoidheanan*, 'saithes', or *adhaichean*, 'livers'.

Alloa (Clackmannan), Allamhagh. This may be 'wild or rocky plain'.

Alloway (Ayr). *See* **Alloa**.

Alltgobhlach (Arran), Allt Gobhlach. 'Forked stream'. In several Arran names comprising a noun and qualifying adjective, there is no accompanying definite article, which would be expected and is the norm elsewhere in Scotland as well as in Arran.

Allt-nan-Subh (Ross), Allt nan Subh. 'The stream of the berries'.

Alltnaharra (Sutherland), Allt na h-Eirbhe. 'The stream by the boundary wall'.

Alltnaharrie (Ross), Allt na h-Airbhe. *See* **Alltnaharra**.

Alness (Ross), Alanais. 'Allan place'.

Altandhu (Ross), An t-Alltan Dubh. 'The black streamlet'.

Altanour (Perth), An t-Alltan Odhar. 'The dun-coloured streamlet'.

Altass (Sutherland), Alltais. 'Rock place'.

Altavaig (Skye), Alltabhaig. 'Swan bay', from Norse.

Altgaltraig (Argyll), Allt Galtraig. 'The stream at hogs' bay', from Gaelic/Norse.

Altnabreac (Caithness), Allt nam Breac. 'The stream of the trout'.

Altnacealgach (Sutherland), Allt nan Cealgach. 'The stream of the cheats'.

Altnamain (Ross), Taigh a' Mhonaidh. The English form, which also appears as 'Aultnamain', is from *Allt na Mèinn*, 'the ore stream', while the Gaelic name is 'the house on the moor'.

Alturlie (Inverness), Allt Rollaidh. The defining element of this stream name is unclear. Alturlie Point is *Gob Allt Rollaidh*.

Altyre (Moray), Alltar. This appears to contain *allt*, 'stream', but is unclear in whole.

Alva (Clackmannan). *See* **Alloa**.

Alvah (Banff). *See* **Alloa**.

Alves (Moray), An Àbhas. This may be 'water place'.

Alvie (Inverness), Albhaidh or Allamhaigh. *See* **Alloa**.

Alyth (Perth), Àilt or Allaid. The root of this name may be *ail*, 'rock'.

Amar (Skye), An t-Amar. 'The channel'.

Amat (Ross, Sutherland), Àmait. 'Confluence', from Norse. In Ross, North Amat is *Àmait na h-Eaglais*, 'Amat of the church', and South Amat

is *Àmait na Tuath*, 'Amat of the laity'. Amat in Sutherland is *Àmait nan Cuilean*, 'Amat of the pups'.

Amhuinnsuidhe (Harris), Abhainn Suidhe. 'River Suidhe'. The English form is from an older Gaelic spelling.

Amulree (Perth), Àth Maol Ruibhe. 'St Maol Rubha's ford'. Amulree church is *Cill Maol Ruibhe* or *Cill Mo Ruibhe*.

An Ard (Ross), An Àird. 'The headland'. This refers to a group of settlements in Gairloch.

Anaheilt (Argyll), Àth na h-Eilde. 'The ford of the hind'.

Anancaun (Ross), Àth nan Ceann. 'The ford of the heads'.

Angus, Aonghas or Siorrachd Aonghais. This may commemorate Aonghas, the leader of one of the Dal Riada groups. Coastal Angus is known as *Machair Aonghais*, 'plain of Angus', while the area of the Glens is *Bràigh Aonghais*, 'upland of Angus'. Angus and the Mearns together were known as *Cìrcheann*, 'Circenn'.

Ankerville (Ross), Cinn Déis Bhig. The English name comes from an 18th century owner, while the Gaelic name is 'little Kindeace'.

Annan (Dumfries), Anainn. This is primarily a river name, dedicated to the goddess Anu. The phrase *eadar Cataibh is Anainn* is a Gaelic equivalent of *from Lands End to John O'Groats*. Annandale is *Srath Anann*.

Annat (Ross), An Annaid. 'The mother church'. Local people were known as *daoine uaisle*, 'gentlefolk'.

Annathill (Lanark). This may represent a hill at an *annaid*, 'mother church', from Gaelic.

Annet (Ayr). 'The mother church', from *An Annaid*.

Annishader (Skye), Anaiseadar or Arnaiseadar. 'Eagle township', from Norse.

Anstruther (Fife). The root of this name may be *sruthair*, 'stream' or 'current', which is common in Ireland, but rarer in Scotland. This town's name is pronounced as 'Enster' by local people.

Appin (Argyll, Perth), An Apainn. 'The abbey lands'. Appin in Argyll, which probably belonged to the religious community of Lismore, is also known as *Apainn nan Stiùbhartach*, 'Appin of the Stewarts', and *Apainn Mhic Iain Stiùbhairt*, 'Appin of John Stewart's son', and the inhabitants were nicknamed *cearcan-tomain*, 'partridges'. Appin in Perthshire is also known as *Apainn man Mèinnearach*, 'Appin of the Menzies'.

Applecross (Ross), A' Chomraich. The English form comes from an older Gaelic, *Abar Crosain*, 'mouth of the cross river', while the present Gaelic name is 'the sanctuary', with a longer form *A' Chomraich Abrach*, 'the sanctuary of Abar Crosain'. It used also to be known as *Comraich Maol Ruibhe*, 'St Maol Rubha's sanctuary'. To express 'in Applecross', Gaelic uses *air a' Chomraich*, 'on the sanctuary'. A native of the area is an *Abrach*, also nicknamed a *boc*, 'buck'. Applecross Mains is *Borghdal*, 'fort valley', from Norse, and the north coast is *Na Cealan*, possibly from Norse.

Aquhorties (Aberdeen). 'Field of the standing stone', from *Achadh Coirthe*.

Arabella (Ross), Am Bog. The English name commemorates the wife of an owner, and the Gaelic name is 'the bog'.

Araird (Ross), An Araird. 'The prominent headland'.

Arbirlot (Angus). 'The mouth of the Elliot Burn', containing Brythonic *aber* or *obar*.

Arboll (Ross), Àrbol. 'River farm' or 'seal farm', from Norse.

Arbroath (Angus), Obar Bhrothaig. 'The mouth of the Brothock'.

Arbuthnot (Kincardine), Obar Bhuadhnait. 'The mouth of the Buadhnat'.

Arcandeith (Ross), Arcan Duibh. 'Very black place'.

Ardachu (Sutherland), Àrd Achadh. 'High field'.

Ardachvie (Inverness), Àird Eachaidh or Àird Eachbhaidh. 'The point on the horse plain'.

Ardachy (Inverness), Àrdachaidh. This appears to be 'high field' with an intrusive 'i' near the end of the name, but may alternatively be 'high place'.

Ardalanish (Mull), Àird Dealanais. This Gaelic/Norse name may be 'headland at valley point'.

Ardanashaig (Argyll, Scalpay), Àird an Aiseig. 'The headland of the ferry'.

Ard an Runair (North Uist), Àird an Rùnair. This appears to mean 'the headland of the secretary', but the element, *rùnair*, may be from Norse for 'rowan' or 'rough'.

Ardargie (Perth). 'Point on the Farg', from *Àird Fhargaidh*. The same river name appears in 'Aberargie'.

Ardarroch (Ross), Àird Daraich. 'Oak headland'.

Ardbeg (Argyll, Bute, Islay), An Àird Bheag. 'The small headland'.

Ardbrecknish (Argyll), Àird Breicinis. 'Slope headland', from Norse with Gaelic *àird*, 'headland', added later.

Ardcharnich (Ross), Àird Cheatharnaich. 'Warrior headland'.

Ardchattan (Argyll), Àird Chatain. 'Catan's headland'.

Ardchivaig (Jura), Àird Chiabhaig. This Gaelic/Norse name is 'headland of enclosure bay'.

Ardchrishnish (Mull), Àird Chraoisinis. This has both Gaelic and Norse words for 'point', but the first Norse element is unclear.

Ardchronie (Ross), Àird Chrònaidh. 'The headland at the swarthy place'.

Ardchuing (Benbecula), An Àird Chumhang. 'The narrow headland'. This is also known as 'Ard Cumhang'.

Ardchyle (Perth), Àrd Choille. 'High wood'.

Ardclach (Nairn), Àird Chlach. 'Stony high point'.

Ard Cumhang (Benbecula), An Àird Chumhang. *See* **Ardchuing**.

Ardeer (Ayr). This may be 'west headland', from *Àird Iar*.

Ardelve (Ross), Àird Eilbh. This may be 'the headland at fallow land'.

Ardencaple (Dunbarton), Àird nan Capall. 'Headland of the horses'.

Ardentallen (Argyll), Àird an t-Sàilein. 'The headland at the small inlet'.

Ardentinny (Argyll), Àird an t-Sion-naich. 'The headland of the fox'.

Ardentrive (Kerrera), Àird an t-Snàimh. 'The headland of the swimming'.

Ardeonaig (Perth), Àird Eódhanaig or Àird Eónaig. 'Adamnan's headland'. The local church is *Cill Mo Charmaig*, 'St Cormac's church'. This area used to be known as 'Ardewnan', from *Àird Eódhanain* or *Àird Eónain*, but possibly by analogy with nearby places the final consonant changed from 'n' to 'g'.

Ardersier (Inverness), Àird nan Saor. 'The headland of the joiners'. This village is also known as *Am Baile Ùr*, 'the new village', and was earlier known as *Baile nan Caimbeulach*, 'the Campbells' village'.

Ardessie (Ross), Àird Easaidh. 'Head-land at the waterfall place'.

Ardfenaig (Mull), Àird Fìneig. This may be from one of two sources. If it is a wholly Gaelic name, it may be 'headland of the Fìneag', a diminutive form of *Fìne*, 'Fyne'. It could, however, be Gaelic/Norse, containing Gaelic *àird*, 'headland', and Norse *vík*, 'bay'.

Ardfern (Argyll), Àird Fheàrna. 'Alder headland'.

Ardfernal (Jura), Àird Fheàrnail. If this is a wholly Gaelic name it may mean 'alder headland', but the second part could be Norse for 'far hill', giving 'headland of the far hill'.

Ardfour (Ayr). 'Pasture point', from *Àird Phùir*.

Ardgay (Ross), Àird Ghaoithe. 'Windy or marshy point'.

Ardgour (Argyll), Àird Ghobhar. 'Goats' headland'. Local people were known as *gobhair*, 'goats'.

Ardgye (Moray). *See* **Ardgay**.

Ardhallow (Argyll), Àrd-Thalamh. 'High land'.

Ardhasaig (Harris), Àird Àsaig. This Gaelic/Norse name is 'headland at ridge bay'.

Ardheisker (North Uist), Àird Heillsgeir. 'The headland of the flat or holy rock', from Gaelic/Norse.

Ardheslaig (Ross), Àird Heisleag. 'Headland of hazel bay', from Gaelic/Norse. A local person is a *Cràiceanach*.

Ardincaple (Argyll, Dunbarton), Àird nan Capall. 'Horses' headland'.

Ardindrean (Ross), Àird an Dreagh-ainn. 'The headland with the thorn bush'.

Ardintoul (Ross), Àird an t-Sabhail. 'The headland by the barn'.

Ardivachair (South Uist), Àird a' Mhachaire. 'The headland on the machair'.

Ardkenneth (South Uist), Àird Choinnich. 'Coinneach's headland'.

Ardkinglas (Argyll), Àird Chonghlais. 'Point on the Conglass'.

Ardlair (Ross), Àird Làir. 'Mare headland'.

Ardlamont (Argyll), Àird MhicLao-mainn. 'Lamont's headland'.

Ardlui (Dunbarton), Àird Laoigh. 'The point on the Lui or Loy'.

Ardlussa (Jurra), Àird Lusa. 'The point on the Lussa'.

Ardmaddy (Argyll), Àird a' Mhadaidh or Àird Mhadaidh. 'The headland of the wolf or fox'.

Ardmair (Ross), Àird Mhèar. This may be 'finger headland'.

Ardmaleish (Bute), Àird Mo Laoise. 'St Mo Laoise's headland'.

Ardmarnock (Argyll), Àird Mhearnaig. 'St Ernoc's or M' Ernoc's headland'.

Ardmeanach (Mull), An Àird Mheadh-anach. 'The middle headland'.

Ardmenish (Jura), Àird Mhèanais. 'The headland of the narrow point', from Gaelic/Norse.

Ardmhor (Barra), An Àird Mhór. 'The large headland'.

Ardminish (Gigha), Àird Mhèanais. *See* **Ardmenish**.

Ardmore (several), An Àird Mhór. 'The large headland'.

Ard More Mangersta (Lewis), Àird Mhór Mhangartaidh. 'The large headland of Mangersta'.

Ardnacroish (Lismore), Àird na Croise. 'The headland of the cross'.

Ardnacross (Mull), Àird na Croise. *See* **Ardnacroish**.

Ardnadam (Argyll), Àird nan Damh. 'The point of the deer or oxen'.

Ardnagoine (Ross), Àird nan Gaimhne. 'The point of the stirks'.

Ardnagrask (Ross), Àird nan Crasg. 'The point of the crossing places', from older *Àird na gCrasg*.

Ardnahoe (Islay), Àird na Hogh. 'The headland of the burial mound', from Gaelic/Norse.

Ardnakille (Scalpay), Àird na Cille. 'The headland by the church'.

Ardnamonie (South Uist), Àird na Mònadh. 'The headland of the peat'.

Ardnamurchan (Argyll), Àird nam Murchan. 'The headland of the sea hounds'. Ardnamurchan Point is *Rubha Àird nam Murchan* or *An Rubha Murchanach*. A local person is a *Murchanach*, nicknamed a *cnòdan*, 'gurnet'. The rivalry between Ardnamurchan and neighbouring Sunart is recorded in the saying, *Sùrd le Suaineart! Chaidh Àird nam Murchan a dholaidh!*, 'Let Sunart rejoice! Ardnamurchan has been ruined!'. Within Ardnamurchan, a by-word for a detour is *rathad nam Mealla Ruadh chun na Ranna*, 'via Mealla Ruadh to Ranna'.

Ardnaneaskan (Ross), Àird nan Easgann. 'The point of the headland of eels'. Ardnaneaskan Point is *Rubha Àird nan Easgann*.

Ardnarff (Ross), Àird an Arbha. 'The headland with the corn'.

Ardnastruban (Grimsay), Àird nan Srùban. 'The headland of the cockles'.

Ardnave Point (Islay), Rubha Àird Néimh. 'The point of Ném's headland'.

Ardnish (Inverness), Àird Nis. 'The high point on the Ness'.

Ardoch (Moray, Perth). 'High place', from *Àrdach*. The Roman camp at Ardoch in Perthshire was known in Gaelic as *Cathair Mhaothail*, 'Muthil fort'.

Ardoe (Aberdeen). This is probably from *Àrdach*, 'high place', as Gaelic names ending is *-ach* often become anglicised as *-o* in the north-east.

Ardpatrick (Argyll), Àird Phàraig. 'Patrick's headland'. Ardpatrick Point is *Rubha Àird Phàraig*.

Ardradnaig (Perth), Àird Radanaig. This may be 'point on the rat stream'.

Ardrishaig (Argyll), Rubha Àird Driseig. The English name is 'briar headland', while the Gaelic name is 'the point on the briar headland'. A local person is a *Rubhach*, known in English as a 'Pointer'.

Ardroag (Skye), Àird Ròdhaig. 'The headland of Roag', from Gaelic/Norse.

Ardroil (Lewis), Eadra Fhadhail. 'Between two sea fords', from *Eadar Dhà Fhadhail*.

Ardross (Fife); (Ross), Àird Rois. The name in Fife is 'high point' from *Àrd Ros*, whereas the Ross name is 'the headland or high point of Ross'.

Ardrossan (Ayr), Àird Rosain. 'The point of the small promontory'.

Ardruairidh (South Uist), Àird Ruairidh. 'Roderick's headland'.

Ardsheal (Argyll), Àird Seile or Àird Sheile. This headland name contains the pre-Gaelic river name *Seile*, quite common in the west.

Ardskenish (Colonsay), Àird Sgithinis. This may be 'Skiði's headland' from Norse, with Gaelic *àird* added.

Ardslave (Harris), Àird Léimhe. This may be 'moor headland'.

Ardtalla (Islay), Àird Talla. 'Rock point'.

Ardtalnaig (Perth), Àird Talanaig. The second part of this name is unclear although the name denotes a headland.

Ardteaghanish (Scalpay), Àird Adhanais. This Gaelic/Norse may be 'the headland of tongue point'.

Ardtoe (Argyll), Àird Tobha. 'Howe headland', from Gaelic/Norse.

Ardtornish (Argyll), Àird Tòirinis. 'The headland of Thorir's or Thora's promontory', from Gaelic/Norse.

Ardtun (Mull), Àird Tunna. This may be 'enclosure headland', from Gaelic/Norse.

Arduaine (Argyll), An Àird Uaine. 'The green headland'.

Ardullie (Ross), Àird Ilidh. 'The headland of the Ilidh', a name also found further north. *See* **Helmsdale**.

Arduthie (Kincardine). 'Duthac's point', from *Àird Dhubhthaich*, possibly referring to the saint commemorated in **Tain**.

Ardvannie (Ross), Àird Mhanaigh. This is said to be 'monk's headland'.

Ardvar (Sutherland), Àird Bhàirr. This may be 'top headland'.

Ardvasar (Skye), Àird a' Bhàsair. This headland name may contain Norse *voss*, 'current', although locally believed to contain a word based on *bàs*, 'death'. Local people are known as *cearcan*, 'hens'.

Ardveenish (Barra), Àird Mhèanais. 'The headland of the narrow point', from Gaelic/Norse.

Ardverikie (Inverness), Àird Mhair-gidh. This may be 'the high point of the merkland'.

Ardvey (Harris), Àird Mhighe. 'The headland at the narrow place', from Gaelic/Norse. There are two places in Harris with this name, each with a more complete Gaelic form, namely *Àird Mhighe Leacan Lì* near Lackalee and *Àird Mhighe Fhionnasbhaigh* near Finsbay.

Ardvorlich (Perth), Àird Mhùrlaig. 'The point at the rounded inlet'.

Ardvorran (North Uist), Àird a' Bhorrain. It is not clear what this name of this headland means. *Borran* is 'buttock' or 'haunch', but it may be related to the word found in *Caolas a' Mhòrain*, the Gaelic name for the Sound of Boreray.

Ardvourlie (Harris), Àird a' Mhulaidh. This name may be 'lip headland'. A house nearby is named 'Mulag House'.

Ardvreck (Sutherland), An Àird Bhreac. 'The speckled headland'.

Ardyne (Argyll), Àird Fhìne. 'The point on the Fyne'.

Arevegaig (Argyll), Àirigh Bheagaig. This name is unclear, but contains *àirigh*, 'sheiling', and Norse *vík*, 'bay'.

Argyll, Earra-Ghàidheal. 'The coastland of the Gaels'. Mid Argyll is *Dal Riada*, named after the territory in Ireland where the Scots originated. At its peak, Argyll stretched from Kintyre to Loch Broom. South of Ardnamurchan was known as *an t-Oirthir a Deas*, 'the south coast', with the northern area called *an t-Oirthir a Tuath*, 'the north coast'. A by-name for Argyll is *Dùthaich Mhic Chailein*, 'the land of the Duke of Argyll'. Argyll and Bute together are *Earra-Ghàidheal agus Bòid*.

Arichamish (Argyll), Àirigh a' Chamais. 'The sheiling by the bay'.

Arichastlich (Argyll), Àirigh Chastulaich. 'The sheiling by the steep green hill'.

Aridrisaig (Ross), An Àirigh Dhris-each. 'The briar sheiling'.

Arienas (Argyll), Àirigh Aonghais. 'Angus's sheiling'.

Arileod (Coll), Àirigh Leòid. 'Leòd's sheiling'.

Arinacrinachd (Ross), Àirigh nan Cruithneachd. 'The sheiling of the Picts', from an earlier form, *Àirigh nan Cruithneach*. Local people were called *druinich*, 'druids', possibly a corruption of *Cruithnich*.

Arinagour (Coll), Àirigh nan Gobhar. 'The goats' sheiling'.

Arisaig (Inverness), Àrasaig. 'River mouth bay', from Norse. The sheltered nature of the bay was known to fishermen who would recommend *dèan Eige no Àrasaig dheth*, 'head for Eigg or Arisaig', in event of a storm.

Ariundle (Argyll), Àirigh Fhionndail. 'The sheiling in the fair valley', from Gaelic/ Norse.

Arivirig (Coll), Àirigh Mhaoraich. This appears to mean 'shellfish sheiling', but the name may have become corrupted from an original Norse word.

Arivruich (Lewis), Àirigh a' Bhrutha-ich. 'The sheiling on the brae'.

Armadale (several), Armadal. 'Arm valley', from Norse, referring to a bay. Armadale in West Lothian was named after Armadale in Sutherland.

Arnabol (Sutherland), Àrnabol. 'Eagle farm' or 'Arne's farm', from Norse.

Arnipol (Inverness), Àrnapol. *See* **Arnabol**.

Arnabost (Coll), Àrnabost. *See* **Arnabol**.

Arnclay (Perth), Earrann a' Chlaidh. 'The portion (of land) at the graveyard'.

Arnclerich (Perth). 'The cleric's portion of land', from *Earrann a' Chléirich*.

Arndean (Kinross). 'The dean's portion of land', from *Earrann an Deadhain*.

Arndilly (Moray). 'The point at the green hill', from *Àird an Tulaich*.

Arnisdale (Inverness), Àrnasdal. 'Arne's valley', from Norse.

Arnish (Lewis), Àirinis; (Raasay), Àrnais. 'Eagle headland', from Norse.

Arnisort (Skye), Àrnasort. 'Arne's firth', from Norse.

Arnmannoch (Kirkcudbright). 'The monks' portion of land', from *Earrann nam Manach*.

Arnol (Lewis), Àrnol. 'Eagle hill', from Norse.

Arnprior (Stirling). 'The prior's portion of land'. This was earlier known on English as 'Erne-frear', showing more clearly the Gaelic derivation, *Earrann a' Phriair*.

Arnvicar (Perth). 'The vicar's portion of land', from *Earrann a' Bhiocair*.

Aros (Mull), Àros or Àras. 'River mouth', from Norse.

Arpafeelie (Ross), Arpa-philidh. This name is unclear.

Arran, Arainn. This is unclear and said to be unrelated to the name 'Aran' in Ireland which is *Árainn* with a long initial 'a'. However, if the names are linked they mean 'kidney shaped'. Arran has the poetic name, *Arainn nan Aighean Iomadh*, 'Arran of the many stags'. A native of Arran is an *Arannach* or *Arainneach* also called *coinean mór*, 'big rabbit'. In Arran the people of various settlements had their own nicknames as in the rhyme, *Meanbh-chuileagan Acha-Rà, coilich dhubha an Dubh Ghearraidh, stùcanaich /tùiteallaich Achadh a' Charra, cuileagan-ime Chatagail, feannagan Achadh a' Ghallain*, 'Midges from Achara, black cocks from Dougrie, stuckup/awkward folk from Auchencar, butter flies from Catacol, crows from Achagallon'. The coast between North Thundergay and Whitefarland is called *an Luirgeann*, 'the shank'. The Cock of Arran is also known as *an Coileach Arannach*, 'the Arran cock' and *an Coileach Clachaig*, 'the stone cock'. In olden times sailors would have been considered lucky if in one day's sailing they had seen *a' Chearc Leódhasach, an Coileach Arannach agus an Eireag Mhanannach*, 'the Lewis Chicken, the Cock of Arran and the Manx Pullet'.

Arrivain (Perth), Àirigh a' Mheadhain. 'The sheiling in the middle'.

Arrochar (Dunbarton), An t-Àrar or An Tairbeart Iar. The English and first Gaelic names are obscure but may be related to 'Ben Arthur'. The second Gaelic name is 'the west isthmus', Tarbet Loch Lomond lying to the east.

Arscaig (Sutherland), Àrsgaig. 'Strip of land by a river', from Norse.

Artafallie (Ross), Àirde Fàillidh. This may be 'high point of the sods'.

Aruadh (Islay), An t-Àth Ruadh. 'The red-brown ford'.

Ascog (Bute), Àsgaig. 'Ash bay', from Norse.

Ashaig (Skye), Aiseag. 'Ferry'. The full name is *Aiseag Maol Ruibhe*, 'St Maol Rubha's ferry', the saint commemorated in Applecross. The initial vowel can be pronounced long, giving *Àiseag*, which might point to a Norse origin suggesting 'ash bay' rather than the Gaelic derivation which would normally be expected to contain the definite article.

Ashcraig (Arran), Baile Uachdrach. The English name is 'ash rock', but the Gaelic name is 'upper farm'.

Ashentilly (Kincardine). 'Stream at the green hill', from *Eas an Tulaich*.

Ashfield (Argyll), Learg na h-Uinnsinn. The Gaelic name is 'the ash slope'.

Ashintully (Perth). 'The stream at the green hill', from *Eas an Tulaich*.

Ashmore (Perth), An t-Eas Mór. 'The big waterfall'.

Askernish (South Uist), Àisgearnais. This may be 'ash field point', from Norse.

Asknish (Argyll), Aisginis. 'Ash tree point', from Norse.

Assynt (Ross, Sutherland), Asaint or Asainn. 'Ridge end', from Norse. Mid Assynt is *Meadhan Asaint*, 'the middle of Assynt', and Upper Assynt is *Àrd Asaint*, 'high Assynt'. An Assynt person is an *Asainteach*.

Astle (Sutherland), Àsdal. 'Aspen valley', from Norse.

Atholl (Perth), Athall. 'New Ireland', from *Àth Fhótla*, *Fótla* being a poetic term for Ireland. A local person is an *Athallach*. The Forest of Atholl is *Frìth Athaill*. A short ditty from the early days of coaching outlines the progress made in a day's travel from Atholl to Badenoch, *Bracaist am Baile Chloichrigh, lunch an Dail na Ceàrdaich, dìnneir an Dail Chuinnidh 's a' bhanais ann an Ràt*, 'Breakfast in Pitlochry, lunch in Dalnacardoch, dinner in Dalwhinnie and the wedding in Raitts'.

Attadale (Ross), Atadal. This may be 'fight valley', from Norse.

Auch (Argyll), Achadh Innis Chalainn. The English form is from 'field'. The Gaelic name is 'the field at the meadow of Calann'.

Auchabrick (Wigtown). 'Speckled field', from *Achadh Breac*.

Auchagallon (Arran), Achadh a' Ghallain. 'The field of the standing stone'. An alternative derivation is found in *Achadh a' Ghaillinn*, 'the field of the storm'.

Auchaleffan (Arran), Achadh an Leth-pheighinn. 'The field of the half pennyland'.

Auchallater (Aberdeen). *See* **Achallater**.

Auchareoch (Arran), Achadh Riabhach; (Bute), An t-Achadh Riabhach. 'Brindled field'. The Arran name lacks the expected definite article.

Aucharrigill (Sutherland), Achadh Uraigil. This Gaelic/Norse name is 'the field at the stony ravine'.

Auchenbegg (Lanark). 'Small field', from *Achadh Beag*. This name shows how 'Auchen-' or 'Auchin-', which should mean 'field of the', came to replace 'Auch', 'field', as the generic in many place-names.

Auchenblae (Kincardine). 'Field of blossoms', from *Achadh nam Blàth*.

Auchenbowie (Stirling). 'Yellow field', from *Achadh Buidhe*. See **Auchenbegg**.

Auchenbrack (Aberdeen). 'Speckled field', from *Achadh Breac*. See **Auchenbegg**.

Auchenbrain (Ayr), Achadh na Bràthann. 'The field of the quern'. See **Mauchline**.

Auchencairn (Arran, Kirkcudbright), Achadh a' Chàirn. 'The field with the cairn'. In Arran, Auchencairn is sub-divided into *Baile Ìochdrach*, 'lower farm', and *Baile Uachdrach*, 'upper farm'.

Auchencar (Arran), Achadh a' Charra. 'The field with the standing stone'. Locals were known as *stùcanaich*, 'stuck up people', or *tùiteallaich*, 'awkward people'.

Auchenclech (Aberdeen). 'The field with the stone', from *Achadh na Cloiche*.

Auchencorth (Midlothian). 'The field with the standing stone', from *Achadh na Coirthe*.

Auchencrosh (Ayr). 'The field of the cross', from *Achadh na Croise*.

Auchencrow (Berwick). This looks like a Gaelic field name, but in the 14th century the name was 'Aldenecraw' and more likely of English origin.

Auchencruive (Ayr). 'The field with the tree', from *Achadh na Craoibhe*.

Auchendarg (Aberdeen). Possibly 'red field', from *Achadh Dearg*. See **Auchenbegg**.

Auchendinny (Midlothian). 'Field of the fire' from *Achadh an Teine* or 'field of the fox', from *Achadh an t-Sionnaich*.

Auchendryne (Aberdeen). Ach an Droighinn. 'The field with the thorn bush'.

Auchenfedrick (Dumfries). 'Patrick's field', from *Achadh Phàdraig*. See **Auchenbegg**.

Auchengavin (Dunbarton), Achadh nan Gamhainn. 'The field of the stirks'.

Auchenhalrig (Moray). 'The field at the deer trap', from *Achadh na h-Eilreig*.

Auchenhard (West Lothian). 'The field at the high point', from *Achadh na h-Àirde*.

Auchenharvie (Ayr). 'The field at the boundary wall', from *Achadh na h-Eirbhe*.

Auchenlay (Perth). This may be 'the doctor's field', from *Achadh an Léigh*, or 'the field of the calf', from *Achadh an Laoigh*, but it is uncertain.

Auchenlochan (Argyll), Achadh an Lochain. 'The field by the small loch'.

Auchenlongford (Ayr). 'The field of the encampment', from *Achadh an Longphuirt*.

Auchenreath (Banff). 'The field on the slope', from *Achadh na Ruighe*.

Auchenrioch (Argyll), Achadh na Riabhach. 'Brindled field'. The Gaelic name does not make grammatical sense, but shows how *Achadh na*, 'field of the', appears to have superceded plain *Achadh*, 'field', as a generic in place-names, in a way paralleled in English forms starting with 'Auchen-' and 'Auchin-'.

Auchenrivock (Dumfries). 'Brindled field', from *Achadh Riabhach*. See **Auchenbegg**.

Auchenroy (Ayr). 'Russet field', from *Achadh Ruadh*. See **Auchenbegg**.

Auchensavil (Argyll), Achadh nan Sabhal. 'The field with the barns'.

Auchenshuggle (Glasgow). This may be 'the rye field', from *Achadh an t-Seagail*.

Auchentaggart (Dumfries). 'The priest's field', from *Achadh an t-Sagairt*.

Auchentiber (Ayr). 'The field with the well', from *Achadh an Tiobair*.

Auchinairn (Dunbarton). 'The field of the alder', from *Achadh an Fheàrna*.

Auchinbo (Aberdeen). 'Field of the cows', from *Achadh nam Bó*.

Auchindachy (Banff), Ach Choinneachaidh. This may be 'the meeting field'.

Auchindarroch (Argyll), Achadh nan Darach. 'The field of the oaks'.

Auchindoir (Aberdeen), Ach an Tòrr. 'The field by the hill', but the English form hints at the possibility of *dobhar*, 'water', rather than *tòrr* as the second element.

Auchindoun (Banff). 'The field at the hill(fort)', from *Achadh an Dùin*.

Auchindownie (Fife). Older forms of the name suggest that this was originally *Aodann Dùnaidh*, 'hill face of Dùnaidh', rather than deriving from *achadh*.

Auchindrain (Argyll), Achadh an Droighinn. 'The field with the thorn bush'.

Auchindrum (Aberdeen). 'The field at the ridge', from *Achadh an Droma*.

Auchineden (Stirling). 'The field at the hill face', from *Achadh an Aodainn*.

Auchinhove (Aberdeen). 'The field at the cave or hollow', from *Achadh na h-Uamha*.

Auchinleck (Ayr). 'Field with slabs or flagstones', from *Achadh nan Leac*.

Auchinleith (Aberdeen). This was formerly written as 'Auchincleith' and 'Auchincleche', suggesting 'the field with the stone', from *Achadh na Cloiche*.

Auchinloch (Dunbarton). 'Field by the loch', from *Achadh an Locha*.

Auchinreoch (Kirkcudbright, Stirling). *See* **Auchareoch**.

Auchintarph (Aberdeen). 'The field of the bull or bulls', from *Achadh an Tairbh* or *Achadh nan Tarbh*.

Auchintoul (Aberdeen), Ach an t-Sabhail. 'The field at the barn'.

Auchleuchries (Aberdeen). 'Reedy field', from *Achadh Luachrach*.

Auchleven (Aberdeen). 'Elm field', from *Achadh Leamhan*.

Auchlyne (Perth), Achadh Loinne. This may mean 'stack-yard field', as *loinn* had the meaning of 'stack-yard' in Perthshire Gaelic. Normally, however, *loinn* means 'good condition or appearance', which may be what is intended. The old chapel at Auchlyne was *Caibeal na Fairg(e)*, 'the chapel of the shrine'.

Auchmachor (Aberdeen). 'St Machar's field', from *achadh* and *Madhchar*, 'St Machar'.

Auchmore (Aberdeen, Arran). *See* **Achmore**.

Auchmuir (Fife). Although apparently a name beginning with *achadh*, 'field', older forms of the name suggest that this was *Àth Mór*, 'big ford'.

Auchnaclach (Aberdeen). 'The field of the stones', from *Achadh nan Clach*.

Auchnaclache (Islay), Achadh nan Clach. 'The field of the stones'.

Auchnacloich (Argyll), Achadh na Cloiche. 'The field with the stone'.

Auchnafree (Perth), Achadh na Frithe. 'The field at the deer forest'.

Auchnagallin (Moray). This may be 'the field of the standing stones', from *Achadh nan Gallan*.

Auchnagatt (Aberdeen). 'The field of the cats', from *Achadh nan Cat*. The older Gaelic spelling, *Achadh na gCat*, shows the voicing of initial voiceless consonants in certain situations.

Auchnahannet (Moray). 'The field at the mother church', from *Achadh na h-Annaid*.

Auchnarrow (Banff). 'The corn field', from *Achadh an Arbha*.

Auchness (Moray). 'The field at the stream or waterfall', from *Achadh an Easa*.

Auchnoon (Midlothian). 'The field of the lambs', from *Achadh nan Uan*.

Aucholzie (Aberdeen), Ach Choille. 'Wood field'.

Auchrannie (Arran), Achadh an Rainigh. 'The field of bracken', showing the older form of the genitive of *raineach*, still found in the southern Gaelic-speaking areas.

Auchreddy (Aberdeen), Achadh Reite. The first part of the name is 'field', but the second is unclear. *Achadh Reite* is also the Gaelic name of New Deer.

Auchroisk (Banff, Moray). 'The field at the crossing place', from *Achadh a' Chroisg*.

Auchtascailt (Ross), Achadh Dà Sgaillt. This may be 'field with two bald patches'.

Auchterarder (Perth), Uachdar Àrdair. 'The upland of the Arder'.

Auchteraw (Inverness), Uachdar Abha. 'Upland of the Oich'. This name shows that the river flowing into Loch Oich was called *Abha* before the name altered to *Obhaich*.

Auchterderran (Fife). This was not originally a name containing 'auchter' or *uachdar*, 'upland', but may be related to the element found in **Urchany**. The second element is *deòradh*, 'dewar, relic-holder'.

Auchterflow (Ross), Uachdar Chlò. This may be 'windy upland'. This place is mentioned in a saying found with local variants in a number of places, *Buntàta proinnt' is uachdar leotha, biadh bodaich Uachdar Chlò*, 'Mashed potatoes and cream, the food of the old men of Auchterflow'.

Auchtergavan (Perth), Uachdar Ghamhair. 'The upland of the winter land'.

Auchterless (Aberdeen). 'The upland of the fortified enclosure', from *Uachdar Leasa*.

Auchtermuchty (Fife), Uachdar Mucadaidh. 'The upland of the pig place'.

Auchterneed (Ross), Uachdar Niad. This may be 'the upland of the stream',

with a cognate of Brythonic *nant*, 'stream'.

Auchtertool (Fife). This may be 'Tuathal's upland', from *Uachdar Thuathail*, but a nearby river might instead be the defining element.

Auchtertyre (Moray, Ross), Uachdar Thìre. 'The top of the land'. In Ross, the name was locally pronounced as *Uachdar Ìridh*.

Auchtogorm (Moray), An t-Ochdamh Gorm. 'The green octave or eighth-land'.

Auldcharmaig (Ross), Allt Charmaig. 'Cormac's stream'.

Auldearn (Nairn), Allt Éire or Allt Éireann. 'The stream of Ireland'. *See* **Strathearn**.

Aulich (Perth), Abhlaich. 'Water place'.

Auliston Point (Argyll), Rubha nan Amhlaistean. This appears to mean 'the headland of the circumventions'.

Aultachruinn (Ross), Allt a' Chruinn. 'Stream of the tree'.

Aultanrynie (Sutherland), Allt an Reidhinidh. This stream name is unclear although *reidhneach* is applied to a cow yielding no milk. Nearby Loch More is *Loch an Reidhinidh*.

Aultbea (Ross), An t-Allt Beithe or Am Fàn. The English and first Gaelic names are 'the birch stream' and originally applied to the stream running through the village. The second Gaelic name is 'the slope'. To express 'in Aultbea' Gaelic uses *air an Allt Bheithe* or *air an Fhàn*, 'on Aultbea'. An older Gaelic name for Aultbea was *Am Fàn Braonach*, 'the slope of the Loch Broom area'. Local people are known as *rodain*, 'rats' or *Fànaich*, 'slope people'.

Aultgrishan (Ross), Allt Ghrìsean. 'Brindled stream'. *Grìsean* is a contraction of *grìs-fhionn*. Locals are known as *crùbagan*, 'crabs', or *Grìseanaich*, 'brindled ones'.

Aultguish (Ross), An t-Allt Giuthais. 'The pine or fir stream'.

Aultiphurst (Sutherland), Allt a' Phuirt. 'The stream by the port'.

Aultivulin (Sutherland), Allt a' Mhuilinn. 'The stream of the mill'. This village is also known as Millburn.

Aultmore (Banff). 'Big stream', from *Allt Mór*.

Aultnagar (Sutherland), Allt nan Car. 'The stream with the turns', from older *Allt na gCar*.

Aultnamain (Ross), Taigh a' Mhonaidh. *See* **Altnamain**.

Aultnaskiach (Inverness), Allt nan Sgitheach. 'The stream of the hawthorns'.

Aultonrea (Aberdeen). 'The stream on the slope', from *Allt an Ruighe*.

Aultroy (Ross), An t-Allt Ruadh. 'The red-brown stream'.

Aultsigh (Inverness), Allt Saidhe. 'Bitch stream', streams often being named after animals.

Aundrary (Ross), Anndrairigh. The first part of this Norse field or sheiling name is unclear.

Avernish (Ross), Abhairnis. 'Bulky headland', from Norse. Local people were nicknamed *faoileagan*, 'gulls'.

Avielochan (Inverness), Aghaidh an Lochain. 'The hill face by the small loch'.

Aviemore (Inverness), An Aghaidh Mhór. 'The big hill face'.

Avoch (Ross), Abhach. 'Water place'. The local church is *Cill Ainndreis*, 'St Andrew's church'.

Avonbridge (Stirling). 'Avon' is a common element in the Celtic languages denoting a river and is found as *abhainn* in Gaelic and Irish and *afon* in Welsh.

Ayr, Inbhir Àir. 'The mouth of the River Ayr'. Ayrshire is *Siorrachd Inbhir Àir*.

Back (Lewis), Am Bac. 'The bank', from Norse. To express 'in Back', Gaelic uses *air a' Bhac*, 'on Back'. A native of Back is a *Bacach*, also

nicknamed an *adag*, 'haddock'.

Backhill (Berneray), Cùl na Beinne. 'The back of the hill'.

Backies (Sutherland), Na Bacannan. 'The banks', from Norse.

Back of Keppoch (Inverness), Cùl na Ceapaich. 'The back of Keppoch'.

Badachonachar (Ross), Bad Chonachair. *Bad* is a 'spot' or 'copse' and *conachair* can mean 'uproar', but the second part may be a genitive of the personal name *Conchobhar*, to give 'Conchobhar's spot'.

Badachro (Ross), An Caolas. The Gaelic name is 'the strait', but the English form comes from *Bad a' Chrò*, 'the copse or clump by the sheep-fold', which Gaelic uses as the name of Badachro Farm only.

Badagyle (Ross), Bad a' Ghoill. 'The copse of the non-Gael'.

Badanluig (Ross), Bad an Luig. 'The copse in the hollow'.

Badantional (Ross), Bad an Inneail. 'The copse of the tackle or instrument'.

Badbea (Ross), Am Bad Beithe. 'The birch copse'.

Badcall (Ross), Bada Call. 'Hazel copse'.

Baddoch (Aberdeen), A' Bhadach. 'The copse place'.

Badenloch (Sutherland), Bad an Locha. 'The copse by the loch'.

Badenoch (Inverness), Bàideanach. 'Drowned place'. A short ditty from the early days of coaching outlines the progress made in a day from Atholl to Badenoch, *Bracaist am Baile Chloichrigh, lunch an Dail na Ceàrdaich, dìnneir an Dail Chuinnidh 's a' bhanais ann an Ràt*, 'Breakfast in Pitlochry, lunch in Dalnacardoch, dinner in Dalwhinnie and the wedding in Raitts'.

Badenscoth (Aberdeen). 'The copse of the flowers', from *Bad nan Sgoth*.

Badentarbat (Ross), Bad an Tairbeirt. 'The copse at the isthmus'.

Badenyon (Aberdeen). This appears to be 'the copse of the bird', from *Bad an Eòin*, but is uncertain.

Badfearn (Ross), Am Bad Feàrna. 'The alder copse'.

Badicaul (Ross), Bada Call. 'Hazel copse'.

Badinluchie (Ross), Bad an Fhliuchaidh. 'The copse or spot of the wetting'.

Badintagairt (Sutherland), Bad an t-Sagairt. 'The priest's copse'.

Badluachrach (Ross), Am Bad Luarach or Am Bad Luachrach. 'The reedy copse'.

Badnegie (Caithness), Bad na Gaoithe. 'The windy or marshy copse'.

Badour (Argyll), Bad Odhair. This appears to be 'dun copse', but may have originally been *Bad Dobhair*, 'water or river copse'.

Badralloch (Ross), Am Bad Ràilleach or Am Bad Tràilleach. The first Gaelic name may be 'the oak copse', but the second appears to contain *tràill*, 'slave'.

Badscally (Ross), Bad Sgàlaidh. 'Eerie spot or copse'.

Badvo (Perth), Bad a' Bhoth. 'The copse at the hut'.

Badvoon (Ross), Gràdal. The English form may come from *Bad a' Mhuin*, 'the copse at the hilly clump', while the Gaelic form is 'grey valley', from Norse.

Baile Boidheach (Argyll), Am Baile Bòidheach. 'The beautiful farm or village'.

Baile Mor (Iona), Am Baile Mór. 'The big farm'.

Bailliemore (Kerrera), Am Baile Mór. *See* **Baile Mor**.

Balachroan (Inverness), Baile a' Chròthain. 'The farm with the small sheep fold'.

Balallan (Lewis), Baile Ailein. 'Alan's township'.

Balanloan (Perth). 'The farm by the pond', from *Baile an Lòin*.

Balanreich (Perth). 'The heather farm', from *Baile an Fhraoich*.

Balantyre (Perth), Baile an t-Saoir. 'The joiner's farm'.

Balarumindhu (Colonsay), Baile Raomainn Dubh. 'Raomann's black farm'.

Balaruminmore (Colonsay), Baile Raomainn Mór. 'Raomann's big farm'.

Balavetchy (Colonsay), Baile a' Mhaide. 'The farm of the stick'.

Balavil (Inverness, Ross), Baile a' Bhile. 'The farm at the sacred tree or rock edge'.

Balbaird (Fife). 'The poet's farm', from *Baile a' Bhàird*.

Balbairdie (Fife). This may be 'the poet's farm', from *Baile a' Bhàird*, but if the Gaelic was *Baile Bàrdaidh* it may be 'the farm at the poet's place'.

Balbardie (West Lothian). *See* **Balbairdie**.

Balbeg (Inverness), Am Baile Beag. 'The small farm'.

Balbeggie (Fife, Perth). This may be 'place of the small farm', from *Baile Beagaidh*.

Balblair (Nairn, Ross), Baile a' Bhlàir. 'The farm on the moor'.

Balcaskie (Fife). This may be 'the farm at the projecting ridge', from *Baile Gasgaidh*, earlier *Baile Gasgain*.

Balchalum (Perth), Baile Chaluim. 'Calum's farm'.

Balcherry (Ross), Baile a' Cheathraimh. 'The farm on the quarter-land'.

Balchladich (Sutherland), Baile a' Chladaich. 'The farm by the shore'.

Balchrick (Sutherland), Baile a' Chnuic. 'The farm at the hill'.

Balchristie (Fife). 'Christopher's farm', from *Baile Chrìsdein*.

Balcladich (Caithness). 'Farm by the shore', from *Baile a' Chladaich*.

Balcomie (Fife). 'Colman's farm', from *Baile Cholmain*.

Balconie (Ross), Bailcnidh. 'Strong place'.

Balconish (Inverness), Baile a' Chonais. 'The farm of the dispute'. Local people were nicknamed *gearran beaga*, 'little hares'.

Balcormo (Fife). 'Cormac's farm', from *Baile Charmaig*, as an older English form, 'Balcormak', would attest.

Balcruvie (Fife). 'Wooded farm', from *Baile Craobhaigh*. This was also 'Pit-cruvie', showing Pictish *pett*, 'lands', which changed to Gaelic *baile*.

Baldernock (Dunbarton). 'Ernoc's or D' Ernoc's farm', from *Baile Dearnaig*.

Baldinnie (Fife). This may be 'the farm of the sons of Donnacan or Donnachan', from *Baile Mac Dhonnacain/Dhonnachain*.

Baldoon (Ross), Baile an Dùin. 'The farm by the hill(fort)'.

Baldornoch (Perth). 'Pebbly farm', from *Baile Dòrnach*.

Baldovan (Angus). 'Deep spot or place', from *Ball Domhain*.

Baldutho (Fife). 'Dubhthach's farm', from *Baile Dhubhthaich*.

Balechurn (Raasay), Baile a' Chùirn. 'The farm at the cairn'.

Baledmund (Perth), Baile Admainn. 'Admann's farm'.

Balegra (Arran), Baile Ìochdrach. 'Lower farm'. There is a corresponding Baluagra or *Baile Uachdrach*, 'upper farm'.

Baleloch (North Uist), Baile an Locha. 'The farm by the loch'.

Balemartin (Tiree), Baile Mhàrtainn. 'Martin's farm'.

Balemeanach (Skye), Am Baile Meadhanach. 'The middle farm'.

Balephuil (Tiree), Baile a' Phuill. 'The farm by the bog or pool'.

Balerno (Midlothian). 'Sloe-tree farm', from *Baile Airneach*.

Baleshare (North Uist), Am Baile Sear. 'The east farm'.

Balevulin (Tiree), Baile a' Mhuilinn. 'The farm at the mill'.

Balfour (several). 'Pasture farm', from *Baile Phùir*.

Balfron (Stirling). This may be from *Baile Freòin* and connected with the river name in Glen Fruin which seems to stem from *freòine*, 'fury', but older anglicised forms of the name go against this derivation.

Balgarva (South Uist), Baile Gharbhaidh. 'Garbhach's farm'.

Balgaveny (Banff). 'The farm with the stirk', from *Baile a' Ghamhna*.

Balgaverie (Fife). 'Winter farm', from *Baile Geamhraidh*.

Balgay (Angus). 'Windy or marshy farm', from *Baile Gaoithe*.

Balgeddie (Fife). *See* **Bargeddie**.

Balgone (East Lothian). This may be 'the farm of the dogs', from *Baile nan Con*, earlier spelled *Baile na gCon*.

Balgonie (Fife). *See* **Balgown**.

Balgorney (West Lothian). 'Miry farm', from *Baile Gronnaigh*.

Balgour (Perth). 'The farm with the goats', from *Baile nan Gobhar*.

Balgove (Fife). 'The smith's farm', from *Baile a' Ghobha*.

Balgown (Skye), Baile a' Ghobhainn. 'The smith's farm'.

Balgownie (Aberdeen). *See* **Balgown**.

Balgrummo (Fife). 'Gormag's farm', from *Baile Ghormaig*.

Balgy (Ross), Balgaidh. 'Bag-shaped place'. Local people are known as *balgairean*, 'foxes'.

Balhagarty (Kincardine). This may be 'farm at the priest's place', from *Baile Shagartaidh*.

Balhalloch (Aberdeen). This is said to be 'old womens' farm', from *Baile Chailleach*, although the name may refer to nuns

Balharvie (Fife). 'The farm with the boundary wall', from *Baile na h-Airbhe*.

Baligarve (Lismore), Am Baile Garbh. 'The rough farm'.

Baligrundle (Lismore), Baile Grunndail. This may be 'the farm at Grunndal', this being Norse for 'green valley'.

Balindore (Argyll), Baile an Dobhair. 'The farm by the water or river'.

Balinoe (Tiree), Am Baile Nodha. 'The new farm'.

Balintore (Angus, Inverness, Ross), Baile an Todhair. 'The farm of seaweed or bleaching'. Balintore in Angus is some distance from the sea, and the name here probably refers to bleaching. The old name of Balintore in Ross is *Port an Ab*, 'the abbot's port', which led to local people being known as *abaich*, 'abbot people', as well as *sgalltairean*, 'jellyfish'. Residents of the area of Balintore known as *am Bàrd*, 'the Park', were known as *bàrdanaich*.

Balintraid (Ross), Baile na Tràghad. 'The farm by the beach'.

Balivanich (Benbecula), Baile a' Mhanaich. 'The monk's farm'. Nearby is Nunton or *Baile nan Cailleach*.

Balkaithley (Fife). 'Cathalan's farm', from *Baile Chathalain*.

Balkeith (Sutherland), Baile na Coille. 'The farm by the wood'. The English form suggests that this may have been formed with Brythonic *coed* rather than *coille*, 'wood'.

Balknock (Skye), Baile nan Cnoc. 'The farm in the hills'.

Balla (Eriskay), Am Baile. 'The village'.

Ballachrosk (Aberdeen). 'The farm at the crossing place', from *Baile a' Chroisg*.

Ballachulish (Argyll), Baile a' Chaolais. 'The village at the narrows'. The old name was *Caolas Mhic Phàdraig*, 'the narrows of Patrick's son'.

Ballachurn (Banff). 'The farm at the cairn', from *Baile a' Chùirn*.

Ballagan (Stirling). 'The farm in the hollow', from *Baile an Lagain*.

Ballaglas (Grimsay), Am Baile Glas. 'The grey-green township'.

Ballanlish (Banff). 'The farm with the garden or fortified enclosure', from *Baile an Leis*.

Ballantrae (Ayr), Baile na Tràgha. 'The farm by the beach'. The old name was *Cill Chuithbeirt*, 'St Cuthbert's

church', which is also the Gaelic name of Kirkcudbright.

Ballantruan (Banff). 'The farm by the little stream', from *Baile an t-Sruthain*.

Ballantrushal (Lewis), Baile an Truiseil. 'The farm at the Truiseal stone', a standing stone the name of which comes from Norse *thrus*, 'goblin'.

Ballater (Aberdeen), Bealadair or Bealdair. This name is unclear except from the fact that it is not a *baile* name. Easter Ballater is *Bealadair Shìos* and the Pass of Ballater is *Creagach Bhealadair*, 'the rocky place of Ballater'.

Ballaterach (Aberdeen), Baile Leitreach. 'The slope farm'.

Ballchladdich (Sutherland), Baile a' Chladaich. 'The farm by the shore'.

Ballchraggan (Ross), Lòn nam Ban. The English form is from *Baile a' Chreagain*, 'the farm at the small rock', while the Gaelic name is 'the women's meadow'.

Ballechin (Perth), Baile Eachainn. 'Eachann's farm'.

Balleigh (Ross), Baile an Lighe or Baile an Lighiche. 'The doctor's farm'.

Ballencrieff (East Lothian, West Lothian). 'The farm by the tree', from *Baile na Craoibhe*.

Ballentoul (Perth), Baile an t-Sabhail. 'The farm with the barn'.

Balliefurth (Moray). 'The farm at the port', from *Baile a' Phuirt*.

Balliekine (Argyll), Bàinleacainn; (Arran) A' Bhàinleacainn. 'White broad slope'. People from the Arran place of this name were nicknamed *calmain*, 'pigeons', while the place itself was sub-divided into *Baile Ìochdrach*, 'lower farm', and *Baile Uachdrach*, 'upper farm'.

Balliemeanoch (Argyll), Am Baile Meadhanach. 'The middle farm'.

Balliemore (Argyll), Am Baile Mór; (Inverness) A' Bhealaidh Mhór. In Argyll this is 'the big farm', but the

Inverness name is 'the big broom', referring to the type of bush.

Ballieward (Inverness), Baile a' Bhàird. 'The farm with the meadow'.

Ballifeary (Inverness), Baile na Faire. 'The farm of the watch or guard'.

Balligill (Sutherland), Bàiligil. This may be 'grassy ravine', from Norse.

Ballinaby (Islay), Baile an Aba. 'The abbot's farm'.

Ballindeoir (Argyll), Baile an Deòir. 'The farm of the relic keeper'.

Ballindewar (Perth). *See* **Ballindeoir**.

Ballingrew (Perth), Baile nan Craobh. 'The farm by the trees', from older *Baile na gCraobh*.

Ballinakill (Argyll), Baile na Cille. 'The farm at the church'.

Ballindalloch (Banff), Baile na Dalach. 'The farm at the haugh'.

Ballindean (Fife, Perth). Possibly 'the dean's farm', from *Baile an Deadhain*.

Ballindeor (Argyll). 'The pilgrim's farm', from *Baile an Deòir*.

Ballindollo (Angus). *See* **Ballindalloch**.

Ballingall (Fife). 'Farm of the non-Gaels', from *Baile nan Gall*.

Ballinlagg (Moray). This appears to be 'the farm in the hollows', from *Baile nan Lag*.

Ballinloan (Perth). 'The farm by the pond', from *Baile an Lòin*.

Ballinluig (Perth), Baile an Luig. 'The farm in the hollow'.

Ballinroich (Ross), Baile an Rothaich. 'Munro's farm'.

Ballintomb (Moray). *See* **Ballintuim**. There are two places with this name, the one near Knockando being the site of the planned village of Archiestown, built for Sir Archibald Grant.

Ballintuim (Perth), Baile an Tuim. 'The farm at the hillock'.

Ballivicar (Islay), Baile a' Bhiocair. 'The vicar's farm'.

Ballo (Fife). 'Pass', from *Bealach*.

Balloan (Inverness, Nairn). 'The farm by the pond', from *Baile an Lòin*.

Balloch (Dunbarton), Bealach; (Inverness), Baile an Locha. In Dunbarton, the name means 'pass'. In Inverness it is 'the farm by the loch'.

Ballochbuie (Aberdeen), Bealach Buidhe. 'Yellow pass'. Ballochbuie Forest is *Frìth Bhealaich Bhuidhe*.

Ballochgoy (Ayr, Bute). This is probably 'windy pass', from *Bealach Gaoithe*.

Ballochmartin (Cumbrae). 'Martin's pass', from *Bealach Mhàrtainn*.

Ballochmyle (Ayr). 'Blunt pass', from *Bealach Maol*.

Ballochyle (Argyll), Baile a' Chaoil. 'The farm at the strait'.

Ballogie (Aberdeen). 'The farm in the place of the hollow' or rather 'the farm of Logie', from *Baile Lagaidh*.

Ballygown (Arran, Mull), Baile a' Ghobhainn. 'The smith's farm'.

Ballygrant (Islay), Baile a' Ghràna. This may be 'the grain farm'.

Ballygrogan (Argyll), Baile Ghrogain. 'Grogan's farm'.

Ballygrundle (Lismore), Baile Grunndail. *See* **Baligrundle**.

Ballyhaugh (Coll), Baile Hogh. 'The farm at Hogh', this being Norse for 'mound'.

Ballyhennan (Dunbarton). 'Seanan's farm', from *Baile Sheanain*.

Ballymeanoch (Arran), Baile Meadhanach. 'Middle farm'. It is worth noting that the definite article is missing from this name, a common feature of Arran place-names.

Ballymichael (Arran), Baile Mhìcheil. 'Michael's farm'.

Ballymony (Islay), Baile a' Mhonaidh. 'The farm at the hill or upland'.

Balmacaan (Inverness), Baile Mac Cathain. 'The farm of the son of Cathan'.

Balmacara (Ross), Baile Mac Ara or Baile Mac Carra. 'The farm of the son of Ara or Carra'.

Balmachree (Inverness). This may be 'Mo Chridhe's farm', from *Baile Mo*

Chridhe, in memory of a Gaelic saint, but *Baile mo chridhe* could be 'my beloved farm', although this is unlikely.

Balmaclellan (Kirkcudbright). 'Maclellan's farm', from *Baile MhicIllFhaolain* or 'the farm of GillFhaolain's son', from *Baile Mac IllFhaolain.*

Balmacnaughton (Perth), Baile Mac Neachdain. 'The farm of Neachdan's son'.

Balmacqueen (Skye), Baile MhicCuithein. 'MacQueen's farm'.

Balmaghie (Kirkcudbright). 'MacGhie's farm', from *Baile MhicAoidh*, or 'the farm of Aodh's son', from *Baile Mac Aoidh.*

Balmaglaister (Inverness), Baile Mac Glasdair. This appears to mean 'the farm of the son of Glasdar', but the name was originally *Bad a' Ghlaistir*, 'the grassy copse'.

Balmaha (Stirling), Baile Mo Thatha. 'St Mo Thatha's farm'. The generic element here may originally have been *bealach*, 'pass'.

Balmain (Fife, Perth). 'Middle farm', from *Baile Meadhain.*

Balmainish (Skye), Baile Mhànais. 'Magnus' farm'.

Balmakeith (Nairn), Baile MacCàidh or Baile MacDhàidh. 'Davidson's farm'.

Balmakewan (Kincardine). 'MacEwan's farm', from *Baile MhicEóghainn*, or 'Ewan's son's farm', from *Baile Mac Eóghainn.*

Balmalcolm (Fife) 'Malcolm's farm'. The forename here is probably *Maol Chaluim* rather than just *Calum.*

Balmanno (Perth). 'The monks' farm', from *Baile Manach* in earlier Gaelic, now *Baile Mhanach.*

Balmartin (North Uist), Baile Mhàrtainn. 'Martin's farm'.

Balmedie (Aberdeen). This may be 'the middle farm' from *Baile a' Mheadhain*, which would give the same meaning as Pitmedden in the same area.

Balmenach (Banff). *See* **Balemeanach**.

Balmerino (Fife). The first element is *baile* and the second is said to refer to a saint Merinach.

Balmoral (Aberdeen), Baile Mhoireil or Both Mhoireil. This is said to mean 'majestic farm', but the phonetics do not support this. Locally the name was *Both Mhoireil*, which suggests that the place was named after a saint.

Balmore (Dunbarton); (Inverness), A' Bhuaile Mhór. For the interpretation of the Dunbarton name, *see* **Baile Mor**. The Inverness name (on the south side of Loch Ness) is 'the big fold'.

Balmuchy (Ross), Baile Mhuchaidh. It has been suggested that name contains a Brythonic personal name, but there is an old Gaelic word *much*, 'mist', which might be the origin here.

Balmuckety (Angus). 'The farm at the pig place', from *Baile Mucadaidh.*

Balmule (Fife). 'The farm of Maol's son', from *Baile Mac Mhaoil.*

Balmullo (Fife). 'The farm at the summit or summits', from *Baile a' Mhullaich* or *Baile Mullach*, the latter being the plural form which would be *Baile Mhullach* in modern Gaelic.

Balmungie (Ross), Baile Mhungaidh. 'The farm at the place of mugwort', from *mong.*

Balmungo (Fife). *See* **Balmungie**.

Balmyle (Perth). This was earlier Balmain, which may represent *Baile Meadhain*, 'middle farm'.

Balnaba (Wigtown). 'The abbot's farm', from *Baile an Aba.*

Balnabeen (Ross), Baile na Binn. 'The farm of judgement'. This was located near a gallows hill.

Balnaboath (Ross), Baile nam Both. 'The farm with the huts'.

Balnabreich (Banff). Possibly 'the farm on the bank', from *Baile na Bruaiche.*

Balnabroich (Perth). *See* **Balnabreich**.

Balnabruich (Caithness). *See* **Balnabreich.**

Balnacarn (Inverness), Baile nan Càrn. 'The farm at the cairns'.

Balnaclash (Moray). 'The farm at the ditch', from *Baile na Claise*.

Balnacoil (Sutherland), Baile na Coille. 'The farm at the wood'.

Balnacoole (Arran), Baile na Cùil. 'The farm in the secluded spot'.

Balnacoul (Banff, Moray). *See* **Balnacoole.**

Balnacra (Ross), Beul-àtha na Crà. 'The ford of the salmon trap'.

Balnacraig (Inverness, Perth), Baile na Creige. 'The farm at the rock'.

Balnadelson (Sutherland), Baile an Dìollaid. 'The farm of the saddle'.

Balnafettack (Inverness), Baile nam Feadag. 'The farm of the plovers'.

Balnagall (Ross), Baile nan Gall. 'The farm of the non-Gaels'.

Balnageith (Moray). 'Windy or marshy farm', from *Baile na Gaoithe*. *Gaoth* means 'wind', but in older place-names can also stand for 'marsh'.

Balnaglach (Inverness), Baile nan Clach. 'The farm of the stones', from older *Baile na gClach*.

Balnagore (Arran), Baile nan Gobhar; (Ross), Baile nan Corr. In Arran this is 'the farm of the goats', while in Ross the name is 'the farm of the cranes' from an older *Baile na gCorr*.

Balnagowan (Lismore), Baile nan Gobhann. 'The smiths' township'.

Balnagown (Nairn, Ross), Baile nan Gobhainn. *See* **Balnagowan.**

Balnagrantach (Inverness), Baile nan Granndach. 'The Grants' farm'.

Balnaguard (Perth), Baile nan Ceàrd. 'The tinkers' farm', from older *Baile na gCeàrd*.

Balnaguisich (Ross), Baile na Giuth-saich. 'The farm at the pine wood'.

Balnaha (Perth, Ross). 'The farm with the barn or kiln', from *Baile na h-Àtha.*

Balnahard (Mull), Baile na h-Àirde. 'The farm on the headland'.

Balnain (Inverness), Baile an Fhàin and Beul an Àthain. The first Gaelic name is that of Balnain by Loch Ness and is 'the farm on the slope'. The second is near the Spey and is 'the mouth of the small ford'.

Balnakeil (Sutherland), Baile na Cill. 'The farm at the church'.

Balnakeilly (Perth), Baile na Cille. *See* **Balnakeil.**

Balnakilly (Perth), Baile na Cille. *See* **Balnakeil.**

Balnakyle (Ross), Baile na Coille. 'The farm at the wood'.

Balnald (Perth), Baile nan Allt. 'The farm at the streams'.

Balnamoan (Perth). This is probably 'the peat farm' from *Baile na Mòna*.

Balnamoon (Angus). *See* **Balnamoan.**

Balnapaling (Ross), Baile nam Péiling. 'The township of the palings', where plots of land were thus separated.

Balnasuim (Perth), Baile nan Sum. 'The farm of the soumings', the method of calculating the ratio of cattle to sheep on a given piece of land.

Balnault (Ross), Baile an Uillt. 'The farm at the stream'. The English pronunciation suggests that it came from an earlier Gaelic form *Baile nan Allt*, 'the township at the streams', or includes the genitive *n* sound referred to in **Achanalt.**

Balnespick (Inverness), Baile an Easbaig. 'The bishop's farm'.

Balniel (Fife). 'Neil's farm', from *Baile Néill*.

Balno (Moray), Am Baile Nodha. 'The new farm'.

Balnoe (Aberdeen). *See* **Balno.**

Balnuig (Ross), Baile an Aoig. This is said to mean 'the township of death'.

Balnuilt (Nairn), Baile an Uillt. 'The farm at the stream'.

Balole (Islay), Baile Olla. 'Olaf's farm'.

Balornock (Glasgow). This is said to be 'Louernoc's hut', from Brythonic, and not a Gaelic *baile* name.

Balphetrish (Tiree), Baile Pheadrais. 'Petrus's farm'.

Balquhidder (Perth), Both Chuidir or Both Phuidir. The meaning of this name is unclear except that *both* is a 'hut'. A native of the area is a *Puidreach*, which may be the origin of the Perthshire surname, Buttar. Balquhidder Fair was known as *Féill Aonghais*, 'St Angus's Fair'. The Braes of Balquhidder is *Srath Bhoth Phuidir*.

Balranald (North Uist), Baile Raghnaill. 'Ranald's farm'.

Balrymonth (Fife). 'The farm on the royal moor', from *Baile Rìmhinn*. *See* **St Andrews**.

Baltersan (Wigtown). This may be 'cross farm', from *Baile Tarsainn*, 'township across'.

Baluagra (Arran) Baile Uachdrach. 'Upper farm', also known in English as Meadowside. There is a corresponding Balegra or *Baile Ìochdrach*, 'lower farm'.

Baluain (Perth), Am Baile Uaine. 'The green farm'.

Balvaird (Ross), Baile a' Bhàird. 'The poet's farm' or 'the farm at the meadow', as *bàrd*, which usually means 'poet', is found in Ross with the meaning of 'meadow'.

Balvaron (Inverness), Baile a' Bharain. 'The baron's farm'.

Balvarran (Perth), Baile a' Bharain. 'The baron's farm', possibly referring to the Baron of Straloch.

Balvatten (Inverness), Baile a' Bhadain. 'The farm at the little copse'.

Balvenie (Banff), Baile Bhainidh or Both Bhainidh. 'St Beathan's farm', in memory of the 11th century Bishop of Mortlach. Braemar Gaelic pronunciation suggests spellings such as *Bail' Bhìnidh* and *Both Bhìnidh*.

Balveolan (Argyll), Baile Bheòlain or Baile a' Bheòlain. 'Beòlan's farm'. This personal name is found in the Irish *Ó Beoláin*, 'Boland'.

Balvicar (Seil), Baile a' Bhiocaire. 'The vicar's farm'.

Balvonie (Inverness), Baile a' Mhonaidh. 'The farm at the uplands or hills'.

Balvraid (Inverness), Baile Bhràid. 'Upland farm', containing a genitive form of *bràigh*.

Bamff (Perth), Banbh. *Banbh*, with *Eilg*, *Éire* and *Fòtla*, were poetic names for Ireland and applied commemoratively to several places in Scotland, as here.

Banavie (Inverness), Bainbhidh or Banbhaidh. 'Pig place', although this may be a reference to Ireland. *See* **Bamff**.

Banbeath (Fife). 'The farm at the birch', from *Baile na Beithe*.

Banchor (Nairn), Beannchar. 'Horn-shaped place'. This is a name common to Scotland, Ireland and Wales. In English, in the other countries, it is known as 'Bangor', but in Irish it is *Beannchar*, as here.

Banchory (Kincardine), Beannchar. This is also known in English as Banchory Ternan, named after *Torranan*, as opposed to Banchory Devenick near Aberdeen, where Devenick, an associate of Machar, is commemorated. *See* **Banchor**.

Bandon (Fife). 'The farm at the hill(fort)', from *Baile an Dùin*.

Bandrum (Fife). 'Farm at the ridge', from *Baile an Droma*.

Bandry (Dunbarton), Am Bàn-Doire. 'The fair oak grove'. This name was understood locally to derive from *Am Bàn-Àirigh*, 'the fair sheiling', but this appears to have not to have been the original form.

Banff (Banff), Banbh. *See* **Bamff**. Banffshire is *Siorrachd Bhanbh*. Upper Banffshire is *Bràigh Bhanbh*, 'the upland of Banff'.

Bangour (West Lothian). This may represent *Beinn Ghobhar*, 'hill of goats'.

Bankhead (Perth), Dul Corrachaidh. 'The head of the bank' in English, but the Gaelic name is 'the haugh of the odd field'. This place used to be known as Dalcorachy.

Banknock (Stirling). 'The farm at the hills', from *Baile nan Cnoc*, as confirmed in an older form of the anglicised name, Ballinknok.

Bannachra (Dunbarton), Beannchar. *See* **Banchory**.

Bannockburn (Stirling), Allt a' Bhonnaich. 'The bannock stream'. The Gaelic name has taken the 'bannock' of the English form to mean 'scone', although the origin may be different. The Battle of Bannockburn is *Blàr Allt a' Bhonnaich* in Gaelic.

Bantaskin (Stirling). 'The farm or place of the gospel'. Earlier evidence shows that this name included the Pictish element *pett* together with *soisgeul* 'gospel'.

Barassie (Ayr). Folk etymology has it that this name came from the 'braw sea'. The origin of the name may be *Bàrr Fhasaidh*, 'the top of the stance or place'.

Baravullin (Argyll), Bàrr a' Mhuilinn. 'The summit by the mill'.

Barbaraville (Ross), An Cladach. The English name commemorates the wife of a former proprietor. The Gaelic name is 'the shore'.

Barbauchlaw (East Lothian). This is said to be 'the farm of the crozier' from *Baile Bachlach*, as seen more clearly in the an older English form, 'Balbaghloch'.

Barcaldine (Argyll), Am Barra Calltainn. 'The hazel summit'. Barcaldine House was known a *Taigh Inbhir Dheargain*, 'the house at the mouth of the red stream'.

Bardrochat (Ayr). This name probably means 'the farm at the bridge' from *Baile na Drochaid*. In place-names of the south-west, *baile*, which is generally anglicised as 'Bal-', often appears as 'Bar-', causing confusion with names deriving from *bàrr*, 'summit or hill'.

Barevan (Nairn), Bréibhinn. 'Éibhinn's summit', from an earlier *Bàrr Éibhinn*, commemorating a saint.

Bargeddie (Lanark). An older form of the name shows this to contain *baile* rather than *bàrr* and to be 'the farm at the strip of arable land', from *Baile Geadaidh*.

Barglass (Aberdeen), Am Blàr Glas. 'The grey-green field'.

Bargrennan (Kirkcudbright). This may mean 'the township at the sunny spot' or 'the hill at the sunny spot', from *baile* or *bàrr* and *grianan*. *See* **Bardrochat**.

Barjarg (Dumfries). 'Red hill' or 'red township', from *bàrr* or *baile* and *dearg* (red).

Barlanark (Glasgow). This apparently hybrid Gaelic/Brythonic name suggests 'the hill at the clearing' from *bàrr* and Brythonic *lanerc*, 'clearing'.

Barleyport (Ross), Port an Eòrna. The Gaelic and English names are self-explanatory.

Barlinnie (Glasgow). Like nearby Barlanark, this may be a hybrid Gaelic/Brythonic name or a wholly Gaelic name meaning 'the hill by the pool', from *bàrr* and either Brythonic *llyn* or Gaelic *linn*, 'pool'.

Barmuckity (Moray). 'The summit at the pig place', from *Bàrr Mucadaidh*.

Barmulloch (Glasgow). This appears to be 'the hill of the summit', from *bàrr* and *mullach*, but earlier forms of the name suggest a Brythonic origin with a different meaning.

Barnacarry (Argyll), Bàrr na Cairidh. 'The hill by the weir' or 'the top of the weir'.

Barnakill (Argyll), Bàrr na Coille. 'The top of the forest'.

Barnhill (Angus); (Jura), Cnoc an t-Sabhail. 'Hill of the barn'. Barnhill in Angus was earlier known as Ecclesmonichto, from *eaglais* (church) dedicated probably to St Nechtan, using a diminutive form.

The Gaelic name above only applies to Barnhill in Jura.

Barnultoch (Wigtown). 'The hill or farm of the Ulstermen', from *Bàrr nan Ultach* or *Baile nan Ultach*. See **Bardrochat**. However, this name may be *Bàrr n-Ultach* or *Baile n-Ultach* without the definite article.

Barra, Barraigh. 'Finbar's island', from Norse. A native of Barra is a *Barrach*. The island's isolation is mentioned in the saying, *Ged's fhada a-muigh Barraigh, ruigear e*, 'Although Barra is far out, it can be reached'. Barra Head on the southerly island of Berneray is *Ceann Bharraigh*.

Barrapoll (Tiree), Goirtean Dòmhnaill. The English name is 'the farm at the rocky mound', from Norse. The Gaelic name is 'Donald's enclosed field', named after an official of the Duke of Argyll.

Barrhill (Ayr). In the south-west *bàrr* appears to be used for 'hill' although in the north it is restricted to 'top' or 'summit'. Thus this is an example of the Gaelic element *bàrr* being later defined by the addition of English 'hill'.

Barrisdale (Inverness), Bàrrasdal. 'Barr's valley', from Norse.

Barrlockhart (Wigtown). This may be 'the hill of the encampment' from *bàrr* and *longphort/longart*, 'encampment'. There is a place in Argyll also known as *Bàrr an Longairt*. See **Bardrochat**.

Barsolus (Dumfries). This is thought to be 'light or bright hill' from *bàrr* and *solas*, but *see* **Bardrochat**.

Barthol Chapel (Aberdeen). The older name of this place was Fithkil from *Fiodh-Chill*, 'wooden church'.

Barvas (Lewis), Barbhas or Barabhas. 'The fort by the river mouth', from Norse. The second spelling shows the epenthetic vowel between *r* and *bh* not normally shown in Gaelic orthography. A local saying, *iasgach*

muinntir Bharbhais, 'the fishing of the Barvas folk', refers to the alleged habit of the people here of waiting to see how other areas got on with the fishing before starting themselves.

Bassaguard (Fife). 'The priest's farm', from *Baile an t-Sagairt*.

Batabeg (Moray). 'Little boat', from *Bàta Beag*, referring to the small ferry which used to operate across the mouth of the Findhorn.

Baugh (Tiree), Am Bàgh. 'The bay'.

Bayble (Lewis), Pabail. 'Priest village', from Norse. Lower Bayble is *Pabail Iarach* and Upper Bayble is *Pabail Uarach*.

Bayfield (Ross), Croit Seocaidh (Black Isle), Cinn Déis Bhig or Cinn Déis Robson Shuas (Nigg); An Sligneach (Skye). While the English name is simply 'field by the bay' in all cases, the Gaelic names vary from place to place. Bayfield in the Black Isle is 'Jockie's croft', while in Nigg it is 'big Kindeace' or 'Robertson's upper Kindeace', referring to a Robertson who lived here in the 17th century. *See* **Kindeace**. In Skye, Bayfield is 'the shell place'.

Bayhead (North Uist), Ceann a' Bhàigh. 'The head of the bay'.

Bayherivagh (Barra), Bàgh Shiarabhagh. This is a Gaelic/Norse name, containing both languages' words for 'bay' and an unclear first Norse element.

Baymore (Grimsay), Am Bàgh Mór. 'The big bay'.

Bays (Harris), Na Bàigh. 'The bays'. The hilly area inland from Bays is *Bràigh nam Bàgh*, 'the upper part of Bays'.

Beach (Mull), Am Beitheach. 'The birch wood'.

Beachan (Aberdeen, Moray), Am Beitheachan. 'Little birch wood'.

Beacravik (Harris), Beicribhig. 'Stream bay', from Norse.

Beaufort Castle (Inverness), Caisteal

Dhùnaidh. The seat of the Lovats was renamed from *Dùnaidh*, 'fort place', to *Beaufort*.

Beauly (Inverness), A' Mhanachainn. The English name is said to be 'beautiful place', from French *beau lieu*, and was probably imported from England. The Gaelic name is 'the monastery', an abbreviated form of *Manachainn Mhic Shimidh*, 'Lovat's monastery'. A more poetic name was *Manachainn nan Lios*, 'the monastery with the enclosed gardens'. The fair held here was known as *Féill na Manachainn*.

Bedersaig (Harris), Beudarsaig. This may be 'pasture land bay', from Norse.

Bedrule (Roxburgh). 'Bethóc's rule', referring to lands owned by Bethóc or Beathag, the wife of a nobleman from Nithsdale. The order of elements in the place-name changed from Celtic 'Rulebethock' through 'Bethrowll' to its present form, marking the change in language from Celtic to Germanic.

Beglan (Inverness), Beag Ghleann. 'Small glen'.

Beldorney (Aberdeen), Baile Dòrnaigh. 'The farm at the pebbly place', one time home of poet Sìleas na Ceapaich.

Belgaverie (Wigtown). This is believed to represent *Baile Geamhraidh*, 'winter township'.

Belhelvie (Aberdeen). 'Sealbhach's farm', from *Baile Shealbhaigh*.

Belivat (Nairn), Buaile Fhiodhaid. 'The cattle fold at the wooded place'.

Bellabeg (Aberdeen). 'Small township', from *Baile Beag*.

Bellie (Moray). 'Broom place', from *Bealaidh*.

Belliheglish (Banff). 'Farm at the church', from *Baile na h-Eaglais*, near to Marypark, named after the Virgin Mary.

Bellochantuy (Argyll), Bealach an t-Suidhe. 'The pass at the seat'.

Bell Rock (Fife), Innis Ceap. This is also known in English as Inchcape

from Gaelic, meaning 'island of the stumps'.

Bellsgrove (Argyll), Doire nan Clag. 'The grove of the bluebells'.

Bellyclone (Perth). 'The farm of Gill-Eòin's son', from *Baile Mac Ghill-Eòin*.

Belmaduthy (Ross), Baile Mac Duibh. 'The farm of Dubh's son'.

Belnacraig (Aberdeen), Baile na Creige. 'The farm by the rock'.

Belnahua (Luing), Beul na h-Uamha. 'The mouth of the cave'.

Benadrove (Lewis), Beinn na Dròbh. 'Hill of the cattle sale'.

Ben Armine (Sutherland), Beinn Àrmainn. This Gaelic/Norse name is 'mountain of the steward or commander'.

Benbecula, Beinn nam Fadhla or Beinn a' Bhaoghla. 'Mountain of the sea fords'. As Benbecula is mainly low-lying, the name may have originated in *Peighinn nam Fadhla*, 'the pennyland of the fords'. Poetically the island is known as *an t-Eilean Dorcha*, 'the dark island'. A local is a *Badhlach* or *Baoghlach*.

Benbuie (Dumfries). 'Yellow mountain', from *Beinn Bhuidhe*.

Benderloch (Argyll), Meudarloch. 'Mountain between two lochs', a contraction of *Beinn eadar dà loch*. Local people were nicknamed *eireagan dathte*, 'coloured pullets'.

Bendochy (Perth). This may be 'horn place', referring to the horn-like bends on the River Isla, from *Beannachaidh*. However, Bennochy in Fife is 'blessing place', possibly an area of church lands, and the Perth name might be from the same source.

Benlister (Arran), Peighinn an Fhléisteir. 'The pennyland of the archer'.

Benmore (Argyll), A' Bheinn Mhór. 'The big mountain'.

Bennan (Arran), Am Beannan. 'The cliff'. Bennan Head is *Ceann a' Bheannain*.

Bennecarrigan (Arran), Beinn na Cànraigeann. The meaning of the second part of this name is unclear, although the first is 'mountain'.

Bennetfield (Ross), Baile Bheineit. Although 'Benedict's field' in English, the Gaelic name is 'Benedict's township'.

Bennochy (Fife). *See* **Bendochy**.

Benside (Lewis), Beinn na Saighde. 'The mountain of the arrow'.

Benvie (Angus). *See* **Banavie**.

Berie (Lewis), A' Bheirgh. 'The rock or stone', from Norse.

Berisay (Lewis), Beirgheasaigh. 'Rock island' or 'stone island', from Norse.

Bernera (Great Bernera), Beàrnaraigh. 'Bjørn's island', from Norse. Bernera or Great Bernera is also known as *Beàrnaraigh Ùig* , 'Bernera of Uig', and *Beàrnaraigh Leódhais*, 'Bernera of Lewis'. A local is a *Beàrnarach*.

Berneray (Barra, Berneray), Beàrnaraigh. 'Bjørn's island', from Norse. The full names of Berneray near Barra are *Beàrnaraigh Cheann Bharraigh*, 'Berneray of Barra Head', and *Beàrnaraigh an Easbaig*, 'Berneray of the bishop'. Berneray between Uist and Harris is known as both *Beàrnaraigh Na Hearadh*, 'Berneray of Harris', and *Beàrnaraigh Uibhist*, 'Berneray of Uist'. A native of this island is known as a *Beàrnarach* or *Bagan*.

Bernisdale (Skye), Beàrnasdal. 'Bjørn's valley', from Norse.

Berriedale (Caithness), Bearghdal. This may be Norse 'valley at the rocky hill'.

Berwickshire (Berwick), Siorrachd Bhearaig. Berwick itself is 'barley village', from English. For some time the town of Berwick was known as South Berwick to distinguish it from North Berwick. Berwick town is known in Gaelic as *Bearaig* and *Abaraig*.

Bettyhill (Sutherland), Am Blàran Odhar. The English name is in memory of Elizabeth, a Countess of Sutherland, while the Gaelic name is 'the dun-coloured field or moor'.

Bighouse (Sutherland), Bìogas. 'Barley house', from Norse.

Big Sand (Ross), Sannda Mhór. 'Big sand river', from Norse/Gaelic.

Bindal (Ross), Bindeil. 'Sheaf valley', from Norse.

Birchburn (Arran), An t-Allt Beithe. 'The birch stream'.

Birchfield (Inverness), Cùl a' Mhuilinn; (Ross), Achadh na h-Uamhach. The English name is self-explanatory, but the two places have different Gaelic names. In Inverness this is 'the back of the mill', whilst in Ross it is 'the field at the cave'.

Birichen (Sutherland), Bioraichean. This may mean 'sharp points'.

Birkhall (Aberdeen), Tòrr Beatha or Tòrr Beithe. The English name is 'birch haugh', while the Gaelic names are 'birch hill'.

Birkisco (Skye), Birceasgo. 'Birch wood', from Norse.

Birnam (Perth), Biorman or Biornam. This may be 'homestead by the stream', from English.

Birness (Aberdeen). This may be 'damp place', from *Braonais*.

Birnie (Moray), Braonaigh. 'Damp place'. Birnie was earlier known as Brenach, from *braonach*, 'damp'.

Birse (Aberdeen), Braois or Breis. This may be from *preas*, 'bush' or 'thicket'. The parish is Sgìre Bhraois or Sgìre Bhreis.

Bishopbriggs (Dunbarton), Drochaid an Easbaig. This was originally 'the bishop's riggs' although it now appears to be 'the bishop's bridges'.

Blackfold (Inverness), Am Buaile Dubh. 'The black fold', referring to a fold for cattle or other animals. *Buaile* is usually feminine in gender, but appears to have been masculine in this area.

Blackford (Perth), Srath Gaoithe. 'Black ford' in the English name is not reflected in the Gaelic name of 'marshy or windy strath', which is the source of the older English name, Strageath.

Black Isle (Ross), An t-Eilean Dubh. 'The black island', although this is a peninsula. It was known as *Eilean Dubhthaich*, 'Duthac's island', from which the name nowadays is a contraction. The area used also to be known as *An Àird Mheadhanach*, 'the middle headland' and *Eadar Dhà Dhàil*, 'between two haughs'.

Blacklunans (Perth), Bealach Glùinneig or Bealach Lùnaig. This name may be 'the pass of jointed-grass'.

Blackmill (Luing), Am Muileann Dubh. 'The black mill'.

Blackwaterfoot (Arran), An Dubh-Abhainn, Bun na Dubh-Abhann or Bun na h-Abhann. 'The mouth of the black river', a translation of the second Gaelic name. The first Gaelic name translates as 'the black river', whilst the third is 'the river mouth'.

Blaich (Argyll), Blàthaich. This may be 'blossom place'.

Blair (Fife). 'Field, plain', from *Blàr*.

Blair Atholl (Perth), Blàr Athaill or Blàr Athall. 'The plain of Atholl'. Old Blair is *Seann Bhlàr* and Upper Blair is *Blàr Uachdar*.

Blairbeg (Arran), Am Blàr Beag. 'The small plain'.

Blairboych (Arran), Blàir Bòidheach. 'Beautiful plain', showing an unexpected form of *blàr* and no definite article.

Blairdaff (Ayr). 'Field of oxen', from *Blàr Damh* which would be *Blàr Dhamh* in modern Gaelic.

Blairfettie (Perth), Blàr Pheitigh. 'The moor of the place of pits', referring to the Pictish term *pett*.

Blairfindie (Banff), Blàr Fionndaidh. This may be 'the field at the white place'.

Blairfoid (Ross), Blàr Choighde. This may be a Gaelic/Brythonic name, 'the plain at the wood'.

Blairgowrie (Perth), Blàr Ghobharaidh. 'The plain of Gowrie'. This was also known locally as *Blàr na Gobharaidh*, with the same meaning.

Blairhullichan (Stirling), Blàr Thulachain. 'The field at the small green hill'.

Blairingone (Kinross). 'The plain of the hounds', from *Blàr nan Con*, earlier *Blàr na gCon*.

Blairinroar (Perth). This may be 'the plain of the skirmish', from *Blàr an Ruathair*.

Blairish (Perth), Blàrais. 'Plain place'.

Blairlogie (Stirling). 'Field or plain of Logie', from *Blàr Lagaidh*.

Blairmore (Argyll, Arran, Nairn, Sutherland), Am Blàr Mór. 'The big field or plain'.

Blairnamarrow (Banff), Blàr nam Marbh. 'The field of the dead'.

Blairnavaid (Stirling). 'The field of the peats', from *Blàr nam Fàd,* formerly *Blàr na bhFàd*.

Blairninich (Ross), Blàr an Aonaich. 'The moor of the market'.

Blair Uachdar (Perth), Blàr Uachdar. 'Upper Blair'.

Blairy (Inverness), Blàiridh or Blàraidh. 'Field or plain place'.

Blarmachfoldach (Inverness), Blàr Mac Faoilteach. This is not clear and, although the Gaelic name seems to mean 'field of the son of Faoilteach', it may have altered through the centuries.

Blarmore (Inverness), Am Blàr Mór. 'The big field or plain'.

Blarnaleavoch (Ross), Blàr na Leitheach or Blàr na Leamhach. The first Gaelic name is 'field of the half place' while the second is 'the elm field'.

Blarour (Inverness), Blàr Dhobhair. 'The water or river field'.

Blashaval (North Uist), Blathaiseabhal. 'Blue sea mountain', from Norse.

Bleaton Hallet (Perth), Am Plàdan.
This was originally a hill name to
which a previous proprietor added
his surname.

Blebo (Fife). This is said to be from
Blàth-Bholg, 'bag-shaped blossom
land'.

Blelack (Aberdeen). *See* **Blebo**. Diack
recorded local Gaelic pronunciation
of this name as 'bllalak'.

Blochairn (Glasgow). This appears to
be 'the farm by the cairn', from *Baile
a' Chàirn*.

Blughasary (Ross), Blaoghasairigh.
The first element of this Norse name
is unclear although a field or sheiling
is referred to.

Boath (Angus, Ross), Na Bothachan
(Ross). The Angus name appears to
be from *Both Mhearnaig*, 'St Ernoc's
or M' Ernoc's hut', while the Ross
name is 'the huts'.

Boat of Garten (Inverness), Coit a'
Ghartain or A' Choit. 'The boat at
Garten' or 'the boat', where a ferry
operated prior to the construction of
the bridge.

Bochastle (Perth), Both Chaisteil. 'The
hut at the castle'.

Bochonie (Perth), Both Chòmhnaidh.
This may be 'St Comhghan's hut'.

Bogach (Barra), A' Bhogach. 'The
boggy place'.

Bogallan (Ross), Bog Alain. 'The bog
of Allan'.

Bogary (Arran), Na Bogaire. This
may be 'the bog place', although the
Gaelic name is a plural.

Bogbain (Inverness), Am Bog Bàn;
(Ross), Am Bac Bàn. In Inverness
this is 'the fair bog', but in Ross, 'the
fair bank', from Norse *bakki*.

Bogbuie (Ross), Am Bog Buidhe. 'The
yellow bog'.

Bogindollo (Angus). 'The bog in the
haugh', from *Bog na Dalach*.

Bognie (Aberdeen). 'Boggy place',
from *Boganach* or *Boganaidh*.

Bog of Gight (Aberdeen). 'The windy

or marshy bog', from *Bog na Gaoithe*.

Bogrow (Ross), Am Bogaradh. 'The
bog place'.

Bohally (Perth), Both Àlaidh. This
hut name probably has the corrupted
name of a saint as its second element.

Boharm (Banff), Both Sheirm. *See*
Bohally.

Bohenie (Inverness), Both Shinidh.
See **Bohally**. A saying about local
place-names goes, *Tha cóig bothan
an Loch Abar, cóig gasgan ann am
Bàideanach's cóig cóigean ann an
Srath Éireann*, 'There are five boths
in Lochaber, five gasgs in Badenoch
and five cóigs in Strathdearn'. The
five boths in Lochaber are Bohenie,
Bohuntine, Bolyne, Both Chàsgaidh
and Both Lugha.

Bohespick (Perth), Both Theasbaigh.
'Bishop's hut'.

Bohuntine (Inverness), Both
Fhionndain. 'Fintan's hut', possibly
referring to the saint of that name.
See **Bohenie**.

Boisdale (South Uist), Baghasdal.
'Baegi's valley', from Norse. North
Boisdale is *Baghasdal* or *Baghasdal
a Tuath*, while South Boisdale is *An
Leth Mheadhanaich*, 'the middle half'.

Boleskine (Inverness), Both Fhleis-
ginn. This refers to a hut, but the
second element is unclear though
may contain *fleasg*, 'withe'.

Bolfracks (Perth), Both Bhrac or Both
Frac. This name is unclear although
the Gaelic form contains 'hut'.
Locally the name is pronounced *Both
Frac* and this may be related to *Leitir
Fraic*, 'Letterfrack', in County Galway
which contains a personal name.

Bolnabodach (Barra), Buaile nam
Bodach. 'The old men's fold or pen'.

Boltachan (Perth), Bualtachan. 'Sheep
or cattle pens'.

Bolyne (Inverness), Both Fhloinn.
'Flann's hut'. *See* **Bohenie**.

Bomakellock (Banff), Both Mo
Cheallaig. 'St Ceallag's hut'.

Bona (Inverness), Am Bànath. 'The fair ford'.

Bonahaven (Islay), Bun na h-Abhainn. 'The mouth of the river'. The English form of the name appears to have gone out of use.

Bonar Bridge (Sutherland), Drochaid a' Bhanna. 'The bridge at Bonar', meaning 'bottom ford', from *am Bannath*. The site of the present-day village was formerly known as *Baile na Croit*, 'farm of the hump'.

Bonaveh (Colonsay), Bun a' Bheithe. 'The foot of the birch'. This may refer to the root of a birch tree, but might actually mean 'mouth of the birch stream'.

Bonawe (Argyll), Bun Abha. 'The mouth of the Awe'.

Bonhard (Fife, West Lothian). 'Farm at the high point', from *Baile na h-Àirde*.

Bonhill (Dunbarton), Bun Olla. This appears to be a gaelicisation of an English name.

Bonjedward (Roxburgh). The second part of this name contains the older English form of the name 'Jedburgh', and the first element appears to be *bun*, 'river mouth'.

Bonnavoulin (Argyll), Bun a' Mhuilinn. 'The river mouth of the mill'. This is also spelled 'Bunavullin' in English.

Bonskeid (Perth), Both na Sgaod. The second part of this hut name is unclear.

Boor (Ross), Bùra. 'Bower river', from Norse.

Boreland (Perth), Am Borlainn or A' Bhorlainn. This appears to be 'the sloping land', but may have originated in English, referring to land used to feed the landlord's household, as in the name in Dumfries.

Borenich (Perth), Both Reithnich. This name sounds as though it is 'bracken hut', but the second element might be the name of a saint, which also

appears to form the defining element in the church name 'Kilrenny'.

Boreraig (Skye), Boraraig. 'Fort bay', from Norse.

Boreray, (North Uist), Boighreigh; (St Kilda), Boraraigh. 'Fort island', from Norse. A native of Boreray by Uist is a *Boighreach* or *sgarbh*, 'cormorant'. There is a saying *Na toir bó á Paibeil's na toir bean á Boighreigh* 'Don't take a cow from Paible or a wife from Boreray'.

Borgie (Sutherland), Borghaidh. 'Fort river', from Norse.

Borline (Inverness, Skye), Borlainn. *See* **Boreland**.

Borlum (Inverness), Bòrlum. 'Strip of arable land'.

Borneskitaig (Skye), Borgh na Sgiotaig. 'Fort at the division bay', from Gaelic/Norse.

Bornish (South Uist), Bòirnis. 'Fort headland', from Norse.

Borrisdale (Harris), Borghasdal. 'Fort valley', from Norse.

Borriston (Lewis), Borghasdan. This Norse name contains 'fort'.

Borrobol (Sutherland), Borghbol. 'Fort farm', from Norse.

Borrodale (Argyll, Skye, South Uist), Borghdal. 'Fort valley', from Norse.

Borsham (Harris), Boirseam. This Norse name may be 'fort holm'.

Borve (Harris), Na Buirgh; (Skye), Borbh; (elsewhere), Borgh. The Harris name is 'the forts'. Elsewhere it is 'fort', from Norse.

Bosta (Bernera), Bostadh. 'Small farm', from Norse. Local pronunciation suggests a preferable spelling of *Bòstadh*.

Bothkennar (Stirling). 'St Cainnear's hut', from *Both Cainneir*, referring to a saint also commemorated in Glen Cannel.

Bot na h-Acaire (Perth), Both Uachdair. 'Upper hut'. The English form came from a misreading of earlier anglicisation, 'Bothvechtar'.

Botriphnie (Banff). Local Gaelic pronunication was transcribed by Diack as 'vatreini', suggesting spellings such as *Bhad Reidhnigh* or *Bhoth Draighnidh*, both open to interpretation. The first element could be *bad*, 'copse' or *both*, 'hut', whilst the second is unclear, but may include *reidhneach*, 'cow yielding no milk', or *droigheann*, 'thorn'.

Bottacks (Perth), Na Botagan. 'The peat banks'.

Bottle Island (Ross), Eilean a' Bhotail. 'The island of the bottle', so called because of its shape. An alternative name was *Eilean Druim Briste*, 'broken ridge island'.

Bousd (Coll), Babhsta. 'Small farm', from Norse.

Bovain (Perth), Both Mheadhain. 'The middle hut'.

Bower (Caithness), Bàgair. The origin of this Norse name may be the plural of 'bower'.

Bowglass (Harris), Am Bogha Glas. 'The grey reef'.

Bowmore (Islay), Bogha Mór or Am Bogha Mór. 'Big reef'.

Boyndie (Banff), Bòinndidh. This was originally the name of a river which may be 'eternal goddess', from old Gaelic *buandea*. The current Gaelic name, used in Easter Ross, could simply be a gaelicisation of the English form. Boyndie beach is *Tràigh Bhòinndidh* in Gaelic.

Boysack (Angus). This is said to be from *Baile Iosaig*, 'Isaac's township'.

Bracadale (Skye), Bràcadal. 'Slope valley', from Norse.

Bracla (Inverness). *See* **Brackloch**.

Brackla (Nairn). *See* **Brackloch**.

Brackletter (Inverness), Breac-Leitir. 'Speckled slope'.

Brackley (Argyll), Am Bracal. 'Slope field' or 'slope valley', from Norse.

Brackloch (Sutherland), A' Bhraclaich. 'The badger's sett'.

Brae (Ross), A' Bhruthach or A'

Bhruthaich. 'The brae'.

Braebost (Skye), Bréabost. 'Broad farm', from Norse.

Braedownie (Angus). This seems to be from *Bràigh Dhùnaidh*, 'the upper part of Downie'.

Braegarrie (Aberdeen), Bràigh a' Ghàraidh. 'The upper part of the Garrie'.

Braegrudie (Sutherland), Bràigh Ghrùididh. 'The upper part of Grudie'.

Braehorrisdale (Ross), Bràigh Thòrasdail. 'The upper part of Torrisdale'.

Braeintra (Ross), Bràigh an t-Sratha. 'The upper part of the strath'.

Braelangwell (Ross), Bràigh Langail. 'The upper part of Langwell'.

Brae Leny (Perth), Bràigh Lànaigh 'The upper part of Leny'.

Brae Lochaber (Inverness), Bràigh Loch Abar. 'Upper Lochaber'. A native is a *Bràigheach*.

Braelude (Perth), Bràigh Leòid. 'The upper part of Lude'.

Braemar (Aberdeen), Bràigh Mhàrr (district), Baile a' Chaisteil (village). The district is 'the upper part of Mar' and the village is 'village at the castle'. The village comprises *Ach an Droighinn* or Auchendryne, 'field of the thorn bush' west of the river and *Baile a' Chaisteil* or Castleton to the east. The village was earlier known as *Cinn Drochaid*, 'bridge end'.

Brae Moray (Moray), Bràigh Mhoireibh. 'The upper part of Moray'.

Braemore (Caithness, Ross), Am Bràigh Mór. 'The large upland'.

Brae Rannoch (Argyll, Perth), Bràigh Raineach. 'The upper part of Rannoch'.

Braes (Skye), Am Bràighe. 'The upper part'. The full name is *Bràighe Thròndairnis*, 'upper Trotternish', or *Bràighe Phort Rìgh*, 'the upper part of Portree'.

Braes of Abernethy (Inverness), Bràigh Obar Neithich. 'The upper part of Abernethy'.

Braes of Balquhidder (Perth), Srath Bhoth Phuidir. The Gaelic name is 'the strath of Balquhidder'.

Braes of Callander (Perth), Bràigh Chalasraid. The upper part of Callander'.

Braes of Cromar (Aberdeen), Bràigh Crò Mhàrr or Bruthaichean Crò Mhàrr. 'The upper part of Cromar' or 'the braes of Cromar'. The second Gaelic form may be a re-translation into Gaelic from a mistranslation into English assuming *bràigh* to mean 'brae'.

Braes of Doune (Perth), Bràigh Dhùin. 'The upper part of Doune'.

Braes of Foss (Perth), Bràigh Fasaidh. 'The upper part of Foss'.

Braes of Glen Orchy (Argyll), Bràigh Ghlinn Urchaidh. 'The upper part of Glen Orchy'.

Braes of Mause (Perth), Bruthaichean Mheallaibh. 'The braes of Mause'.

Braes of Ullapool (Ross), Bruthaichean Ulapuil. 'The braes of Ullapool'.

Brae Tongue (Sutherland), Bràigh Thunga. 'The upper part of Tongue'.

Bragar (Lewis), Bràgar. This Norse name may be 'pretty field'. Local pronunciation suggests a spelling of *Bràgair*.

Braglen (Argyll), Bràigh a' Ghlinne. 'The upper part of the glen'.

Brahan (Ross), Brathann. This may be 'quern place'.

Braichlie (Aberdeen), Brachlach. This may be the same name as in **Brackloch**.

Branahuie (Lewis), Bràigh na h-Aoidhe. 'The upper part of the Eye isthmus'. *See* **Point**.

Branault (Argyll), Bràigh nan Allt. 'The upper land at the streams'

Brawl (Sutherland), Breitheal. 'Broad field or hill', from Norse.

Breacachadh (Coll), Breac-Achadh. 'Speckled field'.

Breaclete (Bernera), Breacleit. 'Broad cliff', from Norse. Local pronuncia-tion collected by Oftedal suggests a preferable spelling of *Britheacleit*.

Breadalbane (Perth), Bràid Albainn or Bràghaid Albainn. 'The upper part of Alba or Scotland'. A native of the area is a *Bràighdeach*.

Breakish (Skye), Breacais. This may be 'speckled place'. Lower Breakish is *Breacais Ìosal* and Upper Breakish is *Breacais Àrd*.

Breakough (Cumbrae). 'Speckled place', from *Breacach*.

Breasclete (Lewis), Briascleit or Brèascleit. 'Cliff with the broad ridge', from Norse. Local pronuncia-tion collected by Oftedal suggests a preferable speeling of *Britheascleit*.

Brechin (Angus), Breichin or Brichin. This name is said to represent a dedication to the Brythonic St Brychan. An earlier Gaelic form appears as *Breichne*, probably with the same derivation.

Breckrey (Skye), Am Breacaradh. The Gaelic name suggests that this may be 'the speckled place' (*see* **Bogrow**), but given its location, this may be of Norse origin and contain the element *brekkr*, 'slope'.

Breich (West Lothian). 'Bank', from *Bruaich*.

Brenachie (Ross), Breanagaich. The meaning of this name is unclear.

Brenachoil (Perth), Breun-Choille. 'Putrid wood'.

Brenchoille (Argyll), Breun-Choille. See **Brenachoil**.

Brenish (Lewis), Bréinis. 'Broad headland', from Norse.

Brevig (Barra, Lewis), Bréibhig. 'Broad bay', from Norse. Brevig in Lewis is situated on Broad Bay also known as *an Loch a Tuath*.

Bridgend (Arran), Ceann an Drochaid; (Inverness), Ceann na Drochaid; (Islay) Beul an Àtha. The Arran and Inverness names are 'the end of the bridge', while the Islay name is 'the ford' or 'the mouth of the ford'. It is interesting that the Arran name shows *drochaid*, 'bridge', to be masculine as it is in Irish, although generally this is a feminine noun in Scottish Gaelic.

Bridge of Awe (Argyll), Drochaid Abha. 'The bridge over the Awe'.

Bridge of Balgy (Perth), Drochaid Bhalgaidh. 'The bridge at Balgy'. The old churchyard here is *Cladh Bhranno*, 'Brandubh's churchyard'.

Bridge of Brown (Banff), Drochaid Bhruthainn. 'The bridge over the Brown', a river name unconnected with English 'brown'.

Bridge of Cally (Perth), Drochaid Challaidh. 'The bridge at Cally', meaning 'hazel place'.

Bridge of Dee (Aberdeen, Kincardine, Kirkcudbright). 'The bridge over the Dee', possibly from *Drochaid Dhé*.

Bridge of Don (Aberdeen), Drochaid Dheathain. 'The bridge over the Don'.

Bridge of Earn (Perth), Drochaid Éireann. 'The bridge over the Earn'.

Bridge of Fiddich (Banff). 'The bridge over the Fiddich', possibly from *Drochaid Fhiodhaich*.

Bridge of Gaur (Perth), Drochaid Ghamhair. 'The bridge over the Gaur'.

Bridge of Marnoch (Aberdeen), Drochaid na Màrnaich. This is said to mean 'St Ernoc's or St M' Ernoc's bridge', but might be 'the bridge of the Mar men'.

Bridge of Orchy (Argyll), Drochaid Urchaidh. 'The bridge over the Orchy'.

Bridge of Tarf (Perth), Drochaid Tairbh. 'The bridge over the Tarf'.

Brig O'Turk (Perth), Ceann Drochaid. The English name mentions the 'Turk' or 'boar river', but the Gaelic name is 'bridge end'. In Gaelic this place was also known as *Àird Cheann-Chnocain* or *Allt Cheann-Chnocain* which is 'point or stream at the hillock head', either of which is possible. In some dialects, such as that of Jura, *allt* and *àird* were interchangeable.

Brin (Inverness), Braoin. This name may refer to damp ground. Brin Mains is *Cnoc nan Cnaimhseag*, 'the hill of the whortleberries'.

Broadford (Skye), An t-Àth Leathann. 'The broad ford'.

Brochel (Raasay), Brochaill. This name is unclear, but may be from Norse 'fort hill' or 'fort field'.

Brochroy (Argyll), Am Bruthach Ruadh. 'The red-brown brae'.

Brock (Tiree), Am Brog. 'The fort', from Norse.

Brockies Corner (Inverness), Taigh Bhròcaidh. The Gaelic name is 'Brockie's house'.

Brodick (Arran), Tràigh a' Chaisteil. The English form is 'broad bay', from Norse. This has been gaelicised as *Breadhaig* but is used only to refer to the part of the village known as 'Douglas Row' in English. The Gaelic name is 'the beach by the castle'.

Brogaig (Skye), Brògaig. 'Fort bay', from Norse.

Broker (Lewis), Brocair. This may be 'forts', from Norse.

Brolass (Mull), Bròlas. This name is unclear.

Brolum (Lewis), Brothluim. This name appears to contain Norse for 'holm'.

Broomhill (Ross), Àird nan Cathag (Kindeace), Cnoc a' Bhealaidh or An Cnoc Bealaidh (Urray). The Kindeace Gaelic name is 'the high point of the jackdaws', whilst the Urray names both mean 'the broom hill'.

Broomton (Ross), Baile a' Bhealaidh. 'The farm of the broom', referring to the plant.

Brora (Sutherland), Brùra. 'Bridge river', from Norse, a name originally applied to the river and then to the village which was earlier *Inbhir Bhrùra*, 'mouth of the Brora'. Brora is also called locally, *Brùra nam maraichean*, 'Brora of the mariners'.

Broughdarg (Aberdeen), A' Bhruthach Dhearg. 'The red brae'.

Broxburn (West Lothian). 'Badger stream'. The village was earlier known as Easter Strathbroc, the latter part of which is from Gaelic *Srath Broc*, 'badger strath'. *See* **Uphall**.

Bruachaig (Ross), Bruachaig. 'Small bank'.

Bruachbane (Perth), Am Bruthach Bàn. 'The white brae'.

Bruachrobie (Sutherland), Bruthach Robaidh. 'Robbie's brae'.

Bruar (Perth), Bruthar. It is unclear what is meant in this name, although it may contain an old Gaelic element for 'heat', possibly referring to the whirlpools at the Falls of Bruar.

Brucefield (Ross), Cnoc an Tighearna. The Gaelic name is 'the hill of the lord', while the English name commemorates the proprietor, Robert Bruce MacLeod. North Brucefield is *Loch Sirr*.

Brue (Lewis), Brù. 'Bridge', from Norse.

Bruernish (Barra), Bruthairnis. This may be 'bridge headland', from Norse, showing a plural of *brú*, 'bridge'.

Bruichladdich (Islay), Bruach a' Chladaich. 'The bank of the shore'. Locally the name is pronounced as *Bruach a' Chladaigh*. *See* **Acharanny**.

Bruichnain (Ross), Bruach an Éidhinn. 'The ivy bank'.

Bruist (Berneray), Brùsta. 'Bridge village', from Norse.

Brunigil (Skye), Brùnaigil. 'Brown ravine', from Norse.

Brybeg (Ross), Am Bràighe Beag. 'The small upper part'. *See* **Alligin**.

Buailedhubh (South Uist), A' Bhuaile Dhubh. 'The black pen'.

Buaile-uachdrach (South Uist), A' Bhuaile Uachdrach. 'The upper pen'.

Buailnaluib (Ross), Buaile na Lùib. 'Pen at the bend'.

Bualintur (Skye), Buaile an Todhair. 'The bleaching pen' or 'seaweed fertiliser pen'. Given this place's location by the sea, the latter interpretation is more likely.

Buchan (Aberdeen), Buchan or Bùchainn. This name may stem from Brythonic *bwch*, 'cow'. The name was recorded as *Búkan* in Norse, although not of Norse origin.

Buchanan (Stirling), Bochanan. 'The hut of the canon', from an older *Both a' Chanain*.

Buchanty (Perth), Buchantaidh. This name is unclear, although it may be a locative form of the name, 'Buchan'.

Buckie (Banff), Bucaidh. This may be 'buck place', from *boc*, 'buck'. A native of this area and the north-east coast generally is a *Bucach*.

Bught (Inverness), Cill Bheathain. The English name is 'pen', while the Gaelic name is 'Bean's church'. Bught Park is known as *Pàirc nam Bochd*, 'the park of the poor', but this may be an attempt to interpret Bught as a Gaelic word.

Buinach (Moray), Buidheanach. 'Yellow place'.

Bullion (West Lothian). This name refers to boggy land, from English. The older name was Croftangry, from *Croit an Rìgh*, 'the king's croft'.

Bunacaimb (Inverness), Bun na Caime. 'The mouth of the crooked stream'.

Bunachton (Inverness), Both Neachdain. 'Nechtan's hut'.

Bunanuisg (Islay), Bun an Uisge. 'The mouth of the water'.

Bunarkaig (Inverness), Bun Airceig. 'The mouth of the Arkaig'.

Bunavoneddar (Harris), Bun Abhainn Eadarra. 'The mouth of the Eadarra river'.

Bunavullin (Argyll, Eriskay), Bun a' Mhuilinn. 'The river mouth of the mill'. The place in Argyll is also spelled Bonnavoulin in English.

Bunchrew (Inverness), Bun Chraoibh. 'The foot of the tree'.

Bundalloch (Ross), Bun Dà Loch. 'The mouth of two lochs'.

Bunessan (Mull), Bun Easain. 'The base of the little waterfall'. Local people here were nicknamed *othaisgean*, 'sheep'.

Bunloit (Inverness), Bun Leothaid. 'Slope foot'.

Bunnabhain (Islay), Bun na h-Abhainn. 'The mouth of the river'. This was formerly known in English as Bonahaven.

Bunoich (Inverness), Bun Obhaich. 'The mouth of the Oich'.

Bunrannoch (Perth), Bun Raineach. 'The mouth of the Rannoch'.

Bunree (Inverness), Bun an Ruighe. 'The foot of the slope'.

Bunzion (Fife). 'Peak', from *Binnean*.

Burghead (Moray), Am Broch. The English name is 'head of the fort', with Norse *borg*. The Gaelic name is from the local English name, The Broch, a name also applied to Fraserburgh.

Burgie (Moray). This appears to be Norse *borg*, 'fort', with a Gaelic locative.

Burnhervie (Aberdeen). 'The stream at the boundary wall', with *eirbhe* preceded by Scottish English 'burn'. The whole name may be a part-translation from a Gaelic name. *See* **Alltnaharra**.

Burnside (Ross), Taigh an Daimh. The English name refers to the 'side of the stream', but the Gaelic name is 'the house of the stag or ox'. This Gaelic name only applies to the place in Ross.

Burrelton (Perth), Both Bhùirnich or Both Bhùirm. The English name commemorates the founder of the planned village, George Burrel. The Gaelic names are unclear although they contains *both*, 'hut', and possibly reference to a saint.

Bute, Bód or Bòid. This name may have its source in old Gaelic *bót*, 'fire'. A native of Bute is a *Bódach* or *Bòideach* which gives the anglicised surname 'Boyd'. A saying claims, *Chan ann am Bòid uile a tha an t-olc;*

tha cuid dheth sa Chumaradh bheag làimh ris, 'Not all evil is in Bute; there is some in little Cumbrae nearby'.

Butt (Arran), Am Buta. 'The short rig (in a field)', from Norse.

Butterston (Perth). 'Buttar's farm', from English. Buttar is a surname which may be related to *Puidreach*, an adjective connected to Balquhidder.

Buttock Point (Bute), A' Phutaig. This may be 'the small ridge of land'.

Butt of Lewis (Lewis), Rubha Robhanais. The English name refers to this headland's location at the tip of Lewis, while the Gaelic name is 'the point of the hole headland', the latter element being from Norse, and referring to the hole known as the Eye of the Butt through which the sea pushes.

Cabaan (Ross), An Cadha Bàn. 'The white pass'.

Cabrach (Banff, Jura), A' Chabrach. 'The antler place'.

Cabrich (Inverness). *See* **Cabrach**.

Cadboll (Ross), Cadabal. 'Cat village', from Norse. An alternative spelling and pronunciation is given as *Cathabul*. This is possibly a tribal reference to the people usually associated with Caithness and Sutherland.

Caensa (Tiree), Ceòsaibh. 'Hollows', from the Norse term also found in 'Keose'.

Caillach Head (Argyll), Sròn na Caillich. 'The old woman's or witch's promontory'.

Caiplich (Inverness), A' Chaiplich. 'The horse place', from *capall*.

Cairnaqueen (Aberdeen), Càrn na Cuinge. 'The cairn at the narrow pass'. This is often rendered as *Càrn na Cuimhne*, 'the memorial cairn', which sounds similar.

Cairnbaan (Argyll), An Càrn Bàn. 'The white cairn'.

Cairnbanno (Aberdeen). This may be 'peaked cairn', from *Càrn Beannach*.

Cairnbrogie (Aberdeen). 'Brogan's cairn', from *Càrn Bhrogain*.

Cairnbulg (Aberdeen). 'Bag shaped cairn'. *See* **Cairnwell**.

Cairndow (Argyll), An Càrn Dubh. 'The black cairn'.

Cairney (Perth). 'Copse place', from Pictish *carden* with a Gaelic ending.

Cairngall (Aberdeen). 'The cairn of the non-Gaels', from *Càrn nan Gall*.

Cairngate (Fife). 'The cairn of the cats', from *Càrn nan Cat*.

Cairnie (Aberdeen). There are two places with this name in Aberdeen. The first, near Skene, derives from Pictish *carden*, and is 'copse place', while the second, in Strathbogie, comes from *càrn* and is 'cairn place'.

Cairn na Burgh Beg (Mull), Cearnaborg Beg. 'Small Cearnaborg', a Norse name possibly meaning 'fort on good land'.

Cairnoch (Stirling). 'Cairn place', from *Càrnach*.

Cairnryan (Wigtown). This fairly recent English name refers to a cairn on Loch Ryan. Previously the village was called Macheraskeoch, from *Machair an Sgithich*, 'the hawthorn machair or plain'.

Cairns (Fife). 'Corner place', from *Ceàrnais*.

Cairntradlin (Aberdeen). 'Triduana's cairn', from *Càrn Traillein*.

Cairnwell (Aberdeen), Càrn a' Bhalg or An Càrn Bhailg. 'The bag-shaped cairn'. The bad weather associated with this area is summed up in the rhyme, *Cur is cathadh am Bealach Dearg, sneachd is reòthadh an Càrn a' Bhalg, cùl ri gaoith air Làirig Bhealaich, grian gheal am Maoilinn*, 'Drifts and storms at Bealach Dearg, snow and frost at the Cairnwell, back to the wind at Làirig Bhealaich, bright sun at Moulin'.

Caithness, Gallaibh. The English name is 'cat headland', referring to the tribal name of the people of Caithness and Sutherland. The Gaelic name is 'territory of the foreigners or non-Gaels', namely the Norse who settled in large numbers in this area. The extreme north-east of Caithness is *Roinn Ghallaibh*, 'the point of Caithness', from *rinn*, 'point'. A person from Caithness is a *Gallach*.

Calbha Beag (Sutherland), Calbha Beag. 'Small calf island', from Norse/Gaelic.

Calbost (Lewis), Calbost. 'Kalfi's farm', from Norse.

Calgary (Mull), Calgarraidh. This may be 'Kali's sheiling or pasture land', from Norse.

Caliach Point (Mull), Rubha na Caillich. 'The old woman's or witch's headland'.

Callander (Moray), Caladar; (Perth), Calasraid. The name in Moray is 'hard water', a common river name, while in Perth it is 'harbour street', possibly referring to the town's riverside location, and pronounced *Caltraid* in local Gaelic. The fair held at Callander in Perthshire was *Féill Mo Cheasaig*, 'St Kessock's Fair' and *Féill Chalasraid*, 'Callander Fair'. The Braes of Callander are known as *Bràigh Chalasraid*, 'the upper part of Callander'.

Callanish (Lewis), Calanais. This may be 'Kali's headland', from Norse. The Standing Stones of Callanish are *Tursachan Chalanais*, possibly from Norse *thrus*, 'goblin', as also found in 'Ballantrushal'.

Callert (Inverness), Callaird. 'Hazel headland'.

Calligarry (Skye), Cailigearraidh. *See* **Calgary**. People from Calligarry are known as *cearcan breaca*, 'speckled hens'.

Callyons (Fife). 'Small wood', from *Coillean*.

Calnakill (Ros), Cal na Cille or Cal 'a Cille. 'The meadow at the church'. Local people are known as *slatan-mara*, 'tangle stems'. A Wester

Ross saying lists the nicknames of people from a number of Applecross settlements as follows, *Slatan-mara Cal na Cille, Bodaich bhiorach an Lòin Bhàin, Rùcanaich Chùthaig agus tùchanaich na Feàrn*, 'Tangle-stems from Calnakill, sharp old men from Lonbain, rumblers from Cuaig and the hoarse folk of Fearns'.

Calrossie (Ross), Calrosaidh. This may be 'meadow wood place'.

Calvay (South Uist), Calbhaigh. 'Calf island', from Norse.

Calvine (Perth), Cail Mhinn or Cail Mhìn. 'Kids' meadow' or 'smooth meadow'.

Camasine (Argyll), Camas Éidhinn. 'Ivy bay'.

Camaslongart (Ross), Camas Longairt. 'Encampment bay'.

Camasnacroise (Argyll), Camas na Croise. 'Cross bay'.

Camasnaharry (Ross), Camas na h-Eirbhe. 'The bay at the boundary wall'.

Cambus (Stirling). 'River bend', from *Camas*.

Cambusbarron (Stirling). This may be 'the baron's river bend', from *Camas a' Bharain*.

Cambuscurrie (Ross), Camas Curaidh. This appears to be 'coracle bay'.

Cambuskenneth (Stirling). This appears to be 'Kenneth's river bend', but the personal name was not *Coinneach* but *Cionnaith*, which is no longer current in modern Gaelic.

Cambuslang (Lanark). 'River bend of ships', from *Camas Long*. This was the furthest point up the Clyde navigable by large vessels.

Cambusmore (Perth, Sutherland), An Camas Mór. In Perth this name means 'the large river bend', but in Sutherland is 'the large bay'.

Cambusnethan (Lanark). 'The bend on the Nethan'.

Cambus O'May (Aberdeen), Camas a' Mhuigh. 'The river bend on the plain'.

Camdell (Aberdeen), Camdhail. 'Crooked meadow'.

Camelon (Stirling), Camlan. This name is unclear, but said to be where King Arthur met his death. Locally in English the first syllable is pronounced locally as in 'came'.

Camghouran (Perth), Camgharan. 'Crooked river', from older *Cam Dhobhran*.

Camisky (Inverness), Camuisgidh. 'Crooked water'.

Cammachmore (Kincardine). 'Big bent place', from *Camach Mór*.

Cammo (Midlothian). 'Bent place', from *Camach*.

Camore (Sutherland), An Cadha Mór. 'The big pass'.

Campbeltown (Argyll), Ceann Loch Chille Chiarain or Ceann Loch. The planned settlement was named after Archibald Campbell, but was earlier known as Lochhead, a translation of *Ceann Loch*. The full Gaelic name is 'the head of the loch at St Ciaran's church'.

Campsie (Perth), Camais or Camas. 'River bend'.

Camuscross (Skye), Camas Cros. 'Cross bay'.

Camusinas (Argyll), Camas Aonghais. 'Angus's bay'.

Camusluinie (Ross), Camas Luinge. 'Ship bay'.

Camusmore (Skye), An Camas Mór. 'The large bay'.

Camusnagaul (Argyll, Ross), Camas nan Gall. 'The bay of the non-Gaels'.

Camusrory (Inverness), Camas Ruairidh. 'Roderick's bay'.

Camusteel (Ross), Camas Teile. 'Linden bay'.

Camusterrach (Ross), Camas Tearach. 'Eastern bay'.

Camustianavaig (Skye), Camas Dìonabhaig. This Gaelic/Norse name contains both languages' words for 'bay', while the first Norse element may be *dyn*, 'noisy'.

Candacraig (Aberdeen), Cionn na Creige. 'The end of the rock'. This is basically the same name as 'Kennacraig' and 'Kincraig'.

Canna, Canaigh. This may be 'can island', referring to the shape of a rock near the harbour. A native of Canna is a *Canach*, and the Laird of Canna is *Fear Chanaigh*.

Cannich (Inverness), Canaich. 'Bog cotton place'.

Cantray (Inverness), Canntra. This Brythonic name may be 'white settlement'

Cantraydoune (Inverness), Canntra an Dùin. 'Cantray by the hill(fort)'.

Caol (Inverness), An Caol. 'The narrows'. The full name is *Caol Loch Abar*, 'narrows of Lochaber'.

Caolasnacon (Argyll), Caolas nan Con. 'The narrows of the dogs', referring to the small waves caused by the tide against the wind.

Caoles (Coll, Tiree), An Caolas. 'The narrows'. The full name of Caoles in Coll is *An Caolas Colach*, 'the Coll narrows', while in Tiree it is *An Caolas Tiristeach*, 'the Tiree narrows'.

Caol Ila (Islay), Caol Ìle. 'The Islay narrows'. This was originally the name of the strait separating Islay and Jura and was given to the distillery founded here. The settlement's original name was *Ruadhphort*, 'red-brown port' ostensibly, and the village was divided into *Ruadhphort Beag* and *Ruadhphort Mór*.

Caolis (Vatersay), An Caolas. *See* **Caoles**.

Cape Wrath (Sutherland), Am Parbh or An Carbh. The Gaelic and English names come from a Norse word for 'turning', where ships would turn south after passing along the north coast. The second Gaelic name is used in Lewis whilst the first is more widespread.

Capisdale (Skye), Capasdal. This may be 'champion's valley', from Norse.

Cappenoch (Dumfries). 'Tillage place', from *Ceapanach*.

Caputh (Perth), Capaig or a' Cheapaich. The first Gaelic name may be from a Brythonic word for 'birch wood', while the second is 'the tillage land', from Gaelic.

Cara (Gigha), Cara. This Norse name may be 'Kari's island'.

Caradal (Skye), Càradal. 'Copse valley' or 'Kari's valley', from Norse.

Caragrich (Harris), Caragraich. The meaning of this name is unclear.

Carberry (East Lothian). Given this place's location, the name is most likely of Brythonic origin, denoting a fort.

Carbeth (Stirling). This may be 'birch cairn', from *Càrn Beithe*, as the name was 'Carnbeth' in the 16th century.

Carbisdale (Sutherland), Càrbasdal. 'Copse farm valley', from Norse. This is also the old name of nearby Culrain.

Carbost (Skye), Càrbost or Carabost. 'Copse farm', from Norse.

Cardhu (Moray). *See* **Cardow**.

Cardnach (Moray). 'Copse place', from Pictish *carden* with a Gaelic suffix.

Cardno (Aberdeen). *See* **Cardnach**.

Cardonald (Glasgow). This may be 'Donald's fort', from *Cathair Dhòmhnaill*, but may have originated in Brythonic.

Cardow (Moray). This may be 'black mossy land', from *Càthar Dubh*. The name is also spelled 'Cardhu' in English.

Cardross (Dunbarton). 'Copse headland', from Gaelic *Càrdainn-Ros*, containing Pictish *carden*.

Carfin (Lanark). An old form of the name is 'Carnefyn' which appears to suggest a Brythonic derivation such as 'Nefyn's fort or cairn'. However, the stress in the English name is on the second syllable which might suggest Gaelic *Càrn Fionn*, 'white cairn'.

Cargill (Perth), Car Ghàidheal. This may be 'seat of the Gaels'.

Carie (Perth), Càraidh. *Cairidh* is 'weir', and this may be a corruption of that.

Carinish (North Uist), Càirinis. 'Kari's headland', from Norse.

Carlo (Arran), Rubha na Beithe. The English name dates from the late 19th century and replaced the earlier 'Birchpoint' which was a translation of the Gaelic name.

Carloway (Lewis), Càrlabhagh. 'Karl's bay', from Norse. Upper Carloway is *Mullach Chàrlabhaigh*, 'the top of Carloway'.

Carluke (Lanark). This appears to contain Brythonic *caer*, 'fort', and may also have a dedication to the saint Lughaidh, also known as Mo Luag. Around the 13th century Carluke was known as *Eaglais Mo Luaig*, 'St Mo Luag's church'.

Carmahome (Arran). This is said to be from *Cathair Mo Choilm*, 'the seat of St Columba'.

Carmichael (Lanark). 'Michael's fort', from Brythonic. In the 12th and 13th centuries this place was known as 'Kermichel' and 'Karemigal', cognate with Gaelic *Cathair Mhìcheil*.

Carminish (Harris), Cairiminis. This Norse headland name is unclear.

Carmunnock (Lanark). This may be 'monks' seat' from Brythonic as suggested by an old form of the name, 'Cormannoc', cognate with older Gaelic *Cathair Manach*, now *Cathair Mhanach*.

Carmyle (Lanark). 'Blunt fort', from Brythonic, cognate with Gaelic *Cathair Mhaol*.

Carmyllie (Angus), Càrn Mhìlidh. This may be 'warriors' cairn', a name known to Gaelic speakers in Glenshee and Braemar.

Carna (Argyll), Càrna. This may be 'Kari's island', from Norse.

Carnach (Argyll, Ross), Càrnach. 'Cairn place'.

Carnan (South Uist), An Càrnan. 'Small cairn'. The full name is *Càrnan an Ìochdair*, 'small cairn of Iochdar'.

Carnasserie (Argyll), Càrn Asaraidh. 'Cairn at the path'.

Carnbee (Fife). This may be 'mountain cairn', from *Càrn Beinne*.

Carndearg (Muck), An Càrn Dearg. 'The red cairn'.

Carnish (Lewis), Càrnais. This may be 'Kari's headland', from Norse.

Carnoch (Argyll), A' Chàrnach; (Ross), A' Chàrnaich. 'The stony place'.

Carntyne (Glasgow). This may be 'fire cairn', from Gaelic *Càrn Teine* or a Brythonic cognate.

Carnwath (Lanark). An old form of the name, Carnewyth, suggests 'new fort' from *Caer Newydd*, a Brythonic cognate of Gaelic *Cathair Nuadh*.

Caroy (Skye), An Cadha Ruadh. 'The red-brown pass'.

Carradale (Argyll), Càradal or Càradail. 'Copse valley' or 'Kari's valley', from Norse. Carradale House is *Taigh Mór Chàradail*.

Carr Brae (Ross), Bruthach Charra. 'The slope at the rock shelf'.

Carrbridge (Inverness), Drochaid Chàrr or Drochaid Charra. Both names are found, the former being preferred locally and said to mean 'the bridge at the marsh'. An alternative derivation for the latter form is 'the bridge at the rock shelf'.

Carrick (Argyll, Ayr), Carraig. 'Rock'.

Carriden (Midlothian). While this was believed to be Brythonic 'fort of Eidyn', containing the personal name found in 'Edinburgh' and *Dùn Éideann*, it may stem from Pictish *carden*, 'thicket'.

Carishader (Lewis), Càiriseadar. 'Kari's dwelling' or 'Kárinn's dwelling', from Norse. Local pronunciation suggests a preferable spelling of *Càiriseadair*.

Carron (Moray); (Stirling), Carrann. The Stirling name is from 'rough water' and the Moray name may be from the same source or from *carr*, 'rock shelf'.

Carron Valley (Stirling), Srath Carrann. *See* **Strathcarron**. This was the site of a battle referred to in early Gaelic documents.

Carsaig (Argyll), Càrsaig. This may be 'Kari's bay', from Norse.

Carse of Bayhead (Ross), Moroich Chinn Déis. The Gaelic name is 'the carse of Kindeace'.

Carse of Gowrie (Perth), Cars Ghobharaidh. The English name is self-explanatory, and the Gaelic form is a translation of it. *See* **Gowrie** form.

Carsie (Perth). This is either an English diminutive of 'carse' or a name based on English 'carse' with a Gaelic locative.

Carskiey (Argyll), Carraig Sgéithe. 'Wing rock', first applied to a rock in the bay.

Carsphairn (Kirkcudbright). This name is unclear, but presumably Gaelic. The first element is *cars*, 'carse', from English, and the second may be *feàrna*, 'alder', but this name is under debate.

Carstairs (Lanark). 'Castle of Tarras', probably from Brythonic. The name was 'Casteltarras' in the 12th century but had altered to 'Carstaris' by the 16th.

Cartomy (Ross), Càthar Tomaidh. This may be 'mossy ground at the hillock place'.

Carwhin (Perth), Coire Chunna. 'Cunna's corrie'. Cunna is also commemorated at the graveyard of *Cladh Chunna* in Glen Lyon.

Cashel (Dunbarton), Caiseil; (Stirling). 'Stone fort', from *Caiseal*.

Cashel Dhu (Sutherland), An Caiseal Dubh. 'The black stone fort'.

Cashlie (Perth), Caislidh. 'Place of the stone fort'.

Cassilis (Ayr). This is from *caiseal*, 'stone fort', with an English plural attached.

Cassindonald (Fife). 'Donald's projecting ridge', from *Gasg Dhòmhnaill*.

Castlebay (Barra), Bàgh a' Chaisteil.

'The bay of the castle', referring to Kisimul Castle.

Castle Campbell (Clackmannan), Caisteal a' Ghlòim. While the English name mentions the owners of the castle, the Gaelic name is 'castle in the chasm'.

Castle Coeffin (Lismore), Caisteal Chaifeann. This name allegedly commemorates a Norse noble called *Caifeann* in Gaelic.

Castle Corbet (Ross), An Caisteal Dearg. The English name mentions the owners of the castle, but the Gaelic name is 'the red castle'.

Castlecraig (Ross), Taigh na Creige (Black Isle); Caisteal Chrag (Nigg). The English name means 'castle rock', similar to the Gaelic name in Nigg. The Black Isle name is 'the house by the rock' in Gaelic.

Castle Douglas (Kirkcudbright), Caisteal nan Dùghlasach. 'Castle of the Douglases', referring to nearby Threave Castle.

Castle Heather (Inverness), Caisteal Leathoir. 'Castle on the slope'. The English name is a corruption of the Gaelic.

Castle Leod (Ross), Cùl Dà Leothaid or Cùltaigh Leòid. This name does not refer to a castle held by Leòd, but is a corruption in English of the Gaelic names which both mean 'at the back of two slopes'.

Castleton (Arran), Baile a' Chaisteil. 'The village by the castle'.

Castletown (Caithness). *See* **Castleton**.

Catacol (Arran), Catagal. This Norse name refers to a ravine, but the first part of the name is unclear. People from here were known as *cuileagan-ime*, 'butter flies'. The coast between Catacol and Lochranza is *an Luirgeann*, 'the shank'.

Cathkin (Lanark). 'Common land', from *Coitcheann*.

Catlodge (Inverness), Caitleag. 'Sheep cote'.

Cattadale (Sutherland), Catadal. 'Cat

valley', from Norse, referring to the tribal name of the people of Caithness and Sutherland.

Causamul (North Uist), Cabhsamul. This may be 'cow island', from Norse.

Causer (Moray), Cabhsair. 'Constructed pathway'.

Caversta (Lewis), Cabhartaigh. 'Kofri's farm', from Norse.

Caw (Scalpay), An Cadha. 'The pass'.

Cawdor (Nairn), Caladar. 'Hard water', a name usually applied to rivers. This was the seat of a sept of the Campbells known as *Caimbeulaich bhoga Chaladair*, 'the soft Campbells of Cawdor'.

Ceannacroc (Inverness), Ceann nan Cnoc or Ceanna-Chnoc. 'The end of the hills'.

Cellar Head (Lewis), An Seilear. This name may refer to shells, from Norse.

Ceres (Fife). 'West or back place', from *Siarais*.

Challoch (Wigtown). 'Anvil', from *teallach*, as in the hill name *An Teallach*.

Challochmunn (Ayr). This may be 'Munna's anvil', from *Teallach Mhunna*. *Munna* is a by-name of the saint also known as *Fionntan* or Fintan.

Changue (Ayr). This may be 'tongue', from *teanga*, referring to strip of land.

Chanonry Point (Ross), Gob na Cananaich or Rubha na Cananaich. 'The point of the chanonry', which is at Fortrose or *A' Chananaich*, 'the chanonry', referring to the abbey of *Curadan*, also known as St Boniface.

Chapelhill (Ross), Cnoc an t-Seipeil. 'The hill at the chapel'.

Chapelpark (Inverness), Croit Mo Luaig or Pàirc an t-Seipeil. Gaelic has two names, 'St Mo Luag's croft' and 'the field at the chapel'.

Chapelton (Inverness), Baile an t-Seipeil. 'The farm at the chapel'.

Charleston (Inverness, Ross), Baile Theàrlaich. 'Charles's farm'. Charleston in Inverness used to be known

as *Achadh nam Bodach*, 'field of the old men'.

Charleston of Aberlour (Banff), Obar Lobhair. The English name commemorates the founder of the planned village. *See* **Aberlour**.

Charlestown (Ross), Am Baile Dearg. The English name commemorates a former owner, while the Gaelic name is 'the red farm'. Formerly this was known as *an Clachan*, 'the church-yard'. Charlestown House is *An Taigh Dearg*, 'the red house'.

Cheesebay (North Uist), Bàgh a' Chàise. 'Spume bay'. *Càise*, 'spume', is an uncommon word of Norse origin which sounds identical to the word for 'cheese', hence the English mistranslation.

Chesthill (Perth), Seasdal. 'Terraced meadow', of which the English form is an approximation in sound.

Chicken Head (Lewis), A' Chearc. The Gaelic name of this headland is simply 'the hen', so called because of its shape. Some say the name comes from the Norse 'kierke' because of an early Christian cell on the headland.

Chipperton (South Uist), Tiobartan. 'Well place', containing *tiobar* rather than the usual *tobar* for 'well'. The well itself was *Tobar Thiobartain* and said to be *air fìor iomall an domhain*, 'at the very edge of the world'.

Chirmorie (Ayr). This appears to be 'St Mary's land', from *Tìr Mhoire*.

Churchtown (Raasay), An Clachan. 'The churchyard' or 'the village with a church'. *Clachan* is often anglicised as 'Kirkton'.

Cilmalieu (Argyll), Cill Mo Liubha. 'St Mo Liubha's church'.

Clabhach (Coll), A' Chlabaich. This name is unclear but may mean something like 'the open mouthed place', referring to a topographical feature.

Clachaig (Argyll), Clachaig. 'Stone place'.

Clachamish (Skye), Clach Amais. This appears to mean 'target stone', but an older form of the name shows that it was *Cladh a' Chamais*, 'graveyard by the bay'.

Clachan (Argyll, Lismore, North Uist, Seil), An Clachan. 'The churchyard' or 'the village with a church', also anglicised as 'kirkton'. In North Uist the full Gaelic name is *Clachan na Lùib* or *Clachan a' Ghlùib*, 'the churchyard at the glebe'. In Seil the full name is *Clachan Saoil*, 'the kirkton of Seil'.

Clachan of Campsie (Stirling), Clachan Chamais. 'The kirkton of Campsie'.

Clachan of Glendaruel (Argyll), Clachan Ghlinn Dà Ruadhail. 'The kirkton of Glendaruel'.

Clachan Sands (North Uist), Clachan Shannda. 'The churchyard of Sanda', which is 'sand river', from Norse. The graveyard here is called *Cladh a' Chlachain*, 'the graveyard of Clachan'.

Clachieran (Bute), Cladh Chiarain. 'The graveyard of St Ciaran'.

Clachnacuddin (Inverness), Clach na Cùdainn. 'The stone of the tub', where local women did their washing.

Clachnaharry (Inverness), Clach na h-Aithrigh. 'Repentance stone'.

Clachtoll (Sutherland), Clach Toll. 'Stone with holes'.

Clachuil (Ross), Clach Thuill. 'Stone with a hole'.

Clackmannan Clach Mhanainn. 'The stone of Manau', a district of the Brythonic people of the Forth area. Clackmannanshire is *Siorrachd Chlach Mhanainn*.

Clackriach (Aberdeen). 'Brindled stone', from *Clach Riabhach*.

Cladach (Arran), An Cladach. 'The shore'.

Claddach (Bute), An Cladach. 'The shore'.

Claddach Baleshare (North Uist), Cladach a' Bhaile Shear. 'The shore opposite Baleshare'.

Claddach Carinish (North Uist), Cladach Chàirinis. 'The shore opposite Carinish'.

Claddach Illeray (North Uist), Cladach Iolaraigh. 'The shore opposite Illeray'.

Claddach Kirkebost (North Uist), Cladach Chirceboist. 'The shore opposite Kirkebost'.

Claddach Knockline (North Uist), Cladach Chnoc an Lìn. 'The shore opposite Knockline'.

Claddach Kyles (North Uist), Cladach a' Chaolais. 'The shore at the narrows'.

Cladich (Argyll), An Cladach. 'The shore'.

Cladoch (Arran), An Cladach. 'The shore'.

Claggan (Argyll, Inverness), An Claigeann. 'The skull', a word used to denote the most productive field on a farm.

Claigen (Skye), An Claigeann. *See* **Claggan**.

Claonaig (Argyll), Claonaig. This Norse name denoting a bay has an unclear initial element.

Clare (Ross), An Clàr. 'The small plain'.

Claremont (Fife). 'Flat hill' or 'rough pasture', from *Clàr Mhon(adh)*.

Clashindarroch (Aberdeen). 'Ditch by the oak', from *Clais an Daraich*.

Clashmahew (Wigtown). 'St Mo Chua's ditch', from *Clais Mo Chua*.

Clashmore (Sutherland), A' Chlais Mhór. 'The big ditch'.

Clashnabuiac (Ross), Clais nam Buidheag. 'The ditch of the yellow flowers'.

Clashnamuiach (Ross), Clais nam Maigheach. 'The ditch of the hares'.

Clashnessie (Sutherland), Clais an Easaidh. 'The ditch by the small waterfall'.

Clauchaneasy (Wigtown). 'Jesus's churchyard', from *Clachan Ìosa*.

Clauchlands (Arran). This may be from *clachlann*, 'stone enclosure'.

Clauchog (Arran), Clachaig. 'Stony place'.

Clava (Inverness), Clabhalag. The meaning of this name is unclear.

Claybokie (Aberdeen), Cladh Bhò-caidh. 'The graveyard of the ghost'.

Clay of Allan (Ross), Criadhach Alain Mhóir. 'Claylands by the big Allan'.

Claypark (Lewis), A' Bhuaile Chrèadha. The Gaelic name is 'the clay pen'.

Cleadale (Eigg), Clèadail. This Norse name refers to a valley, and the first element may refer to a ridged slope.

Cleascro (Lewis), Cliasgro. This Norse name may be 'river pit at ridged slope'.

Cleland (Lanark). This is probably 'clay land', from English.

Clerkhill (Sutherland), Cnoc a' Chléirich. 'The clerk's or cleric's hill'.

Cliad (Barra), Cliaid; (Coll), Cliad. This Norse name may be a form of *klettr*, 'rock' or 'cliff'.

Cliasmol (Harris), Cliasmol. This Norse name contains *holm*, 'small island', but the first part is unclear although it may contain a personal name.

Cliff (Lewis), Clibh; (Ross), A' Chliubh. These Norse names mean 'cliff'. Cliff House in Ross is *Taigh na Cliubhann*.

Clifton (Perth), Achadh nan Tuirigh-nean; (Ross), Baile na Creige. The English name is 'cliff village' which is also the meaning of the Ross Gaelic name. In Perth the Gaelic name is 'the field of the kings'.

Clochan (Banff). 'Churchyard' or 'kirkton', from *Clachan*.

Clochfoldich (Perth), Cloich Phol-laich. 'Indented stone'.

Cloch Point (Renfrew). 'Point of the stone', possibly a part-translation of *Rubha na Cloiche*, of which there are several.

Cloddach (Moray). 'River meadow', from *Cladach*. This word normally means 'shore', but is the usual term in Manx Gaelic for a river meadow.

Closeburn (Dumfries). 'St Osbran's or Osbern's church', from *Cill Osbrain*, as reflected in the 12th century form of the name, 'Kyleosbren'. It is unclear whether St Osbran of Ireland or St Osbern of England is the saint in question.

Clova (Angus), Clàbha. The meaning of this name is unclear.

Clovulin (Argyll), Cladh a' Mhuilinn. This appears to mean 'the cemetery at the mill'.

Cluanie (Arran, Ross), Cluainidh. 'Meadow place'.

Cluer (Harris), Cluthair. This Norse name appears to be in plural form, but its meaning is unclear.

Clunas (Nairn), Cluanais. 'Meadow place'.

Clune (Inverness), An Cluain or A' Chluain. 'The meadow'.

Clunes (Inverness), Na Cluainean. 'The meadows'. The old name was *Fionn-Ghaisg*, 'white Gask', referring to a strip of land projecting from a plateau.

Clunie (Perth), Cluainidh. 'Meadow place'.

Cluniemore (Perth), Cluainidh Mhór. 'Big Cluny'.

Cluniter (Argyll), Claon-Oitir. 'Sloping promontory'.

Cluny (Aberdeen, Fife). *See* **Clunie**.

Clydebank (Dunbarton), Bruach Chluaidh. 'The bank of the Clyde'.

Clydesdale (Lanark), Dail Chluaidh. 'The valley of the Clyde'.

Clynder (Dunbarton), An Claon Dearg. 'The red slope'.

Clyne (Sutherland), Clìn. 'Slope'. Clyne parish is *Sgìre Chlìn*.

Cnocantubha (Arran), Cnocan an Tugha. 'The hillock of the thatch'.

Cnocbreac (Jura), An Cnoc Breac. 'The speckled hill'.

Coalsnaughton (Clackmannan). This may be 'Nechtan's land', from *Cas Neachdain*, where *cas* is used for 'land' rather than 'foot', as happens in Irish place-names.

Coast (Ross), An t-Eirtheaire. 'The coast'. First Coast is *an t-Eirtheaire Shìos*, 'the lower coast', and Second Coast is *an t-Eirtheaire Shuas*, 'the upper coast'. Gaelic uses *air an Eirtheaire* to express 'in Coast'.

Cochno (Dunbarton). This may mean 'place of little hollows', from Gaelic *Cuachanach*, but may also be from a Brythonic source based on *coch*, 'red'.

Cockbridge (Aberdeen), Drochaid a' Choilich. This appears to be 'the bridge of the cockerel', but *coileach* also means 'eddy', which may be the intended meaning.

Cockenzie (East Lothian). This appears to be 'Kenneth's secluded spot', from *Cùil Choinnich*.

Coigach (Ross), Cóigeach. 'Fifth part', referring to a land division. The area is also known as *Sgìre na Cóigich*, 'the district of Coigach'.

Coignafearn (Inverness), Cóig na Feàrna. 'The fifth of the alder'. This is located in Strathdearn which contains five cóigs, Coignafearn, Coignascallan, Cóig na Sithe, Cóig a' Mhuilinn and Cóig nam Fionndaraich. *See* **Strathdearn**.

Coignascallan (Inverness), Cóig nan Sgàlan. 'The fifth of the shelters or huts'. *See* **Coignafearn**.

Coilacreich (Aberdeen), Coille a' Chrithich. 'The aspen wood'.

Coilleag (Eriskay), A' Choilleag. 'The cockle beach'.

Coillemore (Arran), Coille Mór. 'Large wood'. This name is unusual in that the definite article would be expected as would *mhór*, the feminine form of the adjective, rather than the masculine *mór*.

Coillore (Skye), Coille Òra. This was originally the name of a wood, but the spelling in Gaelic and English obscure the meaning of the second element.

Colaboll (Sutherland), Colabol. 'Coal farm', from Norse.

Colbost (Skye), Cealabost or Caileabost. This may be 'keel farm' or 'farm with a drying shed', from Norse.

Coldbackie (Sutherland), Callbacaidh. 'Cold bank' or 'charcoal bank', from Norse.

Coldwells (Ross), Am Bealaidh. The 'cold wells' referred to in the English name are absent from the Gaelic, which means 'the broom', referring to the shrub.

Col Glen (Argyll), An Caol-Ghleann. 'The narrow glen'.

Colintraive (Argyll), Caol an t-Snàimh. 'The narrows of the swimming', where cattle were swum across between Cowal and Bute.

Coll (Coll), Cola; (Lewis), Col. The island of Coll has a pre-Celtic name and is known by the epithet, *Cola Chreagach Chiar*, 'dark rocky Coll'. A native of the island is a *Colach*. The character of the people is referred to disparagingly in a couple of rhymes such as, *Chan fhaic am Muileach nach sanntaich am Muileach; na shanntaicheas am Muileach, goididh an Colach; 's na ghoideas an Colach, cuiridh an Tiristeach am folach*, 'What the Mull man sees, he wants; what the Mull man wants, the Coll man steals; what the Coll man steals, the Tiree man hides'. Another is *Chan eil an cùil no an cuilidh nach fhaic sùil a' Mhuilich, 's chan eil an àird no 'n ìosal nach laimhsich làmh an Ìlich. Na dh'fhàgadh am Muileach, ghrad-sgrìobadh an Colach bhuaithe, ach 's mairg a dh'earbadh a chuid no anam ris a' chealgaire Bharrach*, which has similar sentiments, but manages to disparage the people of Islay and Barra too. *Cola* is frequently spelt as *Colla* although this latter form does not reflect the pronunciation. Coll is Lewis is 'summit', from Norse. Upper Coll is *Col Uarach*, Inner Coll is *Ceann a-Staigh Chuil*, and Outend Coll is *Ceann a-Muigh Chuil*. The nearby beach is *Tràigh Chuil*.

Collam (Harris), Colam. This may mean 'summit holm', from Norse.

Collychippen (Dunbarton), Cùil a' Chipein. 'The secluded spot at the place of (tree) stumps'.

Colmonell (Ayr). The saint Colman Eala is commemorated in this name.

Colnabaichin (Aberdeen), Cùil nam Bàthaichean. 'The secluded spot at the byres'.

Colonsay, Colbhasa. 'Kolbein's island', from Norse. A native of Colonsay is a *Colbhasach*, also nicknamed a *coinean mór*, 'big rabbit'.

Colzium (Midlothian). 'Narrow leap', from *cuingleum*.

Comer (Stirling). This may be 'confluence', from *comar*.

Comrie (Perth) Cuimrigh; (Ross), Comraigh. 'Sanctuary'. The fair in Comrie in Perthshire was known as *Féill Mo Cheasaig*, 'St Kessock's Fair'.

Conaglen (Argyll), Conghleann. 'Hound valley'.

Conchra (Argyll, Ross), Conchra. 'Place of cruives', a type of pen or fold.

Conicavel (Moray). This may be 'narrow place at the fish trap' from *Cong a' Chabhail*.

Conisby (Islay), Còmhnaidh nan Easbaig. Despite the Germanic appearance of the English form of this name, this Gaelic name is 'residence of the bishops'.

Connage (Inverness), A' Choinnis. This may mean 'the joint meadow'.

Connel (Argyll), A' Chonghail. 'The whirlpool', the full name being *A' Chonghail Latharnach*, 'the Lorn Connel'.

Connista (Skye), Conasta. The first part of this Norse farm name is unclear.

Conon (Skye), Connain. This commemoration of the saint Connan was originally applied to the nearby river and then to the township.

Cononbrae (Ross), Bog Domhain. The English name refers to the river

Conon, whilst the Gaelic name means 'deep bog'.

Conon Bridge (Ross), Drochaid Sguideil. The English name refers to the River Conon, and while the Gaelic also mentions a bridge, its second part is a Norse valley name although its defining element is unclear. Local people were nicknamed *geòcairean*, 'gluttons'.

Conon House (Ross), Taigh Chonainn. 'House of the Conon', a river name possibly meaning 'hound stream'.

Conordon (Skye), An Còmhnardan. 'The small plain'.

Conrick (Dumfries); (Inverness), A' Chòmhrag. The Inverness name means 'the confluence' and the Dumfries name may be from the same source.

Contin (Ross), Cunndainn. This may be 'confluence'. The local fair was *Féill Ma Ruibhe*, 'St Maol Rubha's fair', later relocated to Dingwall.

Contullich (Ross), Conntulaich. 'Place of joint hills'.

Conveth (Kincardine), Coinmheadh. 'Free quartering'. This refers to the obligation placed on the area to provide sustenance free of charge to passing troops. Conveth is the old name of the parish of Laurencekirk.

Convinth (Inverness), An Confhadhach. 'The place of storms'.

Coppay (Harris), Copaigh. 'Cup island', from Norse, a reference to the island's shape.

Corarder (Inverness), Coire Àrdair. 'Corrie of the Arder'.

Corgarff (Aberdeen), Corr Garaidh. This appears to mean 'end of the den'.

Corkamull (Mull), Corcamul. 'Oat ridge', from Norse.

Corkisary (Ross), Corcasairigh. This may be 'oat sheiling', from Norse, or it might be a Norse sheiling or field name with a personal name as the first element.

Cornabus (Islay), Còrnabus. 'Corn

farm', from Norse.

Cornaig (Tiree), Còrnaig. 'Corn bay', from Norse. Cornaigbeg is *Còrnaig Bheag*, 'little Cornaig' and Cornaigmore is *Còrnaig Mhór*, 'big Cornaig'.

Corncattrach (Aberdeen). 'The corrie with the stone fort', from *Coire na Cathrach*.

Corndavon (Aberdeen), Coire an Dà Bheinn. 'The corrie in the two mountains'.

Cornton (Ross), Baile an Loch. While the English name is 'corn farm', from English, the Gaelic name is 'the farm by the loch'.

Coroghan (Canna), An Corra-Dhùn. 'The uneven hill(fort)'.

Corpach (Inverness), A' Chorpaich. 'The place of bodies', possibly meaning that the dead were ferried from here for burial.

Corran (Inverness, Skye), An Corran. 'The narrow spit'. The full name of Corran by Ardgour is *Corran Àird Ghobhar*, 'the narrow spit of Ardgour'.

Corrie (Arran), An Coire. 'The corrie'. The full name used to be *Coire Cnoc Dubh*, 'the corrie of the black hill', from which the genitive case is absent. Upper Corrie is *Achag*, possibly 'little field', also known as Achag in English. High Corrie is *An Coire Àrd*, whilst North High Corrie is *Guala Bàn*, 'white shoulder'.

Corriecravie (Arran), Coire Chraobh-aidh. 'Corrie at the tree place'. Corriecravie Moor was known locally as *An Cnoc Reamhar*, 'the fat hill', after a prominent nearby feature.

Corriehiam (Arran), Coire Chaim. This appears to be 'crooked corrie'.

Corriemoillie (Ross), Coire Mhuillidh. 'Milling corrie'.

Corriemulzie (Ross), Coire Mhuillidh. *See* **Corriemoillie**.

Corrievorrie (Inverness), Coire Mhóruigh. 'The corrie on the big slope'.

Corrour (Inverness), Coire Odhar. 'Dun corrie', but the original name may have been *Coire Dhobhair*, 'corrie by the water'.

Corry (Ross), An Coire. 'The corrie'.

Corrygills (Arran), Coire Ghoill. Although this appears to be 'corrie of the non-Gael', it may be from Norse *korfagil* (raven gully) or *karigil* (Kari's gully).

Corrynahera (Jura), Coire na h-Earadh. 'The corrie at the division'.

Corry of Ardnagrask (Ross), Coire Àird nan Crasg. 'The corrie of Ardnagrask'.

Corskie (Moray). This may be 'crossing place', from *Crasgaidh*.

Coruanan (Inverness), Coire Uanain. 'Lamb's corrie'.

Corunna (North Uist), Corùna. This was named after the battle in Spain during the Napoleonic wars

Corvost (Ross), Coire-Bheist. This name is locally interpreted as 'corrie of the beast', but since the stress is on the first syllable the name's origin must lie somewhere else.

Coshieville (Perth), Cois a' Bhile. 'By the rock edge or sacred tree'.

Cotterton (Ross), Achadh nan Coitear. The English name is 'cotters' farm', but the Gaelic name is 'the cotters' field'.

Coul (Ross), A' Chùil. 'The secluded spot'.

Coulags (Ross), Na Cùileagan. 'The little secluded spots'.

Coulhill (Ross), Cnoc na Cùil. 'The hill at the secluded spot'. The old name was *Baile na Cùil*, 'farm at the secluded spot'.

Coulin (Ross), Cùmhlainn. 'Place of enclosures'. The old name was *Teamradal*, 'timber valley', from Norse.

Coull (Aberdeen), A' Chùil or Cùil. 'The secluded spot'. Coull parish is *Sgìre Chùil*.

Coulport (Dunbarton), An Cùl-Phort. 'The back port', possibly referring to its location at the back of Rosneath peninsula.

Coulregrein (Lewis), Cùl ri Gréin. 'Back to the sun'.

Coupar Angus (Perth), Cùbar Aonghais. 'The *cùbar* of Angus', *cùbar* being a Brythonic word maybe meaning 'confluence'.

Cour (Argyll), An Cùr. This is unclear, but if from Norse, may refer to cattle folds.

Courthill (Ross), Cnoc a' Mhòid. 'The hill of the meeting place or court'.

Couttie (Perth). 'The *cùbar* of Ultan's son', from *Cùbar Mac Ultain*. See **Coupar Angus** and **Cupar**.

Cove (Ross), An Uamhghaidh. The Gaelic name is 'the place of caves'. Local people are known as *buic*, 'bucks'.

Cowal (Argyll), Comhal or Comhghall. 'Comhghall's land', the leader of one of the four sections of Dal Riada. A local is a *Comhalach*. The Kerry or Kyles district is *An Ceathramh Comhalach*, 'the Cowal quarterland', and a native of that area is a *Ceathrach*.

Cowden (Perth), A' Challtainn. 'The hazel wood'.

Cowie (Kincardine, Stirling). This may be 'hazel place', from *Collaidh*.

Coylet (Argyll), Cuingleathad. 'Narrow slope'.

Coylumbridge (Inverness), Drochaid na Cuingleum. 'The bridge of Coylum', which means 'narrow leap'.

Crackaig (Jura), Cracaig; (Sutherland), Crachdaig. 'Crow bay', from Norse.

Craggan (Perth). 'Small rock', from *Creagan*.

Cragganmore (Banff), An Creagan Mór. 'The big rock'.

Craggie (Sutherland), Cragaidh. 'Rock place'.

Craig (Ross), Creag Ruigh Mhorghain or A' Chreag. 'The rock at Morgan's slope' or 'the rock'. An alternative interpretation is based on *morghan*, 'gravel' or 'shingle'. Another form

of the name is *Creag Ni Mhorghain*, 'Morgan's daughter's rock'. The Craig River is *Abhainn na Creige* or *Abhainn Bràigh Thathaisgeail*.

Craigellachie (Banff), Creag Eileachaidh. 'The rock at the stony place'.

Craigellie (Aberdeen). This may be 'the rock at the stony place', from *Creag Eilidh*.

Craigendoran (Dunbarton), Creag an Dobhrain. 'The rock of the otter'.

Craigengall (West Lothian). 'Rock of the non-Gaels', from *Creag nan Gall*.

Craigentinny (Midlothian). This may be 'the rock of the fox', from *Creag an t-Sionnaich*.

Craigesk (Midlothian). 'The rock at the Esk', from *Creag Easg*.

Craighouse (Jura), Taigh na Creige. 'The house by the rock'.

Craigie (Angus, Ayr, Perth, West Lothian). 'Rock place', from *Creagaidh*.

Craigievar (Aberdeen), Creag Mhàrr. 'The rock of Mar'.

Craigleith (East Lothian). 'The rock of Leith', from *Creag Lìte*.

Craiglumphart (Fife). This is 'the rock at the encampment' from *creag* and *longphort*.

Craigmaddie (Dunbarton), Creag a' Mhadaidh. 'The rock of the fox or wolf'.

Craigmailing (West Lothian). This may be 'rock at the smooth rounded hill', from *Creag Mhaoilinn*.

Craigmarry (West Lothian). This may be 'the rock of killing', from *Creag a' Mharbhaidh*.

Craigmawhannel (Ayr). This appears to be 'St Conall's rock', from *Creag Mo Chonaill*.

Craigmore (Bute), A' Chreag Mhór. 'The big rock'.

Craigmyle (Aberdeen). 'Rounded rock', from *Creag Mhaol*.

Craignavie (Perth), Creag Neamhaidh. 'The rock at the sacred place'.

Craignish (Argyll), Creiginis. 'Rocky

headland', from Norse. Local people were nicknamed *òigich*, 'youngsters', and *fithich dhubha*, 'black ravens'. Craignish Point is *Rubha Chreiginis*.

Craignure (Mull), Creag an Iubhair. 'The rock of the yew'.

Craigo (Angus). 'Rock place', from *Creagach*.

Craig Phadrig (Inverness), Creag Phàdraig or Làrach an Taigh Mhóir. The English and first Gaelic names are 'Patrick's rock', whilst the second Gaelic name, used by local Gaelic speakers, is 'the site of the big house'.

Craigs (Ross), Taigh na Creige. The English name is 'rocks', while the Gaelic name is 'the house by the rock'.

Craigston (Barra), Baile na Creige. 'The village by the rock'.

Craigstrome (Benbecula), Creaga-strom. 'Rocky current', from Norse.

Craigton (Ross, Sutherland), Baile na Creige. 'The village by the rock'. There is a Craigton in Glasgow and in Angus which may contain the surname 'Craig' rather refer to a rock.

Crail (Fife). 'Fort at the rock', from Brythonic *Cair Al* or Gaelic *Cathair Ail*. An older form of the name, 'Caraile', shows the derivation more clearly.

Cramond (Midlothian). 'Fort on the Almond', from Brythonic. The derivation is clear in an old form of the name, 'Caramonth'.

Cranachan (Inverness), Crannachan. 'Tree place'.

Crandart (Angus), Crannaird. 'Tree point'.

Cranloch (Moray). 'Tree place', from *crannlach*. There is no reference to a loch in the name.

Crannach (Aberdeen), Crannach. 'Tree place'.

Crarae (Argyll), Carr Eighe. The elements in the Gaelic name can be interpreted as 'rock ledge' and 'file', giving an overall meaning of 'file-shaped rock ledge' but, if the English form is an accurate reflection of an older name, an alternative interpretation might include *crò* or *crà*, 'enclosure' and *réidh*, 'level'.

Crask (Sutherland), An Crasg or A' Chrasg. 'The crossing'.

Crathes (Kincardine), Crathais. This appears to mean 'shaking place'.

Crathie (Aberdeen), Craichidh. This may mean the same as **Crathes** and **Cray**.

Craw (Arran), An Crà, An Cràdha or A' Chré. All the variations in the name stem from *crò*, 'sheep pen', originally a Norse word.

Cray (Perth), Crathaidh. 'Shaking place'.

Creagan (Argyll), An Creagan; (Perth). 'The small rock'.

Creagorry (Benbecula), Creag Ghoraidh. 'Godred's rock'.

Creich (Mull), Crèich; (Sutherland), Craoich. This may mean 'tree place'.

Cremannan (Stirling). This is thought to stem from either *Crò Mhanainn*, 'the enclosure of Manau', a Brythonic district around the Forth, or from *Crò Mheannan*, 'kids' enclosure'.

Crepkill (Skye), Creipigil. This was originally Norse *Cresgil*, 'cross ravine'.

Cretshengan (Argyll), Croit Shean-gain. 'Seangan's croft'.

Crianlarich (Perth), A' Chrìon-Làraich. This appears to be 'the wasted site', but the first element may originally have been *critheann*, 'aspen', rather than *crìon*, 'wasted or feeble'.

Crieff (Perth), Craoibh. 'Tree place'.

Crimond (Aberdeen). This may be 'shaking moor' or 'boundary moor', from *crith* or *crìoch* and *monadh*.

Crinan (Argyll), An Crìonan. This seems to be 'the wasted or debilitated place'. Crinan Moss is *A' Mhòine Mhór*, 'the big peat moss'.

Croachy (Inverness), Cruachaidh. 'Hard field'.

Crobeg (Lewis), Crò Beag. 'Small enclosure', from Norse/Gaelic.

Crochandoon (Arran), An Cnocan Donn. 'The brown hillock'.

Croe Bridge (Ross), Drochaid a' Chrò. 'The bridge at the enclosure'.

Croft (Ross), Croit Thollaidh. The Gaelic name is 'croft at Tollie'.

Croftamie (Stirling), Croit Sheumaidh. This appears to be 'Jamie's croft'.

Croftjames (Ross), Croit Sheumais. 'James's croft'.

Croftmore (Perth), A' Chroit Mhór. 'The big croft'.

Croftnahaven (Inverness), Croit na h-Abhann. 'The croft by the river'.

Croggan (Mull), An Crògan. This name seems to refer to a paw-shaped piece of land, from *cròg*, 'paw'. Local people were nickamed *eich dhonna*, 'brown horses'.

Croick (Ross), A' Chròic. 'The antlers', possibly referring to a branch in the glen or river.

Croir (Bernera), Crothair. 'Enclosures', from Norse.

Cromar (Aberdeen), Crò Mhàrr. 'The enclosure of Mar'. Braes of Cromar is *Bràigh Crò Mhàrr* and *Bruthaichean Crò Mhàrr*.

Cromarty (Ross), Cromba. 'Crooked bay'. The Cromarty Firth is *Caolas Chrombaigh*. The saying, *Ged a rachadh Cromba leis a' mhuir*, 'Even though Cromarty were to slip into the sea', was used to denote an unlikely occurrence.

Cromasaig (Ross), An Cromasadh or Cromasaig. 'The crooked stance'.

Crombie (Fife). 'Crooked river'. The older name was Abercrombie, from *Obar Chrombaidh*, 'mouth of the crooked river'.

Cromdale (Moray), Crombail. 'Crooked haugh'. The original form of the name, *Cromdhail*, shows the component parts more clearly. The parish was known as *Sgìr' Mo Luaig*, 'St Mo Luag's parish', and the Cromdale Hills are *Beinn Chrombail* or *Beinn Chromdhail*.

Cromlix (Perth). This may refer to standing stones and come from either Gaelic *crom leac* or Brythonic *cromlech* with an English plural attached.

Cromore (Lewis), Crò Mór. 'Large enclosure', from Norse/Gaelic.

Cromra (Inverness), Cromrath. 'Crooked circular fort'.

Cross (Lewis), Cros. 'Crossing place', from Norse.

Crossaig (Argyll), Crosaig. 'Cross bay', from Norse.

Crossal (Skye), Crosal. 'Cross hill', from Norse.

Crossapoll (Tiree), Crosabol. 'Cross farm', from Norse.

Crossbost (Lewis), Crosabost. 'Farm of the crosses', from Norse.

Crosscraig (Perth), Troisearraig. Both Gaelic and English names contain a reference to some kind of crossing, but the Gaelic name says nothing about a rock or craig.

Crossmyloof (Glasgow). This may be 'St Mo Liubha's cross', from *Crois Mo Liubha*. Locally the name is believed to stem from the saying 'cross my loof with silver', where 'loof' is said to mean 'hand'.

Cross Skigersta Road (Lewis), An Rathad Ur. The road between Cross and Skigersta is known as 'the new road' in Gaelic.

Crowlin Islands (Ross), Na h-Eileanan Cròlaigeach or Na h-Eileanan Cròlainneach. The 'Crowlin' part of the name may mean 'hard land'.

Crowlista (Lewis), Crabhlasta. This may be 'farm of the meadow with a pen', from Norse.

Croy (Ayr, Dunbarton, Nairn), Crothaigh. This is said to stem from *cruaidh*, 'hard'.

Crubenmore (Inverness), Crùbainn Mhór. 'Large crouching place', possibly a reference to the nearby hills.

Crulivaig (Lewis), Crùlabhaig. This Norse name may be 'bay at the meadow with a pen'.

Cuach (Inverness), A' Chuach. 'The hollow'.

Cuagach (Eigg), A' Chuagach. This is said to be 'twisted place', but may originate from Norse for 'bay at the enclosure'.

Cuaig (Ross), Cùthaig. 'Cow bay', from Norse. The bay itself is called Òb Chùthaig. Local people are known as rùcanaich, 'rumblers', or tùthagan, 'patches'.

Cuderish (Perth), Cudrais. This may mean 'common land'.

Cuidrach (Skye), A' Chuidreach. This may be 'common land'. South Cuidrach is Peighinn an Dùine, 'pennyland of the hill fort'.

Cuier (Barra), Cuithir. 'Cattle folds', from Norse.

Cuigeas (Tiree), Cu-dhéis. This may contain Norse kví, 'enclosure'. An alternative English name is 'Quaish'.

Cuil (Argyll, Ross), A' Chùil. 'The secluded spot'.

Cuilghailtro (Argyll), Cùil Ghailltreo. 'Secluded spot of the non-Gaels' settlement'. This name appears to contain Brythonic tref, 'settlement', although the location is far from the main groupings of Brythonic names.

Cuillich (Ross), Cuinglich. 'Narrow place'.

Cuithe (Arran), An Cuithe. 'The cattle fold', from Norse kví.

Culaneilan (Ross), Cùl an Eilein. 'The back of the island'.

Culbin Sands (Moray), Bar Inbhir Éireann. The sands here are called 'the sand bar at the mouth of the Findhorn' in Gaelic.

Culbo (Ross, Sutherland), Cùrabol. 'Knob-shaped farm', from Norse.

Culbokie (Ross), Cùil Bhòcaidh or An Cùil Bhàicidh. 'The secluded spot of the ghost or goblin'.

Culburnie (Ross), Cùil Braonaigh. 'Secluded spot at the damp place'.

Culcabock (Inverness), Cùil na Càbaig. This name appears to mean 'the quiet spot of the kebbuck of cheese', but the original name was possibly Cùl na Ceapaich, 'the back of the tillage land'. The name Capaig is found in **Caputh**, and this may be another origin of the name. An older name of this place was Clachan Donnchaidh, 'Duncan's village'.

Culchonich (Ross), A' Chùil Chóintich. 'The mossy secluded spot'.

Culduie (Ross), Cùil Duibh. 'Black secluded spot'.

Culduthel (Inverness), Cùl Daothail or Cùil Daothail. This name's meaning is unclear although it includes cùl, 'back', or cùil, 'quiet spot'. Daothail is said to come from tuathail, 'north side', however there is a personal name, Tuathal, which may be the origin of this name.

Culeave (Ross), Cùil Liabh. 'The back of the moors', from sliabh.

Culisse (Ross), Cùl an Lios. 'The back of the fortified enclosure'.

Culkein (Sutherland), An Cùl-cinn. 'The common grazings'.

Culkein Drumbeg (Sutherland), Cùl-cinn an Droma Bhig. 'The common grazings of Drumbeg'.

Cullen (Banff), Cùillean. The old English form was Invercullen which was said to mean 'the mouth of the holly stream', from Inbhir Cuilinn. The Gaelic name is that used by speakers of Banffshire and Braemar Gaelic, and does not support the 'holly' source. However, the pronunciation of Gaelic place-names in marginal areas can be unreliable.

Cullerne (Moray). 'The back of the Findhorn', from Cùl Éireann.

Cullicudden (Ross), Cùl a' Chùdainn. 'The back of the tub', referring to some topographical feature.

Cullipool (Luing), Culapul. This Norse name may be 'coal farm'.

Culloden (Inverness), Cùil Lodair. This may be 'the secluded spot at the shelving slope'.

Culmaily (Sutherland), Cùil Mhàilidh. *Cùil* is a 'secluded spot', but the second element is unclear. However, *see* **Dalmally** and **Kilmallie**.

Culnacraig (Ross), Cùl na Creige. 'The back of the rock'.

Culnaknock (Skye), Cùl nan Cnoc. 'The back of the hills'.

Culnamean (Skye), Cùl nam Beann. 'The back of the mountains'.

Culrain (Sutherland), Cùl Ràthain. 'The back of the small circular fort'. The older name was *Càrbasdal*, 'copse farm valley', from Norse, now applied to Carbisdale.

Culross (Fife), Cuileann-Ros. 'Holly point'.

Culsh (Aberdeen), A' Chùilt. 'The secluded spot'.

Culter (Aberdeen, Kincardine), Cùldair. This may be 'back water'. Peterculter is on the north side of the Dee with Maryculter on the southern bank in Kincardineshire.

Cults (Aberdeen, Fife). *See* **Culsh**.

Culzie (Ross), Caolaisidh. 'Place of the narrow meadow'.

Cumbernauld (Dunbarton), Comar nan Allt. 'The confluence of the streams'. *See* **Achnalt**.

Cumbrae, Cumaradh. 'Place of the Cymric people', referring to the Brythonic people of Strathclyde. A derogatory saying about Bute also takes a side swipe at Cumbrae, *Chan ann am Bòid uile a tha an t-olc; tha cuid dheth sa Chumaradh bheag làimh ris*, 'Not all evil is in Bute; some is in little Cumbrae nearby'. Cumbrae is also known as 'Great Cumbrae' or *Cumaradh Mór*, while Little Cumbrae is *Cumaradh Beag*. The fair held in Great Cumbrae was known as *Féill Mo Cheasaig*, 'St Kessock's Fair'.

Cummingston (Moray). 'The town of the Cummings'. This is locally known as 'the Collach', perhaps from *an coileach* meaning 'the eddy'.

Cuniside (Sutherland), Caonasaid.

'Lady's farm', from Norse.

Cunninghame (Ayr), Coineagan. The meaning of this name is unclear, but predates the arrival of English and is thus not a *ham* or 'homestead' name.

Cupar (Fife), Cùbar or Cùbar Fìobha. *Cùbar* is a Brythonic word, maybe meaning 'confluence'. In Gaelic, Cupar was known as *Cùbar Fìobha*, 'Cupar of Fife', to distinguish it from *Cùbar Aonghais*, 'Coupar of Angus'. The town cross is known as *Crois Chùbair*.

Curin (Ross), Caorthainn. 'Rowan place'.

Curragh (Ayr). 'Wet plain', from *Currach*.

Currie (Midlothian). *See* **Curragh**.

Cushnie (Aberdeen). This may mean 'cold place'. *See* **Troup Head**.

Cyderhall (Sutherland), Siara. 'Sigurd's howe', from Norse. The English form of the name was 'Sydera' before the ornate creation of 'Cyderhall'. This is the burial place of Sigurd Eysteinson who subjugated Caithness and Sutherland for the Norse.

Daan (Ross), Dathan. 'Small davoch'.

Dailly (Ayr), Dail Mhaol Chiarain. The English form is is an abbreviation of the Gaelic, 'the haugh of the devotee of St Ciaran'.

Dailuaine (Banff), An Dail Uaine. 'The green haugh'.

Dairsie (Fife). 'Oak stance', from *dair* and *fasadh*. This is also known as Osnaburgh.

Dalachale (Banff). 'The kail haugh', from *Dail a' Chàil*.

Dalarossie (Inverness), Dail Fhearghais. 'Fergus's haugh'. The English version comes from an older Gaelic form with the same meaning, *Dail Fhearghasa*.

Dalavich (Argyll), Dail Abhaich. 'Haugh at the water place'.

Dalavil (Skye), Dail a' Bhil. This may be 'haugh at the rock edge' from

Gaelic, or 'valley at the rock edge' from Norse/Gaelic.

Dalbeattie (Kirkcudbright). This contains *dail*, 'haugh', but the second element is unclear. It is said to be from *beithe*, 'birch', but the phonetics do not suggest this. It may represent *biataiche*, 'provider of food'.

Dalbeg (Lewis), Dail Beag or An Daile Beag. 'Small valley', from Norse/Gaelic. Dalbeg and Dalmore are together known as *Na Dailean*, 'the valleys'.

Dalbeth (Glasgow). This may be 'birch haugh', from *Dail Bheithe*.

Dalblair (Ayr). 'The haugh on the plain', from *Dail a' Bhlàir*.

Dalcataig (Inverness), Dail Cataig. The second element of this haugh or meadow name is unclear.

Dalcharn (Sutherland), Dail Chàirn. 'Cairn haugh'.

Dalchlachaig (Perth), Dail Chlachaig. 'Haugh at the stone place'.

Dalchork (Sutherland), Dail Choirce. 'Oat haugh'.

Dalchosnie (Perth), Dail Chosnaidh. This may be 'haugh of the defender or defending'.

Dalchreichart (Inverness), Dul Chreachaird or Dail Chreachaird. This appears to be 'the haugh at the raiding point'.

Dalcrombie (Inverness), Dail Chrombaidh. 'The haugh at the crooked river'.

Dalcross (Inverness), Dealgros. 'Thorn point'. Influenced by English, a new Gaelic name has arisen for this place, *Dail Chrois*, which appears to mean 'cross haugh'.

Daldhu (Perth), An Dail Dubh. 'The black haugh'.

Dalgety (Fife). 'Thorn place', from *Dealgadaidh*.

Dalginch (Fife). 'Thorn meadow', from *Dealg-Innis*.

Dalginross (Perth), Dealganros. 'Thorn point'. This is similar to the Gaelic name of Dalcross, but shows the plural form of *dealg*.

Dalguise (Perth). This may be 'pine haugh' from *Dail Ghiuthais*.

Dalhalvaig (Sutherland), Dail Healabhaig. 'The haugh of Healabhaig, a Norse name possibly meaning 'flat bay'.

Daliburgh (South Uist), Dalabrog. 'Valley fort', from Norse. Until recently this was known as Dalibrog in English.

Dalilea (Argyll), Dail an Léigh. 'The doctor's haugh'. Another Gaelic name is *Dail Eildhe*, the second part of which is unclear and which would be stressed on the first syllable of the second word.

Dalintart (Argyll), Dail an Tairt. This appears to be 'the haugh of the thirst or dryness'.

Dalintober (Argyll), Dul an Tobair. 'The haugh of the well'.

Dalivaddy (Argyll), Dail a' Mhadaidh. 'The haugh of the wolf'.

Dalkeith (Midlothian), Dail Chéith. 'Valley with the wood', from Brythonic.

Dall (Perth), An Dail. 'The haugh'.

Dallachy (Moray). 'Haugh field or place', from *Dalachaidh* or *Daileachaidh*.

Dallas (Moray), Dalais. 'Haugh place'. The present village replaced the older Dolais Mychel or *Dalais Mhìcheil*, 'Dallas of St Michael', which was located at Torechastle.

Dalleagles (Ayr). 'Church haugh', from *dail* and *eaglais*.

Dallyfour (Aberdeen), Dail a' Phùir. 'Haugh at the pasture land'.

Dalmagarry (Inverness), Dail Mac Gearraidh. 'Gearraidh's son's haugh'.

Dalmahoy (Midlothian). 'St Mo Thua's haugh', from *Dail Mo Thua*.

Dalmaik (Aberdeen). 'St Mayota's haugh', from *Dul M' Aodhaig*.

Dalmally (Argyll), Clachan an Dìseirt. The English name is from *Dul Mhài-*

lidh, a haugh name with an unclear second element which is said to be the name of a saint. *See* **Culmaily** and **Kilmallie**. The Gaelic name is 'the churchyard of the hermitage', and refers back to an older name, *Dìseart Chonnain*, 'St Connan's hermitage'. The parish of Glen Orchy was known as *An Dìseart*, 'the hermitage'.

Dalmarnock (Glasgow, Perth). 'St Ernoc's or M' Ernoc's haugh', from *Dail Mhearnaig*.

Dalmellington (Ayr). 'Meling's farm', from English, to which Gaelic *dail*, 'haugh', was later prefixed, suggesting that Gaelic replaced English for a time in the area, giving rise to a conjectural Gaelic form such as *Dail Mheileangtain*, 'the haugh at Melingtun'

Dalmeny (West Lothian). Although this appears to be a haugh name possibly containing the name of the saint commemorated in **Kilmeny**, earlier forms of the name such as 'Dunmanyn' and 'Dunmany', suggest a hill(fort). The second element may be that found in 'Slamannan' and 'Clackmannan', giving a conjectural *Dùn Mhanainn* as the original basis of the name.

Dalmigavie (Inverness), Dail Mhigeachaidh. 'Haugh at the marshy hill face'.

Dalmore (Lewis), Dail Mór or An Daile Mór; (Ross), An Dail Mór; (Sutherland) Dail Mhór. In Lewis, the name means 'the big valley', from Norse/Gaelic. *See* **Dalbeg**. In Ross and Sutherland it is 'big haugh'.

Dalmuir (Dunbarton). This suggests 'St Mary's haugh', from *Dail Mhoire*.

Dalmunzie (Perth), Dail Mhungaidh. 'Mungo's haugh'.

Dalnabreck (Argyll, Perth), Dail nam Breac. 'The haugh of the trout'.

Dalnacardoch (Perth), Dail na Ceàrdaich. 'The haugh of the smithy'. *See* **Atholl**.

Dalnacloich (Ross), Dail na Cloiche. 'The haugh of the stone'.

Dalnafree (Sutherland), Dail na Frìthe. 'The haugh at the deer forest'.

Dalnagairn (Perth), Dail nan Càrn. 'The haugh of the cairns', from older *Dail na gCàrn*.

Dalnaglar (Perth), Dail nan Clàr. 'The haugh of the slabs', from older *Dail na gClàr*.

Dalnamein (Perth), Dail na Mèinn. 'The haugh with the mine or ore'.

Dalnaspidal (Perth), Dail na Spideil. 'The haugh at the hospice'. The old name was simply *An Spideal*, 'the hospice or spittal'.

Dalnatrat (Argyll), Dail na Tràghad. 'The haugh by the beach'.

Dalnavert (Inverness), Dail nam Feart. 'The haugh of the graves', from older *Dail na bhFeart*.

Dalnavie (Ross), Dail Neimhidh. 'The haugh of the sacred place'.

Dalneigh (Inverness), Dail an Eich. 'The horse haugh'.

Dalness (Argyll), Dail an Easa. 'The haugh at the waterfall'.

Dalnessie (Sutherland), Dail an Easaidh. 'The haugh at the waterfall place' or 'the haugh at the little waterfall'.

Dalpatrick (Lanark, Perth), Dail Phàdraig. 'Patrick's haugh'.

Dalraddy (Aberdeen, Inverness), Dail Radaidh. This may mean 'dark or ruddy haugh', from a dialect word, *rodaigh*. A saying concerning the Inverness place depends on word play in Gaelic, *Bha cailleach ann an Dail Radaidh, dh'ith i adag 's i marbh*, 'There was an old woman in Dalraddy who ate a haddock dead.'

Dalreavoch (Sutherland), An Dail Riabhach. 'The brindled haugh'.

Dalreoch (Ayr, Dunbarton). *See* **Dalreavoch**.

Dalrigh (Perth), Dail Rìgh. 'King's haugh'. This name may originally have contained *ruigh* (slope), but is now understood to refer to King Robert Bruce after a battle fought here. *See* **Clifton**.

Dalry (Ayr, Kirkcudbright, Midlothian). 'The haugh at the slope', from *dail* and *ruigh*. The village in Kirkcudbright is also known as St John's Town (of Dalry) and *Clachan Eòin*.

Dalserf (Lanark). 'St Serf's haugh', possibly from *Dail Sheirbh*.

Dalswinton (Dumfries). 'Swine farm', from English, to which Gaelic *dail*, 'haugh', was prefixed later when Gaelic replaced English in the area, giving rise to a conjectural form *Dail Suantain*, 'the haugh at the swine farm'

Dalvorar (Aberdeen), Dail a' Mhorair. 'The lord's haugh'.

Dalvoulin (Inverness), Dail a' Mhuilinn. 'The haugh at the mill'.

Dalwhinnie (Inverness), Dail Chuinnidh. 'Warrior's haugh'. *See* **Atholl**

Dalziel (Inverness, Ross), Dail Ghil; (Perth), Dail Gheollaidh. The name in Inverness and Ross is 'white haugh', while in Perth it is 'haugh at the white or bright place'.

Dandaleith (Moray). This may be 'the hill(fort) of two halves', from *Dùn Dà Leth*.

Danna Island (Argyll), Danna. This Norse island name is unclear.

Dares (Inverness), Daras. 'Door'. A local measure is *mìle o Dhubhras gu Daras*, 'a mile from Dores to Dares'.

Dargill, (Perth), Deargail. 'Red place' or 'red rock'.

Darnaway (Moray), Taranaich. 'Thunder plain'.

Dava (Moray), An Damhath. 'The ox or stag ford'

Davaar Island (Argyll), Eilean Dà Bhàrr. 'Barr's island'.

Davidston (Ross), Baile Dhàidh. 'David's farm'.

Daviot (Aberdeen, Inverness), Deimhidh. The Inverness name is

cognate with that of the Demetae tribe, similar to *Dyfed* of Wales and is of Brythonic origin. It is unclear whether the Aberdeen name is from the same source.

Davoch (Banff). A davoch was a measurement of land used in the former Pictish areas. In Gaelic, *dabhach* is also a 'vat' or 'tub'.

Deanich (Ross), An Dianaich. 'The steep place'.

Dechmont (West Lothian). This is said to be 'good hill', from *deagh mhon(adh)*.

Deecastle (Aberdeen), Ceann na Coille. The English name is unrelated to the Gaelic one which means 'wood end'.

Deeside (Aberdeen, Kincardine), Oir Dhé. 'The side or edge of the Dee'. Upper Deeside is *Bràigh Dhé*, 'the upper part of the Dee', while Lower Deeside is *Inbhir Dhé*, 'the mouth of the Dee'. The Dee itself is *Uisge Dhé*, 'the water of Dee', a name with connotations of divinity, and occurs in the saying, *Spé, Dé is Tatha, na trì uisge as motha fon adhar*, 'Spey, Dee and Tay, the three greatest rivers under the sun'.

Delavorar (Banff), Dail a' Mhorair. 'The lord's haugh'.

Delfour (Inverness, Moray), Dail Phùir. *See* **Dallyfour**.

Delgaty (Aberdeen). 'Thorn place', from *Dealgadaidh*.

Dell (Inverness), An Dail; (Lewis), Dail. In Inverness the name is 'the haugh', also known by the full name *Dail MhicEachainn*, 'MacEachen's haugh'. The Lewis name is 'valley', from Norse. In Lewis, North Dell is *Dail bho Thuath*, South Dell is *Dail bho Dheas* and Aird Dell is *Àird Dhail*, 'headland of Dell'.

Delliefour (Inverness), Dail a' Phùir. *See* **Dallyfour**.

Dell of Morile (Inverness), Baile nam Bodach. The English name refers to a dale near Morile, while the Gaelic name is 'the old men's farm'.

Delmore (Inverness). 'The big haugh or valley', from *An Dail Mór*.

Delnabo (Banff), Dail nam Bó. 'The haugh of the cows'.

Delnadamph (Aberdeen), Dail nan Damh. 'The haugh of the oxen or stags'.

Delnashaugh (Banff). 'The haugh of the willows', from *Dail nan Seileach*.

Delny (Inverness), Deilgnidh. 'Prickly place'.

Dennyhogles (Fife). 'Hill(fort) of the church', from *Dùn na h-Eaglais*.

Dereneneach (Arran), Doire nan Each. 'The oak grove of the horses'.

Derraid (Moray), An Doire Roid. 'The bog myrtle grove'.

Derry (Aberdeen), An Doire. 'The oak grove'.

Dervaig (Mull), Dearbhaig. This Norse name may be 'deer bay'.

Desher (Inverness), Deisear. 'North facing land'.

Deskford (Banff), Deasgart. This is pronounced 'Deskart' locally and does not refer to a ford. It may mean 'south field', from Gaelic *deas* and *gart*, but is uncertain.

Dhoon (Kirkcudbright). 'Hill fort', from *dùn*.

Diabaig (Ross), Dìobaig. 'Deep bay', from Norse. *Upper Diabaig* is *Dìobaig an Àird*, but Gaelic has no specific name for *Lower Diabaig*. A saying stresses its isolation in earlier times: *'S fhada bhon lagh Dìobaig, 's fhaide na sin sìos Mealbhaig*, 'Diabaig is far from the law and Melvaig even further'. Locals are known as *cnòdain* or *cnùdanan*, 'gurnards'. The weather locally is referred to in *Fras agus ialach, earrach muinntir Dhìobaig*, 'Showers and sunny spells, the Diabaig people's springtime'.

Dibidale (Lewis, Rum), Dìobadal. 'Deep valley', from Norse.

Diebidale Forest (Ross), Frìth Dhìobadail. 'Deer forest of Diebidale', which itself is 'deep valley', from Norse.

Dieraclete (Harris), Dìricleit. 'Deer cliff', from Norse.

Digg (Skye), An Dìg. 'The ditch or furrow'.

Dingwall (Ross), Inbhir Pheofharain. The English name is 'court field', from Norse. The Gaelic name is 'mouth of the Peffer'. The town has the by-name of *Baile a' Chàil*, 'the kail village', anglicised as 'Balechaul'. The fair here, formerly held at Contin, was *Féill Ma Ruibhe*, 'St Maol Rubha's fair', while the fair held in July was *Féill Choluim*, referring possibly to Columba.

Dinnet (Aberdeen), Dùnaidh. 'Fort place'. The English version seems to derive from an older Gaelic or possibly Brythonic form. The Moor of Dinnet is *Sliabh Muileann Dùnaidh*, 'the moor of Dinnet mill'.

Dippen (Argyll), Duipinn; (Arran), An Dipinn. This may be 'black pennyland', from *dubh* and *peighinn*, or 'two pennyland', from *dà* and *peighinn* although in both cases one would expect *f* rather than *p* in the names.

Diriebught (Inverness), Tìr nam Bochd. 'Land of the poor', apparently because this was owned by the church which donated the profit as alms to the poor. Originally, however, this may have been *Doire nam Bochd*, 'oak grove of the poor', or even *Doire nam Boc*, 'oak grove of the bucks'.

Dirnanean (Perth), Doire nan Eun. 'Oak grove of the birds'.

Divach (Inverness), Dìobhach. The meaning of this name is unclear.

Dochanassie (Argyll), Dabhach an Fhasaidh. 'The davoch at the stance'.

Dochcarty (Ross), Dabhach Gartaidh. This may be 'the davoch at the place of the enclosed field'.

Dochfour (Inverness), Dabhach Phùir. 'The davoch of pasture land'.

Dochgarroch (Inverness), Dabhach Gairbheach. 'The davoch at the rough place'.

Dochmaluag (Ross), Dabhach Mo Luaig. 'St Mo Luag's davoch'.

Dochnaclear (Ross), Dabhach nan Cliar. 'The davoch of the clerics'.

Dochnalurg (Inverness), Dabhach na Lurgainn. 'The davoch of the shank'.

Dola (Sutherland), Dóla. The meaning of this name is unclear, but may feature a river.

Doll (Sutherland), An Dail. 'The haugh'.

Dollar (Clackmannan). This may be 'haugh place', from *Dolar*.

Dollerie (Perth), Doillearaidh. 'Dark place'. This name is the opposite of 'Soilzarie' or *Soillearaidh* near Glenshee.

Donavourd (Perth), Dùn a' Bhùird. 'The table hill(fort)'.

Donibristle (Fife). This may be 'Breasal's or Uí Bhreasail's fortress', from *Dùnadh Bhreasail* or *Dùn Uí Bhreasail*.

Dores (Inverness), Dubhras. 'Black wood' or 'black headland'. A local saying measures *mìle o Dhubhras gu Daras*, 'a mile from Dores to Dares'.

Dorlin (Argyll), An Dòirlinn. 'The tidal isthmus or promontory'.

Dornie (Ross), An Dòrnaidh. 'The pebble place'. Dornie ferry was known as *Aiseag na h-Àirde* referring to its landing place at Ardelve. Gaelic uses *air an Dòrnaidh* to express 'in Dornie'.

Dornoch (Sutherland), Dòrnach. 'Pebble place'. This was known as *Dòrnach na goirt*, 'Dornoch of starvation' and the fair held here was *Fèill Bhàrr*, 'St Barr's fair'.

Dornock (Dumfries). *See* **Dornoch**.

Dorusduan (Ross), Doras Dubhain. 'Door of the black stream', referring to the mouth of the stream.

Dosmuckeran (Ross), Dos Mucaran or Dos Mhucarain. This suggests 'thicket of the pig place'. Dosmuckeran House is *Taigh Dhos Mhucarain*.

Douglas (Lanark), Dùghlas. 'Black stream', from an older *Dubhghlas*.

Dougrie (Arran), An Dubh-Gharadh or An Dubh-Ghearraidh. 'The black dyke' or 'the black fertile land', though probably the former. Local people were nicknamed *coilich dhubha*, 'black cocks'.

Doularg (Ayr). 'Black slope', from *Dubh-Learg*.

Doune (Perth, Ross), An Dùn. 'The hill(fort)'. Doune in Perth is known as *Baile an Dùine*, 'the town of Doune', and the Braes of Doune are *Bràigh Dhùin*.

Doune Carloway (Lewis), Dùn Chàrlabhaigh. 'The fort of Carloway', referring to the broch. This township is usually referred to as *An Dùn*, 'the hill(fort)'. Local people are referred to in the saying *Muinntir an Dùin, bidh iad fada gun èirigh*, 'the people of Doune Carloway never get up early'.

Dounie (Perth), An Dùnaidh; (Ross), Dùnaidh. 'Hill(fort) place'. Easter Dounie in Perth is *Dùnaidh Shìos*.

Dounreay (Caithness), Dùnrath. 'Fortified mound'.

Dowally (Perth). This may be 'place at the black rock', from *Dubhailigh*.

Downies (Perth), Dùnais. 'Hill(fort) place'.

Draikies (Inverness), Dreigidh. The meaning of this name is unclear.

Drainie (Moray). 'Thorn place', from *Droighnidh*, as in Drynie.

Drem (East Lothian). 'Ridge', from *Druim*.

Drimindarroch (Inverness). 'The ridge of the oak or oaks', from *Druim an Daraich* or *Druim nan Darach*.

Drimnin (Argyll), Na Druimnean or Na Drumainean. 'The ridges'.

Drimsdale (South Uist), Dreumasdal. The first part of this Norse valley name is unclear, although it may be a personal name.

Drishaig (Argyll), Driseig. This appears to be from Gaelic *dris*, 'briar' or 'bramble', but given its location may be a Norse bay name.

Droman (Sutherland), An Droman. 'The small ridge'.

Dron (Perth), Drongaidh or An Dronn. 'Ridge place' or 'the ridge'. The saying, *Rathad mór leathann réidh, rathad muileann Drongaidh*, 'A smooth broad main road, the road to Dron mill', referred to something which did not exist.

Drudaig (Ross), Drùdaig. The first part of this Norse bay name is unclear.

Druimachoish (Argyll), Druim a' Chòthais. 'The ridge at the cave or lair'.

Druimarbin (Inverness), Druim Earbainn. 'Roe-deer ridge'.

Druimavuic (Argyll), Druim a' Bhuic. 'The ridge of the buck'.

Druimdrishaig (Inverness), Druim Driseig. 'Briar or bramble ridge'.

Drum (Aberdeen, Kinross). 'Ridge', from *Druim*.

Drumachine (Arran), Druim a' Chaoin; (Perth), Druim a' Chaoine. This may be 'smooth ridge'.

Drumadoon (Arran), Druim an Dùin. 'The ridge by the hill(fort)'. Druma-doon Point is *Rubha a' Bharra*, 'the point at the extremity' or *Rubha an Dùin*, 'the point at the hill(fort)'.

Drumain (Fife), 'Middle ridge', from *Druim Meadhain*.

Drumaird (Fife). 'The high ridge', from *Druim Àrd*.

Drumbeg (Sutherland), An Druim Beag; (West Lothian). 'The small ridge'.

Drumblade (Aberdeen). The first part of this name is Gaelic *druim*, 'ridge', while the second may be from Brythonic for 'flower' or 'blossom'.

Drumbowie (West Lothian). *See* **Drumbuie**.

Drumbroider (Stirling). 'Bruadar's ridge', from *Druim Bhruadair*.

Drumbuie (Inverness, Ross), An Druim Buidhe. 'The yellow ridge', Drumbuie in Ross is known jocularly as *Druim Buidhe nan deargannan*, 'Drumbuie of the fleas'.

Drumcarro (Fife). 'Rocky or uneven ridge', from *Druim Carrach*.

Drumchapel (Glasgow). 'Horse ridge', from *druim* and *capall*.

Drumchardine (Inverness), Druim Chàrdainn. 'Copse ridge', from Gaelic/Brythonic.

Drumchork (Ross, Sutherland), Druim a' Choirc. 'The oat ridge'.

Drumclog (Lanark). This includes Brythonic *colg*, 'rock', and also either Brythonic or Gaelic for 'ridge', giving an overall meaning of 'rock ridge'.

Drumcross (West Lothian). 'Ridge of the cross', from *druim* and *crois*.

Drumcroy (Ross), Druim Chruaidh. 'Hard ridge'.

Drumcudden (Ross), Druim a' Chùdainn. 'The ridge of the tub'.

Drumdelgie (Aberdeen). 'Prickly ridge', from *Druim Dealgaidh*.

Drumderfit (Ross), Druim a Diar. This is said to be 'ridge of tears', the local story being that the old name was *Druim Dubh*, 'black ridge', until a battle was fought which gave rise to the saying, *Bu Druim Dubh an-dé thu, ach's Druim a Deur an-diugh*, 'You were Black Ridge yesterday, but today you are the Ridge of Tears'. It is more likely, given the English form, that the second part originated in Pictish and was adapted by Gaelic speakers.

Drumdevan (Inverness), An Druim Dìomhain. 'The idle ridge'. This is a ridge on which nothing will grow. *An Druim Dìomhain* was the original name of the Drummond area of Inverness.

Drumdow (Ayr). 'Black ridge', from *Druim Dubh*.

Drumduff (West Lothian). *See* **Drumdow**.

Drumdurno (Aberdeen). This may be

'pebbly ridge', from *Druim Dòrnach*.

Drumfearn (Skye), An Druim Fheàrna. 'The alder ridge'. Local people are known as *coin*, 'dogs'.

Drumfin (Fife). 'White ridge', from *Druim Fionn*.

Drumforber (Kincardine). This appears to be 'Cairbre's ridge', from *Druim Chairbre*.

Drumguish (Moray), Druim Giuthais. 'Pine ridge'.

Drumlamford (Ayr). 'Encampment ridge', from *druim* and *longphort*.

Drumlanrig (Dumfries). 'Ridge at the clearing', from *druim* and *lannraig*, the latter from Brythonic *lanerc*.

Drumlean (Perth), An Druim Leathann. 'The broad ridge'.

Drumloist (Perth), An Druim Loisgte. Although this is literally 'burnt ridge', this term was used to indicate an ancient cooking site.

Drummin (Inverness), Drumainn. 'Ridge place'.

Drummond (Inverness), An Druim-ein; (Perth, Ross), Drumainn. The Perth and Ross names mean 'ridge place', while the Inverness name is simply 'the small ridge'. *See* **Drumdevan**.

Drummonernoch (Perth). 'The Drummond of Earn or Ireland', from *Drumainn Éireannach*.

Drummore (Wigtown). *See* **Drumore**.

Drumnadrochit (Inverness), Druim na Drochaid. 'The ridge at the bridge'.

Drumoak (Aberdeen). 'St Mayota's ridge', from *Druim M' Aodhaig*.

Drumochter (Inverness, Perth), Druim Uachdair. 'Top ridge'. This is also known as *Druim Uachdair nam Bó*, 'Drumochter of the cattle'.

Drumore (Argyll, Nairn), An Druim Mór. 'The big ridge'.

Drumossie (Inverness), Druim Athaisidh. 'Ridge of the great haugh'. Nearby Loch Ashie is *Loch Athaisidh*.

Drumpellier (Lanark). 'Ridge of the spear shafts', from Brythonic. Earlier forms of the name point to *din*, 'fort', as the Brythonic first element.

Drumrunie (Ross), Druim Raonaidh. 'Ridge at the field place'.

Drumry (Dunbarton). 'Slope ridge'. Nearby is Kingsridge, the name of which developed through confusion between *ruigh*, 'slope', and *rìgh*, 'king', which both sound alike. The same confusion occurred in the names of Kingseat and Portree.

Drums (Aberdeen), Druim Airgididh. The English form is 'ridges', while the Gaelic name is 'ridge at the silver place' or 'silver ridge'.

Drumsallie (Inverness), Druim na Saille. 'The willow ridge'.

Drumsleet (Kirkcudbright). This may be 'the ridge of hills', from *druim* and *sléibhte*.

Drumsmittal (Ross), Druim Smiotail. This second part of this ridge name is unclear.

Drumtuthil (Fife). 'Tuathal's ridge', from *Druim Tuathail*, a personal name found in 'O'Toole'.

Drumuie (Skye, Sutherland), Druim Muighe. 'The ridge on the plain'. Drumuie in Sutherland was known as *Druim Muighe a' bhàrr*, 'Drumuie of the cream'.

Drumullie (Inverness), Druim Mùil-lidh. 'Milling ridge'. An alternative derivation given by Watson is *Druim Ulaidh*, 'treasure ridge', relating to a tale of treasure known locally.

Drumwhirn (Kirkcudbright). This may be 'rowan ridge', from *Druim a' Chaorthaim*.

Dry Harbour (Raasay), An Acarsaid Thioram. 'The dry anchorage'.

Drymen (Stirling), Druiminn. 'Ridge place'.

Drynachan (Nairn), Droighneachan. 'Thorn place'.

Drynan (Skye), Droighnean. 'Thorns'.

Drynie (Ross), Droighnidh. 'Thorn place'.

Drynoch (Skye), An Droighneach. 'The thorn place'.

Dualin (Perth), Dubh-Àilean. 'Black meadow'.

Duart (Mull), Dubhaird. 'Black headland'.

Duartbeg (Sutherland), Dubhaird Bheag. 'Small Duart'.

Duartmore (Sutherland), Dubhaird Mhór. 'Large Duart'.

Dufftown (Banff). The planned village here was named after the Duff family of Banffshire. Previously the settlement had been known as **Balvenie**.

Duffus (Moray), Dubhais. 'Black place'.

Duible (Sutherland), Daigheabal. This may be 'bog farm' from Norse.

Duiletter (Argyll), An Dubh-Leitir. 'The black slope'.

Duirinish (Ross, Skye), Diùranais or Diùirinis. 'Deer headland', from Norse. Duirinish in Skye is known as *dùthaich nam mogan*, 'land of the mogan shoes', and the locals as *moganaich*. In Ross, the village is known as *Diùranais an eòrna*, 'Duirinish of the barley', and is close to *Port an Eòrna* or Barleyport.

Duisdale (Skye), Dùisdeil. The first part of this Norse valley name is unclear, but may be the same element as found in 'Dusary'. Duisdalebeg is *Dùisdeil Bheag*, 'little Duisdale', and Duisdalemore is *Dùisdeil Mhór*, 'big Duisdale'.

Duisky (Argyll), Dùisgidh. 'Black water'.

Dull (Perth), Dul. 'Haugh' or 'meadow'. Appin of Dull is *Apainn nam Mèin-nearach*, 'The Menzies' Appin'.

Dullater (Dunbarton). *See* **Duiletter**.

Dulnain Bridge (Inverness, Moray), Drochaid Thulnain. 'The bridge over the Dulnain'.

Duloch (Fife). 'Black loch', from *Dubh-Loch*.

Dulsie Bridoge (Nairn), Drochaid Dhulfhasaidh. 'The bridge at the haugh place'.

Dumbarton (Dunbarton), Dùn Breatann or Dùn Breatainn. 'Fort of the Britons', as mentioned in the saying, *Trì gearastain na h-Albann - Dùn Breatann, Dùn Chailleann is Madaigein na Mòin*, 'Three fortresses of Scotland - Dumbarton, Dunkeld and Rannoch Moor'. Dumbarton Rock is *Ail Chluaidh*, 'the rock of the Clyde', and was the capital of the Brythonic territory of Strathclyde. Dunbartonshire is *Siorrachd Dhùn Breatann* or *Siorrachd Dhùn Breatainn*.

Dumbreck (Glasgow). 'Speckled hill(fort)', from *Dùn Breac*.

Dumcrieff (Dumfries). 'Hill(fort) of the tree(s)', from *dùn* and *craobh*.

Dumfin (Dunbarton), Dùn Fhinn. 'Fionn or Fingal's fort'.

Dumfries, Dùn Phris. 'Hill(fort) at the thicket'. However, old forms of the name suggest *druim* or *dronn*, 'ridge', rather than *dùn*, 'hill(fort)'. Dumfriesshire is *Siorrachd Dhùn Phris*.

Dunaad (Argyll), Dùn Athad. 'Fort on the Add'.

Dunach (Argyll), Dùnach. 'Hill(fort) place'.

Dunain (Inverness), Dùn Eun. This appears to be 'birds' hill', but could be 'John's hill(fort)', from *Dùn Eathain*. Local Gaelic speakers pronounced the name as *Dùn Ian*. Dunain Mains is *Baile Mór Dùn Eun*, 'the big farm of Dunain'. Craig Dunain is *Creag Dhùn Eun*.

Dunalister (Perth), Dùn Alasdair. 'Alasdair's fort'. The old name was *Mùrbhlagan*. *See* **Murlaggan**.

Dunan (Arran, Skye), An Dùnan. 'The hillock'.

Dunans (Skye), Na Dùnanan. 'The hillocks'.

Dunaverty (Argyll), Dùn Àbhartaich. 'Àbhartach's fort'.

Dunbar (East Lothian), Dùn Barra. This appears to be a Gaelic name meaning 'Barr's fort', but given the town's location, this is probably a name of Brythonic origin.

Dunbartonshire (Dunbarton), Siorrachd Dhùn Breatann or Siorrachd Dhùn Breatainn. This name, with 'Dun-' rather than 'Dum-', was created to distinguish the county from the town of Dumbarton. The part of the county between Loch Lomond, Loch Long and the Clyde was known to local Gaelic speakers as *An t-Eilean Leamhnach*, 'the Leven Island'.

Dunbeath (Caithness), Dùn Beithe. 'Birch hill(fort)'.

Dunbeg (Argyll), An Dùn Beag. 'The small hill(fort)'.

Dunblane (Perth), Dùn Bhlàthain. 'Blane's hill(fort)'.

Dunbog (Fife). This looks like a Gaelic name meaning 'soft or damp hill', but an older form suggests that it is from *dùn* and *bolg* and means 'bag hill', possibly referring to its shape.

Duncansby (Caithness), Dùn Gasbaith. This English form suggests 'Duncan's farm', from Norse. The Gaelic name, which contains the term for a hill(fort) and an obscure second element, is simply a gaelicisation of the Norse name, and is also applied to Duncansby Head.

Duncanstown (Ross), Bog a' Mhiodair. The Gaelic name is 'the bog at the pasture land', but since *miodar*, 'pasture land' is similar to the word for a mitre, a local story arose about a bishop losing his mitre in the bog here.

Duncow (Dumfries). 'Hazel hill', from *Dùn Choll* in modern Gaelic, previously *Dùn Coll*. An old form of the anglicised name, 'Duncoll', shows this derivation very clearly.

Duncraig (Ross), Dùn Creige. 'Rock hill'. This name is fairly recent and supplanted the earlier *Am Fasadh Àlainn*, 'the beautiful spot'.

Dundarave (Argyll), Dùn Dà Ràmh.

This appears to mean 'fort of two oars', but may have become corrupted over the centuries.

Dundas (Stirling, West Lothian). 'South hill' or 'pretty hill', from *Dùn Deas*.

Dundee (Angus), Dùn Deagh or Dùn Dé. It was believed that this contained a personal name based on 'fire', but it is now believed that the second part of the name is a by-form of 'Tay' or *Tatha*, giving an overall meaning of 'fort on the Tay'. Dundee was known to Gaelic speakers in Aberdeenshire as *Baile Ailleag* which is unclear.

Dundonald (Ayr, Fife). 'Donald's hill(fort)', from *Dùn Dòmhnaill*.

Dundonnell (Ross), An Srath Beag, An Locha Beag or Achadh Dà Dhòmhnaill. The English form is 'Donald's fort', from an older Gaelic *Dùn Dòmhnaill*. The first Gaelic name is 'the little strath', and the second is 'the little loch', also the name of Little Loch Broom. The third Gaelic name is 'the field of two Donalds'. Dundonnell Lodge is *An t-Eilean Daraich*, 'the oak island', while Dundonnell Hotel is *Taigh-òsta an t-Sratha Bhig*, 'the hotel of the small strath'.

Dun Dornadilla (Sutherland), Dùn Dornaigil. This mixed Gaelic/Norse name is 'hill(fort) at the thorny ravine'.

Dundreggan (Inverness), Dul Dreagain. 'Dragon haugh', a term used to denote a warrior or hero.

Dundrennan (Kirkcudbright). 'Thorn hill', from *dùn* and *droighnean*.

Dunduff (Ayr, Fife). 'Black hill(fort)', from *Dùn Dubh*.

Dundurcus (Moray). 'The hill(fort) at the place of boars', from *Dùn Turcais*.

Dundurn (Perth), Dùn Dùirn. 'Fort of the fist', a former Pictish stronghold.

Dunearn (Fife); (Nairn), Dùn Éireann. 'Hill(fort) on the Findhorn'.

Dunfermline (Fife), Dùn Phàrlain.

This is generally understood to be 'Pàrlan's fort', a personal name usually translated as 'Bartholomew'. However, the name is older and possibly tribal or belonging to a kin-group.

Dungainachy (Benbecula), Dùn Gainmheacha. 'Sandy hill'.

Dungavel (Ayr). 'Forked hill', from *dùn* and *gobhal*.

Dunglass (Berwick, East Lothian). 'Grey-green hill', from either Gaelic or more probably Brythonic.

Dunhallin (Skye), Dùn Hàlainn. 'Hill(fort) of Hallin'.

Dunidea (Perth), Dùnaidh Dé. This name may mean the same as 'Dundee' although it appears to mean 'fortress of god' or 'fortress on the Dee'. *See* **Dundee**.

Dunino (Fife). This may be the fort on the prominent hill', from *Dùn an Aonaich*.

Dunira (Perth), Dùn Iarath. 'Hill(fort) at the west ford'.

Dunkeld (Perth), Dùn Chailleann. 'Hill(fort) of the Caledonians', a tribal name also occurring in 'Rohallion' and 'Schiehallion'. The name occurs in the saying, *Trì gearastain na h-Albann - Dùn Breatann, Dùn Chailleann is Madaigein na Mòin*, 'Three fortresses of Scotland - Dumbarton, Dunkeld and Rannoch Moor'.

Dunlichity (Inverness), Dùn Fhlicheadaidh. 'Hill(fort) of Flichity'.

Dunlop (Ayr). This may be '(hill)fort at the bend', from *Dùn Lùib*.

Dunlossit (Islay), Dùn Losaid. 'Hill by the Lossit'.

Dunlugas (Aberdeen). This may be 'slug hill', from *Dùn Lùgais*.

Dunmaglass (Inverness), Dùn Mac Glais. This appears to be 'the fort of Glas's son'.

Dunmore (Fife, Stirling); (Argyll), An Dùn Mór. 'The big hill(fort)'.

Dunneaves (Perth), Taigh Neimhidh. 'The house at the sacred place'.

Dunnet (Caithness), Dùnaid.

Although the Gaelic name suggests 'hill(fort) place', the origin of this name may be Norse, given its location in north-east Caithness.

Dunnichen (Angus), Dùn Eachainn. The Gaelic name suggests 'Eachann's hill(fort)', but the original was *Dùn Neachdain*, 'Nechtan's hill(fort)', as this is near the site of the 7th century battle at Nechtansmere or *Linn Garan*.

Dunnivaig (Islay), Dùn Naomhaig. 'Naomhag's or Naomhan's fort'

Dunollie (Argyll), Dùn Ollaigh. 'Onlach's or Ollach's fort'.

Dunoon (Argyll), Dùn Omhain. 'Hill(fort) on the river'.

Dunork (Fife). 'Hill(fort) of the swine', from *Dùn Orc*.

Dunottar (Kincardine). This may be 'fort on the shelving slope', from *dùn* and *fothair*. The name was previously 'Dunfoeder', which may indicate a Pictish cognate of *fothair*.

Dunphail (Moray), Dùn Fàil. 'Palisade fort'.

Dunragit (Wigtown), Dùn Reicheit. 'The fort of Rheged', a Brythonic territory in Galloway.

Dunringell (Skye), Dùn Ruingeil. This Gaelic/Norse name may be 'fort at the rough ravine'.

Dunrobin (Sutherland), Dùn Robain. 'Robin's fort' was known as *Dùn Robain a' chàil*, 'Dunrobin of the kail'.

Duns (Berwick). This is Brythonic or Gaelic for 'fort' with an English plural.

Dunscore (Dumfries). If this is a Gaelic name, it may mean 'hill(fort) at the pinnacle', but as there are Norse names in this area, this may be Gaelic/Norse for 'Hill(fort) at the wood'.

Dunsgaith (Skye), Dùn Sgàthaich. 'The fort of Sgàthach', who trained Cù Chulainn in the martial arts.

Dunskeath Ness (Ross), Rubha Dhùn Sgàth. 'Promontory at the fort of

Sgàth', which may be a personal name connected with that of *Sgàthach* in Skye.

Dunskellar (North Uist), Dùn Sgealair. This Gaelic/Norse name is 'fort by the sheilings'.

Dunstaffnage (Argyll), Dùn Stafhainis. 'Fort by the staff headland', from Gaelic/Norse.

Duntarvie (West Lothian). 'Hill(fort) at the bull place', from *Dùn Tarbhaidh*.

Duntelchaig (Inverness), Dùn Deilcheig. 'Snail hill'.

Duntocher (Dunbarton). 'Fort at the causeway', from *Dùn Tòchair*. However, an earlier form of the name was 'ridge at the causeway', from *Druim Tòchair*.

Duntroon (Argyll), Dùn Treò or Dùn Treòin. This fort be have been named after someone called *Treun*, 'mighty'.

Duntulm (Skye), Dùn Tuilm or Dùn Thuilm. 'Fort at the island', from Gaelic/Norse.

Dunure (Ayr). 'Yew hill', from *Dùn Iubhair*.

Dunvegan (Aberdeen), Dùn Bheathagain or Dùn Mheagain; (Skye), Dùn Bheagain. In Skye this is 'Beagan's fort'. Dunvegan Head is *Ceann Dhùn Bheagain*. The Aberdeenshire names, although spelt differently may be from the same source.

Dunvornie (Ross), Dùn Bhoirinidh. 'Hill(fort) in the stony place'. *An Bhoireann*, 'the Burren', is a stony area of County Clare.

Dupplin (Perth), Dubh-Linn. The Gaelic name suggests 'black pool', which is also the origin of 'Dublin'.

Durie (Fife). 'Water place', from *Dobharaidh*, earlier *Dobharan*.

Durine (Sutherland), Dubhrinn. 'Black headland'. *See* **Durness**.

Durnamuck (Ross), Doire nam Muc. 'The oak grove of the pigs'.

Durness (Sutherland), Diùirnis. 'Deer headland', from Norse. An alternative

name was *Dubhrinn*, 'black headland', which still exists as the Gaelic origin of 'Durine'.

Durno (Aberdeen). This may be 'pebbly place', from *Dòrnach*.

Duror (Argyll), Dùror or Dùrar. 'Hard water'. The complete name is *Dùror na h-Apann*, 'Duror of Appin'.

Durris (Kincardine), Duras or Dòrs. This may be 'black wood'.

Dusary (North Uist), Duthasaraidh. This Norse field name may contain the same personal name as in 'Duisdale'.

Dutchman's Cap (Mull), Am Bac Mór. The island's shape gave rise to its English name, but the Gaelic means 'the big bank', from Norse *bakki*, 'bank'.

Duthil (Inverness), Daothal. This may be a by-form from *tuathail*, 'north side', but *See* **Culduthel**.

Dyke (Moray), Dìg. 'Ditch' or 'furrow'. The parish was known as *Sgìre Dhìg*.

Dysart (Fife). 'Hermitage', from *dìseart*.

Eaglescairnie (East Lothian). This may be 'church at the cairn place', and although it can be interpreted from Gaelic sources as *Eaglais Chàrnaich*, it is probably Brythonic given its location.

Eaglesfield (Dumfries). 'Church field', from Gaelic or Brythonic and English 'field'.

Eaglesham (Renfrew). 'Church homestead', from Gaelic or Brythonic and English *ham*.

Eagleton (Lewis), Baile na h-Iolaire or Cnoc na h-Iolaire. The Gaelic names are 'eagle farm' and 'eagle hill', although the Gaelic names are probably translations from an original English.

Earlish (Skye), Eàrlais. This Norse name may be 'earl's river mouth' or 'earl's ridge'.

Earshader (Lewis), Iorseadar or Iarsadar. 'Beach farm' or 'Ævarr's farm', from Norse. Local pronunciation collected by Oftedal suggests *Iarsadar* as the preferable spelling.

Easdale (Easdale), Èisdeal. 'Horse dale', from Norse.

Easter Ross (Ross), Ros an Ear. This eastern part of Ross is also known in Gaelic as *Taobh Sear Rois*, 'the east side of Ross', although this is not used locally.

Easterton (Perth), Easgardan. 'East farm', from English. The Gaelic name is an adaption of the English.

Eastertyre (Perth), Ìochdar Thìre. 'Bottom of the land'.

Easter Tulloch (Inverness), Baile nan Cròigean or Baile nan Groigean. The present Gaelic name is said locally to mean 'farm of the puddocks'. It is in the east part of Tulloch and was earlier known as *Tulach Ìochdarach*, 'lower Tulloch'.

East Kilbride (Lanark), Cille Bhrìghde an Ear; (South Uist), Taobh a' Chaolais. The English name is 'St Bridget's church', with 'east' to distinguish these places from West Kilbride. In Lanark the Gaelic name is the same and differentiates this place from West Kilbride in Cunninghame. In South Uist the Gaelic name is 'the side of the strait', referring to the place's location on the shore of the Sound of Barra. The English form distinguishes it from the next township known in English as West Kilbride but in Gaelic as simply *Cille Bhrìghde*, 'St Bridget's church' or 'Kilbride'.

Eathie (Ross), Àthaigh. 'Ford place' Upper Eathie is *Bràigh Àthaigh*, 'upper part of Eathie'.

Ebost (Skye), Eubost. 'Isthmus farm', from Norse.

Ecclefechan (Dumfries). This is most likely Brythonic for 'small church'.

Eccles (Berwick). 'Church', originally from Brythonic rather than Gaelic *eaglais*.

Ecclesmachan (West Lothian). 'St Machan's church', from Gaelic *Eaglais Mhachain* or Brythonic sources. Locally the place was also known as Inchmachan, from *Innis Mhachain*, 'St Machan's haugh or meadow'

Echline (West Lothian). 'Paddock', from *eachlann*.

Edderton (Ross), Eadardan. 'Between-fort', from *eadardùn*. Edderton Farm is *Baile nam Foitheachan*, 'farm with the lawns or greens'.

Eddleston (Peebles). 'Edulf's farm', from English. This place has had several names, reflecting the linguistic groups who settled here. The oldest was Brythonic 'Penteiacob', 'the head of Jacob's house', followed by 'Gilmertoun', 'Gille-Mhoire's farm', from English but containing a Gaelic personal name. Finally came the English name which developed into the present form.

Eddrachillis (Sutherland), Eadarra-Chaolas or Eadar Dhà Chaolas. 'Between two straits'.

Ederline (Argyll), Eadarlinn. 'Between two pools', from *Eadar dhà Linn*.

Edinample (Perth), Aodann Ambail. 'Hill face by the vat or cauldron'.

Edinbane (Skye), An t-Aodann Bàn. 'The white hill face'. Upper Edinbane is *An Uaig*, possibly 'the cave'.

Edinburgh (Midlothian), Dùn Éide-ann. 'Eidyn's fort', from Brythonic *Din Eidyn*, of which the Gaelic name is a cognate form which was part-translated into English to form 'Edinburgh'. It is commonly believed that the English name is 'Edwin's burgh', but the name existed before the English language and names were introduced into the area.

Edinchip (Perth), Aodann a' Chip. 'The hill face with a block'.

Edingight (Banff). 'The windy hill face', from *Aodann na Gaoithe*.

Edinkillie (Moray). 'The hill face at the wood', from *Aodann na Coille*.

Edinvillie (Banff). 'The hill face at the rock edge', from *Aodann a' Bhile*.

Edrachalda (Sutherland), Eadarra-Chalda or Eadar Dhà Chalda. 'Between two Caldas', referring to the land between rivers Calda Beag and Calda Mór. The river name is Norse for 'cold river'.

Edradour (Perth), Eadarra-dhobhar or Eadar Dhà Dhobhar. 'Between two rivers'.

Edradynate (Perth), Eadarra-dhoimh-nid or Eadar Dhà Dhoimhnid. 'Between two deep places'.

Edragoul (Perth), Eadarra-ghobhal or Eadar Dhà Ghobhal. 'Between two forks'.

Edramucky (Perth), Eadarra-mhuc-aidh or Eadar Dhà Mhucaidh. 'Between two pig streams'.

Edzell (Angus), Eigill. The meaning of this name is unclear.

Eigg, Eige. This may be 'notch', referring to the shape of Sgùrr Eige or to the depression running across the island. Eigg was known as *Eilean nam Ban Móra*, 'the island of the great women', and a native of the island is an *Eigeach*, also nicknamed a *fachach*, 'puffin'.

Eilean Aigas (Inverness), Eilean Àigeis. 'The island or meadow of Aigas'.

Eilean Anabuich (Harris), An t-Eilean Anabaich. 'The unripe island', referring to poor soil.

Eilean Clourig (Sutherland), Eilean Clobhraig. This may be Norse 'cloven bay' or 'cleft bay', with Gaelic 'island' attached. This is often seen on maps as *Eilean Cluimhrig*.

Eilean Fladday (Raasay), Eilean Fhladaigh. 'Flat island', from Norse, with Gaelic 'island' attached.

Eilean Imersay (Islay), Eilean Iomar-saigh. This Norse island name may contain a personal name with Gaelic 'island' attached.

Eilean Tigh (Raasay), Eilean Taighe. 'House island'.

Eishken (Lewis), Éisgean. This Norse name may contain 'ash tree'.

Elachnave Islands (Argyll), Na h-Eileacha Naomha. 'Holy rocks'.

Elchies (Moray), Eileachaidh. 'Rocky place'. The English name is a plural.

Elcho (Perth). This is said to be stony or rocky place', from *ailcheach*.

Eldrable (Sutherland), Eilldreabal. 'Beacon farm' or 'altar farm', from Norse.

Elgin (Moray), Eilginn. 'Ireland'. *Eilg*, like *Banbh*, *Éire* and *Fótla*, was a by-name for Ireland, attached by the Scots to many places during their settlement. An area of Elgin was known as 'Little Ireland' until recently. A native of Elgin was known as an *Eilgneach*, the same term applied to Glenelg people. The full Gaelic name is *Eilginn Mhoireibh*, 'Elgin of Moray', and it is called *Eilginidh* in Wester Ross.

Elgol (Skye), Ealaghol. This may be a Norse name for a field, and might include the word for wild angelica.

Elie (Fife). If this is a Gaelic name it means 'landing place', from *Ealaidh*. From neighbouring Earlsferry there was a sea link to Lothian. In Mull there is also a place on the shore known as *An Ealaidh*, 'the landing place'.

Elishader (Skye), Eiliseadar. 'Dwelling by the cave', from Norse.

Ellenbeich (Seil), Eilean nam Beath-ach. This appears to be 'island of the animals or cattle', but the original may have been *Eilean nam Beitheach*, 'island of the birch woods'.

Ellister (Islay), Aolastradh. 'Dwelling by the cave', from Norse.

Ellon (Aberdeen), Eilean. 'Meadow'. *Eilean* is normally 'island' but the meaning was extended to cover 'meadow' as was also the case with *innis*.

Elphin (Sutherland), Ailbhinn. 'Rock peak'.

Elrick (Aberdeen). 'Deer trap', from *Eilreig*.

Elrig (Wigtown). 'Deer trap', from *Eilreig*.

Embo (Sutherland), Earabol. This seems to be 'beach farm', from Norse, but an older form, 'Ethenboll', suggests 'Eyvind's farm' originally, also from Norse. Embo was *Earabol nan coileagan*, 'Embo of the cockles'.

Enaclete (Lewis), Èinicleit. 'Brow cliff', from Norse.

Englishtown (Inverness), A' Ghall-Bhaile. The Gaelic name is 'the non-Gaels' farm'.

Enoch (Dumfries). This is from *Aonach* which covers meanings such as 'moor', 'hill' and 'market place'.

Enochdhu (Perth), An t-Aonach Dubh. 'The black moor or hill'.

Ensay (Harris), Easaigh. 'Ewe island', from Norse.

Enzie (Banff), An Éinne or An Éinnidh. 'The angular piece of land'.

Eochar (South Uist), An t-Ìochdar. *See* **Iochdar**.

Eoligarry (Barra), Eòlaigearraidh. This Norse name might be 'pasture land of wild angelica'.

Eorodale (Lewis), Eòradal. 'Jórunn's valley', from Norse.

Eoropie (Lewis), Eòrapaidh. 'Jórunn's farm', from Norse.

Eorsa (Mull), Eòrsa. 'Beach island', from Norse.

Erbusaig (Ross), Earbarsaig. 'Erp's bay', from Norse, although apparently containing a non-Norse personal name. The place was known as *Earbarsaig nan con clomhach*, 'Erbusaig of the scabby dogs'.

Erchite (Inverness), Earchoighd. 'Wood side', probably from Pictish.

Erchless (Inverness), Earghlais. 'River side'.

Eriboll (Sutherland), Earabol. 'Beach farm', from Norse.

Eriska (Argyll), Aoraisge. 'Erik's island', from Norse.

Eriskay, Éirisgeigh. 'Erik's island', from Norse. Eriskay is known as *Eilean na h-Òige*, 'island of youth', and a native of the island is an *Éirisgeach*.

Erista (Lewis), Eireasta. This Norse name appears to mean 'farm at Harris', and lies close to the boundary between Uig and Harris.

Erracht (Inverness), An t-Eireachd. 'The meeting place'.

Erradale (Ross), Earradal. 'Beach valley'. North Erradale is *Earradal a Tuath* or *Earradal Shìos*, the latter being 'lower Erradale', and South Erradale is *Earradal a Deas* or *Earradal Shuas*, the latter being 'upper Erradale'. Inver in Erradale is *Inbhir Earradail*.

Erraid (Mull), Eilean Earraid. 'Foreshore island'. This is similar to the pre-Norse name of Shona.

Errogie (Inverness), Earaghaidh or Earagaidh. It is unclear whether this name contains *aghaidh* (hill face).

Ersary (Barra), Earsaraidh. This may be 'beach field', from Norse.

Erskine (Renfrew), Arasgain. This apparently Brythonic name is unclear but may contain an element meaning 'side'.

Eskadale (Inverness), Éisgeadal. 'Ash valley', from Norse.

Esknish (Islay), Easganais. This is most likely 'ash point', from Norse.

Essengael (Perth), Easan Geal. 'White or bright streamlet'.

Essendy (Perth). 'Place at the streamlet', from *easan* with a locative or diminutive ending such as *Easandaidh*, a formation regularly found locally.

Essich (Inverness), Easaich. 'Stream or waterfall place'.

Esslemont (Aberdeen). 'Low hill', from Brythonic *iselfynydd* or Gaelic *Ìosal-Mhonadh*.

Ethie (Angus). 'Ford place', from *Àthaigh*.

Ettridge (Inverness), Eadrais. 'Between

two streams or waterfalls', from an older *eadar dà eas*.

Evanton (Ross), Am Baile Nodha or Am Baile Ur. The English name is 'Ewan's village' while the Gaelic names are both 'the new village', to distinguish it from the older settlement across the river.

Evelix (Sutherland), Éibhleag. 'Ember', referring to a sparkling stream. The English name is a plural.

Ewe Island (Ross), Eilean Iubh. 'The island of Ewe', meaning 'yew'.

Ewich (Perth), Iubhaich. 'Yew wood'. *Deòradh a' Choigrich*, 'the keeper of St Fillan's staff', lived here.

Exmagirdle (Perth). 'St Mo Ghrill's church', from *Eaglais Mo Ghrill*, comemmorating one of Columba's disciples.

Eye Peninsula (Lewis), An Aoidh. 'The isthmus', from Norse. This area is also known as *An Rubha*, 'Point'. People from here are *Rubhaich*, also *sùlairean*, 'gannets'.

Eynort (Skye), Aoineart. 'Sea loch at the isthmus', from Norse.

Eyre (Raasay), Eighre. 'Beach' or 'sand spit', from Norse.

Faddoch (Ross), An Fhàdaich. 'The place of peat sods'.

Faichem (Inverness), Faicheam. This may contain *faiche*, 'lawn' or 'green'. Lower Faichem is *Faicheam Ìosal* and Upper Faichem is *Faicheam Àrd*.

Fain (Ross), Na Féithean. 'The bog channels'.

Faindouran (Banff). This may be 'the bog channel of the otter' or 'the channel of the little river', from *Féith an Dobhrain*.

Fairybridge (Skye), Beul-àtha nan Trì Allt. The English name is a reminder of the Fairy Flag in Dunvegan Castle, while the Gaelic name is 'the ford of the three streams'.

Falkirk (Stirling), An Eaglais Bhreac. 'The speckled church'. The name

of this place was first recorded as 'Ecclesbrith', from Brythonic, meaning 'speckled church'. As Gaelic replaced Brythonic, the cognate Gaelic form, *An Eaglais Bhreac*, superceded it. This was later translated into Scots 'Fawkirk' with the same meaning, later amended to the present English form. The Latin, *Varia Capella*, has the same meaning. A Wester Ross form of saying 'clear off' is *Thoir an Eaglais Bhreac ort*, 'get yourself to Falkirk'.

Falkland (Fife), Fàclann. Although generally believed to represent 'falcon land', from English, this name is now believed to derive from *Falclann*, with connotations of washing or scrubbing.

Falside (Sutherland), Feallasaid. 'Mountain sheiling or dwelling', from Norse.

Fanagmore (Sutherland), An Fheannag Mhór. This appears to be 'the large lazybed', a lazybed being a narrow strip of cultivable soil built up in rocky ground.

Fanmore (Sutherland), Am Fàn Mór. 'The large slope'.

Fannyfield (Ross), Am Bog Riabhach. The English name commemorates the daughter of a former proprietor while the Gaelic name is 'the brindled bog'.

Faolin (Ross), An Fhaoilinn; (Skye), Fadhlainn or Faolainn. 'Field or stony place by the shore'.

Farlary (Sutherland), Fàrrlaraidh. The meaning of this name is unclear.

Farness (Ross), Feàrnais. 'Alder place'.

Farout Head (Sutherland), An Fharaird. 'The projecting headland'. The English name is a corruption and has 'head' added.

Farquhar's Point (Argyll), Rubha Fhearchair. The English form is a translation from Gaelic.

Farr (Inverness, Sutherland), Fàrr. The meaning of this name is unclear.

Fasach (Skye), Fàsach or Am Fàsach. '(The) wilderness'. Upper Fasach is *Bràigh an Fhàsaich*, 'the upper part of Fasach'.

Fasag (Ross), Am Fasag. 'The place or stance'.

Fasagrianach (Ross), An Fhasadh Chrìonaich. 'The place of the rotten tree'. Local people were *muinntir na Fasadh Chrìonaich*, showing an unusual genitive form.

Faskally (Perth), Fas-Choille. This appears to mean 'wood place'.

Fasnacloich (Argyll), Fas na Cloiche. 'The place of the stone'.

Fasnakyle (Inverness), Fas na Coille. 'The place by the wood'.

Fasque (Kincardine), Fàsg. It is unclear what this name means.

Fassiefern (Inverness), Am Fasadh Feàrna. 'The alder place'.

Fassock (Perth), Am Fasadh. 'The place or stance'.

Fealar (Perth), Féith Làir. This may be 'ground channel'.

Fearder (Aberdeen), Féith Àrdair. 'Bog channel of the Arder'.

Fearn (Ross), Manachainn Rois. The English form is 'alder' from Gaelic *feàrn*. The Gaelic name is 'the monastery of Ross', distinguishing it from *Manachainn Mhic Shimidh*, 'Lovat's monastery', at Beauly. Fearn is recorded as *Nova Farina* in Latin. Easter Fearn is *Feàrn Àrd*, 'high Fearn', Wester Fearn is *Feàrn Ìochdarach*, 'lower Fearn', and Mid Fearn is *Feàrn Meadhanach*. Hill of Fearn is *Baile an Droma*, 'township on the ridge', while the parish of Fearn is *Sgìre na Manachainn*, 'the parish of the monastery'. The market here was *Féill na Manachainn*, 'the market of the monastery'.

Fearnach (Argyll), Feàrnach. 'Alder place'.

Fearnan (Perth), Feàrnan. 'Alders'. The old name was *Sròn Feàrnain*, 'promontory of Fearnan', and the churchyard was *Cladh na Sròine*, 'the graveyard at the promontory'.

Fearnbeg (Ross), Na Feàrna Beaga. 'The small alders'. Local people are known as *eireagan*, 'pullets'.

Fearnmore (Ross), Na Feàrna Móra. 'The large alders'. Local people are known as *coin*, 'dogs'.

Fearns (Raasay), Na Feàrnaibh; (Ross), Na Feàrna or Na Feàrnan. 'The alders'. In Ross, Fearns comprises Fearnbeg and Fearnmore, and local people are known as *tùchanaich*, 'hoarse folk'.

Feaull (Coll, Skye), Feall. 'Mountain', from Norse. In Coll, a byword for a detour was *Rathad Feall do dh'Ameireaga*, 'to America via Feaull'.

Febait (Ross), An Fhéith Bhàite. 'The drowned bog channel'.

Fender Bridge (Perth), Drochaid Aindridh. The English name refers to the River Fender, while the Gaelic name is 'Andrew's bridge'.

Fendom (Ross), Na Fànaibh. 'The gentle slopes'.

Fenechrich (Inverness), Féith na Crìche. 'The bog channel at the boundary'.

Feochaig (Argyll), Feòchaig. This Norse name refers to a bay, but the first element is unclear.

Feolin (Jura), Fadhlainn or Faolainn. 'Field or stony place by the shore'.

Feorlig (Skye), Feòirlig. 'Farthing land'.

Feorlin (Argyll), Feòirling. 'Farthing land'.

Feorline, Feòirling (Argyll), An Fheòrlainn (Arran). 'The farthing land'.

Ferindonald (Ross, Skye), Fearann Dòmhnaill. 'Donald's land'.

Feriniquarrie (Skye), Fearann MhicGuaire. 'MacQuarrie's land'.

Ferintosh (Ross), Sgìre na Tòiseachd. The Gaelic name is 'the chief's district', while the English is from an earlier Gaelic form, *Fearann na Tòiseachd*, 'the chief's land'.

Fernaig (Ross), Feàrnaig. 'Alder place'.

Ferness (Nairn). 'Alder place' from *Feàrnais*.

Fernilea (Skye), Fearann an Leagha or Fearann an Lighiche. 'The doctor's land'.

Fernoch (Argyll), Feàrnach. 'Alder place'.

Fersit (Inverness), Fearsaid Mhór. 'Large sand spit'.

Ferter (Ayr). 'Fortress', from *fartair*.

Feshiebridge (Inverness), Drochaid Fhéisidh. 'Bridge over the Feshie'.

Fetterangus (Aberdeen). 'Angus's shelving or terraced slope', from *Fothair Aonghais*.

Fettercairn (Kincardine), Fothair Chàrdainn. 'Shelving or terraced slope at the copse', containing Pictish *carden*.

Fetteresso (Kincardine). This may be 'waterfall slope', from *fothair* and *easach*, as suggested by an earlier anglicised form of the name, Fodresach.

Fetterletter (Aberdeen). 'Terraced or shelving slope', from *fothair* and *leitir*.

Fetternear (Aberdeen). This may be 'west shelving slope', from *fothair an iar*.

Fiaray (Barra), Fiaraigh. 'Ebb-tide island', from Norse.

Fidden (Mull), Na Fìdean. 'The sea meadows', from Norse with a Gaelic plural.

Fiddes (Kincardine). This may be 'wood place', from *Fiodhais*.

Fidigarry (Lewis), Fidigearraidh. 'Fertile sea meadow', from Norse.

Fife, Fìobh or Fìobha. This appears to be an old tribal or personal name, and first appears as *Fib*, one of the divisions of Pictland. Fife Ness is *Rubha Fìobha*, 'the headland of Fife'. A Fife person is a *Fìobhach*.

Finaltan (Ross), Na Fionnalltan. 'The fair streams'.

Finary (Islay), Fìneairigh. The first element of this Norse name is unclear, whilst the second denotes a field or sheiling.

Finavon (Angus). 'Wooden sanctuary or sacred lands', from *Fiodh-Neimh-eadh*.

Fincastle (Perth), Fonn a' Chaisteil. 'The land of the castle'.

Findhorn (Moray), Inbhir Éireann. 'The mouth of the Findhorn'. The Culbin Sands are *Bar Inbhir Éireann*, 'the sand bar of the mouth of the Findhorn'.

Findochty (Banff). The Braemar and Upper Banffshire Gaelic pronunuciation of this place's name was recorded by Diack as 'fanna-güchti', which is unclear in meaning.

Findo Gask (Perth). A *gasg* is a projecting tail or strip of land. The first element may refer to Findoca, a saint commemorated locally.

Findon (Ross), Fionndun or Fionndan. 'White hill(fort)'.

Findrossie (Moray), Fiondrosaigh. 'Place of the great wood'.

Finegand (Perth), Féith nan Ceann. 'The stream of the heads', from earlier *Féith na gCeann*.

Finlaggan (Islay), Port an Eilein. The English form comes from Gaelic *Fionn-Lagan*, 'white hollow', which was attached in corrupted form to the nearby loch as *Loch Bhìollagain*. The Gaelic name is 'the island port', referring to *Eilean na Comhairle*, 'the island of the council', in the loch where *Comhairle nan Eilean*, 'the Council of the Isles' met during the Lordship of the Isles.

Finlarig (Angus). 'White pass', from *Fionn-Làirig*.

Finmont (Fife). 'White or fair upland', from *Fionn-Mhonadh*. This name is also found in **Kininmonth**.

Finnart (Argyll, Perth), Fionnaird. 'White point'. Finnart Lodge in Perthshire is *Dail MhicRath*, 'Mac-Rae's haugh', and Finnart Church is *Eaglais a' Bhràighe*, 'Brae church', referring to Brae Rannoch.

Finsbay (Harris), Fionnasbhagh.

'Finn's bay', from Norse.

Fintray (Aberdeen). 'White settlement', from Gaelic *fionn*, 'white', and *treabh,* a gaelicisation of Brythonic *gwyn* and *tref.*

Fintry (Angus, Stirling). *See* **Fintray**.

Finzean (Aberdeen), Fìnnean. It is unclear what this name means.

Fionnphort (Mull), Fionnphort. 'White harbour'.

Firmor (Ross), An Fhaighear Mhóir. 'The great raised beach'.

First Coast (Ross), An t-Eirtheaire Shìos. 'The lower coast'.

Fiscary (Sutherland), Fìosgairidh. 'Fish sheiling', from Norse.

Fisherfield (Ross), Innis an Iasgaich. The Gaelic name is slightly different as 'the fishing meadow'.

Fishnish (Mull), Fìsinis. 'Fish point', from Norse.

Fiskavaig (Skye), Fìosgabhaig. 'Fish bay', from Norse.

Fiunary (Argyll), Fionnairigh. 'White sheiling'.

Fivepenny (Lewis), Na Cóig Peighin-nean. 'The five-penny land'. The full name of Fivepenny near Borve is *Cóig Peighinnean Bhuirgh* while in Ness it is *Cóig Peighinnean Nis.*

Fivig (Lewis), Fìbhig. 'Sheep bay', from Norse.

Fladabay (Harris), Fleòideabhagh. 'Float bay', from Norse.

Fladda (Mull), Flada. 'Flat island', from Norse.

Fladda-chuain (Skye), Flada a' Chuain. 'Flat island of the Minch', from Norse/Gaelic.

Flanders Moss (Stirling), A' Mhòinteach Fhlànrasach. 'The Flanders peat moss', a reminder that many Flemish people settled in the east of the country. Flanders itself is *Flànras, Flannras* and *Flairisg* in Gaelic.

Flannan Isles (Lewis), Na h-Eileanan Flannach. This may be 'the red islands'.

Flashader (Skye), Flaiseadar. 'Flat farm', from Norse.

Fleenas (Nairn), Flìonais. The meaning of this name is unclear.

Fleenasnagael (Nairn), Flìonais nan Gàidheal. 'Fleenas of the Gaels'.

Flesherin (Lewis), Na Fleisirean. 'The flat skerries', from Norse, with a Gaelic plural.

Flichity (Inverness), Flicheadaidh. 'Wet place'. A saying warns, *Fhad 's a bhios an t-allt aig Flicheadaidh a' ruith dhan taobh tuath, bidh mallachd air Flicheadaidh,* 'As long as the Flichity stream runs northwards, Flichity will be cursed'. Nearby is *Dùn Fhlicheadaidh* or Dunlichity, 'hill(fort) of Flichity'.

Flisk (Fife). This may be from *fleasg,* 'withe', found as a river name in Ireland. Nearby is Fliskmore, 'big Flisk', probably from *Fleasg Mòr.*

Flodda (Benbecula), Flodaigh. 'Float island', from Norse.

Flodday (Barra, Benbecula), Flodaigh. 'Float island', from Norse.

Floddaybeg (North Uist), Flodaigh Beag. 'Little Flodday', from Norse/Gaelic.

Floddaymore (North Uist), Flodaigh Mór. 'Big Flodday', from Norse/Gaelic.

Flodigarry (Skye), Flòdaigearraidh. 'Wet meadow or pasture land', from Norse.

Flowerdale (Ross), Am Baile Mór. The English name is 'flower dale', and the Gaelic name, 'the big farm'. Flowerdale House is *An Taigh Dìge* or *An Taigh Gìge,* 'the moat house', the full name being *Taigh Dìge nan Gorm Leac,* 'moat house with the blue slates'.

Fluchlady (Ross), Fliuch-Leathadaidh. 'Wet slope place'.

Fochabers (Moray), Fachabair or Fothabair. The meaning of this name is unclear although it contains an element suggesting marshy or muddy land.

Fodderletter (Banff, Moray), Foirleitir; (Nairn), Farrleitir. 'Terraced or

shelving slope', from *fothair* and *leitir*.
In Banffshire, Easter Fodderletter
is *Foirleitir Shìos* while Wester Fodderletter is *Foirleitir Shuas*.

Fodderty (Ross), Fodhraitidh. 'Lower
fort place'.

Foindle (Sutherland), An Fhionndail.
'The fair valley or haugh'.

Fonab (Perth), Fonn an Aba. 'The
abbot's land'.

Ford (Argyll), Àth na Crà or An t-Àth.
'The ford with the salmon trap' or 'the
ford'. Local people were nicknamed
coin-odhar, 'otters'.

Fordell (Fife). 'Over-haugh', from
Fordail.

Fordoun (Kincardine), Fordun.
'Over-fort'. This is a Gaelic equivalent
of the Brythonic/Pictish-based
'Gourdon' situated further south.

Forest Lodge (Argyll), Taigh na Frìthe.
The type of forest referred to here is a
treeless deer forest, from French *forêt*.

Forfar (Angus), Baile Fharfair. This
may be 'shelving slope'. The Gaelic
name has *baile*, 'town' attached.

Forgandenny (Perth). 'Eithne's place
above the bog', from *Forgrann Eithne*.

Forgie (Banff). This may be 'shelving
slope at the marsh' or 'windy shelving
slope', from *Fothair Gaoithe*.

Formartine (Aberdeen), Fearann
Mhàrtainn. 'Martin's land'.

Formont (Fife). 'Great or projecting
hill', from *Formhon(adh)*.

Fornighty (Nairn), Achadh Ghoididh.
The Gaelic name is 'the field of theft',
but the English name which was
recorded earlier as 'Fathenachten' is
unclear.

Forres (Moray), Farrais. 'Small copse'.

Forsinain (Sutherland), Fors an Fhàin.
'Waterfall at the slope', containg
Norse *fors*, 'waterfall'.

Forsinard (Sutherland), Forsan
Àrd. This appears to be 'high little
waterfall'.

Forss (Caithness). 'Waterfall', from
Norse.

Fort Augustus (Inverness), Cille Chui-
mein. The English name commemorates William Augustus, the Duke of
Cumberland, whose troops won the
Battle of Culloden. The Gaelic name
is 'St Cuimein's church'.

Forter (Angus), Fortair. 'Fortress'.

Forteviot (Perth), Fothair Tabhaicht.
'Tabhacht's shelving slope'. This was
the capital of the southern Picts.

Fort George (Inverness), An Gearasdan or Dùn Deòrsa. The English and
second Gaelic name refer to King
George of Britain, on the throne
when this fort was built in 1748. The
first Gaelic name is a gaelicisation
of English 'garrison' and is also the
Gaelic name of Fort William.

Forth Valley (Stirling), Srath For. 'Valley of the Forth'. *For*, the river's name
in Perthshire Gaelic, was applied to
the lower stretches of the river only,
the upper part being known as *An
Abhainn Dubh*, 'the black river'.

Fortingall (Perth), Fartairchill. 'Fort
church'.

Fortrie (Aberdeen, Banff). 'Big settlement', from Gaelic *for* and *treabh*,
giving *Foirtreabh*.

Fortry (Aberdeen, Banff). *See* **Fortrie**.

Fortrose (Ross), A' Chananaich.
The English name may be 'over-
headland' or 'great headland', from
Gaelic, while the Gaelic name is
'the chanonry', after the religious
settlement here which led to
Fortrose being poetically termed
Cananaich nan clag, 'Fortrose of the
bells'. Chanonry Point is *Rubha na
Cananaich* or *Gob na Cananaich*.

Fort William (Inverness), An Gearasdan. The current English name refers
to the fort at Achintore named after
William of Orange. The town then
became known as Maryburgh after
William of Orange's wife until it
came into the hands of the Duke of
Gordon and was renamed Gordons-
burgh. Later, it was named Duncans-

burgh after Sir Duncan Cameron of Fassfearn, and lastly reverted to its current English name in memory of the Duke of Cumberland. The Gaelic name is a gaelicisation of 'garrison' and, as this is also one of the names of Fort George, has a more complete version in *Gearasdan Loch Abar*, 'the garrison of Lochaber'.

Foss (Perth), Fasadh. 'Place' or 'stance'.

Fossoway (Kinross), Fasadh-Mhaigh. This may be 'stance plain'.

Foula (Shetland). 'Bird island', from Norse.

Foveran (Aberdeen), Fobharan. 'Place of wells'.

Fowlis (Aberdeen, Angus, Perth, Ross), Foghlais or Fólais. 'Small stream' or 'sub-stream'.

Foxhole (Inverness), A' Bhogsolamh or A' Bhog-Solla. The Gaelic name is not clear, but may refer to damp ground and willow trees. The English form is an adaptation from Gaelic.

Foy (Ross), An Fhothaidh. 'Lawn', from *faiche*. Foy Lodge, also known as Inverbroom Lodge, is *Taigh na Fothaidh*.

Foyers (Inverness), Foithear. 'Shelving slope'. The Falls of Foyers are *Eas na Smùide*, 'the smoky waterfall'. The Laird of Foyers was *Fear Foithreach*.

Foynesfield (Nairn), Seipeil Fhìonain. The Gaelic name is 'Finan's chapel' rather than 'field'.

Fraserburgh (Aberdeen), A' Bhruaich. The English name commemorates Sir Alexander Fraser of Philorth in the 16th century. Earlier the place had been known as Faithlie in English, as well as the local name, The Broch. The Gaelic name means 'the bank', and is an attempt by Gaelic speakers to substitute a Gaelic word for an unclear English one, in this case, 'broch'.

Freeburn (Inverness), Allt na Frithe. 'The stream by the deer forest'. The English name is a part-translation from Gaelic.

Frendraught (Aberdeen). This appears to be 'the land at the bridge', from *Fearann na Drochaid*.

Fresgill (Caithness), Freasgail. 'Noisy gully', from Norse.

Freuchie (Fife). 'Heather place', from *Fraochaidh*, also the old name of Grantown on Spey in Moray.

Friesland (Coll), Freaslan. This name comemmorates Friesland in the Netherlands.

Friockheim (Angus). This was earlier 'Friock', from *fraoch*, 'heather', until German *heim* was added in the 19th century by the landowner.

Frobost (South Uist), Fròbost. This Norse farm name contains an unclear initial element.

Fuday (South Uist), Fùideigh. The first part of this Norse island name is unclear.

Fuiay (Barra), Fùidheigh. 'House island', from Norse.

Furnace (Argyll, Ross), An Fhùirneis. 'The furnace' was an early industrial site. Furnace in Argyll was earlier known as *Inbhir Leacainn* or Inverleacain, 'river mouth at the broad hill face'.

Fyal (Perth), Féith Mheall. 'Boggy channel among the lumpy hills'.

Fyrish (Ross), Faoighris. This may be from Norse, containing the word for 'pine tree'.

Gaick (Inverness), Gàdhaig. 'Cleft'. Gaick is known as *Gàdhaig nam feadan fiar*, 'Gaick of the crooked streams', and features in the saying, *'S mór a b' fheàrr leam a bhith an Druim Uachdair na bhith an Gàdhaig nan creagan gruamach*, 'I would rather be in Drumochter than in Gaick of the gloomy crags'. A local curse was *Dìol Bhaltair an Gàdhaig ort*, 'Walter's fate in Gaick to you', referring to Walter Comyn who was pecked to death here by eagles. An incident known as *Call Ghàdhaig* occurred in 1799 when a party of people perished here in a storm.

Gairloch (Ross), Geàrrloch. 'Short loch'. Gairloch Hotel was known as *Taigh-òsta Acha Deuthasdal* and the Old Inn was *Taigh-òsta Cheann an t-Sàil*. The Strath of Gairloch is *Srath Gheàrrloch*. Local people are known as *truisg*, 'cod'.

Gairlochy (Inverness), Geàrr Lòchaidh. 'The short Lochy'.

Gairnshiel (Aberdeen), Àirigh Gharthain. 'Sheiling at the Gairn'.

Gallanach (Argyll), A' Ghallanach; (Coll), A' Ghallanaich. 'The colts-foot place' or 'the place of the standing stone'.

Gallan Head (Lewis), An Gallan Ùigeach. *Gallan* is a prominent rock or headland. The Gaelic name is 'the Uig rock'.

Gallin (Perth), Gealainn. 'White or bright place'.

Gallovie (Inverness), Gealaghaidh. 'White or bright hill face'.

Galloway (Kirkcudbright, Wigtown), Gall-ghàidheil. 'Foreign Gaels', referring to Gaels of mixed Gaelic-Scandanavian origin. The Mull of Galloway is *Maol Ghall-ghàidheil*, 'rounded headland of Galloway', or *Maol nan Gall*, 'rounded headland of the non-Gaels'; the Machars are *Machair Ghall-ghàidheil*, 'plain of Galloway'; and the Rhinns are *Ranna Ghall-ghàidheil*, 'divisions of Galloway', or *Na Rannaibh*, 'divisions'.

Galmisdale (Eigg), Galmasdal. This Norse valley name appears to contain a personal name as its first element.

Galson (Lewis), Gabhsunn. 'Pig sound', from Norse. North Galson is *Gabhsunn bho Thuath* and South Galson is *Gabhsunn bho Dheas*.

Galtrigill (Skye), Galtraigil. This may be 'hog ravine', from Norse.

Ganavan (Argyll), A' Ghaineamh Bhàn. 'The white sand'.

Garbat (Ross), An Garbh Bad. 'The rough copse'. Garbat Forest is *Frìth a' Gharbh Bhaid*.

Garbole (Inverness), An Garbuil. 'The rough boll', from *garbh* and *boll* referring to the amount of seed required to sow the land.

Garelochhead (Dunbarton), Ceann a' Ghearrloch. 'The head of the short loch'.

Garenin (Lewis), Na Gearrannan. 'The fertile lands by the sea'.

Gargadale (Arran), Gargadail. 'Warriors' valley', from Norse.

Garguston (Ross), Baile Ghargaidh. 'Gargach's township'.

Garioch (Aberdeen), Gairbheach. 'Place of roughness'. The Battle of Harlaw is known in Gaelic as *Cath Gairbheach*, 'Battle of Garioch', showing that *Gairbheach* does not decline in the genitive case.

Garlogie (Aberdeen). 'Short Logie', from *Geàrr Lagaidh*.

Garmond (Aberdeen). This may be 'rough hill', from *Garbh-Mhon(adh)*.

Garmoran (Argyll, Inverness), A' Gharbh Mhorbhairne. 'The rough sea gap' or 'rough Morvern'.

Garmouth (Moray), A' Ghairmich. It is unclear whether this name originated in Gaelic or in English. The village is near the mouth of the Spey, and this may be reflected in the English form of the name. However, if the Gaelic name is original, the English may be a corruption or rationalisation of a name based on 'calling', possibly with reference to the sound of the Spey or the sea.

Garnock Valley (Ayr). *See* **Glen Garnock**.

Garrabost (Lewis), Garrabost. 'Enclosed farm', from Norse.

Garrafad (Skye), An Garradh Fada. This may be 'the long field', from Norse *garðr* and Gaelic *fada*.

Garrick Bridge (Ross), Drochaid Gharaig. 'Bridge over the Garag'.

Garrisdale (Canna), Gàrrasdal. 'Field

valley', from Norse.

Garros (Skye), Gàrros or Gearas. 'River mouth at the enclosed field', from Norse.

Garrydhu (North Uist), An Gearraidh Dubh. 'The black fertile land'.

Garrygall (Barra), An Gearraidh Gadhal. This name refers to fertile land but the defining element is unclear.

Garrygannichy (South Uist), Gearraidh Gainmheacha. 'Sandy fertile land'.

Garryhallie (South Uist), Gearraidh Sheilidh. 'Fertile land with willows'.

Garscadden (Glasgow). This appears to be from *Gart Sgadain*, 'herring field', which is improbable, but the *sgadan* element may have become corrupted.

Garscube (Glasgow). 'Sheaf field', from *Gart Sguaib*.

Gartally (Inverness), Car Dàlaidh. This name may refer to a 'rock ledge' and a 'haugh'.

Gartchonzie (Perth). This appears to be 'Kenneth's field', from *Gart Choinnich*.

Gartcosh (Lanark). This field name from *gart*, with a second element maybe from *còs*, 'cave' or 'hollow', gives 'field at a cave or hollow'.

Garth (Perth), Gart. 'Field'. The castle here is *Caisteal Ghairt*, 'Garth Castle', but was also known as *Caisteal a' Chuilein Chursta*, 'castle of the cursed whelp', referring to the son of the Wolf of Badenoch.

Garthonzie (Stirling). This may be 'Kenneth's field', from *Gart Choinnich*.

Gartincaber (Perth). This may be 'the field of the stakes or horns', from *Gart nan Cabar*.

Gartloch (Lanark). 'Enclosed field by the loch', from *Gart Locha*.

Gartly (Aberdeen), Gartaidh. 'Field place' or 'small field', from *gart*.

Gartmore (Perth), An Gart Mór. 'The large enclosed field'.

Gartnatra (Islay), Gart na Tràgha.

'Enclosed field by the beach'.

Gartnavel (Glasgow), Gart nan Abhall. 'Enclosed field of the apple trees'.

Gartness (Stirling), Gart an Easa. 'Enclosed field by the stream'.

Gartocharn (Dunbarton), Gart a' Chàirn. 'Enclosed field with a cairn'.

Gartsherrie (Lanark). This may be 'colt field', from *Gart Searraich*, but *Searrach* here may be a personal name.

Gartymore (Sutherland), Gartaidh Mór. 'Big field place'.

Garvaig (Ross), Garbhaig. 'Small rough place' or 'small rough stream'.

Garvald (East Lothian). This seems to be 'rough stream', from *Garbh Allt*.

Garvamore (Inverness), An Garbhath Mór. 'The large rough ford'.

Garvan (Argyll), An Garbhan. 'The small rough one', refer to a stream or piece of land.

Garve (Ross), Gairbh. 'Rough place'. The Strath of Garve is *Srath Ghairbh* and the loch is *Loch Mhaol Fhinn*, 'loch of Fionn's devotee'. Local people were called *buic*, 'bucks'.

Garvellachs (Argyll), Na Garbh-Eileacha. 'The rough rocks'.

Garvock (Fife). 'Rough place', from *Garbhag*.

Garynahine (Lewis), Gearraidh na h-Aibhne. 'The fertile land by the river'.

Garynamonie (South Uist), Gearraidh na Mònadh. 'The fertile land by the peat'.

Garyvard (Lewis), Gearraidh a' Bhàird. 'The poet's fertile land'.

Gask (Aberdeen, Fife, Perth), Gasg. 'Projecting tail or strip of land'.

Gaza (Ross), Gàsa. This is a biblical reference prompted by the sandy hills here.

Geanies (Ross), Gàthan. 'Sea ravine', from Norse, with Gaelic then English plurals attached.

Geary (Skye), Geàrraidh. 'Fertile land'.

Gearymore (Skye), An Gearraidh Mór. 'The large piece of fertile land'.

Geddes (Nairn), Geadais. 'Place of the plot'.

Gedintailor (Skye), Gead an t-Sailleir. 'Plot of the salter'.

Gedloch (Moray). This may be 'plot place', from *Geadlach*. It is not a loch name.

Geisgeil (Sutherland), Gìsgil. 'Gushing ravine', from Norse.

Gella (Angus). 'White ford', from *Gealath*.

Gellovie (Inverness), Gallabaidh. This name is unclear and appears not to be the same as *Gallovie*.

Gelston (Kirkcudbright). 'Gill-Ìosa's farm', from English with a Gaelic personal name meaning 'devotee of Jesus'.

Geocrab (Harris), Geocrab. 'Crab ravine', from Norse.

Georgetown (Perth), Na Barrags. The English name commemorates a King George, while the Gaelic is a transliteration of 'barracks'.

Gergask (Inverness), Garbh-Ghaisg. 'Rough tail of land projecting from a plateau'. A ditty about names of various neighbouring districts goes, *Tha cóig bothan an Loch Abar, cóig gasgan ann am Bàideanach's cóig cóigean ann an Srath Éireann*, 'There are five boths in Lochaber, five gasgs in Badenoch and five cóigs in Strathdearn'. The gasgs, which are tails of land projecting from a plateau, are Gergask, Gasga Mhór, Gasga Bheag, Drumgask and Gasg an Lóin.

Gerinish (South Uist), Géirinis. This Norse name may mean 'pasture headland'. East Gerinish is *Caolas Liubharsaigh*, 'strait of Liursay', while West Gerinish is simply *Géirinis*.

Geshader (Lewis), Géiseadar. 'Goat township', from Norse. Local pronunciation as collected by Oftedal suggests a preferable spelling of *Géiseadair*.

Gesto (Skye), Geusdo or Geusto. 'Goat farm' or 'goat harbour' from Norse.

Gigalum (Gigha), Gioghalum. 'Holm of Gigha'.

Gigha, Giogha. 'God's island', from Norse. A Gigha person is a *Gioghach*, also nicknamed a *gamhainn*, 'stirk'.

Gighay (Barra), Gioghaigh. 'God's island', from Norse.

Gilberts Bridge (Perth), Drochaid Ghilbeart. 'Gilbert's bridge'.

Gillen (Skye), Na Gilean. 'The ravines', from Norse with a Gaelic plural.

Gilmerton (Midlothian, Perth). 'Gille-Moire's farm', from English but with a Gaelic personal name meaning 'devotee of Mary'.

Gilston (Midlothian, Moray). 'Gille's farm', from English, but with a Gaelic personal name meaning 'devotee'.

Girvan (Ayr), Inbhir Gharbhain. This was previously Invergarvane, from the Gaelic name meaning 'mouth of the rough river'. The current English name is simply that of the river.

Gisla (Lewis), Giosladh. 'Hostage river' or 'Gisl's river', from Norse.

Gizzen Briggs (Ross), Drochaid an Obh. The English name of this sandbar is 'leaky bridge' from Norse, while the Gaelic name also refers to a bridge allegedly once linking Ross and Sutherland.

Glackour (Ross), A' Ghlaic Odhar. 'The dun-coloured hollow'.

Gladsmuir (East Lothian), Sliabh a' Chlamhain. 'The kestrel moor', from English gled, 'kestrel'. The Battle of Prestonpans in Gaelic is *Blàr Sliabh a' Chlamhain*, 'battle of Gladsmuir'.

Glaick (Ross), A' Ghlac. 'The hollow'.

Glame (Raasay), Glàm. This may be a form of *glòm*, 'chasm'.

Glamis (Angus), Glàmais. This may be 'chasm place'.

Glascarnoch (Ross), A' Ghlas Càrnach. This may be 'the rocky hollow' or 'hollow of cairns'.

Glasgo (Aberdeen). *See* **Glasgow**. The village of Blackburn was formerly known as Broadford of Glasgo, and the local area contains names such as Glasgoforest and Glasgoego, the latter apparently containing the surname Eggo (*Ciogach* in Gaelic).

Glasgow, Glaschu. 'Green hollow', from Brythonic.

Glasnakille (Skye), Glas na Cille. 'The stream at the church'.

Glasphein (Skye), Glas-Pheighinn. 'Grey-green pennyland'.

Glass (Aberdeen). 'Stream' or 'meadow', from *glas*.

Glassans (Islay), Na Glasfhasadhnan. 'The grey-green stances'.

Glassard (Colonsay), Glasaird. 'Grey-green headland'.

Glassaugh (Banff). 'Grey-green place', from *Glasach*.

Glassel (Kincardine). This may be 'grey-green place', from *glasail*.

Glassingall (Perth). This may be 'the stream of the non-Gaels', from *Glas nan Gall*.

Gledfield (Ross), Leth Chlamhaig or Lòn na Speireig. The English name is 'kestrel field', from Scottish English gled, 'kestrel'. The first Gaelic name is 'the half strath of the kestrel', and the second is 'wet meadow of the sparrowhawk'.

Glen (Barra), An Gleann. 'The glen'.

Glenachulish (Argyll, Inverness), Gleann a' Chaolais. 'The glen at the narrows'.

Glen Affray (Perth), Gleann Aifrinn. 'The glen of the offering'.

Glen Affric (Inverness), Gleann Afraic. 'The glen of the Affric'. This glen contains *Coille Ruigh na Cuileig*, 'wood at the midge slope', the largest remaining portion of the Caledonian Forest.

Glen Allachie (Banff), Gleann Aileachaidh. 'The glen at the rocky place'.

Glen Alladale (Argyll), Gleann Athaladail. This may mean 'eel valley', from Norse with *gleann* added.

Glen Almond (Perth), Gleann Amain. 'The glen of the Almond'.

Glen Ample (Perth), Gleann Ambail. 'The glen at the cauldron or vat'.

Glenapp (Ayr). 'Alpin's glen', from *Gleann Ailpein*.

Glen Aray (Argyll), Gleann Aora. 'The glen of the Aray'.

Glen Arklet (Stirling), Gleann Aircleid. 'The glen of the difficult slope'.

Glen Aros (Mull), Gleann Àrois. 'Glen at the river mouth', from Gaelic/Norse.

Glen Artney (Perth), Gleann Artanaig. This may be 'Artanag's glen', based on old Gaelic *art*, 'bear'.

Glen Ashdale (Arran), Gleann Éisdeal. 'Ash valley', from Norse with *gleann*, 'glen' attached. The Gaelic name looks coincidentally like that of the island of Easdale, but comes from a different source.

Glen Aven (Banff), Gleann Athfhinn. 'The glen of the very bright river'.

Glen Baloch (Inverness), Gleann a' Bhealaich. 'The glen at the pass'.

Glen Banchor (Inverness), Gleann Bheannchair. 'The glen at the horned place'.

Glenbarr (Argyll), Am Bàrr. The Gaelic name is 'the summit' or 'the hill', while the English may be from an older Gaelic form meaning, *Gleann a' Bhàrr*, 'the glen at the summit/hill'.

Glen Barton (Dumfries). This may be 'the glen of the Britons', from *Gleann Breatann* or *Gleann Breatainn*.

Glen Batrick (Jura), Gleann Badraig. 'The glen at pasture bay', from Gaelic/Norse.

Glenbeg (Moray), An Gleann Beag. 'The small glen'.

Glen Bernisdale (Skye), Gleann Bheàrnasdail. 'The glen of Bernisdale'.

Glenbervie (Kincardine). 'The glen of the boiling water', from *Gleann Biorbhaigh*.

Glen Birnie (Midlothian). 'The glen

at the damp place', from *Gleann Braonaigh*.

Glen Borrodale (Argyll), Gleann Bhorghdail. 'Fort valley', from Norse with *gleann* added.

Glen Breakerie (Argyll), Gleann Breacairidh. If this name is wholly Gaelic, it is 'the glen at the speckled place', but if Gaelic/Norse, means 'the glen at the slope field or sheiling'.

Glenbreck (Peebles). 'Speckled glen', from *An Gleann Breac*.

Glen Brerachan (Perth), Gleann Bhriathrachain or Gleann Briathrachain. 'The glen of the little talkative stream'.

Glen Brittle (Skye), Gleann Breadail. This may be 'broad valley', from Norse, with *gleann* added.

Glen Buchat (Aberdeen), Gleann Buichead. 'Buichead's glen'.

Glen Buckie (Perth), Gleann Bucaidh. 'The glen of the buck stream'.

Glen Callater (Aberdeen), Gleann Chaladair. 'The glen of Callater'. *See* **Aberchalder**.

Glen Calvie (Ross), Gleann Chailbhidh. This may contain *calbh*, 'plant stalk', and mean 'glen at the plant stalk place'. A Glen Calvie person is a *Cailbheach*.

Glen Cannel (Mull), Gleann Cainneir. 'St Cainnear's glen'.

Glencaple (Dumfries). 'Horse glen', from *Gleann Chapall*.

Glen Carragrich (Harris), Gleann Tharmasaig. The defining elements in the English and Gaelic names are unclear, but the Gaelic name ends in Norse 'bay'.

Glen Cassley (Sutherland), Gleann Charsla. 'The glen at the castle place'.

Glen Clova (Angus), Gleann Chlàbhaidh. The meaning of this glen name is unclear.

Glen Cloy (Arran). This appears to be *Gleann Cloiche*, 'stony glen'.

Glencoe (Argyll), Gleann Comhan or Gleanna Comhan. 'The glen of

the Coe'. This is often said to be 'glen of weeping' as a result of the Massacre of Glencoe, but the name existed long before that event. The river name appears to be pre-Gaelic. Glencoe Village is *A' Chàrnach*, 'the stony place', the English name being a fairly recent invention.

Glen Convinth (Inverness), Gleann a' Chonfhadhaich. 'The glen in the stormy place'.

Glencorse (Midlothian). This may be 'glen at the crossing place'.

Glen Creran (Argyll), Gleann Creurain. The second part of this glen name is unclear.

Glen Cribesdale (Argyll), Gleann Creabasdail. This may be 'cliff valley' from Norse, with *gleann* added.

Glen Crossaig (Argyll), Gleann Chrosaig. 'Valley of cross bay', from Gaelic/Norse.

Glendale (Skye, South Uist), Gleann Dail. A Gaelic/Norse name meaning 'valley'. In South Uist, North Glendale is *Ceann a Tuath Ghlinn Dail* and South Glendale is *Ceann a Deas Ghlinn Dail*. A native of Glendale in Skye is a *Daileach*.

Glendaruel (Argyll), Gleann Dà Ruadhail. This was was thought to mean 'glen of the two red places', but recent research suggests that the site of the church here may be pre-Christian and commemorate Dà Ruadha, a deity possibly connected with Dà Dearga. This would give a meaning of 'glen of Dà Ruadha'. Loch Riddon is *Loch Ruadhail* with the same element.

Glen Dee (Aberdeen), Gleann Dé. 'Glen of the Dee', a river name with connotations of divinity.

Glen Derby (Perth), Gleann Geunaid. The Gaelic name is 'glen of the goose stream' which led to the anglicised form of Glen Gennet, later abandoned when a Victorian landowner wished to immortalise his home town of Derby.

Glen Dessary (Inverness), Gleann Deasairidh. 'Glen in the south-facing place'.

Glendevon (Perth). 'The glen of the black river', from *Gleann Duibhe*.

Glendhu (Dumfries). 'Black glen', from *Gleann Dubh*.

Glen Dibidale (Ross), Gleann Dìobadail. 'Deep valley', from Norse with *gleann* added.

Glen Dochart (Perth), Gleann Dochard. The river name in this glen may be that found in the name 'Cart', but with negative connotations of scouring.

Glen Docharty (Ross), Gleann Dochartaich. This may be 'glen of great scouring'.

Glen Doe (Inverness), Gleann Dotha. This is said to commemorate a water sprite named *Dotha* or *Dogha*, but the name may simply be 'bad water'. Glendoebeg is *Gleann Dotha Beag*, 'little Glen Doe'.

Glendoick (Perth), Gleann Doig. 'Cadoc's glen'.

Glen Douglas (Dunbarton), Gleann Dùghlais. 'The glen of the black river'.

Glen Dye (Kincardine), Gleann Dàidh. This appears in Gaelic to be 'David's glen', but the origins are obscure. Cairn Dye is now *Càrn an Tàilleir*, but it is unlikely that 'Glen Dye' is from that source.

Gleneagles (Perth), Gleann Eagas or Gleann na h-Eaglais. The second element of the first Gaelic name connotes a 'notch', while the second is 'glen at the church', although this may be a newer form influenced by English.

Glenegedale (Islay), Gleann Eigeadail. 'Edge valley', from Norse with *gleann* attached.

Glen Elchaig (Ross), Gleann Eilcheig. This meaning of this name is unclear.

Glenelg (Inverness), Gleann Eilg. 'Glen of Ireland', a commemorative name. A person from Glenelg is an *Eilgneach*, and locals were nicknamed *othaisgean*, 'yearlings' or 'hogs'.

Glen Elgin (Moray), Gleann Eilginn. 'The glen of Elgin'.

Glen Ericht (Perth), Gleann Eireachd. 'Assembly glen'.

Glen Errochty (Perth), Gleann Eireachdaidh. 'Assembly glen'.

Glen Esk (Angus), Gleann Easg. 'The glen of the Esk'.

Glen Etive (Argyll), Gleann Éite. 'The glen of the Etive', a name with connotations of foulness. *Éiteag*, a water goddess, is said to have lived in the river. A person from this area is an *Éiteach*.

Glen Ey (Aberdeen), Gleann Eidh. The defining element in this name is unclear.

Glen Eynort (Skye), Gleann Aoineart. 'The glen of Eynort'.

Glen Falloch (Perth), Gleann Falach. 'Ringed glen'.

Glen Farclas (Banff), Gleann Farghlais. 'The glen of the over-stream'.

Glen Farquhar (Kincardine). 'Farquhar's glen', from *Gleann Fhearchair*.

Glen Fender (Perth), Gleann Fhionndair. 'The glen of the Fender'.

Glen Feochan (Argyll), Gleann Faochain. The defining element here is unclear.

Glen Fernate (Perth), Gleann Feàrnaid. 'The glen of the alder stream'.

Glen Feshie (Inverness), Gleann Féisidh. 'The glen of the boggy haugh river'.

Glen Fiddich (Banff), Gleann Fhiodhaich. 'The glen at the wood place'. It is often assumed that this name is based on *fiadh*, 'deer', but in fact the root is *fiodh*, 'wood'.

Glen Finglas (Perth), Gleann Fhionnghlais. 'The glen of the fair stream'. The church here was *Cladh nan Ceasanach*, 'graveyard of Kessock's people', referring to the saint.

Glen Finlas (Argyll), Gleann Fhionnghlais. *See* **Glen Finglas**.

Glenfinnan (Inverness), Gleann Fhionnainn, Gleann Fhionghain or Gleann Fhìonain. The first Gaelic name represents local pronunciation but is unclear. The second and third Gaelic names are 'Fingon's glen' or 'Finan's glen' respectively. There is a certain amount of confusion regarding the personal name here, because the area is also associated with Finan who is commemorated in *Eilean Fhìonain*, 'Island Finnan', in Loch Sheil. Local place-name signs reflect the confusion.

Glen Forsa (Mull), Gleann Forsa. 'Valley of the waterfall river', from Gaelic/Norse.

Glen Fruin (Dunbarton), Gleann Freòin. This name may include that of a river, the name of which is based on *freòine*, 'rage'. The road from Loch Long to Glen Fruin was known as *Rathad Mór nan Gàidheal*, 'high road of the Gaels'. The name of this glen might be related to that of Balfron.

Glen Fyne (Argyll), Gleann Fìne. The river name here appears to be based on *fìon*, 'wine'. A person from the area is a *Fìneach*, also nicknamed a *muc bhiorach*, 'porpoise'.

Glen Gairn (Aberdeen), Gleann Gharthain. 'The glen of the calling river'. Lower Glen Gairn is *Ìochdar Ghlinn Gharthain*. Glen Gairn church is *Cill Mo Thatha*, 'St Mo Thatha's church', a saint commemorated in Balmaha, and the fair held here was *Féill Mo Thatha*.

Glen Garnock (Ayr). 'The glen of the crying river'. *See* **Glen Girnock**.

Glen Garrisdale (Jura), Gleann Gharrasdail. 'Field valley', from Norse with Gaelic *gleann*.

Glen Garry (Inverness), Gleann Garadh or Gleanna Garadh; (North Perthshire), Gleann Gar; (South Perthshire), Gleann Gamhair. In Inverness and North Perthshire, this name is 'copse glen'. In South

Perthshire it may mean 'winter glen'. A person from Glen Garry in Inverness is a *Garranach*.

Glen Garvie (Aberdeen). 'The glen of the rough river', from *Gleann Gharbhaidh*.

Glen Gelder (Aberdeen), Gleann Ghealdair. 'The glen of the white or bright water'.

Glen Gennet (Ayr). 'The glen of the goose stream', from *Gleann Geunaid*. A glen in Perthshire with the same original name was renamed by a 19th century landowner as Glen Derby.

Glen Girnock (Aberdeen), Gleann Goirneig. 'The glen of the crying river'.

Glen Glass (Ross), Gleann Ghlais. 'The glen of the stream'.

Glen Glaster (Inverness), Gleann Ghlasdair. 'The glen of the grey-green water'.

Glen Gloy (Inverness), Gleann Glaoidh. 'The glen of the gluey or viscous river'.

Glen Golly (Sutherland), Gleanna Gollaidh. 'The glen of the blind river', maybe referring to an overgrown river. This is known as *Gleanna Gollaidh nan craobh*, 'Glen Golly of the trees'.

Glen Gorm (Mull), An Gleann Gorm. 'The green glen'. *Gorm* usually means 'blue' but also covers the colour of fresh vegetation.

Glen Goulandie (Perth), Gleann Gobhlandaidh. This may be 'the glen at the forked place'.

Gleann Gour (Argyll), Gleann Ghobhar. 'Goats' glen'.

Glen Gravir (Lewis), Gleann Ghrabhair. 'The glen of Gravir'.

Glen Grivie (Sutherland), Gleann Ghrìobhaidh. 'The glen at the claw place'.

Glen Grudie (Ross), Gleann Ghrùididh. 'The glen of the Grudie', referring to gravel.

Glen Gynack (Inverness), Gleann

Gòineig. This river name here is obscure.

Glen Haultin (Skye), Gleann Shealtainn. This appears to be 'glen of Shetland', and may refer to settlement by Norse people who had come from there.

Glenhinnsdal (Skye), Gleann Hinneasdail. 'Hengist's valley', from Norse with *gleann* attached.

Glen House (Mull), Tìr Chonaill. The Gaelic name is 'Conall's land', and is also the Gaelic name of County Donegal in Ireland.

Glen Isla (Angus), Gleann Ìl or Gleann Ìle. 'The glen of the Isla'. A local is an *Ìleach*.

Glenjorrie (Ayr). 'The pilgrim's or dewar's glen', from *Gleann an Deòraidh*.

Glen Ketland (Argyll), Gleann Ceitilein. This name is unclear but may contain an element cognate with Brythonic *coed*, 'wood'.

Glenkill (Arran). Although commonly derived from *Gleann na Cille*, 'glen of the church', the alternative *Gleann na Coille* is more likely, given the absence of evidence for the existence of a church in the area.

Glenkindie (Aberdeen), Gleann Cinnidh. The name of the river here may be 'champion' or 'warrior'.

Glen Kinglas (Argyll), Gleann Chonghlais. 'The glen of the dog river'.

Glen Kyles (Harris), Gleann a' Chaolais. 'The glen at the narrows'.

Glen Latterach (Moray). 'Sloping glen', from *Gleann Leitreach*.

Glen Lednock (Perth), Gleann Liadnaig. The meaning of this name is unclear.

Glen Leraig (Sutherland), Gleann Leireag. 'Larch glen'.

Glen Levishie (Inverness), Gleann Lìbhisidh. 'The glen of Levishie'.

Glenlia (Inverness), An Gleann Liath. 'The blue-grey glen'.

Glen Liever (Argyll), Gleann Lìbhir. 'The glen of Liever'.

Glenlivet (Banff), Gleann Lìobhait. 'The glen of the Livet'.

Glen Lochay (Perth), Gleann Lòchaidh. 'The glen of the Lochy'.

Glen Lochsie (Perth), Gleann Lòchsaidh. This may be 'the glen at the dark place', from *lòch* and *fasadh*.

Glen Lossie (Moray), Gleann Losaidh. 'The glen of the plant river'.

Glen Loyne (Inverness), Gleann Loinn. 'Loyne' may originate in *loinn*, 'beauty'.

Glenluce (Wigtown), Gleann Lus. *Lus* is 'plant' or 'herb', here perhaps implying an overgrown river. Glenluce Village is *Clachan Ghlinn Lus*.

Glen Lui (Aberdeen), Gleann Laoigh. 'The glen of the calf river'.

Glen Luss (Dunbarton), Gleann Luis. *See* **Glenluce**.

Glen Lyon (Perth), Gleann Lìomhann. 'The glen of the Lyon', a name conveying smoothness. This was also known as *an Crom Ghleann*, 'the crooked glen'. MacGregor's patrimony in Glen Lyon is *an Tòiseachd*, 'the lord's land'.

Glenmallie (Argyll), Gleann Màilidh. *See* **Dalmally** and **Kilmallie**.

Glen Markie (Inverness), Gleann Mharcaidh. 'The glen of the horse river'.

Glen Marxie (Ross), Gleann Mharcfh-asaidh. 'The glen at the horse stance'.

Glen Massan (Argyll), Gleann Masain. 'Masan's glen'. This was the place beloved of Deirdre in legend.

Glen Mazeran (Inverness), Gleann Masarain. This name is unclear.

Glenmeanie (Ross), Gleann Mèinnidh. This name may be related to 'Main' in Ross.

Glenmoidart (Argyll), Gleann Mhùideart. 'The glen of Moidart'.

Glenmore (several), An Gleann Mór. 'The great glen'.

Glen Moriston (Inverness), Gleann

Moireasdan. This is said to be 'the glen of the great water', referring to the river, but the phonetics do not support this.

Glenmoy (Angus). 'Glen at the plain', from *Gleann na Mòighe*.

Glen Muick (Aberdeen), Gleann Muice. 'Glen of the pig river'. The fair here was *Féill Mhoir*, 'St Mary's fair'. A native is a *Mucarnach*.

Glen Nevis (Inverness), Gleann Nibheis. This is commonly believed to be 'the glen of terror' from *uabhas*, but the basis of the name is an Indo-European root with connotations of wetness. Glen Nevis had a negative reputation in one poem is called, *amar sgùrainn an domhain mhóir*, 'slop-pail of the wide world'.

Glen of Lintrathen (Angus), Gleann Tréithean. The second part of this name is unclear, and it is notable that *linn* or Brythonic *llyn*, 'pool', is absent from the Gaelic. 'Lintrathen' itself was recorded by Diack from speakers of Perthshire Gaelic as *lan-tréin* and *lyann-tré-an*.

Glen of Rothes (Moray), Gleann Ràthais. 'The glen of Rothes'.

Glen Ogil (Angus). *See* **Glen Ogle**.

Glen Ogle (Perth), Gleann Ogail. The meaning of this name is unclear, but is unrelated to *òg*, 'young'.

Glen Orchy (Argyll), Gleann Urchaidh. 'The glen of the Orchy'. The glen was called *Gleann Urcha nam badan*, 'Glen Orchy of the copses', showing local pronunciation. The parish of Glen Orchy was known as *An Dìseart*, 'the hermitage', which is referred to in the Gaelic name of nearby Dalmally. The fair held at Glen Orchy was *Féill Chonnain*, 'St Connan's fair', referring to the saint commemorated at Dalmally. The Braes of Glen Orchy are *Bràigh Ghlinn Urchaidh*, 'the upper part of Glen Orchy'.

Glen Ormisdale (Arran), Gleann Ormasdail. 'Orm's valley', from Norse, with *gleann* attached.

Glen Orrin (Ross), Gleann Oirrinn or Gleann Orthainn. 'The glen of the offering', referring to church lands of Urray at the confluence of the Conon and Orrin.

Glen Pean (Inverness), Gleann Peathain. This name is unclear and may be from Pictish.

Glen Prosen (Angus), Gleann Pràsaig or Gleann Pràsain. This name is unclear but may contain a personal name.

Glen Quiech (Angus). *See* **Glen Quoich**.

Glen Quoich (Inverness), Gleann Chuaich. 'The glen of the hollow'. This glen was allegedly haunted by a sprite named *Cuachag*.

Glenramskill (Argyll), Gleann Ramasgail. 'Valley at raven gully', from Gaelic/Norse.

Glenrath (Peebles). 'Glen with a circular fort', from *Gleann an Ràtha*.

Glen Rinnes (Banff), Gleann Ruaidhneis. 'The glen at the red-brown haugh'.

Glen Rosa (Arran), Gleann Ruasaidh. 'Glen of the horse river', from Gaelic/Norse.

Glenrothes (Fife), Gleann Ràthais. *See* **Glen of Rothes**.

Glen Roy (Inverness), Gleann Ruaidh. 'The glen of the Roy'.

Glen Sanda (Argyll), Gleann Shannda. 'The glen of the sand river', from Gaelic/Norse. Glensanda Castle is *Caisteal na Gruagaich*, 'the maiden's castle'.

Glen Scorrodale (Arran), Gleann Sgoradail. 'Skorri's valley', from Norse, with *gleann* added.

Glensgaich (Ross), Gleann Sgathaich. This name may refer to the pruning of branches from trees in the area.

Glen Shant (Arran), Gleann Sianta. 'Holy glen'. Older forms of the name suggest that this was originally *Crann*

Sianta, 'holy tree'.

Glenshee (Perth), Gleann Sìth. 'Fairy glen'.

Glensheil (Ross), Gleann Seile. 'The glen of the Sheil', a pre-Gaelic river name. Glensheil church is *Eaglais Riabhachain*, 'church at the brindled place', and a Glensheil person is a *Seileach*.

Glenshian (Inverness), Gleann an t-Sìthein. 'The glen with the small fairy hill'.

Glen Shira (Argyll), Gleann Siara. 'The glen of the eternal river'.

Glen Sloy (Dunbarton), Gleann Sluagh or Gleann Sluaigh. 'The glen of the host'.

Glenstrae (Argyll), Gleann Sreith. This may be 'the glen of the row'.

Glen Strathfarrar (Ross), Gleann Srath Farair. 'The glen of the strath of the Farrar'.

Glen Tanar (Aberdeen), Gleann Tanair. 'The glen of the thundering river'.

Glen Tilt (Perth), Gleann Teilt. This river name is pre-Gaelic.

Glen Tolsta (Lewis), Gleann Tholastaidh. 'The glen of Tolsta'.

Glen Tromie (Inverness), Gleann Tromaidh. 'The glen of the elder tree river'. A song about this place says, *Gleann Tromaidh nan siantan, leam bu mhiann bhith nad fhasgadh*, 'Stormy Glen Tromie, I wish I were in your shelter'.

Glen Trool (Ayr). 'The glen of the stream', from *Gleann an t-Sruthail*.

Glen Truim (Inverness), Gleann Truim. 'The glen of the elder tree river'.

Glen Turret (Perth), Gleann Turraid. 'The glen of the dry river', one which shrinks in volume in summer.

Glenuig (Inverness), Gleann Ùige. 'Glen at the bay', from Gaelic/Norse.

Glen Urquhart (Inverness), Gleann Urchadain. 'The glen of Urquhart'.

Glenvicaskill (Skye), Gleann MhicAsgaill. 'MacAskill's glen'.

Glenwhinnie (Ayr). This may be 'warrior glen', from *Gleann Chuinnidh*.

Glespin (Lanark). This may be 'grey-green pennyland', from *Glas-Pheighinn*.

Glutton (Ross), Glotan. 'Gorge'.

Goathill (Lewis), Cnoc nan Gobhar. 'The hill of the goats'.

Goat Island (Lewis), Eilean a' Ghobhail. 'The forked island'. The English translation came about through confusion between *gobhal*, 'fork', and *gobhar*, 'goat'.

Gobagrennan (Argyll), Gob a' Ghrianain. 'The promontory at the sunny spot'.

Gobernuisgach (Sutherland), Gob an Uisgich. 'The point at the water place'.

Golspie (Sutherland), Goillspidh. 'Gully village', from Norse. Golspie is *Goillspidh nan sligean dubh*, 'Golspie of the mussels'.

Golval (Sutherland), Golbhal. 'Galli's field' or 'field with a loud stream', from Norse.

Gometra (Mull), Gómastra. 'Godmund's island'.

Gordon (Berwick). *See* **Gourdon**.

Gordonbush (Sutherland), Gar-eisgeig. The more recent English name replaced the Gaelic name based on Gaelic/Norse meaning 'copse at the waste strip of land'.

Gordon Castle (Moray), Bogan Ghaoithe. The site of Gordon Castle occupies land known as 'windy or marshy bog' in Gaelic.

Gordon Hall (Inverness), Lag an Nòtair. The Gordons were landowners here at the site known as 'the notary's hollow' in Gaelic.

Gorstan (Ross), An Goirtean. 'The small enclosed field', also known as *Goirtean Ghairbh*, 'the small enclosed field at Garve',

Gortan (Ross), An Goirtean. 'The small enclosed field'. The full name of Gortan in Lochcarron is *An Goirtean Fraoich*, 'small enclosed heathery field'.

Gortaneorn (Argyll), An Goirtean Eòrna. 'Small enclosed barley field'.

Gortantaoid (Islay), Goirtean an Taoid. 'The small enclosed field of the halter'. An alternative derivation is *Goirtean an t-Saoid*, 'the small enclosed field of the cattle drive'.

Gorthleck (Inverness), Goirtlig. This name is unclear, although the English form suggests that it may have come from *gart/gort* and *leac* to give 'slab field'. Nearby is Loch Garth which contains *gart*.

Gorton (Coll), An Goirtean. 'The small enclosed field'.

Gortonallister (Arran), Goirtean Alasdair. 'Alasdair's small enclosed field'.

Gott (Tiree), Got. This Norse name is unclear. A saying meaning someone stopped halfway through something is, *Ma stad iad mu Ghot, stad iad mu Ghot*.

Gourdon (Kincardine). 'Great fort', from Brythonic. This was previously *Gordoun* and is closely related to *Fordoun* which shows Gaelic *f* rather than Brythonic *g*.

Gourock (Renfrew), Guireag. 'Pimple', referring to the hill above the town.

Govan (Glasgow), Baile a' Ghobhainn. The Gaelic name is 'the smith's farm', and while the name may originally have contained a reference to a smith, it is likely that it stems from Brythonic, with the Gaelic name a subsequent attempt to give the name meaning.

Govig (Harris), Góbhaig. 'Ravine bay', from Norse.

Gowrie (Perth), Gobharaidh. 'Gabhran's land'. Gabhran was king of Dal Riada during the 6th century. The divisions of Gowrie are *Blàr Ghobharaidh*, 'Blair of Gowrie', and *Cars Ghobharaidh*, 'Carse of Gowrie'.

Gramsdale (Benbecula), Gramasdal. 'Gram's valley', from Norse.

Grandtully (Perth), Gar an Tulaich. 'The den at the green hill'.

Granish (Inverness), Grèanais. This name is unclear but contains a suffix meaning 'place'.

Grantown on Spey (Moray), Baile Ùr nan Granndach or A' Bhaile Ùr. The planned town here is 'the new town of the Grants' or just 'the new town' in Gaelic, also referred to locally at one time as 'Valoor'. Prior to this the settlement was known as Freuchie from *Fraochaidh*, 'heather place'.

Grasspoint (Mull), Achadh na Creige. The Gaelic name is 'the field at the rock' and is unrelated to the English one.

Gravir (Lewis), Grabhair. 'Ravines', from Norse.

Grealin (Skye), Grèalainn or Greallainn. The meaning of this Norse name is unclear.

Grean (Barra), Grinn. 'Green', from Norse.

Great Bernera, Beàrnaraigh. 'Bjørn's island', from Norse. Also known as Bernera. 'Great' in the English form distinguishes here from Little Bernera. In Gaelic this is known as *Beàrnaraigh Leódhais*, 'Bernera of Lewis', and *Beàrnaraigh Ùig*, 'Bernera of Uig', the district of Lewis to which Bernera is attached. A Bernera person is a *Beàrnarach*.

Great Cumbrae, Cumaradh Mór. 'Large island of the Cymric people', meaning the Britons of Strathclyde.

Great Glen (Inverness), An Gleann Mór. 'The great glen', also known as 'Glenmore'.

Green, The (Tiree), Biosta or Port Bhiosta. The English name may be from Norse 'green' or 'den'. The Gaelic name may be '(port of) the farm dwelling', from Norse.

Greenhill (Tiree), Grianal. 'Green field', from Norse. The English version of the name came via Gaelic and was rationalised to its present form to give 'meaning' in English.

Greenock (Renfrew), Grianaig. This may be 'sunny place', from Gaelic. Given the town's location, a Norse derivation is highly unlikely. An old Gaelic name of the place was *Gónait*.

Greenstone Point (Ross), Rubha na Cloiche Uaine or Rubha na Lice Uaine. 'The point of the green stone or slab.'

Greep (Skye), An Grìob or An Grìpe. 'The cliff', originally from Norse.

Greinem (Harris), Grianam. 'Green islet', from Norse.

Grenicle (Skye), Gréinigil. This Norse name may be 'green ravine'.

Greshornish (Skye), Grisinis. 'Swine headland', from Norse.

Gress (Lewis), Griais. 'Grassy place'.

Greystone (Aberdeen), Dail Iarainn. The English name may be either 'grey stone' or 'Gray's farm', from English. The Gaelic name is 'iron haugh'.

Gribun (Mull), Grìobainn or Bun na Sgrìob. The meaning of the main name is unclear, but the second Gaelic name, used locally, is 'the foot of the scree'. Local people are *eich*, 'horses'.

Grigadale (Argyll), Griogadal. The first part of this Norse valley name is unclear.

Grimersta (Lewis), Grìomarsta. 'Grima's dwelling', from Norse.

Griminish (Benbecula, North Uist), Grìminis. 'Grima's headland', from Norse.

Grimsay, Griomasaigh. 'Grim's island', from Norse.

Grimshader (Lewis), Grimiseadar. 'Grim's township', from Norse.

Grishapool (Coll), Grìseabol. 'Pig farm', from Norse.

Groay (Harris), Gròaigh or Grothaigh. 'Stream island', from Norse.

Grogarry (South Uist), Gròigearraidh. 'Stream meadow', from Norse.

Grosebay (Harris), Greòsabhagh. 'Grass bay', from Norse.

Grotaig (Inverness), Grotaig. It is unclear what this name means. It has the appearance of a gaelicised Norse name and there is evidence of other Norse names in the wider area.

Grudie (Ross), Grùididh. 'Gravel place'.

Gruids (Sutherland), Na Grùidean. 'The gravelly places'.

Gruinard (Ross), Gruinneard or Gruinneart. 'Shallow firth', from Norse. Wester Gruinard is *Gruinneard Shuas*, 'upper Gruinard'. Big Gruinard is *Gruinneard Mhór* and Little Gruinard is *Gruinneard Bheag*. Gruinard Island, nicknamed 'Anthrax Island' following British government experiments in germ warfare there, is *Eilean Ghruinneart*.

Gruinart (Islay), Gruinneart. *See* **Gruinard**.

Grula (Skye), Grùla. This may be 'stony river', from Norse.

Grulin (Eigg), Grùlainn. 'Stony land'.

Gruline (Mull), Grùilinn. 'Stony land'.

Grumbeg (Sutherland), Gnùb Beag or Grùb Beag. 'Small knob-shaped hill'.

Gualachulain (Argyll), Guala Chuilinn. 'Holly ridge'. *See* **Gualin**.

Gualin (Sutherland), A' Ghualainn. 'Ridge'. This generally means 'shoulder' but is used to mean a long ridge.

Guay (Perth). This may mean 'marsh', from *gaoth*.

Guershader (Lewis), Giùirseadar. 'Farm near a chasm', from Norse. *See* **Stornoway**.

Gullane (East Lothian). This may be 'ridge', from *Gualainn*.

Gunna (Coll, Tiree), Gunna or Gunnaigh. 'Gunnar's island', from Norse. Gunna is mentioned in the lines of a song, *Thoir mo shoraidh thar Ghunnaigh gu Muile nam mór bheann*, 'Farewell beyond Gunna to Mull of the great mountains'.

Guridil (Rum), Giùradal. 'Chasm valley', from Norse.

Gylen (Kerrera), Na Goibhlean. 'Forks' or 'forked places'. This name has appeared in a number of spellings, such as *Gaoidhlean, Gaoilean* and *Goibhlean*. It has been used in literature with the definite article. The castle here was known locally as *Dùn Donnchaidh*, 'Duncan's fort'.

Habost (Lewis), Tàbost. 'High farm', from Norse.

Hacklete, Haclait (Benbecula), Tàicleit (Bernera). 'High rock or cliff', from Norse.

Haddo (Aberdeen). 'Half of a davoch', from English. This is an anglicised or half-anglicised equivalent of the more common 'Lettoch'.

Half Davoch (Moray). *See* **Haddo**.

Halistra (Skye), Halastra. 'Township on a slope', from Norse.

Halkirk (Caithness), Hàcraig. 'Haugh church', from English.

Halladale (Sutherland), Healadal. 'Hallowed valley', from Norse.

Hallaig (Raasay), Halaig. This Norse name may be 'high slope bay'.

Hallin (Skye, South Uist), Hàlainn. 'Sloping land', from Norse.

Halmadary (Sutherland), Halmadairigh. This may be Norse 'Hjalmund's sheiling'.

Hamera (Skye), Hamara. 'Hill' or 'rock', from Norse.

Hameraverin (Skye), Hamara Bhoirein. 'Hollow at the hill or rock', from Norse.

Hamersay (Harris), Hamarsaigh. 'Rock island', from Norse.

Hamilton (Lanark), Hamaltan. 'Hamill's town', from English.

Handa (Sutherland), Eilean Shannda. 'Island at the sandy river', from Gaelic/Norse.

Harlaw (Aberdeen), Arla. 'Hard hill', from English. The Battle of Harlaw is *Cath Gairbheach*, 'the battle of Garioch'.

Harlosh (Skye), Heàrrlois. This Norse name appears to refer to a river mouth, but the first element is unclear.

Harrapool (Skye), Harrapol. 'Hari's farm', from Norse.

Harris, (Harris, Islay, Rum), Na Hearadh. 'Division' or 'portion'. In south Harris, the west side is *a' Mhachair*, 'machair land', as opposed to the east side which is *na Bàigh*, 'bays'. The hilly area above the east coast is *Bràigh nam Bàgh*, 'upland of the bays'. A Harris person is a *Hearach* or *Tearach*.

Hartfield (Ross), Coille Mhùiridh. While the English name refers to a field of deer, the Gaelic name is 'the wood at the rampart place'. However, another version of the Gaelic name is *Coille a' Bhùiridh*, 'the wood of bellowing', which might refer to stags, but may be an attempt to give the name 'meaning'. Hartfield is referred to as *Coille Mhùiridh dà thaobh na h-aibhne*, 'Hartfield on both sides of the river'.

Hasker (North Uist), Haisgeir. 'Ocean rock', from Norse.

Haugh (Inverness), An Talchan. The Gaelic form is a gaelicisation of English 'haugh' with a diminutive ending.

Haun (Eriskay), Na Hann. 'Harbour', from Norse.

Haunn (Mull), Na Hann. *See* **Haun**.

Hayfield (Perth), Gallanach. 'Place of the standing stone' or 'place of colts-foot'.

Heanish (Tiree), Hianais. 'Outlying headland', from Norse.

Heaste (Skye), Heasta. 'Horse farm', from Norse. Local people are nicknamed *mèirlich*, 'thieves'.

Heatherfield (Skye), An Torran Uaine. The Gaelic name is 'the small green hillock'.

Heathfield (Ross), Cail Fhraochaidh. The Gaelic name is 'meadow at the heathery place'.

Hebrides, Innse Gall. The English name is unclear but stems from a misreading of 'Hebudes', itself from

'Ebudae'. The Gaelic name is 'islands of the non-Gaels', referring to the island's once Norse population. The Outer Hebrides are *na h-Eileanan a-Muigh* and the Inner Hebrides *na h-Eileanan a-Staigh*. A Gaelic equivalent of 'carry coals to Newcastle' is *Eich a thoirt a dh'Innse Gall*, 'take horses to the Hebrides'.

Heights of Brae (Ross), Am Bràigh. The Gaelic name is 'the upper part', which often appears as 'brae' in English, despite meaning something different.

Heights of Dochcarty (Ross), Bràigh Dabhach Gartaidh. The Gaelic name is 'the upper part of Dochcarty'.

Heights of Inchvannie (Ross), Bràigh Innis Mheannaidh. The Gaelic name is 'the upper part of Inchvannie'.

Heights of Kinlochewe (Ross), Bràigh Cheann Loch Iùbh. The Gaelic name is 'the upper part of Kinlochewe'.

Heisker (North Uist), Heillsgeir. 'Flat rock', from Norse.

Helensburgh (Dunbarton), Baile Eilidh. Before the construction of the planned town, named after the founder's wife, this was known as Malig, Milrigs and Mulig. The planned town itself was first known simply as 'New Town'.

Hell's Glen (Argyll), Gleann Iarainn or An Gleann Beag. The first Gaelic name is 'iron glen', which led to the English form, because *iarann*, 'iron', sounds like *ifrinn*, 'hell'. The second Gaelic name is 'the small glen'.

Helmsdale (Sutherland), Bun Ilidh. The English name is 'Helm's valley', from Norse. The Gaelic name is 'the mouth of the Ilidh', the Gaelic name of the Helmsdale River. The Strath of Kildonan is *Srath Ilidh* in Gaelic, named again after the river. A person from Helmsdale and district is an *Ileach* as opposed to an *Ìleach* who is someone from Islay, Glen Isla or Strath Isla.

Herbusta (Skye), Hearbusta or Tearbusta. 'Lord's farm', from Norse.

Heribost (Skye), Heireabost. *See* **Herbusta**.

Herishader (Skye), Heiriseadar. 'Lord's place', from Norse.

Hermetray (Harris), Hearmatraigh. 'Hermund's island', from Norse.

Heylipol (Tiree), An Cruairtean or An Cruadh Ghoirtean. The English name is 'flat farm' or 'holy farm', from Norse. The first Gaelic name is an abbreviation of the second, meaning 'hard field'. Heylipol church is *Eaglais na Mòintich*, 'Moss church', named after a neighbouring township.

Hielum (Sutherland), Huilleum. This may be 'hound holm', from Norse.

High Borve (Lewis), Am Baile Àrd. The Gaelic name is 'the high township', its full name being *Baile Àrd Bhuirgh*, 'high township of Borve'.

High Corrie (Arran), An Coire Àrd. 'The high corrie'. North High Corrie is *Guala Bàn*, 'white shoulder'.

Highfield (Ross), Ciarnaig. The 'high field' referred to in English is absent from the Gaelic which is unclear in meaning, but may contain an element meaning 'dark'.

Highlands, A' Ghàidhealtachd. The Gaelic name for the 'high lands' is 'Gaeldom', meaning the area occupied by indigenous Gaelic speakers. These terms are accurately speaking not co-terminous, but the usage is established. Gaelic uses *air a' Ghàidh-ealtachd* for 'in the Highlands'.

Hill of Fearn (Ross), Baile an Droma. The Gaelic name is 'the township on the ridge'.

Hilton of Cadboll (Ross), Baile a' Chnuic. The Gaelic name is 'the township on the hill'. Because of local people's connection to the fishing industry, they were known as *dubhain*, 'hooks'.

Hoebeg (North Uist), Na Hogha

Bheag. 'The small rocky mound', from Norse/Gaelic.

Hogharry (North Uist), Hòigearraidh. 'Field at a rocky mound', from Norse.

Holm (Inverness), An Tuilm; (Lewis), Tolm. The Inverness name refers to a river meadow, from English, while the Lewis name is 'islet', from Norse. Facing the Lewis village of Holm are the rocks known as *Biastan Thuilm*, 'Beasts of Holm', on which the Iolaire troopship sank after World War I.

Holmisdale (Skye), Holmasdal. 'Holm valley', from Norse.

Holoman (Raasay), Holman. 'Small islet', from Norse but apparently with a Gaelic diminutive.

Holy Island (Arran), An t-Eilean Àrd or Eilean Mo Laise. This 'holy island' is 'the high island' or 'Laisren's island' in Gaelic.

Home Farm (Arran). *See* **Mossend**.

Hope (Sutherland), Hòb. 'Bay', from Norse.

Hopeman (Moray), Hudaman. This name may incorporate Norse 'bay'.

Horgabost (Harris), Torgabost. 'Farm at the worship place', from Norse.

Horisary (North Uist), Hórasaraidh. 'Grave sheiling', from Norse.

Horneval (Skye), Hornabhal. 'Horn mountain', from Norse.

Horsaclete (Harris), Horsacleit. 'Horse cliff', from Norse.

Horse Island (Ross), Eilean nan Each. 'The island of the horses'.

Horve (Barra), Na Horgh. 'Cairn', from Norse.

Hosta (North Uist), Hòmhsta. 'Hogni's dwelling', from Norse.

Hough (Tiree), Hogh. 'Rocky mound', from Norse. A local term for a detour is *Rathad Hogh do Haoidhnis*, 'via Hough to Hynish'.

Houston (Renfrew). 'Hugh's town'. This was formerly known as Kilpeter, from Gaelic *Cill Pheadair*, 'St Peter's church'.

Howbeg (South Uist), Togh Beag.

'Small rocky mound', from Norse/Gaelic.

Howe of Alford (Aberdeen), Lagan Athfuirt. 'Hollow of Alford'.

Howe of the Mearns (Kincardine), Lag na Maoirne. 'The hollow of the steward's territory'.

Howmore (South Uist), Togh Mór. 'Large rocky mound', from Norse.

Hughstown (Ross), Cnocan Cruaidh. 'Hugh's town', from English. The Gaelic name is 'hard hillock'.

Humberstone (Ross), Cill Duinn Uachdrach. The English name which is that of a family of landowners replaced the older Gaelic name of 'upper Kildun'. *See* **Kildun**.

Hungladder (Skye), Hùnagladair. The first part of this Norse name may come from a personal name based on *húna*, 'bear cub'. The second element in the name is unclear but may be a plural form. The related name *Ru Hunish/Rubha Hùinis* is nearby.

Hunter's Quay (Argyll), Camas Rainich. The older English form was Camusronich, from the Gaelic name which means 'bracken bay'.

Huntly (Aberdeen), Hunndaidh or Srath Bhalgaidh. The English name was imported from England, and the first Gaelic name is an adaption of it. The second Gaelic name is the same as that of the surrounding area of Strathbogie. Huntly Market was *Féill Srath Bhalgaidh*.

Husabost (Skye), Hùsabost. 'House farm', from Norse.

Hushinish (Harris), Hùisinis. 'House headland', from Norse.

Hynish (Tiree), Haoidhnis. 'High headland', from Norse. West Hynish is *na Cùiltean*, 'secluded spots', the full name being *Cùiltean Haoidhnis* or *Cùiltean Bhaile a' Phuill*, 'secluded spots of Hynish' and the same 'of Balephuil'.

Hysbackie (Sutherland), Heillsbacaidh. 'Flat bank' or 'cave bank', from Norse.

Ibert (Perth, Stirling). 'Offering', relating to church lands, from *Ìobairt*.

Ichrachen (Argyll), Ìochdrachann. 'Bottom or lower place'.

Idrigill (Skye), Ìdrigil. 'Outer ravine', from Norse.

Imachar (Arran), An Iomachar or An t-Iomachar. Folk etymology has it that this is *iomadh char* (many turns) and refers to rowing. However this probably refers to ploughed land. Local people were nicknamed *faoileagan*, 'seagulls'.

Immeroin (Perth), Iomaire Eóghainn. 'Ewen's rigg'.

Inaltrie (Moray). 'Pasture land', from Gaelic *Ionaltraidh*.

Inch (Midlothian). 'Meadow', from Gaelic *innis* which can also mean 'island'.

Inchadnie (Perth), Innis Chailtnidh. 'Meadow at the hard water'.

Inchaffray (Perth), Innis Aifrinn. 'Meadow of the offering'.

Incharvie (Fife). 'Meadow at the boundary wall', from *Innis na h-Airbhe*.

Inchbae (Ross), Innis Beithe. 'Birch meadow'.

Inchbare (Angus). This may be 'St Barr's meadow', from Gaelic *Innis Bharra*.

Inchbelly (Dunbarton). 'Broom meadow', from *Innis Bealaidh*.

Inchberry (Inverness), Innis a' Bhàiridh; (Moray). The Inverness name is 'the hurling meadow', while the Moray name is possibly 'St Bearach's meadow', from *Innis Bhearaigh*.

Inchcailoch (Stirling), Innis Cailleach. 'Nuns' island', showing the old form of the genitive plural.

Inchcolm (Fife). 'St Columba's island', from *Innis Choluim*.

Incheril (Ross), Innis a' Choiril. The defining element of this meadow name is unclear, but may be the name of the saint commemorated in the church at **Roybridge**.

Inchgall (Fife). 'Island of non-Gaels', from *Innis Gall*, which would be *Innis Ghall* in modern Gaelic.

Inchgarvie (West Lothian). 'The island of the rough place' or 'Garbhach's island', from *Innis Gharbhaidh*.

Inchgowan (Ross), Innis a' Ghobhann. 'The smith's meadow'.

Inchgrundle (Angus). This is probably 'meadow of the low haugh', from *Innis Ghrunndail*.

Inchina (Ross), Innis an Àtha. 'The meadow by the ford'.

Inchinnan (Renfrew). 'St Finan's meadow', from *Innis Fhionain*.

Inchkeith (Fife). Possibly 'the island of the wood', from Gaelic *innis* and Brythonic *coed*, giving *Innis Chéith*.

Inchkenneth (Mull), Innis Choinnich. 'St Cainneach's island'.

Inchkinloch (Sutherland), Innis Ceann Loch. 'The meadow at the head of the loch'.

Inchlaggan (Inverness), Innis an Lagain. 'The meadow of Laggan'.

Inchlumpie (Ross), Innis Lombaidh. 'The meadow at the bare place'.

Inchmahome (Perth), Innis Mo Cholmaig. 'St Colman's island' in the Lake of Menteith which is in Gaelic *Loch Innis Mo Cholmaig*.

Inchmarnoch (Aberdeen), Innis Mhearnaig. 'St Ernoc's or M' Ernoc's meadow'.

Inchmarnock (Bute). *See* **Inchmarnoch**.

Inchmartin (Perth). 'Martin's meadow', from *Innis Mhàrtainn*, possibly commemorating St Martin.

Inchmichael (Perth). 'Michael's meadow', from *Innis Mhìcheil*, possibly commemorating St Michael.

Inchnadamph (Sutherland), Innis nan Damh. 'The meadow of the stags'.

Inchnairn (Ross), Innis an Fheàrna. 'The meadow of the alder tree'.

Inchnavie (Ross), Innis Neimhidh. 'The meadow at the sacred lands'.

Inchree (Inverness), Innis an Ruighe.

'The meadow at the slope'.

Inchrory (Banff), Innis Ruairidh. 'Roderick's meadow'.

Inchture (Perth). 'The meadow on north-facing land', from *Innis Tuathair*.

Inchtuthil (Perth). 'Tuathal's meadow', from *Innis Thuathail*.

Inchvannie (Ross), Innis Mheannaidh. 'The meadow at the kids' place'. Heights of Inchvannie is *Bràigh Innis Mheannaidh*.

Inglesmaldie (Kincardine). 'St Màilidh's church', from *Eaglais Mhàilidh*, as seen in an older anglicised form, Eglismaldie. *See* **Dalmally** and **Kilmallie**.

Inishail (Argyll), Innis Fhàil. The name of this island can have two meanings. *Fàl* can refer to a dyke or earth wall construction but also mean 'destiny' as in *Lia Fàil*, the Gaelic name of the Stone of Destiny.

Inishglass (Ross), An Innis Ghlas. 'The grey-green meadow'.

Innercochill (Perth), Inbhir Cochaill or Inbhir Chochall. This is the name of a river mouth, but it is unclear what the name of the river means.

Innergeldie (Perth), Inbhir Gheallaidh. 'The mouth of the bright river'. This is similar to 'Abergeldie' except that the latter contains the Brythonic *aber* rather than Gaelic *inbhir*.

Innergellie (Fife). *See* **Innergeldie**.

Innerhadden (Perth), Inbhir Chadain. 'The mouth of the Caddon', which is 'warlike river'.

Innerleithen (Peebles). 'The mouth of the Leithen'.

Innermessan (Wigtown). 'The mouth of the fruit river', from *Inbhir Mheasain*.

Innerourie (Banff). This may be 'mouth of the river', with the Gaelic element *dobhar*, 'water'.

Innerpeffray (Peebles), Inbhir Pheafraidh. 'The mouth of the bright river', related to the river name in

the Gaelic names of Dingwall and Strathpeffer.

Innisabhaird (Ross), Innis a' Bhàird. 'The poet's meadow'. However, *bàrd* is also found as 'field' in Ross, and it may be the case that *innis* was added after *bàrd* had gone out of popular use to mean 'field'.

Innis a'Chro (Ross), Innis a' Chrò. 'The meadow at the enclosure', referred to in the song about *Crò Chinn Tàile*.

Innisbhuidhe (Ross), An Innis Bhuidhe. 'The yellow meadow'.

Insch (Aberdeen), Innis Mo Bheathain. 'St Bean's meadow'.

Insh (Inverness), Am Baile Ùr. The Gaelic name is 'the new village' and is a short form of *Baile Ùr Sgìre Innis*, 'the new village of Insh district', 'Insh' itself meaning 'meadow'.

Inshes (Inverness), Na h-Innseagan. 'The little meadows'.

Insh Island (Luing), An Innis. This is 'the island' with English 'island' added.

Inshore (Sutherland), Innse Odhar. This appears to mean 'dun-coloured meadows'.

Inver (several), An t-Inbhir. 'The river mouth'. The full name of Inver in Aberdeen is *Inbhir Àrdair*, 'the mouth of the Arder'; in Easter Ross it is *Inbhir Loch Slinn*, 'the river mouth at Loch Slin', and in Wester Ross it is *Inbhir Earradail*, 'the river mouth at Erradale'.

Inverailort (Inverness), Inbhir Ailleart. 'The river mouth at Loch Ailort'. The old Gaelic name for this place was *Cinn a' Chreagain*, 'the end of the little rock'.

Inveraldie (Angus). 'The river mouth at the rocky place', from Gaelic *Inbhir Alltaidh*.

Inveralivaig (Skye), Inbhir Àlabhaig. A Gaelic/Norse name containing 'river mouth' and either 'eel bay' or 'deep river bay'.

Inverallan (Banff), Inbhir Ailein. This looks like 'Alan's river mouth', but is a corruption, possibly of *Inbhir Alain*, 'mouth of the Allan', as suggested by older forms.

Inveralligin (Ross), Inbhir Àiliginn. 'The mouth of the Alligin stream'. This is also known in English as Easter Alligin.

Inverallochy (Aberdeen). 'The river mouth at the rocky place', from *Inbhir Aileachaidh*.

Inveralmond (Perth), Inbhir Amain. 'The mouth of the Almond'.

Inveran (Ross, Sutherland), Inbhirean. 'Small river mouth'.

Inveraray (Argyll), Inbhir Aora. 'The mouth of the Aray'.

Inverardran (Perth), Inbhir Àrdrain. 'The mouth of the high water'.

Inverarish (Raasay), Inbhir Àrais. 'River mouth', containing both the Gaelic and Norse elements for the same feature.

Inverarity (Angus). 'Mouth of the slow river', from *Inbhir Aradaidh*.

Inverarnan (Dunbarton), Inbhir Àirnein. The meaning of the second element is unclear although it might refer to some kidney-shaped topographical feature.

Inverasdale (Ross), Inbhir Àsdail. 'The river mouth in the aspen valley', from Gaelic and Norse. Brae of Inverasdale is *Bràigh Inbhir Àsdail*, 'the upper part of Inverasdale'. Coast of Inverasdale is *Eirtheaire Inbhir Àsdail*.

Inveraven (Banff), Inbhir Athfhinn. 'The mouth of the very bright river'.

Inveravon (West Lothian). 'The mouth of the river', with the Celtic element for a river found as *abhainn* in Gaelic and Irish and as *afon* in Welsh.

Inverbeg (Dunbarton), An t-Inbhir Beag. 'The small river mouth'.

Inverbervie (Kincardine), Inbhir Biorbhaigh. 'The mouth of the boiling river'. The old name of Haberberui shows how Gaelic *inbhir* replaced Brythonic *aber* in some instances.

Inverboyndie (Banff). 'The mouth of the eternal river'. *See* **Boyndie**.

Inverbreakie (Ross), Inbhir Breacaidh. 'The river mouth at the speckled place'. *See* **Invergordon**.

Inverbroom (Ross), Baile an Lòin. The English form refers to Loch Broom, while the Gaelic one is 'farm at the wet meadow'. Inverbroom House, also called Foy Lodge, is *Taigh na Fothaidh*, 'house with the lawn'.

Inverbrough (Inverness), Inbhir Bruachaig. 'The river mouth at the small bank'.

Invercarnaig (Ross), Inbhir Cheatharnaig. 'The mouth of the little warrior river'.

Invercassley (Sutherland), Inbhir Charsla. 'The mouth of the castle place river'.

Invercauld (Aberdeen), Inbhir Call or Inbhir Callaidh. 'Hazel estuary'. The Laird of Invercauld was *Tighearn Inbhir Call*.

Inverchaolain (Argyll), Inbhir Chaolain. 'The mouth of the narrow stream'.

Invercharron (Ross), Inbhir Charrann. 'The mouth of the Carron', which is 'rough water'.

Inverchoran (Ross), Inbhir Chòmhrainn. 'The mouth of the Coran', which is 'high oozing stream'.

Inverchroskie (Perth), Inbhir Chrosgaidh. 'The river mouth at the crossing place'.

Inverclyde (Renfrew), Inbhir Chluaidh. 'The mouth of the Clyde'.

Invercoe (Argyll), Inbhir Comhan. 'The mouth of the Coe'.

Inverdruie (Inverness), Inbhir Dhrùidh. 'The mouth of the Druie'.

Inverebrie (Aberdeen). 'The river mouth at the marshy place', from *Inbhir Eabraigh*.

Inveredrie (Perth), Inbhir Eadrain. 'The mouth of the between-river'.

Invereen (Inverness), Inbhir Fhinn. 'The mouth of the fair river'.

Inverenzie (Banff), Inbhir Fhionnaidh. 'The river mouth at the fair place'.

Invereshie (Inverness), Inbhir Fhéisidh. 'The mouth of the river in the boggy haugh'.

Inveresk (Midlothian). 'The mouth of the river', from *Inbhir Easg*, containing the Brythonic water element *esk*.

Inveresragan (Argyll), Inbhir Easragain. 'The mouth of the Esragan'.

Inverewe (Ross), Inbhir Iubh. 'The mouth of the yew river'. Inverewe House is *Taigh na Plucaird*, 'house at the lump promontory', often over-corrected to *Taigh nam Pluc Àrd*, 'house of the high lumps'.

Inverey (Aberdeen), Inbhir Eidh. 'The mouth of the Ey'. Local people distinguished between *Inbhir Eidh Bheag* and *Inbhir Eidh Mhór* (little and big Inverey).

Inverfarigaig (Inverness), Inbhir Fairgeag or Inbhir Farragaig. 'Mouth of the Farigaig', a river name connected with *fairge*, 'ocean'. Nearby Stratherrick (*Srath Fharragaig*) is named after the same river.

Invergarry (Inverness), Inbhir Garadh. 'The mouth of the Garry'.

Invergelder (Aberdeen), Inbhir Ghealdair. 'The mouth of the white water'.

Invergloy (Inverness), Inbhir Ghlaoidh. 'The mouth of the gluey or viscous river'.

Invergordon (Ross), An Rubha or Inbhir Ghòrdain. 'Point' or 'Gordon's river mouth', named after Sir Alexander Gordon. In Gaelic, 'in Invergordon' is expressed by *air an Rubha*, 'on the point'. An older name was *Rubha Nach Breacaidh*, 'the point on the high speckled moor'. Invergordon ferry left from *Port Nach Breacaidh*, 'the port of the high speckled place', an abbreviation of *Port Aonach Breacaidh*.

Invergowrie (Perth), Inbhir Ghobharaidh. 'The river mouth of Gowrie'.

Invergroin (Dunbarton), Inbhir Dhroighinn. 'The mouth of the thorny river'.

Inverguseran (Inverness), Inbhir Ghùiseirein. The defining element in this river name is unclear.

Inverhaggernie (Perth), Inbhir Chagarnaidh. 'The mouth of the whispering river'.

Inverherive (Perth), Inbhir Thairbh. 'The mouth of the bull stream'.

Inverhope (Sutherland), Inbhir Hòb. 'The river mouth at the bay', from Gaelic/Norse.

Inverie (Fife); (Inverness), Inbhir Aoidh. In Fife this is 'estuary place', from *Inbhiridh*, earlier *Inbhirin*. In Inverness-shire, this may be 'the river mouth at the isthmus', from Gaelic/Norse.

Inverinate (Ross), Inbhir Ìonaid. 'The mouth of the brown river', from the earlier *Inbhir Dhuinnid*. The surrounding area is known as *Leitir Choill*, 'hazel slope'.

Inverinian (Perth), Inbhir Inneoin. 'The mouth of the anvil stream', which is known as *Allt Inneoin*.

Inverkeillor (Angus), Inbhir Chìolair. The meaning of the second element is unclear.

Inverkeithing (Fife), Inbhir Chéitinn. This may be 'the mouth of the wood river', with the second element based on Brythonic *coed*, 'a wood'.

Inverkeithney (Banff). This may be similar to **Inverkeithing**, or alternatively contain the element *Cé* referring to a Pictish district or tribe.

Inverkip (Renfrew). 'The river mouth at the stump', containing Gaelic *ceap*.

Inverkirkaig (Sutherland), Inbhir Chirceig. 'The river mouth at church bay', from Gaelic/Norse.

Inverlael (Ross), Inbhir Lathail. 'The river mouth in the low hollow', from Gaelic/Norse.

Inverlaidnon (Inverness), Inbhir Laidirean. The defining element in this name is unclear.

Inverleith (Midlothian), Inbhir Lìte. 'The mouth of the Leith', a name from Brythonic denoting wetness.

Inverlochlarig (Perth), Inbhir Lòch Làirig. 'The river mouth at the dark pass'.

Inverlochy (Inverness), Inbhir Lòchaidh. 'The mouth of the Lochy'.

Inverlussa (Argyll, Jura), Inbhir Lusa. 'The mouth of the bright river', from Gaelic/Norse.

Invermark (Argyll). 'The mouth of the horse river', containing Gaelic *marc*.

Invermarkie (Aberdeen), Inbhir Mharcaidh. 'The mouth of the horse river'.

Invermoriston (Inverness), Inbhir Moireasdan. 'The mouth of the Moriston', which is often taken to mean 'great water' but does not.

Invermuick (Aberdeen), Inbhir Muice. 'The mouth of the pig stream'.

Invernahyle (Inverness), Inbhir na h-Aidhle. 'The river mouth at the adze', referring to the shape of a piece of land.

Invernauld (Sutherland), Inbhir nan Allt. 'The mouth of the streams'.

Invernaver (Sutherland), Inbhir Nabhair. 'The mouth of the Naver'.

Inverneill (Argyll), Inbhir Néill. This appears to mean 'Neil's river mouth'.

Invernenty (Perth), Inbhir Leanntaidh. 'The mouth of the nettle river'.

Inverness, Inbhir Nis. 'The mouth of the Ness'. Inverness-shire is *Siorrachd Inbhir Nis* and the western part is *na Garbh-Chrìochan*, 'rough bounds', in full *Garbh-Chrìochan Chloinn Raghnaill*, 'rough bounds of Clanranald'.

Inveroran (Argyll), Inbhir Dhobhrain. 'The mouth of the little water'.

Inverpeffer (Angus). 'The mouth of the bright river', from *Inbhir Pheofh-air*. *See* **Strathpeffer** and **Dingwall**.

Inverpolly (Sutherland), Inbhir Pollaidh. 'The mouth of the Polly'.

Inverquharity (Angus). This may

mean 'twin river mouth' and contain *càraid*, 'twin' or 'couple'.

Inverroy (Inverness), Inbhir Ruaidh. 'The mouth of the red-brown river'.

Inversanda (Argyll), Inbhir Shannda. 'Mouth of the sand river', from Gaelic/Norse.

Inversheil (Ross), Inbhir Sheile. 'The mouth of the Sheil'.

Invershin (Sutherland), Inbhir Sin. 'The mouth of the old river'. Locally this was also known as *Inbhir Sìn* and *Port na Lic*, 'port at the flagstone'.

Inversnaid (Stirling), Inbhir Snàthaid. 'The mouth of the needle stream', which is known as *Allt na Snàthaid*.

Invertote (Skye), Inbhir Thobhta. This hybrid Gaelic/Norse name is 'the river mouth at the house site'.

Inverugie (Aberdeen), Inbhir Ùigidh. 'The mouth of the Ugie'. *Inbhir Ùigidh* is the name of Peterhead in eastern Gaelic dialects.

Inveruglas (Dunbarton), Inbhir Dhùghlais. 'Mouth of the Douglas (black stream).

Inverurie (Aberdeen), Inbhir Uaraidh. This may be 'the mouth of the landslip river' if the name is related to that of Strathrory.

Invervack (Perth), Inbhir a' Bhac. It is unclear what the second part means.

Invervar (Perth), Inbhir Bharra. This may mean 'the mouth of the top river'.

Inverveigh (Argyll), Inbhir Bheithe. 'The mouth of the birch stream'.

Inverwick (Inverness), Inbhir Bhuic (Perth), Inbhir Mhuice. The Inverness name is 'the mouth of the buck river' while in Perth it is 'the mouth of the pig river'.

Invery (Kincardine). This is 'estuary place' from *Inbhiridh*, earlier *Inbhirin*.

Iochdar (South Uist), An t-Ìochdar. 'The bottom'. The English name is still occasionally spelled as 'Eochar'.

Iona, Ì, Ì Chaluim Chille or Eilean Idhe. The English name comes from a misreading of *Ioua* which may be 'yew island'. The Gaelic name *Ì* is generally lengthened to avoid confusion to *Ì Chaluim Chille*, 'St Columba's Iona', or *Eilean Idhe*, 'the isle of Iona'. A native of Iona is an *Idheach*, and the island was known as *Ì nam ban bòidheach*, 'Iona of the beautiful women'.

Irongath (West Lothian). 'Portion of the marsh land', from *Earrann Gaoithe*.

Isay (Skye), Ìosaigh. 'Ice island', from Norse.

Islandfinnan (Argyll), Eilean Fhìonain. 'St Finan's island'.

Islay, Ìle. If this is a Gaelic name it may be 'flank shaped'. Islay is known as *Eilean uaine Ìle*, 'green isle of Islay', and has a number of distinct areas. The Rinns of Islay are *Roinn Ìle*, *na Roinn Ìleach* and *na Ranna*, all of which refer to a division. A person from the Rinns is a *Rannach*. The north-east of the island is *Na Hearadh*, which is another word for 'division' also found in 'Harris', while the south-west peninsula of Oa is *an Obha*, 'headland', where the local people were nicknamed *cuthagan*, 'cuckoos'. A native of Islay is an *Ìleach*, a name shared with the people of Glen Isla and Strath Isla. A number of sayings and expressions concern Islay. *Nuair a thréigeas na dùthchasaich Ìle, beannachd le sìth Albainn*, 'When the natives leave Islay, farewell to the peace of Scotland', is a fairly ominous warning. Less ominous is *Muileach is Ìleach is deamhan, An triùir as miosa air an domhain. Is miosa am Muileach na an t-Ìleach, Is miosa an t-Ìleach na an deamhan*, 'A Mull person, an Islay person and the devil, The three worst in the world. The Mull one is worse than the Islay one, The Islay one is worse than the devil'. This is contradicted by *Nam b' eileanach mi, gum b' Ìleach mi, nam b' Ìleach mi, bu*

Rannach mi, 'If I were an islander, I'd want to be from Islay; if I were from Islay, I'd want to be from the Rinns'. Islay's place-names are mentioned in a saying which includes the line, *Tha ceithir busaichean fichead an Ìle*, 'There are twenty-four *buses* in Islay', which shows how Norse names from *bólstaðr*, which when gaelicised usually become *-bost*, end in *-bus* in Islay.

Isle Martin (Ross), Eilean Mhàrtainn. 'Martin's island'.

Isle of Whithorn (Wigtown), Port Rosnait. The Gaelic name is 'port at the small promontory'. *See* **Whithorn**.

Isleornsay (Skye), Eilean Iarmain. The alternative version of the name of the village, *Eilean Dhiarmaid*, 'Diarmid's island', was commonly heard in Skye. The nearby island with the same name in English is *Eilean Orasaigh*, the second element from Norse meaning 'tidal island'. Local people were known by the nickname *eireagan*, 'pullets'.

Isle Ristol (Ross), Eilean Ruisteil. 'Island with the horse valley', from Gaelic/Norse.

Islivig (Lewis), Ìslibhig. 'Ice slope bay', from Norse.

Jamestown (Dumfries, Dunbarton, Ross). Jamestown in Ross in *Baile Sheumais* or *Baile Shiamais*, 'James's village', the latter spelling showing the distinctive local pronunciation.

John O'Groats (Caithness), Taigh Iain Ghròt. 'Jan de Groot's house', in memory of the Dutch merchant who built the first house here. A couple of rather derogatory Gaelic sayings relate to John O'Groats, *Taigh Iain Ghròt ort!*, 'John O'Groats to you' and *Cuiridh mi a Thaigh Iain Ghròt thu!*, 'I'll send you to John O'Groats'.

Jordanhill (Glasgow), Cnoc Iòrdain. A biblical reference.

Jura, Diùra. 'Deer island', from Norse. The island's byname is *An t-Eilean*

Bàn, 'the blessed island', wherein *bàn* has had its usual meaning of 'fair' or 'white' extended . A local person is a *Diùrach* but would also have been known by the nickname *each*, 'horse'.

Kallin (Grimsay), Na Ceallan. 'The cells', as inhabitanted by hermits.

Kames (Argyll), Camas nam Muclach. 'The bay of the pig places'.

Katewell (Ross), Ciadail. 'Cattle fold valley', from Norse.

Keanculish (Ross), Ceann a' Chaolais. 'The head of the strait'.

Kearstay (Harris), Cearstaigh. 'Hart island', from Norse.

Kebbock Head (Lewis), A' Chàbag. 'The kebbuck (of cheese)'. This may refer to the headland's shape.

Keil (Argyll), A' Chill. 'The cell' or 'the church'.

Keill (Muck), A' Chill. *See* **Keil**.

Keills (Argyll), Cill Mhic Ó Carmaig; (Islay), A' Chill. The Argyll name is 'cell or church of the son of O'Cormack', while the Islay name is 'the cell or church'.

Keiloch (Aberdeen), An Caolach. 'The narrow place'.

Keils (Argyll, Jura), A' Chill. 'The cell', with an English plural attached.

Keir (Dumfries, Stirling). 'Fort'. In Dumfries this probably comes from Brythonic, while in Stirling it may be either Brythonic or Gaelic *cathair*.

Keiss (Caithess), Céis. This Norse name may indicate either a rounded ridge or promontory.

Keistle (Skye), Ceasdail or Ciosdal. This Norse name may mean 'low valley'.

Keith (Banff), Baile Chéith. This seems to be from Brythonic *coed*, 'wood', but a local Pictish territorial division was *Cé*, and the name may be related to this. The Gaelic name is prefixed by *baile*, 'town'. The town used to be known as Kethmalruf (*Céith Maol Rubha)*, 'St Maol Rubha's

Keith', this saint's name later becoming confused with that of St Rufus.

Keithick (Perth). 'Small wood', based on Brythonic *coed* with a Gaelic diminutive ending, suggesting *Céitheag*.

Keithmore (Banff), Céith Mhór. 'Large wood', with Brythonic *coed*.

Keithock (Angus). *See* **Keithick**.

Kellas (Angus, Moray), Ceallas. 'Church place'.

Kelso (Roxburgh), Cealsaidh or Cealso. 'Chalk heugh', from English.

Keltneyburn (Perth), Allt Chailtnidh. 'Stream of the hard river'.

Kelty (Fife); (Perth), Cailtidh. In Perth, 'hard place', from the element found in river names such as *Caladar* and 'Calder'. The Fife name may be the same.

Kenary (Grimsay), Ceann Àirigh. 'Sheiling end'.

Kendibig (Harris), Ceann Dìbig. 'Head of the deep bay', from Gaelic/ Norse.

Kendram (Skye), Ceann Droma. 'Ridge end'.

Kendrum (Perth), Ceanndruim. 'Head ridge'.

Kenknock (Perth), Ceannchnoc. 'Head hill'.

Kenmore (Argyll, Ross), A' Cheann-mhor; (Perth), An Ceannmhor. 'Big headed place'. In Ross, people from Kenmore are known as *ceann-phollain*, 'tadpoles'.

Kennacraig (Argyll), Ceann na Creige. 'The end of the rock'.

Kennacreggan (Inverness), Ceann nan Creagan. 'The end of the rocks'.

Kennoway (Fife). Old forms of the name such as Kennochin and Kennoquhy suggest a Gaelic origin from *ceann*, 'end' or 'head', and while the latter part of the name is unclear, it may be related to 'Kenknock' and the old Gaelic name of Brig O'Turk.

Kenovay (Scalpay, Tiree), Ceann a' Bhàigh. 'The head of the bay'.

Kensaleyre (Skye), Ceann Sàil Eighre. 'The head of the inlet at the beach', from Gaelic/Norse.

Kensalroag (Skye), Ceann Sàil Ròdhag or Ceann an t-Sàile. 'The head of Roag inlet'. Gaelic also has the shorter name, 'the head of the inlet'.

Kentallen (Argyll), Ceann an t-Sàilein. 'The head of the small inlet'.

Kentangaval (Barra), Ceann Tangabhail. 'Head of the hill at the sharp point', from Gaelic/Norse.

Kentra (Argyll, Ross), Ceann Tràgha. 'Beach end'.

Kentulavaig (Lewis), Ceann Tùlabhaig or Ceann Thùlabhaig. 'The head of the rocky bay', from Gaelic/Norse.

Kenvar (Tiree), Ceann a' Bhara. 'The head of the cliff', from Gaelic/Norse.

Keoldale (Sutherland), Cealldail. This may be 'keel valley', from Norse.

Keose (Lewis), Ceòs. 'Hollow', from Norse. Keose Glebe is *Glìb Cheòis*.

Keppanach (Inverness), Ceapanach. 'Arable land'.

Keppoch (Inverness, Ross), A' Cheapach. 'The tillage land'. Back of Keppoch is *Cùl na Ceapaich*. Keppoch Muir is *an Sliabh Ceapanach*, 'the moor of the tillage land'.

Kernsary (Ross), Cearnasair. 'Shieling on good land', from Norse.

Kerrera, Cearrara. 'Copse island', from Norse. A Kerrera person is a *Cearrarach*, also nicknamed an *eireag*, 'pullet', and a saying about Kerrera people is, *Tha trì casan deiridh air na h-eireagan an Cearrara*, ('The pullets in Kerrera have three back legs').

Kerrowdown (Inverness), An Ceathramh Donn. 'The brown quarter-land'.

Kerrowgair (Inverness), An Ceathramh Geàrr. 'The short quarter-land'.

Kerry (Argyll), An Ceathramh Comhalach; (Ross), Cearraidh. In Argyll the name means 'the Cowal quarter-land', an inhabitant of which is known as a *Ceathrach*. This word

also appears in *An Caol Ceathrach*, 'the Kerry strait' or West Kyle of Bute. In Ross, the name may be 'copse river', from Norse.

Kerrycroy (Bute), An Ceathramh Cruaidh. 'The hard quarterland'.

Kerrysdale (Ross), A' Chathair Bheag. This may be 'copse valley', from Norse, while the Gaelic name is 'the little fort'.

Kersavagh (North Uist), Cearsabhagh. This may be 'copse bay', from Norse.

Kershader (Lewis), Ceairseadar. 'Copse dwelling' or 'deer farm', from Norse.

Kessock (Inverness), Ceasag. This is named after the saint associated with the Lennox area. *See* **North Kessock** and **South Kessock**.

Kettle (Fife). 'Cat place', from *Catail*.

Khantore (Aberdeen), Ceann Tòrr. 'Hill end'.

Kiel (Argyll), A' Chill. 'The cell' or 'church'.

Kilanallen (Mull), Cill an Àilein. 'The church in the meadow'.

Kilarrow (Islay), Cill A Rubha. 'St Maol Rubha's church'. The *A* in the Gaelic name is not a definite article but a contraction of *Maol*.

Kilaulay (South Uist), Cill Amhlaigh. 'Amhlaigh's church'. There is no Gaelic saint of this name recorded, so the name may be an old dedication to a Norse Olaf, of which *Amhlaigh* is a gaelicisation.

Kilbarchan (Renfrew). 'St Bearchan's church', from *Cill Bhearchain*.

Kilberry (Argyll), Cill Bheiridh or Cill Bhearaigh. 'St Bearach's church'.

Kilbirnie (Ayr). 'St Brendan's church', from *Cill Bhreannain*. St Brennan's Fair was held here each year.

Kilblain (Bute), Cill Bhlàthain. 'St Blane's church'.

Kilblane (Argyll), Cill Bhlàthain. *See* **Kilblain**.

Kilblean (Argyll), Cill Bhlàthain. *See* **Kilblain**.

Kilbowie (Dunbarton). 'Yellow church', from *Cill Bhuidhe*.

Kilbrandon (Argyll, Islay, Mull), Cill Bhrianainn. 'St Brendan's church'.

Kilbrare (Sutherland), Cill nam Bràthair. 'Church of the brothers'.

Kilbrennan (Mull), Cill Bhrianainn. 'St Brendan's church'.

Kilbride (Argyll, Arran), Cille Bhrìghde. 'St Bridget's church'.

Kilbridemore (Argyll), Cille Bhrìghde Mhór. 'Big church of St Bridget'.

Kilbryde (Perth), Cill Bhrìghde. *See* **Kilbride**.

Kilbucho (Peebles). This may be 'St Beagha's church', named after a little known 7th century Irish nun.

Kilcalmonell (Argyll), Cill Cholmain Eala. 'St Colman Eala's church', a saint also commemorated in Colmonell.

Kilchattan (Argyll, Bute, Colonsay, Luing), Cille Chatain. 'St Catan's church'. In Colonsay there are Lower Kilchattan and Upper Kilchattan. Lower Kilchattan comprises both *Baile Ìochdarach*, 'lower farm', and *Baile Uachdrach*, 'upper farm'. Upper Kilchattan is *Baile Mhoire* in Gaelic, 'St Mary's farm'.

Kilcheran (Lismore), Cill Chiarain. 'St Ciaran's church'.

Kilchiaran (Islay), Cill Chiarain. *See* **Kilcheran**.

Kilchoan (Argyll, Inverness, Islay), Cille Chomhghain. 'St Comhghan's church'. The Gaelic name can also be seen spelt *Cill a' Chòthain* which sounds similar but is meaningless.

Kilchoman (Islay), Cill Chomain. 'St Coman's church'.

Kilchousland (Argyll), Cill Chuisilein. 'St Constantine's church'.

Kilchrenan (Argyll), Cill Chrèanain. Although there is no saint recorded as *Crèanan*, there is a Kilmacrenan in Donegal which may refer to a son or devotee of a saint of this name.

Kilchrist (Argyll, Mull, Ross, Skye),

Cille Chrìosd. 'Christ's church'.

Kilchurn (Argyll), Caol a' Chùirn. 'The strait at the cairn'.

Kilconquhar (Fife). 'St Dúnchadh's or St Conchadh's church', from *Cill Dúnchaidh* or *Cill Chonchaidh*.

Kilcoy (Ross), Cùil Challaidh. 'Secluded spot at the hazel place'.

Kildary (Ross), Caoldaraigh. 'Narrow plain'.

Kildavaig (Argyll), Cill Damhaig. 'St Damhóc's church'.

Kildavie (Argyll), Cill Dà Bhì. 'St Dà Bhì's church'. Dà Bhì was a by-name of Bearchan.

Kildermorie (Ross), Cille Mhuire. 'St Mary's church'. Kildermorie Forest is *Frith Chille Mhuire*.

Kildonan (several), Cill Donnain. 'St Donnan's church'. The Kildonan area of Sutherland is *Sgìre Ilidh*, 'district of Ilidh or Helmsdale River'. An old saying is, *Cill Fhinn, Cill Duinn 's Cill Donnain, na trì cilltean as sine as Albainn*, 'Killin, Kildun and Kildonan, the three oldest cells in Scotland'. A person from the Kildonan area in Sutherland, where the fair was known as *Fèill Donnain*, is an *Ileach*.

Kildrochit (Wigtown). 'Bridge end', from an original *Ceann Drochaid*.

Kildrummy (Aberdeen), Cionn Droma. 'Ridge end'.

Kildun (Ross), Cill Duinn. 'Brown church'. *See* **Kildonan**.

Kilduncan (Fife). This appears to be 'St Donnchadh's church', from *Cill Donnchaidh* or *Cill Donnacain*.

Kilduthie (Kincardine). 'St Duthac's church', from *Cill Dubhthaich*.

Kilellan (Argyll), Cill Fhaolain. 'St Fillan's church'.

Kilennan (Islay), Cill Fhìonain. 'St Finnan's church'.

Kilerivagh (Benbecula), Cill Éireabhagh. This Gaelic/Norse name may mean 'church at the bay with a beach'.

Kilfeddar (Wigtown). 'St Peter's church', from *Cill Pheadair*.

Kilfinan (Argyll), Cill Fhìonain. 'St Finnan's church'.

Kilfinnan (Inverness). Cill Fhìonain. *See* **Kilfinan**.

Kilfinnichen (Mull), Cill Fhionnchain. 'St Fionnchan's church'. A local saying describing a detour was *Rathad Mhóirnis do Chill Fhionnchain*, 'via Mornish to Kilfinnichen'.

Kilhenzie (Ayr). *See* **Kilkenneth**.

Kilkenneth (Tiree), Cill Choinnich. 'St Cainnech's church'.

Kilkenzie (Argyll, Ayr), Cill Choinnich. 'St Cainnech's church'. The English form of the Argyll name is pronounced as 'Kilkenny'. In Ayrshire, the name was formerly *Cill Mo Chainnich*, featuring a diminutive, affectionate form of the saint's name.

Kilkerran (Argyll, Ayr), Cill Chiarain. 'St Ciaran's church'.

Killallan (Renfrew). 'St Fillan's church', from *Cill Fhaolain*.

Killanaish (Argyll), Cill Aonghais. 'St Angus's church'.

Killandrist (Lismore), Cill Anndrais. 'St Andrew's church'.

Killean (Argyll, Islay, Lismore), Cill Eathain. 'St John's church'. In Islay, Lower Killean is *Cill Eathain Ìochdrach* and Upper Killean is *Cill Eathain Uachdrach*.

Killearn (Stirling), Cill Earrain. This was originally *Cinn Earrainn*, 'the end of the portion of land', but has changed to a *cill* name, possibly by analogy with other names.

Killearnan (Ross), Cill Iùrnain. 'St Iotharnan's church'. Killearnan Parish is *Sgìre Iùrnain*.

Killegray (Harris), Ceileagraigh. 'Island of the burial place', from Norse.

Killen (Ross), Cill Annaidh or Cill Fhannaidh. It is not clear which saint is commemorated in this name.

Killeonan (Argyll), Cill Eónain or Cill Eódhanain. 'St Adamnan's church'.

Killernandale (Jura), Cill Earnadail or Cill Earradail. 'The valley of St Ern-an's church', a hybrid Gaelic/Norse name where an earlier Gaelic name had Norse *dalr* attached.

Killernie (Fife). 'End of the alder or sloe place', from *Cinn Fheàrna* or *Cinn Àirne*. Originally this name was formed with *ceann/cinn*, 'end', rather than *cill*, 'church'.

Killichonan (Perth), Cille Chonnain. 'St Connan's church'.

Killiechassie (Perth), Cill Chasaidh. 'St Casan's church'.

Killiechonate (Inverness), Cille Chonaid. 'St Conaid's church'.

Killiechronan (Mull), Coille Chrònain. 'The wood of the murmuring sound'. Old Killiechronan is *An Seann Bhaile*, 'the old farm'.

Killiecrankie (Perth), Coille Chreithnich or Coille Chneagaidh. 'Aspen wood' or possibly 'the wood at the knobbly place'. The site of the Battle of Killiecrankie is known as *Raon Ruairidh*, 'Roderick's field'.

Killiehangie (Perth), Cille Chaomhaidh. This may be 'St Kevin's church'.

Killiehuntly (Inverness), Coille Chunndainn. 'Wood at the confluence'.

Killiemacuddican (Kirkcudbright). 'St Mo Chuda's church', showing a diminutive form of the saint's name from *Cille Mo Chudagain*.

Killilan (Ross), Cill Fhaolain. 'St Fillan's church'.

Killin (Inverness, Perth), Cill Fhinn; (Sutherland), Cill Eathain. In Inverness and Perth, the name means 'white church', while in Sutherland it is 'St John's church'. The fair held at Killin in Perth was known as *Féill Faolain*, 'St Fillan's Fair', dedicated to the saint named in nearby Strathfillan. *See* **Kildonan**.

Killinaig (Mull), Cill Fhionnaig. 'St Fionnag's church'.

Killochan (Wigtown). 'St Onchu's church', from *Cill Onchon*.

Killundine (Argyll), Cill Fhionndain. 'St Fintan's church'.

Kilmachalmaig (Bute, Ross), Cill Mo Chalmaig. 'St Mo Chalmag's church', a reference possibly to St Columba.

Kilmachellaig (Argyll), Cill Mo Cheallaig. 'St Mo Cheallag's church'.

Kilmacolm (Renfrew). 'Church of St Columba's devotee', from *Cill Mhaol Chaluim*.

Kilmadoc (Perth), Cill Mo Dog 'St Mo Dog's church'.

Kilmaglass (Argyll). This may be the 'church of Glas's son', from *Cill Mac Glais*.

Kilmahoe (Argyll), Cill Mo Chotha. 'St Mo Chotha's church'.

Kilmahog (Perth), Cill Mo Chùg. 'St Mo Chùg's church'. The fair held here each November was known as *Féill Mo Chùg*, 'St Mo Chùg's Fair'.

Kilmahumaig (Argyll), Cill Mo Chumaig. 'St Mo Chumag's church'.

Kilmaichlie (Banff), Cill Mhèichlidh or Cinn Mheachlainn. This may be a corrupted form of the name of the saint *Maoil-Sheachlainn* as found in the pass of *Làirig Mheachlainn* in Perthshire. *Cinn Mheachlainn* contains *ceann*, 'end or head', rather than *cill*, 'church', but this may not be significant. The English form of the name is also found as 'Kilnmaichlie'.

Kilmain (Sutherland), Cill Mheadhain. 'Middle church', situated between the churches at Killin and Kilbrare.

Kilmallie (Inverness), Cill Mhàilidh. This church name is unclear, but Kilmaley in Co. Clare is *Cill Mháille*, which seems to contain the same personal name as in *Ó Máille* 'O'Malley'. *See* **Culmaily** and **Dalmally**.

Kilmannan (Stirling). This may be 'the church of Manau', from *Cill Mhanainn*. *See* **Clackmannan**.

Kilmany (Fife). *See* **Kilmeny**.

Kilmarie (Skye), Cill Ma Ruibhe. 'St Maol Rubha's church'.

Kilmarnock (Argyll, Ayr), Cill Mhearnaig. 'St Ernoc's or M' Ernoc's church'.

Kilmaronag (Argyll), Cill Mo Chrònaig. 'St Crònan's church'.

Kilmaronock (Dunbarton). 'St Ronan's church', from *Cill Mo Rònaig*.

Kilmartin (Argyll, Ayr), Cille Mhàrtainn. 'St Martin's church'. Local people were nicknamed *coilich*, 'cockrels'.

Kilmaveonaig (Perth), Cill Mo Mh'Eónaig or Cill Mo Bheònaig. This is either 'Adamnan's church' or 'St Beoghna's church', both possible derivations showing a diminutive form of the name.

Kilmelford (Argyll), Cill Mheallaird. This may be 'church at the lumpy headland'.

Kilmeny (Islay), Cill Mheinidh. 'St Eithne's church', from an affectionate form of the name.

Kilmichael (Argyll, Arran), Cill Mhìcheil. 'St Michael's church'.

Kilminning (Fife). This may be 'St Maoineann's church', from *Cill Mhaoininn*

Kilmodan (Argyll), Cill Mhaodhain. 'St Modan's church'.

Kilmoluag (Skye, Tiree), Cille Mo Luaig. 'St Mo Luag's church'.

Kilmolymock (Moray). Older forms of the name, such as Kilmalaman and Kilmalemnock from *Cill Mo Lomain* and *Cill Mo Lomanaig*, suggest that St Loman may be commemorated here.

Kilmonivaig (Inverness), Cill Mo Naomhaig. 'St Naomhan's church'.

Kilmorack (Inverness), Cill Mhóraig. 'St Moroc's church'. The Gaelic version suggests the name *Mórag*, but the dedication is to *Moroc*. The area of East Kilmorack is known as *Leathair nam Manach*, 'the monks' slope'.

Kilmore (Argyll, Skye), A' Chille Mhór. 'The big church'. The manse here was known as *An Taigh Bàn* for its pale colour.

Kilmorich (Argyll, Perth), Cill Mhuirich. 'St Muireadhach's church.

Kilmory (Argyll, Arran, Rum), Cille Mhoire. 'St Mary's church'.

Kilmote (Sutherland), Baile na h-Àtha. The English form suggests a church dedication to St Mayota from an older Gaelic name including *cill*, while the Gaelic name is 'the farm with the stable or kiln'.

Kilmuick (Banff), Cill Muice. This name suggests 'pig church', and may refer to a nearby river or stream.

Kilmuir, Cill Mhoir (Ross), Cille Mhoire (Skye). 'St Mary's church'.

Kilmun (Argyll), Cill Mhunna. 'St Munna's church', using an affectionate by-name of St Fintan.

Kilmure Easter (Ross), Sgìre Mhoire Shìos. The English name refers to the eastern part of Kilmure, while the Gaelic name is 'lower parish of St Mary'.

Kilnaughton (Islay), Cill Neachdain. 'St Nechtan's church'.

Kilnave (Islay), Cill Néimh. 'St Ném's church'.

Kilninian (Mull), Cill Naoi Nighean. 'Church of the Nine Maidens'.

Kilninver (Argyll), Cill an Inbhir. This name appears to mean 'church by the river mouth', however an older form of *Cill Fhionnbhair*, 'St Finbar's church', appears together with an earlier version of *Cill M' Fhionnbhair*, 'Dear St Finbar's church'.

Kiloran (Colonsay), Cill Odhrain. 'St Oran's church'.

Kilpatrick (Ayr); (Arran), Cill Phàraig or Cill Pheadair; (Mull), Cill Phàdraig. 'St Patrick's church'. The Arran names show the confusion between the names *Pàdraig* and *Peadar*, where the former is translated into English as both Patrick and Peter.

Kilpheder (South Uist), Cille Pheadair. 'St Peter's church'.

Kilphedir (Sutherland), Cill Pheadair. 'St Peter's church'.

Kilpunt (West Lothian). This probably originated as Brythonic *pen pont*,

'bridge end', with Brythonic *pen*, 'end, head', changing to Gaelic *ceann* which in turn became *cill*, 'church'. This gaelicisation of Brythonic names also appears in **Kirkintilloch** and **Kinneil**.

Kilquhockadale (Wigtown). This name is 'St Cuaca's church', from Gaelic *Cill Chuaca* to which Norse *dalr*, 'valley', was added.

Kilravock (Nairn), Cill Ràthaig. 'Church at the small circular fort'.

Kilrenny (Fife). 'St Ethernan's church', from *Cill Eatharnain*.

Kilry (Angus), Caol-Ruigh. 'Narrow slope'.

Kilrymonth (Fife), Cill Rìmhinn. *See* **St Andrews**.

Kilslevan (Islay), Cill Sléibheainn. 'St Slevan's church'.

Kilspindie (Perth). 'St Pensandus's church', from a lost Gaelic form.

Kilsyth (Dunbarton), Cill Saidhe. This may be 'St Sadhbh's church', although a number of earlier Gaelic forms may suggest alternative interpretations, e.g. *Cill Saoif*, *Cil Saithe* and *Cill Saighdhe*.

Kiltarlity (Inverness), Cill Targhlain. 'St Talorcan's church'. The Gaelic name is the same as that of the old name of Portree in Skye. The settlement now called by this name was earlier *Allt Feàrna*, 'alder burn'. The Kiltarlity area is known as *Bràigh na h-Àirde*, 'the upper part of the Aird'.

Kiltearn (Inverness), Cill Tighearn. 'The Lord's church'. Kiltearn Parish is *Sgìre Thighearn*.

Kilvaxter (Skye), Cille Bhacastair. This appears to be a Gaelic/Norse name meaning 'the church at the settlement on the bank'.

Kilvickeon (Mull), Cill Mhic Eóghainn. 'Church of Eóghann's son'.

Kilwhannel (Ayr). 'St Conall's church', from *Cill Chonaill*.

Kilwhipnach (Argyll). This may be 'St Coidhbeannach's church', from *Cill Choidhbeannaich*.

Kilwinning (Ayr), Cill Dingeain. 'St Finian's church'. The English form may show a Brythonic rather than Gaelic form of the saint's name.

Kinaldie (Aberdeen). 'Head of the rock', from *Cinn Allaidh*.

Kinaldy (Fife). *See* **Kinaldie**.

Kinbeachie (Ross), Cinn a' Bheathchaidh. 'The head of the birch wood'.

Kinblethmont (Angus). This name may be 'the head of the blossom or smooth moor', from either Brythonic or Gaelic *Ceann Blàthmhon*.

Kinbrace (Sutherland), Ceann a' Bhràist. This may be 'the head of the upland', including a form of *bràigh*, 'upland'.

Kincaldrum (Angus). 'The end of the hazel ridge', from *ceann, coll* and *druim*. This name is very similar to that of **Kingoldrum**.

Kincardine (Fife, Kincardine); (Ross), Cinn Chàrdainn. 'The head of the copse', including the Brythonic/Pictish word *carden*, 'copse'. Kincardineshire is *Siorrachd Chinn Chàrdainn*, the older name of which was the **Mearns**.

Kincardine O'Neil (Kincardine), Cinn Chàrdainn. *See* **Kincardine**. An older name for this was *Eaglais Iarach*, 'Iarchadh's church'.

Kinclaven (Perth), Ceann Cliathain or Cionn Cliobhain. 'The end of the hurdle'.

Kincorth (Aberdeen), Ceann na Coirthe. 'The head of the standing stone'.

Kincraig (Fife, Inverness), Ceann na Creige. 'The head of the rock'.

Kincraigie (Perth), Cionn Chnagaidh. This may be 'the end of the knobbly place'.

Kindallachan (Perth), Ceann Daileachain. 'The end of the little valley'.

Kindeace (Ross), Cinn Déis. The meaning of this is unclear although it contains *ceann* (head) and possibly *dias* (corn).

Kindrochit (Aberdeen). 'Bridge end', from *Ceann Drochaid*.

Kindrogan (Perth), Ceann Drogain. This appears to mean 'dragon head', and may have referred to a river, stream or topological feature.

Kineddar (Moray). 'Between headland', from *Ceann Eadar*.

Kinell (Angus), Ceann an Fhàil. 'The end of the dyke'.

Kingairloch (Argyll), Cinn a' Gheàrrloch. 'The head of the short loch'. Local people were known as *buic*, 'bucks'.

Kingarth (Bute), Ceann a' Gharaidh. 'The end of the den'.

Kingask (Fife). 'The end of the projecting ridge', from *Ceann Ghaisg*.

King Edward (Aberdeen). This name is from the same origin as 'Kineddar', but was adapted to render it meaningful to English speakers.

Kinghorn (Fife). 'End of the marsh', from *ceann* and *gronn*, an earlier spelling of the name being 'Kyngorn'.

Kinglass (West Lothian). This is 'green head or end', from *Ceann Glas*.

Kinglassie (Fife). This may be 'the church at the stream', from *Cill Ghlaise*.

Kingoldrum (Angus), Cionn Colldruim or Druim Cionn Coill. The English form and the first Gaelic name suggest 'the end of the hazel ridge', but the second Gaelic name means 'the ridge at the end of the (hazel)wood'. Both Gaelic names were noted by Diack from speakers of eastern dialects.

Kingsburgh (Skye), Cinnseborg or Cinnseaborg. This may be 'king's castle', from Norse.

Kingscavil (West Lothian). This may be 'headland of the fish catching creel', from *Ceann Cabhail*.

Kingscross (Arran), Rubha na h-Àirde. The English name appears to be from Gaelic *Cinn a' Chrois*, 'end of the crossing place', but earlier forms point to *Peighinn a' Chrois*, 'pennyland of the crossing place'. The modern Gaelic name is 'point of the headland'.

Kingsmuir (Fife). This may be the 'king's moor' referred to as *righ-mhonadh* which became contracted to *rìmhinn* in such names as Balrymonth and the Gaelic name of **St Andrews**.

Kingseat (Perth), Suidhe an Ruighe. 'Seat of the slope'. Gaelic *ruigh* (slope) sounds similar to *rìgh* (king) and in several places, such as Kingsridge and Portree, *ruigh* has been superceded by *rìgh*.

Kingshouse (Argyll), Taigh an Rìgh. Both English and Gaelic names refer to an inn on the king's highway.

Kingussie (Inverness), Ceann a' Ghiuthsaich or Cinn a' Ghiuthsaich. 'End of the pine wood'.

Kinharvie (Dumfries). This suggests 'the end of the boundary wall', from *Ceann na h-Eirbhe*.

Kiniegallin (Perth), Cinn a' Ghealainn. 'The end of the white land'.

Kininmonth (Aberdeen, Fife). 'The end of the white moor', from *Ceann Fhionn-Mhonaidh*.

Kininvie (Banff). This appears to be 'the end of the fair plain', from *Ceann Fhionn-Mhuighe*.

Kinkell (Aberdeen, Perth, Ross), Ceann na Coille. 'The end of the wood'.

Kinloch (Lewis), Ceann an Loch; (Barra, Perth), Ceann Loch; (Rum, Skye), Ceann Locha; (Sutherland), Ceann Loch an Reidhinidh. 'Loch head'. *Reidhinidh* is unclear but may derive from *reidhneach*, 'cow yielding no milk'.

Kinlochard (Perth), Ceann Loch na h-Àirde. 'The head of the loch of the promontory'.

Kinlochbeoraid, (Inverness), Ceann Loch Bheòraid. 'The head of Loch Beoraid'.

Kinlochbervie (Sutherland), Ceann

Loch Biorbhaigh. This may be 'the head of the loch of boiling water', if the second element is related to that in 'Inverbervie'. However if the second element is of Norse origin, which is likely given its location, it may be 'the head of the loch of the rock river'.

Kinlocheil (Inverness), Ceann Loch Iall. 'The head of the thong loch'.

Kinlochetive (Argyll), Ceann Loch Éite. 'The head of the loch of the foul one', referring to *Éiteag*, a water spirit.

Kinlochewe (Ross), Ceann Loch Iubh. 'The head of the yew loch'.

Kinlochgair (Argyll), Ceann Locha Giorra. 'The head of the short loch'.

Kinlochlaggan (Inverness), Ceann Loch an Lagain. 'The head of the loch of Laggan'.

Kinlochleven (Argyll, Inverness), Ceann Loch Lìobhann. 'The head of the loch of Leven'.

Kinlochmoidart (Inverness), Ceann Loch Mhùideart. 'The head of the loch of Moidart'.

Kinlochmorar (Inverness), Ceann Loch Mhórair. 'The head of the loch of Morar'.

Kinlochmore (Inverness), Ceann Loch Mór. 'The big head of the loch'.

Kinlochourn (Inverness), Ceann Loch Shùirn or Ceann Loch Shubhairne. 'The head of the loch of the berry gap'.

Kinlochquoich (Inverness), Ceann Loch Chuaich. 'The head of the loch of the hollow'.

Kinloch Rannoch (Perth), Ceann Loch Raineach. 'The head of the loch of Rannoch'.

Kinlochroag (Lewis), Ceann Locha Ròg. 'The head of the loch of Roag'.

Kinlochsheil (Ross), Ceann Loch Seile. 'The head of the loch of Sheil'.

Kinlochspelve (Argyll), Ceann Loch Spéilbhidh. 'The head of Loch Spelve'.

Kinlochteagus (Argyll), Ceann Loch Tiacais. 'The head of Loch Teagus'.

Kinloid (Inverness), Ceann an Leothaid. 'The end of the slope'.

Kinloss (Moray), Cinn Lois. 'Herb headland'.

Kinmont (Dumfries). 'Head moor', from *ceann* and *monadh*.

Kinmundy (Aberdeen). 'St Munna's church', from *Cill Mhunna*, using a by-name for St Fintan.

Kinmylies (Inverness), Ceann a' Mhìlidh. 'The head of the warrior'. Locally this is known as *Ceann a' Mhìle*, 'Mile end'.

Kinnaber (Angus). 'Marsh end', from *Ceann* and *eabar*.

Kinnabus (Islay), Cionnabus. This Norse name may be 'lady's farm', and is one of the places referred to in, *Tha ceithir busaichean fichead an Ìle*, 'there are twenty-four 'buses' in Islay, *bus* being a shortened form of Norse *bólstaðr*, 'farm'.

Kinnahaird (Ross), Ceann na h-Àirde. 'The end of the high point'.

Kinnaird (Aberdeen). 'High headland', from *Ceann Àrd*.

Kinneil (West Lothian), Ceann an Fhàil. 'The end of the dyke', being located at the end of the Antonine Wall. Originally this name was Penfahel, containing Brythonic *pen*, 'end', rather than Gaelic *ceann*. *See* **Kilpunt**.

Kinnell (Perth), Cinn Alla. 'The end of the rock'.

Kinnettes (Ross), Ceann Iteais. This may be 'the head of the corn place'.

Kinnettles (Angus). The Gaelic pronunciation of this was recorded as 'kynn-nettel', and although it contains *ceann*, 'head' or 'end', the second element is unclear.

Kinnordy (Angus). This appears to be 'the end of the round-hilled place', from *Ceann Òrdaigh*.

Kinnoull (Perth). *See* **Kinnell**.

Kinnudie (Nairn), Cinn Iùdaidh. The meaning of this name is unclear.

Kinrive (Ross), Ceann Ruighe. 'Slope end'.

Kinross (Kinross), Ceann Rois or Cinn Rois. 'Wood end'. Kinross-shire is *Siorrachd Cheann Rois* or *Siorrachd Chinn Rois*.

Kinrossie (Perth), Cinn Rosaidh. 'The end of the wood place'.

Kintail (Ross) Ceann an t-Sàil (Gairloch), Cinn Tàile (Loch Duich); (Sutherland), Ceann Tàile or Cinn Tàile. 'Head of the inlet'. The full name of Kintail by Loch Duich is *Cinn Tàile MhicCoinnich* or *Cinn Tàile MhicRath* , 'MacKenzie's Kintail' or 'MacRae's Kintail'. A saying goes *Cho fad's a bhios monadh an Cinn Tàile, cha bhi MacCoinnich gun àl sa Chrò*, 'as long as there is moorland in Kintail, MacKenzie will have stock in the pen'. Kintail Church is *Clachan Dubhthaich* or *Cill Dubhthaich*, 'Duthac's church or churchyard'. A native is a *Sàileach* or *Tàileach* from which may come the surname *Tallach*. In Sutherland the full name is *Cinn Tàile MhicAoidh*, 'MacKay's Kintail'.

Kintarvie (Lewis), Ceann Tarabhaigh. This compound Gaelic/Norse name is 'head of seaweed bay'.

Kintillo (Perth). 'The end of the green hills', from *Ceann Tulach*.

Kintore (Aberdeen), Ceann Tòrr. 'Hill end'.

Kintra (Argyll, Islay), Cinn Tràgha; (Mull), Ceann na Tràgha. 'The head of the beach'.

Kintradwell (Sutherland), Clìn Trolla. 'Triduana's slope'.

Kintrae (Moray). *See* **Kintra**.

Kintyre (Argyll), Cinn Tìre. 'Land's end'. The older name was *Sàil Tìre*, 'heel of land'. A native of Kintyre is a *Tìreach* or *Cainntireach*, but local people were nicknamed *eich*, 'horses'.

Kinuachdrach (Jura), An Ceann Uachdrach. 'Upper end'.

Kinveachy (Inverness), Ceann a' Bheithich. 'End of the birch wood'.

Kippen (Stirling). 'Small stump', from *ceapan*.

Kippo (Fife). 'Tillage land', from *Ceapach*.

Kirivick (Lewis), Cirbhig. 'Quiet bay', from Norse.

Kirkaboll (Tiree), Circepol. 'Church farm', from Norse.

Kirkandrews (Kirkcudbright). 'St Andrew's church'. A group of place-names in the south-west beginning with 'Kirk-' and ending in a saint's name may originally have been created in Gaelic with *Cill*, then translated into Scandanavian or English, as many of the saints commemorated are of the Gaelic church, and the word order is Celtic rather than Germanic.

Kirkbean (Kirkcudbright). 'St Beathan's church'.

Kirkblane (Dumfries). 'St Blane's church'.

Kirkbride (Ayr). 'St Bridget's church'.

Kirkbuddo (Angus). 'St Buite's church', commemorating a saint who visited Nechtan's court nearby.

Kirkcaldy (Fife), Cathair Chaladain. 'Seat of the hard fort', probably first coined in Brythonic, then adapted to Gaelic then English phonology.

Kirkcarswell (Kirkcudbright). 'St Oswald's church'.

Kirkcolm (Wigtown). 'St Colum's church'.

Kirkconnel (Dumfries). 'St Conall's church'.

Kirkcudbright (Kirkcudbright), Cill Chuithbeirt. 'St Cuthbert's church'. Kirkcudbrightshire is *Siorrachd Chill Chuithbeirt*.

Kirkebost (Bernera, North Uist), Circebost. 'Church farm', from Norse.

Kirkettle (Midlothian). 'Kettil's cairn', created originally in Gaelic perhaps as *Càrn Cheatail*, featuring a Norse personal name.

Kirkfield (Inverness), Achadh na h-Eaglais. 'Church field'.

Kirkhill (Inverness), Cnoc Odhar or Cnoc Mhoire. While the English name is 'church hill', the Gaelic ones are 'dun-coloured hill' and 'St Mary's hill'. The old name was *Dul Bachlach*, which may be 'crozier haugh'. Kirkhill parish is *Sgìre Mhoire*, 'St Mary's parish' and *Sgìre Cnoc na Gaoithe*, ' Windhill parish'.

Kirkiboll (Sutherland), Circeabol. 'Church farm', from Norse.

Kirkinner (Wigtown). 'St Cainnear's church'.

Kirkintilloch (Dunbarton), Cathair Ceann Tulaich. 'Fort at the end of the green hill'. This was originally a Brythonic name, *Caerpentaloch*, which was adapted to Gaelic phonology but carried the same meaning.

Kirklauchline (Wigtown). 'Lachlann's quarterland', from *Ceathramh Lachlainn*.

Kirkmabreck (Kirkcudbright). 'St Broc's church', from a by-form of the saint's name.

Kirkmadrine (Ayr). 'St Draighne's church', from *Mo Dhraighne*, a by-form of the saint's name.

Kirkmahoe (Dumfries). 'St Cua's chuch', from *Mo Chua*, a by-form of the saint's name.

Kirkmaiden (Ayr). 'St Etain's church', from *M' Éadain*, a by-form of the saint's name.

Kirkmartin (Wigtown). 'St Martin's church'.

Kirkmichael (Ayr, Banff, Perth), Cille Mhìcheil. 'St Michael's church'. Kirkmichael parish in Banff is *Sgìre Eaglais Mhìcheil*, 'the parish of St Michael's church'.

Kirkmirran (Kirkcudbright). 'St Mirren's church'.

Kirkoswald (Ayr). 'St Oswald's church'.

Kirkpatrick (Dumfries, Kirkcudbright). 'St Patrick's church'.

Kirksheaf (Ross), A' Chroit Mhór. The Gaelic name is 'the big croft'. A 16th century form of the English name,

Kerskeith, suggests a Gaelic origin, 'hawthorn seat'.

Kirkton (several). 'Churchyard' or 'village with a church'. In Raasay the Gaelic name is *an Clachan*, 'the churchyard' or 'the village with a church', while in Perth and Sutherland it is *Baile na h-Eaglais*, 'village of the church'. Kirkton of Glenisla is *Baile na h-Eaglais Ghlinn Ìl'*, 'the village with the church in Glenisla'. Kirkton of Lochalsh is *an Clachan Aillseach*, 'the Lochalsh clachan'. Kirkton of Skene is *Clachan Sgàin*, and Kirkton of Strathfillan is *Clachan Shraithibh*.

Kirkton Glen (Perth), Làirig Eibhreannach. 'Pass of the castrated goats'. This name has been understood to include the word *Éireannach*, 'Irishman', given that the original word, *eibhreannach*, is obscure.

Kirriemuir (Angus), Cearan Mhoire. 'St Mary's quarter-land'.

Kirtomy (Sutherland), Ciortamaidh. This name is unclear.

Kiscadale (Arran), Cisteal. This name came from Norse *kistudalr*, 'coffin valley'. North Kiscadale is *Cisteal Bheag* while Mid and South Kiscadale collectively are *Cisteal Mhór*.

Kishorn (Ross), Ciseorn. 'Large bulky headland'.

Kisimul (Barra), Cìosamul. 'Castle island'. This is the castle referred to in *Bàgh a' Chaisteil*, 'Castlebay'.

Klibreck (Sutherland), Cleithbrig. Although the second element of this name is clearly Norse *brekkr*, 'stream', the first is obscure.

Knapdale (Argyll), Cnapadal. 'Knob valley', from Norse. The area was known as *Cnapadal a' bhuntàta mhóir*, 'Knapdale of the great potatoes', and local people were nicknamed *crodh maol*, 'hornless cattle'.

Knapp (Perth). 'Lump', from *cnap*.

Kneep (Lewis), Cnìp or Crìp. 'Cliff edge', from Norse.

Knock (several), An Cnoc. 'Hill'. The full name of Knock in Inverness-shire is *Cnoc na h-Àirde*, 'hill of the Aird'. In Lewis, Knock near Carloway is *Cnoc Chàrlabhaigh*, 'the hill of Carloway', while Knock in Point is *Cnoc na h-Aoidhe*, 'the hill of the Eye isthmus'. Knock in Skye is *an Cnoc Uaine*, 'the green hill', or *Cnoc a' Chamais*, 'the hill at the bay', and in Mull is *Cnoc Tìr Mhàrtainn*, 'the hill on Martin's land'.

Knockaird (Lewis), An Cnoc Àrd. 'The high hill'.

Knockan (Sutherland), An Cnocan. 'The hillock'.

Knockando (Moray), Cnoc Cheannachd. 'Market hill'.

Knockandon (Arran), An Cnocan Donn. 'The brow hillock'.

Knockandu (Banff), An Cnocan Dubh. 'The black hillock'.

Knockanduie (Lewis), Cnoc Iain Duibh. 'Black John's hill'.

Knockaneorn (Banff). 'The barley hill', from *Cnoc an Eòrna*.

Knockankelly (Arran), Cnoc a' Choiligh. 'The hill of the cock', referring to a nearby rock.

Knockantivore (Mull), Cnoc an Taigh Mhóir. 'The hill at the big house'.

Knockbain (Ross), An Cnoc Bàn. 'The fair hill'.

Knockban (Ross), An Cnoc Bàn. *See* **Knockbain**.

Knockbreck (Skye), An Cnoc Breac. 'The speckled hill'.

Knockbrex (Kirkcudbright). 'Speckled hill', from *Cnoc Breac*, to which an English plural has been added.

Knockcuien (North Uist), Cnoc Cuidhein or Cnoc Uithein. 'Cuidhean's hill'.

Knockdamph (Sutherland), Cnoc Dhamh. 'Stag hill'.

Knockdon (Islay), An Cnoc Donn. 'Brown hill'.

Knockentiber (Ayr). 'The hill at the well', from *Cnoc an Tiobair*.

Knockespock (Aberdeen). 'The bishop's hill', from *Cnoc an Easbaig*.

Knockfarrel (Ross), Cnoc Fearralaidh or Cnoc Fearghalaigh. 'The hill of the high cliff' or 'Fearghal's hill'.

Knockhill (Fife). This name is an example of where an original name coined in one language has had the same word added in the superceding language as the original element ceased to be understood by the population. In this case Gaelic *cnoc*, 'hill', has had English 'hill' added to it in order to explain the name after Gaelic had died out and been replaced in Fife by English.

Knockintorran (North Uist), Cnoc an Torrain. 'The hill at the little hillock'.

Knockline (North Uist), Cnoc an Lìn. 'The flax hill'.

Knockmore (Fife). 'The big hill', from *An Cnoc Mór*.

Knocknamonie (Benbecula), Cnoc na Mòna. 'The peat hill'.

Knocknavie (Ross), Cnoc Neimhidh. 'Hill of the sacred lands'.

Knockrioch (Argyll), An Cnoc Riabhach. 'The brindled hill'.

Knockrome (Jura), An Cnoc Crom. 'The crooked hill'.

Knockvologan (Mull), Cnoc Mhaolagain. 'Maolagan's hill'. *Maolagan* means 'little tonsured one', denoting a monk.

Knoydart (Inverness), Cnòideart. 'Knut's firth', from Norse. Local people were known as *gobhair*, 'goats'.

Kyle (Ayr), Cuil. This area is named after Coel, a ruler of the Britons locally around 400 AD and immortalised in the rhyme,' Old King Cole'. The same person is also named in Coylton.

Kyleakin (Skye), Caol Àcain. 'Haakon's strait'.

Kyle of Lochalsh (Ross), An Caol or Caol Loch Aillse. 'The strait' or 'the strait of Lochalsh'. Local people were known as *steàrnairean*, 'terns'.

Kylerhea (Skye), Caol Reatha. 'The narrows at the current'. A popular story surrounding this name is that *Reatha*, a member of the legendary band of warriors known as the *Fianna* or *Féinne*, drowned here.

Kyle Rona (Raasay), An Caol Rònach. 'The Rona narrows', referring to the island of South Rona.

Kyles (Argyll), Na Caoil; (Harris), Caolas Stiadar. The Argyll name is 'the kyles or straits', referring to the *Na Caoil Bhódach*, 'the Kyles of Bute'. The Harris name in English is 'the strait', while in Gaelic in full it is 'the strait of Stiadar'.

Kyles Flodday (Benbecula), Caolas Fhlodaigh. 'The strait of Flodday', a Gaelic/Norse name.

Kyles Knoydart (Inverness), Caolas Chnòideart. 'The strait of Knoydart'.

Kylesku (Sutherland), An Caolas Cumhang. 'The narrow strait'.

Kyles Morar (Inverness), Caolas Mhórair. 'The strait of Morar'.

Kyles Scalpay (Harris), Caolas Sgalpaigh. 'The strait of Scalpay'.

Kyles Stockinish (Harris), Caolas Stocainis. 'The strait of Stockinish', a Gaelic/Norse name.

Kylestrome (Sutherland), Caol Sròim. 'The strait of the current', a Gaelic/Norse name.

Kyllachy (Inverness), Coileachaigh. 'Woodcock place'.

Kynachan (Perth), Coinneachan. 'Meeting place' or 'junction'.

Labost (Lewis), Làbost. 'Muddy farm', from Norse.

Lackalee (Harris), Leac an Lì. This appears to be a Gaelic/Norse name meaning 'slab or slabs at the slope'.

Ladybank (Fife). 'Damp slope', from *Leathad Bog*.

Laga (Argyll), Làga. 'Low island', from Norse.

Lagavellie (Arran), Lag a' Bhile. 'The hollow of the rim or edge'.

Lagavulin (Islay), Lag a' Mhuilinn. 'The hollow of the mill'.

Lagg (Arran, Ayr, Jura), An Lag. 'The hollow'.

Laggan (Arran, Inverness), An Lagan. 'The little hollow'. The full name of Laggan in Badenoch is *Lagan Choinnich*, 'Coinneach's little hollow', whilst in the Great Glen it is *Lagan Achaidh Droma*, 'hollow at the field of the ridge'.

Lagganallachie (Perth), Lagan Aileachaidh. 'The hollow at the rock place'.

Laggan Bridge (Inverness), Ceann Drochaid. The Gaelic name is 'bridge end'.

Lagganlia (Inverness), An Lagan Liath. 'The grey-green hollow'.

Lagganmore (Argyll), An Lagan Mór. 'The big hollow'.

Laggantygown (Inverness), Lagan Taigh Ghobhainn. 'The hollow at the smith's house'.

Lagganulva (Mull), Lagan Ulbha. 'The little hollow of Ulva'.

Laggmore (Arran), An Lag Mór. 'The big hollow'.

Laich of Moray (Moray), Machair Mhoireibh. 'The plain of Moray'.

Laid (Sutherland), An Leathad. 'Slope'.

Laide (Ross), An Leathad. *See* **Laid**. Local people are known as *caoraich mhaola*, 'Cheviot sheep'. Coast of Laide is *Eirtheaire an Leothaid* or simple *an t-Eirtheaire*, 'the coast'.

Laig (Eigg), Lathaig. This is possibly 'muddy bay', from Norse.

Laight (Wigtown), Leac Ailpein. This was originally 'Alpin's grave', and the English name has kept only the 'grave' part. *See* **Glenapp**.

Lairg (Sutherland), Luirg. 'Shank'.

Lalathen (Fife). 'Broad half or share', from *Leth Leathann*.

Lamancha (Peebles). *Grange of Romanno* was thus renamed in the 18th century by Admiral Cochrane in memory of the Spanish province. *See* **Romanno**.

Lambhill (Arran), Cnoc nan Uan. 'The hill of the lambs'.

Lamlash (Arran), Loch an Eilein, An t-Eilean or An t-Eilean Àrd. The Gaelic names are 'the loch with the island' or 'the (high) island'. The English form is a contraction of an older, *Eilean Mo Laise*, 'St Laisren's island', referring to Holy Island.

Lanark (Lanark, Perth), Lannraig. 'Clearing', from Brythonic *lanerc*. Lanarkshire is *Siorrachd Lannraig*.

Land, The (Tiree), Lag an t-Seagail. The Gaelic name is 'the rye hollow'.

Langal (Argyll), Langal. 'Long hill', from Norse.

Langamull (Mull), Langamul or Langabhail. 'Long ridge' or 'long field', from Norse.

Langass (North Uist), Langais. 'Long ridge', from Norse.

Langay (Harris), Langaigh. 'Long island', from Norse.

Langley Park (Angus). This name was given by a landlord to replace an earlier name derived from Gaelic *Eaglais Eòin*, 'St John's church'.

Langwell (Caithness, Ross, Sutherland), Langail. 'Long field', from Norse.

Lanrick (Perth), Laraig. 'Clearing', from Brythonic *lanerc*. An earlier Gaelic form was *Lanraig*, showing the derivation more clearly.

Larachantivore (Ross), Làrach an Taigh Mhóir. 'The site of the big house'.

Larachbeg (Argyll), An Làrach Bheag. 'The small site'.

Largie (Argyll), An Learg. 'The slope'.

Largiemore (Bute), An Leargaidh Mhór. 'The big slope-place'.

Largieside (Argyll), Taobh na Leargaich. 'The side or area of the sloping place'.

Largo (Fife). 'Slope place', from *Leargach*.

Largs (Ayr), An Leargaidh Ghallda. The Gaelic original is 'the Lowland sloping place', whilst the English form is based only on 'sloping place'

Largy (Argyll), Leargaich; (Arran), Leargaidh. 'Slope place'. To express 'in Largy' with reference to the place in Argyll, Gaelic uses *air an Leargaich*, 'on Largy'. Largybeg in Arran is *Leargaidh Beag*, 'little Largy'; Largymeanoch is *Leargaidh Meadhanach*, 'middle Largy'; and Largymore is *Leargaidh Mór*, 'big Largy'.

Laroch (Argyll), An Làrfhaich. 'The bottom lawn or green'.

Lary (Aberdeen), Làiridh or Làraidh. This may be 'bottom place'.

Lasgair (South Uist), Laisgeir. This Norse name may be 'low skerry'.

Latheron (Caithness), Latharan or Lathairn. 'Muddy place'. This is believed by some to be from the same origin as *Latharna*, 'Lorne'.

Latheronwheel (Caithness), Latharan a' Phuill or Lathairn a' Phuill. 'Latheron by the pool'.

Lathrisk (Fife). This name appears to derive from *lios* and *riasg*, giving 'boggy enclosure'.

Laudale (Argyll), Labhdal. 'Low valley', from Norse.

Laurencekirk (Kirkcardine). 'St Laurence's church'. Locally this is known as 'Lowrin', a form of the saint's name found as *Labhrann* in Gaelic. The older name of the parish was Conveth, from *Coinmheadh. See* **Conveth**

Lawers (Perth), Labhar. 'Talkative one', referring to a stream. East Lawers is *Labhar Shìos*, 'lower Lawers', West Lawers is *Labhar Shuas*, 'upper Lawers', and Mid Lawers is *Labhar na Craoibhe*, 'Lawers of the tree'. Lawers churchyard is *Cladh Magh Thuaim*, 'the graveyard of Machuim'.

Laxay (Lewis), Lacasaigh. 'Salmon river', from Norse.

Laxdale (Lewis), Lacasdal. 'Salmon valley', from Norse.

Laxford (Sutherland), Lusard. 'Salmon

firth', from Norse.

Leachcan (Harris), Na Leacainn. 'The broad hillsides'.

Leachkin (Inverness), An Leacainn. 'The broad hillside'. The small area known as Pig Row is *Sràid nam Muc*, 'street of the pigs'.

Leachonich (Ross), An Leachanaich. 'The sloping hill face'.

Leacnasaide (Ross), Leac nan Saighead. 'The flat rock of the arrows'.

Leadburn (Midlothian). 'The grave or flat rock of Bernard'. An older form of the name was Leckbernard, from *Leac Bhearnaird*.

Lealt (Jura, Skye), Leathallt. 'Stream with one high bank'.

Lealty (Ross), Leathalltaidh. 'Place of the stream with one high bank'. Wester Lealty is *Leathalltaidh Shuas*, 'upper Lealty'.

Leanachan (Inverness), An Lèanachan. 'The little meadow'.

Leanaig (Ross), Lianaig. 'Meadow'.

Leanish (Barra), Lèanais. This may be 'slope headland', from Norse.

Leargybreck (Jura), An Leargaidh Bhreac. The speckled slope'.

Lebhall (Aberdeen), An Leth Bhaile. 'The half farm'.

Lecht (Aberdeen, Banff), An Leac. 'The flat rock'. The more complete name in Gaelic is *Leac a' Ghobhainn*, 'the flat rock of the smith'.

Leckie (Perth, Ross), Leacaidh. 'Flat rock place'.

Leckmelm (Ross), Leac Mhailm. 'The slab of Mailm,' possibly a personal name and referring to a gravestone.

Ledaig (Argyll), Leideag; (Barra), An Leideag. 'The small slope'. In Argyll, North Ledaig is *Leideag a Tuath* and South Ledaig is *Leideag a Deas*.

Ledbeg (Sutherland), An Leathad Beag. 'The small slope'.

Ledgowan (Ross), Leathad Ghobhainn. 'The smith's slope'.

Ledlanet (Kinross). This may be 'elm slope', from *Leathad Leamhnach*.

Ledmore (Sutherland), An Leathad Mór. 'The big slope'.

Leirable (Sutherland), Lìreabol. 'Muddy farm' or 'tern farm', from Norse.

Leirinbeg (Sutherland), An Leithrinn Bheag. 'The small peninsula'.

Leirinmore (Sutherland), An Leithrinn Mhór. 'The big peninsula'.

Leith (Midlothian), Lìte. The origin of this name is from a Brythonic element signifying wetness or dampness, and may also be found in 'Lithlithgow'.

Lemlair (Ross), Leum na Làir or An Leum. 'The mare's leap'. This is also known as 'the leap', in Gaelic. The old churchyard here is *Cladh Mo Bhrìgh*, 'St Brìgh's graveyard'.

Lemreway (Lewis), Leumrabhagh. This Norse name contains *vágr*, 'bay', but the first element is unclear.

Lendrick (Angus, Kinross). *See* **Lanark**.

Lenimore (Arran). *See* **Thundergay**.

Lennox (Dunbarton, Stirling), An Leamhnachd or Leamhnachd. 'The elm land'. The Lord of Lennox is *Morair Leamhnach* or *Morair Leamhna*, also known in earlier times as *Rìgh Bealaigh*, 'the King of Balloch', A native of the area is a *Leamhnach*.

Leny (Perth), Lànaigh. The meaning of this name is unclear. The Pass of Leny is *Cumhang Lànaigh* and Brae Leny is *Bràigh Lànaigh*.

Lenzie (Dunbarton). This appears to be from *Lèanaidh*, a locative form of *lèana*, 'wet meadow'.

Leochel (Aberdeen). 'Dark place', from *lòchail* or *lòicheil*.

Lephin (Skye), An Leth-pheighinn. 'The half pennyland'.

Lerwick (Shetland), Léiruig. 'Mud bay', from Norse.

Lesmahagow (Lanark). This was originally 'St Mo Chuda's church', from *Eaglais Mo Chuda* which became altered to *Lios Mo Chuda*, 'St Mo Chuda's garden'.

Lesmurdie (Ayr, Moray). 'Murdoch's enclosure', from *Lios Mhuirich*.

Lethen (Nairn), Leathan Dubhthaich. 'Duthac's broad slope'. The Laird of Lethen is *Tighearn Leathan Dubhthaich*.

Lethendy (Perth). 'Place of the broad slope', from Gaelic *Leathandaidh*.

Letter (Arran), Leitir. 'Gentle slope'. The full name is *Leitir nan Canach*, 'gentle slope of the canons'.

Letterewe (Ross), Leitir Iubh. 'The gentle slope of the Ewe'.

Letterfearn (Ross), Leitir Fheàrna. 'Gentle alder slope'.

Letterfinlay (Inverness), Leitir Fhionnlaigh. 'Finlay's gentle slope'.

Lettermorar (Inverness), Leitir Mhórair. 'The gentle slope of Morar'.

Letters (Ross), An Leitir (Loch Broom), Na Leitrichean (Easter Ross). These names are 'the gentle slope' and 'the gentle slopes' respectively.

Lettoch (Perth, Ross), An Leathdach. 'The half davoch', from *leth* and *dabhach*.

Leuchars (Fife, Moray). 'Reeds', from Gaelic *luachair*, with either an English plural or Gaelic locative suffixed.

Leurbost (Lewis), Liùrbost. 'Ljúfa's farm', from Norse. Other interpretations have been suggested for the origin of this name.

Level, The (Moray). 'The half farm', from *An Leth Bhaile*.

Leven (Fife). 'The mouth of the Leven'. The older English name was Innerleven, from *Inbhir Lìobhann*.

Levencorrach (Arran), An Leth-pheighinn Corrach. 'The uneven half pennyland'.

Leverburgh (Harris), An Tòb or An t-Òb. The Gaelic name is 'the bay', from Norse *hóp*. The English name used to be Obbe until it was renamed by the proprietor, Lord Leverhulme.

Levishie (Inverness), Lìbhisidh. This name is unclear, but might be 'smooth meadow place'.

Lewis, Leódhas. One explanation is that this name came from Norse *ljóðahús*, 'song house', which was then applied to the entire island. A native of Lewis is a *Leódhasach*, also nicknamed a *biorach*, 'dogfish'. The island is known as *Eilean Fraoich* or *Eilean an Fhraoich*, 'heather island'.

Lewiston (Inverness), Blàr na Maigh. The English and Gaelic names are unrelated, the Gaelic being 'the field on the plain'.

Leys (Inverness), An Leigheas. This name is unclear.

Lhanbryde (Moray). 'Bridget's church', from *Lann Brìghde. See* **Lathrisk**.

Li (Inverness), Lì. 'Slope', from Norse.

Liddesdale (Roxburgh); (Argyll), Lìdeasal. In Roxburgh, this is the name, from English, of the valley through which the River Leader flows. In Argyll the name appears to be from Norse and may represent a valley named after an individual.

Lienassie (Ross), Lianaisidh. 'Place of the wet meadow'.

Lierinish (North Uist), Lìoranais. 'Muddy headland', from Norse.

Lietrie (Inverness), Liathdoire. 'Grey-blue grove'. This name is surprising in that the *d* did not become *dh* after *liath*.

Lighthill (Lewis), Cnoc an t-Solais. 'Hill of the light'.

Likisto (Harris), Liceasto. 'Body harbour', from Norse, possibly a place from which bodies were ferried for burial.

Limelands (Fife). The older name of this place is from *Innis Cailc*, 'chalk meadow'.

Lindores (Fife). The first part of this name is either Brythonic *llyn* or Gaelic *linn*, 'pool', while the second is unclear but may be *dubhros*, 'dark point' or 'dark wood'.

Lingay (Barra, Harris, South Uist), Lingeigh. 'Heather island', from Norse.

Lingerabay (Harris), Lingearabhagh. 'Heather bay' or 'heather beach bay', from Norse.

Liniclete (Benbecula), Lianacleit or Lìonacleit. 'Flax rock' or 'flax hill', from Norse.

Linicro (Skye), Lianacro. 'Flax land', from Norse.

Liniquie (South Uist), Lianacuidh. 'Flax enclosure', from Norse.

Linlithgow (West Lothian), Gleann Iucha. 'Lake by the wet hollow', from Brythonic. The Gaelic name seems to contain *gleann*, 'valley', but this was a rationalisation on the part of Gaelic speakers to give the name meaning for them. The name occurs in a number of Gaelic sayings, such as *Trì iongantasan na h-Alba: drochaid Obar Pheallaidh, tobraichean Ghlinn Iucha is cluig Pheairt*, 'The three wonders of Scotland: Aberfeldy bridge, the wells of Linlithgow and the bells of Perth', and *tomhas Ghlinn Iucha*, 'a Linlithgow measure', one of the weights and measures which disappeared after 1707.

Linshader (Lewis), Lìseadar or Linnseadar. 'Flax township', from Norse.

Linsidemore (Sutherland), Lianasaid Mhór. 'Large flax township', from Norse/Gaelic.

Lintrathen (Angus). This name was recorded by Diack from speakers of Perthshire Gaelic as *lan-tréin* and *lyann-tré-an*. This suggests that the first element is Brythonic or Gaelic for 'church' or 'pool', but the second element is unclear and may also be Brythonic. The name would be written in Gaelic as either *Lann Tréithean* or *Linn Tréithean*.

Lintrose (Angus). An older form of the name suggests 'shelving slope by the wood', from *fothair* and *ros*.

Lionel (Lewis), Lìonail. 'Flax field', from Norse.

Lismore, Liosmór. 'Big garden'. A

native of Lismore is a *Liosach*, also
nicknamed an *othaisg*, 'yearling sheep'
or 'hog'

Little Bernera (Lewis), Beàrnaraigh
Beag.

Little Colonsay (Mull), Colbhasa
Beag.

Little Cumbrae (Cumbrae), Cumaradh Beag.

Little Daan (Ross), Dathan Bhig.
'Small davoch'.

Little Dunkeld (Perth), Baile a'
Mhuilinn. The Gaelic name is 'the
farm with the mill'.

Little Ferry (Sutherland), Am Port
Beag. The Gaelic name is 'the little
harbour'.

Little Lude (Perth), Leòid Bheag.

Little Sand (Ross), Sannda Bheag.

Little Scatwell (Ross), Sgatail Beag.

Liveras (Skye), Laoras. The meaning
of this is unclear, but it appears in
part of a poem, *bidh cnàmhan nam
fear móra air tràigh bhàn Laorais*, 'the
bones of the big men will be on the
fair beach of Liveras'.

Livingston (West Lothian), Baile
Léibhinn or Baile DhùnLéibhe.
'Leving's village'. The Gaelic name
Baile DhùnLéibhe is common but
erroneous as it is based on the surname *MacDhùnLéibhe*, 'Livingston',
which is unconnected with the name
of the town.

Lix (Perth), Lic. 'Slab place' or 'hard
slope'. Easter Lix is *Lic Ìochdrach*,
Mid Lix is *Lic Meadhanach* and
Wester Lix is *Lic Uachdrach*. Easter
Lix is also known as *Toll Lic*, 'the hole
at Lix'.

Loandhu (Ross), An Lòn Dubh. 'The
black wet meadow'.

Loanreoch (Ross), An Lòn Riabhach.
'The brindled wet meadow'.

Loanroidge (Ross), An Lòn Roid. 'The
wet meadow of bog myrtle'.

Lochaber (Inverness), Loch Abar.
'Muddly or swampy loch'. A native
of the area is an *Abrach*. A Gaelic

equivalent of 'carry coals to Newcastle'
is *fiodhrach a thoirt a Loch Abar*, 'to
take wood to Lochaber'.

Lochailort (Inverness), Loch Ailleart
or Ceann Loch Ailleart. '(Head of)
Lochailort'. This Gaelic/Norse name
contains both languages' elements
for 'sea loch', but the defining Norse
element is unclear. The second
Gaelic name was used to refer to the
settlement rather than the loch, but
has been superceded in recent years
by the first name.

Lochainort (South Uist), Loch
Aoineart. 'Isthmus loch', from Norse
with *loch* added. North Lochainort
is *Taobh a Tuath Loch Aoineart*, 'the
north side of Lochainort', and South
Lochainort is *Taobh a Deas Loch
Aoineart*.

Lochaline (Argyll), Loch Àlainn.
'Beautiful loch', although one would
expect the definite article in a simple
name of this sort. The second element
may originally have been a slightly
different word, rationalised as *àlainn*.

Lochalsh (Ross), Loch Aillse. Possibly
'loch of spume'. Lochalsh parish
is *Sgìre Chomhghain*, 'Comhghan's
parish'. A native of Lochalsh is an
Aillseach. Various villages in the area
and their inhabitants appear in the
ditty, *Steàrnairean a' Chaoil, faoileagan
Abhairnis, taighean dubha Réaraig,
pàilisean Bhaile Mac Ara, Diùranais an
eòrna, clòbhair Ach nan Darach, Druim
Buidhe nan deargannan, Earbarsaig
nan con clomhach*, 'terns from Kyle,
gulls from Avernish, black houses
in Reraig, palaces in Balmacara,
Duirnish of the barley, clover in
Achindarach, Drumbuie of the fleas,
Erbusaig of the scabby dogs'.

Lochardil (Inverness), Loch Àrdail.
'The loch at the high place'.

Lochawe (Argyll), Loch Obha. 'Loch
of the water'. Natives of the area were
nicknamed *liath-chearcan*, 'heath
hens'. This place appears in a number

of sayings, such as *Cha leithne Loch Obha null na nall*, 'Loch Awe is no wider across than back'; *Eireachdas mnathan Loch Obha, am bréid odhar a thionndadh*, 'the ingenuity of the Loch Awe women, to turn the dun-coloured cloth'; *Is fad an éigh o Loch Obha is cobhair o Chlann Ó Duibhne*, 'It's a far cry from Loch Awe and help from the Campbells'.

Lochbay (Skye), Loch a' Bhàigh. 'The loch with the bay'.

Lochboisdale (South Uist), Loch Baghasdail. 'Baegi's loch', containing a Norse personal name. North Lochboisdale is *Taobh a Tuath Loch Baghasdail*, 'the north side of Lochboisdale', and South Lochboisdale is *Taobh a Deas Loch Baghasdail*.

Lochbroom (Ross), Loch Bhraoin. 'The loch of water'. A native of the area is a *Braonach*, also nicknamed a *clamhan*, 'hawk'. Locals from the Little Loch Broom area were known as *crodh*, 'cattle'.

Lochbuie (Mull), Locha Buidhe. 'Yellow loch'.

Lochcarnan (South Uist), Loch a' Chàrnain. 'The loch of the little cairn'.

Lochcarron (Ross), Loch Carrann. 'Loch of the rough water'. A native of the area is a *Carrannach*, also nick-named a *fitheach dubh*, 'black raven'. The old name of the village was *Tòrr nan Clàr*, 'hill of the flat slabs', and changes of name are recorded in the rhyme, *Faire, faire, Tòrr nan Clàr, Baile Séine th' ort an-dràst*'. Chan eil taigh air an téid fàd, nach bi similear air no dhà*, 'Alas Tòrr nan Clàr, now you're called Janetown. Every house burning peat will have a chimney on it or two'. The parish church here is *Clachan Ma Ruibhe*, 'the church of St Maol Rubha'.

Lochcroistean (Lewis), Loch Croistean. The second part of the name is unclear.

Lochdonhead (Mull), Ceann Loch Dona. 'The head of the bad loch', referring to the loch's tendency to dry up.

Lochearnhead (Perth), Ceann Loch Éireann or Ceann Loch Éir. 'Head of the loch of Ireland'.

Lochend (Inverness), Ceann Loch. This settlement was known by two earlier names, *An Dabhach Dearg*, 'the red davoch', and *Dabhach na Creige* 'the davoch by the rock', both now moribund.

Locheport (North Uist), Loch Euphort. 'Loch at the isthmus port', from Gaelic/Norse.

Locheye (Ross), Loch na h-Ùidhe. 'The loch of the isthmus'.

Lochgair (Argyll), An Loch Geàrr. 'The short loch'.

Lochganvich (Lewis), Loch a' Ghainmhich. 'The sandy loch'.

Lochgelly (Fife), Loch Gheallaidh. 'Loch of the white water'.

Lochgilphead (Argyll), Ceann Loch Gilb. 'Head of the chisel loch', referring to its shape. A native is a *Gilbeach* and the parish is *Cill Fhionnbhair*, 'St Finbar's church'.

Lochgoilhead (Argyll), Ceann Loch Goibhle. This appears to be 'the head of the loch of the fork', possibly referring to the split in Loch Long of which Lochgoil is an offshoot. An alternative Gaelic name is found as *Ceann Loch Goill*, 'the head of the non-Gael's loch', but this may be a folk etymology. The church here is *Cill nam Bràithrean*, 'the church of the brothers'.

Lochindorb (Moray), Loch nan Doirb. 'The loch of the minnows'.

Lochinver (Moray, Sutherland), Loch an Inbhir. 'The loch at the river mouth'.

Lochletter (Inverness), Lòch Leitir. 'Dark hillside'.

Lochluichart (Ross), Loch Luinn-cheirt. 'The loch of the encampment'.

Lochmaben (Dumfries). 'Maban's

or Maponos's loch', referring to the
Gaelic equivalent of Apollo.

Lochmaddy (North Uist), Loch nam
Madadh. 'The loch of the wolves',
referring to rocks in the bay known
as *Na Madaidhean*. West Lochmaddy
is *An Rubha Iar*, 'the west point'.

Lochnabo (Moray). 'The loch of the
cows', from *Loch nam Bó*.

Lochnaw (Wigtown). 'The loch of
waters', from an old form *Loch
n-Abha*, or 'the loch of the water',
from *Loch an Abha*, the former being
more likely.

Lochnellan (Moray), Loch an Eilein.
'The loch with the island'.

Lochore (Fife). This loch name
mentions the River Ore.

Lochportan (North Uist), Loch
Portain. 'Loch with a little harbour'.

Lochranza (Arran), Loch Raonasa.
'Loch of the rowan river', a Gaelic/
Norse name. The village used to be
known as *Ceann Loch Raonasa*, 'head
of Lochranza'.

Lochs (Lewis), Na Lochan. 'The lochs'.
The inhabitants are referred to in
*Sùlairean sgìre na h-Aoidhe, 's muinntir
aoigheach nan Loch*, 'The gannets from
the Eye district, and the hospitable
people from Lochs'. South Lochs
contains the district of Park, known
as *A' Phàirc* or *A' Phàirc Leòdhasach*.
To express 'in Lochs', Gaelic uses *air
na Lochan*, 'on Lochs'.

Lochskiport (South Uist), Loch
Sgioport. 'Ship loch', from Norse,
with *loch* added.

Lochslin (Ross), Loch Slinn.   'The
loch of the weaver's sleye', referring
to its shape.

Lochtreighead (Inverness), Ceann
Loch Tréig. 'The head of the loch of
death'.

Lochuisge (Argyll), Loch Uisge.
'Freshwater loch'.

Logan (Ayr). 'Hollow', from *lagan*.

Loggie (Ross), An Lagaidh. 'Place of
the hollow'.

Logie (Moray), Lagaidh. 'Place of the
hollow'.

Logie Almond (Perth). 'The place of
the hollow by the Almond', from
Lagaidh Amain.

Logie Buchan (Aberdeen), Lagan
Talargaidh. The Gaelic name is
'Talorcan's hollow', while the English
form is from *lagaidh*, 'place of the
hollow'.

Logie Coldstone (Aberdeen), Lògaidh.
The English form contains *lagaidh*,
'place of the hollow', while the second
part is said to come from *comhdhail*,
'tryst', which was held at a particular
stone marker. The current Gaelic
form comes from the anglicised
pronunciation of 'Logie'.

Logie Easter (Ross), Lagaidh. The
Gaelic name is 'place of the hollow',
while English distinguishes between
this place and Logie Wester.

Logie Mar (Aberdeen), Lògaidh
Mhàrr. 'The place of the hollow in
Mar'. *See* **Logie Coldstone**.

Logierait (Perth), Lag an Ràtha. 'The
hollow at the circular fort'. The older
name was *Lagan Mo Choid*, 'St Mo
Chuda's hollow'.

Logie Wester (Ross), Lagaidh
Bhrìghde. The Gaelic name is 'St
Bridget's Logie', while English
differentiates between this place and
Logie Easter.

Loinveg (Aberdeen), Loinn Bheag.
'Small enclosure'. An alternative derivation is *Loinn nam Fiodhag*, from
older *Loinn na bhFiodhag*, meaning
'the enclosure of the bird-cherry trees'.

Lonach (Aberdeen), Lònag. 'Small wet
meadow'. The rivalry between Mar
and Lonach is shown in the Mar saying *Olc air mhath le Lònag*, 'whether
Lonach likes it or not'. A native of
Lonach is a *Lònagach*.

Lonbain (Ross), An Lòn Bàn. 'The
fair wet meadow'. Local people are
nicknamed *bodaich bhiorach an Lòin
Bhàin*, 'the sharp old men of Lonbain'.

Londubh (Ross), An Lòn Dubh. 'The black wet meadow'.

Lonemore (Ross, Sutherland), An Lòn Mór. 'The large wet meadow'.

Longa (Ross), Longa. 'Ship island', from Norse.

Longannet (Fife). This may be 'the churchyard of the mother church', from *lann* and *annaid*.

Longay (Ross), Longaigh. *See* **Longa**.

Longforgan (Perth), Forgrann. The Gaelic name is 'the place above the bog', while the English form has 'long' prefixed.

Longformacus (Berwick). 'Macas's camp', from *Longphort Mhacais*, a personal name also found in Maxton.

Longman (Inverness), An Raon Réidh. The Gaelic name is 'the level plain', and unrelated to the English, which is unclear.

Longmorn (Moray). This could be 'the church at the marsh', from *lann* and *morgrann*, although a personal name *Morgrunn* existed.

Longridge (West Lothian). 'Clearing', from Brythonic *lanerc*.

Longrigg (Argyll), An t-Iomaire Fada. 'The long rigg'.

Lonmay (Aberdeen). This may be *Lòn a' Mhaigh* 'wet meadow on the plain', from *lòn* and *magh*.

Lonmore (Skye), An Lòn Mór. 'The big wet meadow'.

Lorgill (Skye), Lobhairgil or Lobhargail. The full meaning of this Norse ravine name is unclear.

Lorne (Argyll), Latharna. 'Loarn's land', referring to the leader of one of the groups of Dal Riada. A person from the area is a *Latharnach*, also nicknamed as a *losgann*, 'frog'. The nicknames applied to inhabitants of various parts of Lorne are found in the rhyme, *Fithich dhubha Chreiginis, coilich Chille Mhàrtainn, liath chearcan taobh Loch Obha's coin-odhar an Àtha*, 'Black ravens from Craignish, cocks from Kilmartin, heath hens from Loch Awe-side and otters from Ford'. Upper Lorne is *Bràigh Latharna* while Nether Lorne is *Latharna Ìochdarach*. The String of Lorne is *An t-Sreang Latharnach*.

Lossiemouth (Moray), Inbhir Losaidh. 'The mouth of the herb river'.

Loth (Sutherland), Loth. 'Mud'. Locals are known as *Lothaich*. Lothbeg is *Loth Beag* while Lothmore is *Loth Mór*.

Lothian, Labhdaidh or Lodainn. This name is apparently of Brythonic origin, and was known as *Machair Labhdaidh*, 'plain of Lothian'. The Perthshire surname 'Lothian' is *Labhdain* or *Loudin* in Gaelic.

Loudon (Ayr), Lughdun. 'Lugh's fort', referring to a pre-Christian deity.

Lovat (Inverness), A' Mhoroich. The English form comes from a Gaelic source suggesting rotting or putrefaction. The Gaelic name is 'the carse' or 'sea plain'.

Lowlands, A' Ghalldachd. 'Non-Gaeldom'. The Lowlands are also known as *Am Machaire Gallda* or *A' Mhachaire Ghallda*, 'the Lowland plain'.

Lubcroy (Ross), An Lùb Chruaidh. 'The hard bend'.

Lubreoch (Perth), An Lùb Riabhach. 'The brindled bend'.

Ludag (South Uist), An Lùdag. 'The little finger', referring to a headland.

Lude (Perth), Leòid. 'Slope place'. A person from here is a *Luidneach*.

Lugar (Ayr). This name was originally that of a river, formerly called Lugdour and meaning 'bright water', from *Lughdhobhar*, later *Lughar*.

Luib (Perth, Ross, Skye), Lùib. 'Bend'. The full name of Luib in Ross is *Lùib a' Ghargain*, 'the bend at the little rough place or stream'. The inn at Luib is mentioned in a ditty, *'S e taigh-òsta Chailein a dh'fhàg mo phòcaid falamh; 'S iomadh stòp is gloinne chuir mi 'n tarraing ann*, 'Colin's inn has left my pocket empty; I had many a stoup and glass there'.

Luibchoinnich (Ross), Lùib a' Chòinnich. 'The bend of the moss'.

Luing, Luinn. This is probably a pre-Gaelic name of unclear meaning. A native of the island is a *Luinneach*, also nicknamed a *piocach*, 'coalfish'.

Lumbo (Fife). 'Bare place', from *Lomach*.

Lumphanan (Aberdeen), Lann Fhìonain. 'St Finan's church'. *See* **Lathrisk**.

Lumphinnans (Fife). *See* **Lumphanan**. The dedication here may have been to *Faolan* (Fillan) rather than *Fìonan* (Finan).

Luncarty (Perth), Longartaidh. 'Encampment place', referring to the camping place of a Danish fleet unable to pass the rapids at Murthly. The Danes are also commemorated in the nearby farm, Denmarkfield.

Lundale (Lewis), Lunndail. 'Roller valley', referring to rollers used to launch ships.

Lundavra (Inverness), Lunn Dà Bhrà. The name has drawn many attempts at interpretation, but none satisfactory. The term *lunnd*, 'marsh', may be the origin.

Lundie (Angus). 'Marshy place', from *Lunndaidh*.

Lundin (Fife). This may come from *Lunndan*, 'small marsh'.

Lundy (Inverness), An Lanndaidh. 'The marshy place'.

Lunga (Argyll, Luing, Mull), Lunga. 'Ship river', from Norse.

Lurg (Fife). 'Shank', from *lurg*, referring to a shank-shaped piece of land.

Luskentyre (Harris), Losgaintìr. This name is unclear.

Luss (Dunbarton), Lus. 'Vegetation'.

Lussa Bridge (Skye), Drochaid Lusaidh. 'The bridge over the bright river', a Gaelic/Norse name.

Lussagiven (Jura), Lusa Dhìomhain. 'Lazy bright river', from Gaelic/Norse.

Lusta (Skye), Lusta. 'Bright farm', from Norse.

Lybster (Caithness), Liabost. This Norse name may be 'slope farm'.

Lynachork (Banff), Lainn a' Choirce. 'The enclosed field of oats'.

Lynchat (Inverness), Lainn a' Chait or Baile a' Chait. 'The enclosed field of the cat' or 'the village of the cat'.

Lynedale (Skye), Lianadail. 'Flax valley', from Norse.

Lyngarrie (Inverness), Lainn Gharaidh. 'The enclosed field in the den'.

Lynwilg (Inverness), Lainn a' Bhuilg or Baile a' Bhuilg. 'The enclosed field of the bellows' or 'the village of the bellows'.

Maaruig (Harris), Màraig. 'Sea mew ridge', from Norse.

Macallan (Moray). 'Fillan's plain', from *Magh Fhaolain*.

Macduff (Banff). The Duff family were prominent landowners locally, but the village was earlier known as Doune, from *Dùn*, 'hill' or 'hill fort'.

Machair Illeray (North Uist), Machair Iolaraigh. 'The machair of Illeray'.

Macharioch (Argyll), Am Machaire Riabhach. 'The brindled machair'. The old name was *Am Baile Sear*, 'the east village'.

Machars of Galloway (Wigtown), Machair Ghall-ghàidheil. 'The plain of the foreign Gaels', a term attached to Gaelic speakers of Scandanavian origin.

Machrie (Arran), Am Machaire or Macharaidh. 'The machair' or 'machair place'.

Machrihanish (Argyll), Machaire Shanais. 'The machair of Sanas' or possibly 'the machair of the old meadow'.

Machrins (Colonsay), Na Machraichean. 'The machairs'.

Machuim (Perth), Magh Thuaim. 'The plain of the tomb'.

MacLean's Nose (Argyll), An t-Sròn

Mhór. In Gaelic this headland is called 'the big nose or point'.

Maggieknockater (Banff). 'The plain of the fuller or waulker', from *Magh an Fhucadair*.

Malaclete (North Uist), Màlacleit. This Norse name may be 'small rock or cliff'.

Maligar (Skye), Màileagar. This Norse name may be 'small bays'.

Mallaig (Inverness), Malaig. This Norse name may be 'small bay'.

Mallaigmore (Inverness) Malaig Mhór. 'Big Mallaig'.

Mallaigvaig (Inverness), Malaig Bheag. 'Little Mallaig'.

Mambeg (Dunbarton), Am Màm Beag. 'The small mountain gap'.

Mandally (Inverness), Manndalaigh or Meanndailidh. This may be 'place of the kids' haugh'.

Mangersta (Lewis), Mangarstaigh. 'Monk place' or 'peddler's place'. Local pronunciation collected by Oftedal suggests *Mangartadh* at an earlier period.

Manish (Harris), Mànais. 'Sea mew headland', from Norse.

Mannel (Tiree), Manal. This Norse name is said to mean 'man field'.

Mar (Aberdeen), Màrr. This may be from a Brythonic personal name. The divisions of the area are Braemar or *Bràigh Mhàrr*, the upland of Mar', Cromar or *Crò Mhàrr*, 'the enclosure of Mar', and Midmar or *Mic Mhàrr*, which may be the 'the bog of Mar'. Mar Lodge is *An Dail Mór*, 'the big haugh', and the place used to be known in English as Dalmore. A native of Mar is a *Màrnach* from which comes the surname, Marnoch.

Marble Lodge (Perth), Taigh a' Mharbail. 'The marble house' in Gaelic.

Marchmont (Berwick). This may be 'horse hill', from Brythonic.

Marganaish (Arran), Marg an Eis. 'The merkland by the stream or waterfall'.

Margmonagach (Argyll), Marg Mòineagach. 'The peaty merkland'.

Margnaheglish (Arran), Marg na h-Eaglais. 'The merkland of the church'.

Marishader (Skye), Mairiseadar. 'Sea village', from Norse.

Markinch (Fife). This is 'horse meadow', from *Marc Innis*, but may originally have contained Brythonic rather than Gaelic *marc* for 'horse'.

Marrel (Sutherland), Maraill. 'Sea field', from Norse.

Marvig (Lewis), Marabhaig. 'Sea bay', from Norse.

Marybank (Ross), An Lagaidh (Logie Easter), Bruach Màiri (Urray). The English name in Logie Easter commemorates Mary Ross of Balnagowan, while the Gaelic name is 'the place of the hollow'. The Urray names mean the same as each other, and the Gaelic is probably a translation from English.

Maryburgh (Ross), Baile Màiri. 'Mary's village'.

Maryculter (Kincardine). 'St Mary's Culter'.

Marykirk (Kincardine), Obar Luathnait. The English name is 'St Mary's church', while the Gaelic name is 'mouth of the swift river'.

Masterton (Fife). This is 'master's farm', but was known earlier as Lethmacdungal, from *Leth Mac Dhùghaill*, 'the slope of the sons of Dùghall or Dùngal'.

Mauchline (Ayr), Machlainn. This name is unclear and may be of Brythonic origin. According to legend it was the site of one of the wonders of Scotland, a miraculous underground quern which worked constantly except on Sundays. Near to Mauchline is Achenbrain or Auchenbrain, 'the field of the quern', from Gaelic *Achadh na Bràthann*.

Maud (Aberdeen). This may be 'meeting place', from Gaelic *Mòd*.

Mauld (Inverness), Màld. The meaning of this name is unclear.

Mause (Perth), Meallaibh. 'Lump-shaped hills'.

Mawhill (Kinross), Magh Chuaich. The Gaelic name is 'the plain of the hollow', while the English name implies the opposite.

Maybole (Ayr). 'Maidens' dwelling', from English. Gaelic *beag* and *mór* were later added to the older 'Mei-bothel' to distinguish two separate places of which there is now no trace.

Mayish (Arran), A' Mhàis. This may be from Brythonic *maes*, 'field' or from the Gaelic equivalent *magh*, 'plain', with the *-ais* ending indicating 'place'.

Meadale (Skye), Miadal. 'Narrow valley', from Norse.

Meadowside (Arran), Baile Uachd-rach; (Inverness), Coille an t-Suidhe. The English name is self-explanatory, whilst the Gaelic name in Arran is 'upper farm' and in Inverness is 'the wood by the seat'. The place in Arran is known also as Baluagra in English.

Mealista (Lewis), Mealasta. 'Bent-grass place', from Norse. Mealista island is *Eilean Mhealasta*.

Mearns (Kincardine), A' Mhaoirn or A' Mhaorainn. 'Territory of the steward'. A native of the Mearns is a *Maoirneach*.

Meavaig (Harris), Miabhaig. 'Narrow bay', from Norse. Meavaig in South Harris has the full name, *Miabhaig nam Bàgh*, 'Meavaig in Bays', while in North Harris the full name is *Miabhaig nam Beann*, 'Meavaig in the mountains'.

Meddat (Ross), Meitheid. 'Soft or spongy place'.

Meggernie (Perth), Migearnaidh. 'Boggy place'.

Megstone (Inverness), Clach Mhair-earad. 'Margaret's stone'.

Meigle (Ayr); (Perth), Mìgeil. In Perth this is 'boggy haugh'. The Ayr name may be the same.

Meikle Daan (Ross), Dathan Mhór. 'Big davoch'.

Meikle Ferry (Sutherland), Port a' Choltair. 'Big ferry', known in Gaelic as 'the port of the coulter'.

Meikleour (Perth). 'Big yew', from English/Gaelic. There was also a Littleour.

Melbost (Lewis), Mealabost. 'Sandbank farm'. The full name of *Mealabost Bhuirgh*, 'Melbost of Borve', distinguishes Melbost on the west side of Lewis from Melbost near Point.

Melgarve (Inverness), Am Meall Garbh. 'The rough lump-shaped hill'.

Mellon Charles (Ross), Meallan Theàrlaich or Na Meallan. 'Charles's lump-shaped hill' or 'the lump-shaped hills'. Local people were known as *rodain*, 'rats'.

Mellongaun (Ross), Meallan a' Ghamhna. 'The lump-shaped hill of the stirk'. This place is also known as Stirkhill in English.

Mellon Udrigle (Ross) Meallan Ùdraigil or Na Meall'. 'The lump-shaped hill of Udrigle', a Gaelic/Norse name, or 'the lump-shaped hill'.

Melness (Sutherland), Taobh Mhealainis 'Bent-grass headland'. The Gaelic name is the same with *taobh*, 'side'. Locally this was also pronounced *Meinleais* and *Taobh Mheinleais*.

Melrose (Selkirk). 'Bald moor', from Brythonic *moelros*, cognate with Gaelic *Maolros*.

Melvaig (Ross), Mealbhaig or Meala-bhaig. 'Bent-grass bay', from Norse. The village is also known by the nickname *A' Bhoilc* and a person from Melvaig is a *Boilceach* or *boc*, 'buck'. A saying concerning Melvaig is *'S fhada bhon lagh Dìobaig, 's fhaide na sin sìos Mealbhaig*, 'Diabaig is far from the law, and Melvaig even further'. The second Gaelic spelling of the name shows the epenthetic vowel between *l* and *bh* which is generally not shown in Gaelic orthography.

Melvich (Sutherland), A' Mhealbhaich or Mealbhaich. This may be 'bentgrass bay', from Norse. To express 'in Melvich', Gaelic uses *air a' Mhealbhaich*, 'on Melvich'.

Menteith (Perth), Tèadhaich. This name is from that of the River Teith. The English form appears to be from an older Gaelic form containing *mon*, 'moor', which in turn may be from Brythonic. A native of the area is a *Tèadhach*.

Meoble (Inverness), Meobal or Miabol. 'Narrow farm', from Norse.

Merkinch (Inverness), Marc Innis. 'Horse meadow', and similar to 'Markinch' in Fife.

Merkland (Arran), Am Marg. 'The merkland'. Merkland Point is *Rubha Shalach*, 'dirty point' or 'willow point'.

Methil (Fife). This may be 'middle church', from an early Gaelic form, *Meadh Chill*.

Methven (Perth), Meadhainnigh or Meithinnigh. 'Middle stone', from Brythonic. The Gaelic name was believed to derive from *meadhan*, 'middle', and Methven Wood was known as *Coille Mheadhain*.

Miagro (Sutherland), Mèathgro or Miagro. 'Narrow river pit', from Norse.

Mial (Ross), Mitheall. 'Narrow field or hill', from Norse.

Mianish (Tiree), Mianais. 'Narrow headland', from Norse.

Miavaig (Lewis), Miabhaig. 'Narrow bay', from Norse. Local pronunciation as collected by Oftedal suggests a preferable spelling of *Mitheabhag*.

Micras (Aberdeen), Miagra. This may be 'boggy circular fort'. The English name was originally 'Micra', with the plural added to reflect the place's division into two parts. Easter Micras is *Miagra Shìos* and Wester Micras is *Miagra Shuas*.

Mid Argyll (Argyll), Dal Riada. The middle part of Argyll was where the Scots' first settlement took place. They brought with them the name of the area in Ireland from which the settlers came, *Dal Riada*, 'Riada's territory'.

Midcalder (West Lothian). Calder is 'hard water', from *Caladar*, a common river name throughout Scotland. Midcalder is part of a larger area along with East Calder and West Calder.

Middlequarter (North Uist), An Ceathramh Meadhanach. 'The middle quarter-land'.

Middle Quarter (South Uist), Na Meadhanan. 'The middle lands' in Gaelic, situated between Boisdale to the south and Iochdar to the north.

Middleton (Inverness), Baile Mheadhain; (Tiree), Am Baile Meadhanach. 'The middle farm'.

Mid Fearn (Ross), Feàrna Meadhanach. 'Middle alder place'.

Midfield (Sutherland), Achadh Mheadhanach. 'Middle field'.

Mid Lawers (Perth), Labhar na Craoibhe. 'Lawers by the tree'.

Mid Lix (Perth), Lic Meadhanach. 'Middle Lix'.

Midlothian, Meadhan Labhdaidh or Meadhan Lodainn. 'The middle of Lothian'.

Midmar (Aberdeen), Mic Mhàrr. This may be 'the bog of Marr'.

Mid Ross (Ross), Ros Meadhanach. 'Middle Ross'.

Midstrath (Aberdeen), Mig Srath. 'Boggy strath'.

Midtown (Ross), Am Baile Meadhain; (Sutherland), Baile Meadhanach. 'Middle farm'.

Midtown of Duntelchaig (Inverness), Bail Shìos. The Gaelic name is 'lower or easter farm'.

Migdale (Sutherland), Migein. The English form is 'boggy valley', while the Gaelic is 'little bog'.

Migger (Perth), Migear. 'Boggy place'.
Migvie (Aberdeen), Migeaghaidh;
(Inverness), Mìgibhidh. 'Boggy hill
face'.
Mile End (Inverness). *See* **Kinmylies**.
This was formerly known as Balachlan
or *Baile Lachlainn*, 'Lachlann's farm'.
Millbuie (Aberdeen), Am Maol
Buidhe. 'The yellow rounded hill'.
Millbuies (Moray). *See* **Millbuie**. In
this case an English plural has been
attached to the basic name.
Millburn (Inverness, Sutherland), Allt
a' Mhuilinn. 'The stream of the mill'.
Millcraig (Ross), Muileann na Creige.
'The mill by the rock'.
Milleur Point (Wigtown). This may
be 'dun-coloured headland', from
Maol Odhar.
Millfield (Arran), Achadh a' Mhuilinn.
'Field of the mill'.
Mill of Sterin (Aberdeen), Muileann
Stairein. 'Mill at the stepping stones'.
Millpark (Raasay), Pàirc na Muilne.
'Field by the mill'.
Millport (Cumbrae), Port a' Mhuilinn.
'The port at the mill'.
Milnafua (Ross), Maol nam Fuath.
'Rounded hill of the ghosts'.
Milngavie (Dunbarton). There are
a number of interpretations of
this name, such as 'Davie's mill',
from Gaelic *Muileann Dhàibhidh*
(although *Muileann Dàibhidh* might
be expected), 'windmill', from Gaelic
Muileann Gaoithe, and 'windy or
boggy rounded hill', from Gaelic
Maol na Gaoithe.
Milovaig (Skye), Mìolabhaig. This
Norse name may be 'bay at the
narrow field'.
Milton (several). There are many places
with this name which means a farm
with a mill (milltown). Normally the
Gaelic equivalent is *Baile a' Mhuilinn*
but this is not always the case. Milton
is Ross is known by the full name
of *Baile Mhuilinn Anndra*, 'Andrew's
milltown', while in South Uist

Milton is known as *Gearra-Bhailteas*,
'fertile land by the river mouth', from
Norse.
Milton Eonan (Perth), Baile Mhuilinn
Eónain. 'Adamnan's milltown'.
Milton of Clova (Angus), Baile
Mhuilinn Chlàbhaidh. 'The milltown
of Clova'.
Milton of Kincraigie (Perth), Baile a'
Mhuilinn. 'The milltown'.
Milton of Roro (Perth), Baile Mhuil-
eann Ruadh-Shruth. 'The farm at the
mill of Roro'.
Minard (Argyll), Mionaird. 'Tiny
headland'.
Mingarry (Argyll), Mìogharraidh;
(South Uist), Mingearraidh. 'Main
field or pasture land', from Norse.
Minginish (Skye), Minginis. 'Main
headland'.
Mingulay (Barra), Miughalaigh. This
Norse name may be 'main hill island'
or 'narrow hill island'.
Minigaig (Perth), Miongag. 'Little
cleft'.
Minish (North Uist), Midhinis. 'Nar-
row headland', from Norse.
Minishant (Ayr). This may mean
'sacred shrubbery', from *Muine Sianta*.
Minmore (Banff), A' Mhon Mhór.
'The big moor'.
Miodar (Tiree), Am Mìodar. This
Norse name may mean 'narrow valley'.
Mishnish (Mull), Misinis. This Norse
name is 'goat headland'.
Modsarie (Sutherland), Modsairidh.
This Norse sheiling name may
include a personal name or 'meeting'
as its first element.
Moidart (Inverness), Mùideart. This
Norse name probably means 'narrow
sea loch'. A native of the area is a
Mùideartach.
Moine (Sutherland), A' Mhòine. 'The
peat bog'. West Moine is *Us-Mhòine*,
'upper Moine'.
Molinginish (Harris), Mol Linginis.
'Shingle beach by the heather
headland', a Gaelic/Norse name.

Moll (Skye), Am Mol. 'The shingle beach'.

Monachylemore (Perth), Monachul. The meaning of this name is unclear. The English form is 'big Monachyle', containing Gaelic *mór*, suggesting that at one time there was a *Monachul Beag* or 'small Monachyle'.

Monaltrie (Aberdeen), Mòine Ailtridh. The first part of the name is 'peat moss', while the second may be 'rocky place'.

Monamore (Arran). This is either *Am Monadh Mór*, 'the big hill-range' or *A' Mhòine Mhór*, 'the big peatbog'.

Moncrieff (Perth). 'Hill or moor of the tree', from Gaelic *Mon(adh) Craoibhe*.

Moniack (Inverness), Mon Itheig. The first part of the name is 'upland' or 'moor', while the second is unclear.

Monifeith (Angus). If this is a Gaelic name it may be 'peat bog by the stream', from *Mòine na Féithe*, however a large number of place-names locally come from Brythonic/Pictish.

Monimail (Fife). This may be 'bald or exposed moor', from Gaelic *Monadh Maol*, but may be from a cognate Brythonic/Pictish source meaning the same.

Monklands (Lanark), Bad nam Manach. The English name is 'land of the monks' while the Gaelic form is 'spot or clump of the monks'.

Monkstadt (Skye), Mogastad. 'Monk village', from Norse. A saying about the hard work involved in harvesting the fertile land around Monkstadt: *Cha do thuig thu a dhol a bhuain a Mhogastad*, 'You didn't realise what harvesting in Monkstadt entailed', is a way of expressing that one has bitten off more than one can chew.

Monorgan (Perth). 'Peat moss on land above a marsh', from *Mòine Fhorgrainn*.

Monquhitter (Aberdeen). The first part of the name suggests Gaelic *mon(adh)*, 'upland' or 'moor', whilst the second is unclear but may be related to the second element in 'Balquhidder', giving a conjectural form of *Mon Chuidir*.

Monreith (Wigtown). This may be 'level moor', from *Mon(adh) Réidh*, or of Brythonic origin.

Montgarrie (Aberdeen). This may be 'the hill of the den', from *Mon(adh) a' Gharaidh*.

Montgreenan (Ayr). 'Hill at the sunny place', from Brythonic and/or Gaelic, *Mon(adh) a' Ghrianain*.

Montrose (Angus), Mon Rois, Monadh Rois or Montròsa. 'The moor by the wood'. The third Gaelic form is a Gaelicised borrowing from the English form. A native of Montrose and the east coast is a *Tròsach*.

Monymusk (Aberdeen), Monadh Musga. The present Gaelic name is probably a gaelicisation of the English which is in turn from a Gaelic original. Given this place's location, the generic is probably *mòine*, 'peat', rather than *monadh*, 'upland, hills'. The second element may refer to dampness or moisture.

Monyquil (Arran), Mon a' Choill. 'The hill of the hazel tree'.

Monzie (Perth), Magh Eadh (Strathearn), Mon Fhiadh (Atholl). *Magh Eadh* is 'corn field' and *Mon Fhiadh* is 'deer moor'.

Monzievaird (Perth), Magh Bhàird. The Gaelic name is 'poet's field', while the English name has amended the first part of the name to link it to 'Monzie'.

Moor of Dinnet (Aberdeen), Sliabh Muileann Dùnaidh. The Gaelic name is 'moor of Dinnet mill'.

Morangie (Ross), Móraistidh. 'Large meadow'. Morangie Forest is *Frìth Mhóraistidh*.

Morar (Inverness), Mórar. 'Great water'. North Morar is *Mórar MhicShimidh*, 'Lovat's Morar'; South

Morar is *Mórar MhicDhùghaill*, 'MacDougall's Morar'.

Moray, Moireibh or Moireabh. 'Sea settlement'. A native of Moray is a *Moireach* which gives the surname 'Murray'.

Morefield (Ross), A' Mhór-Choille. The English name is a corruption of the Gaelic 'the big wood'. Morefield Cottage is *An Ceanna Chruinn*, 'the round head', possibly referring to a headland.

Morenish (Perth), Móirnis. 'Big meadow'.

Morile (Inverness), Móirl. This may be Brythonic/Pictish, meaning 'big clearing'.

Mornish (Mull), Móirnis. This may be Norse for 'sea headland'. An alternative Gaelic derivation would be 'great meadow', but this place's location suggests a more likely Norse origin. A local saying denoting a detour is *Rathad Mhóirnis do Chill Fhionnchain*, 'via Mornish to Kilfinnichen'.

Morsgail (Lewis), Morsgail. This Norse name may be 'sea house'.

Mortlach (Banff), Mórthlach. 'Big green hill'.

Morvern (Argyll), A' Mhorbhairne. 'The sea gap'. This was first applied to Loch Sunart, and Morvern itself was known as *Cineal Bhaodain*, 'Baodan's tribe'. Lower Morvern is *An Leathair Mhorbhairneach*, 'the Morvern slope', and Mull and Morvern together are *An Dreòllainn*. A Morvern person is a *Morbhairneach*.

Morvich (Ross), A' Mhormhoich. 'The carse'.

Moss (Argyll), A' Mhòinteach, (Tiree), A' Mhòinteach Ruadh. In Argyll this is 'the mossy moor', in Tiree, 'the red-brown mossy moor'.

Mossat (Aberdeen). This may be 'stale damp place', from *Musaid*.

Mossend (Arran), Ceann na Mòine. 'The end of the peat moss', also known as Home Farm.

Moss Farm (Arran), An Sliabh. 'The moor'.

Motherwell (Lanark), Tobar na Màthar. 'The well of the mother', referring to the Virgin Mary.

Moulin (Perth), Maoilinn. 'Smooth round hill'. Moulin is known for its good weather as in, *Cur is cathadh am Bealach Dearg, sneachd is reòthadh an Càrn a' Bhalg, cùl ri gaoith air Làirig Bhealaich, grian gheal am Maoilinn*, 'Drifts and storms at Bealach Dearg, snow and frost at the Cairnwell, back to the wind at Lairig Bhealaich, bright sunshine at Moulin'. Moulin fair was called *Fèill Mo Cholmaig*, 'St Colman's Fair'.

Moulinearn (Perth), Maol an Fheàrna. 'The round hill of the alder'.

Mound, The (Sutherland), A' Mhùnd. The English name of this artificial mound was adopted into Gaelic.

Mount Alexander (Inverness), Mùrbhlagan or Mùrlagan. While the English name refers to a landlord, the Gaelic name is 'rounded little inlet'.

Mountblairy (Banff). This may be 'dappled hill', from *Mon(adh) Blàraigh*.

Mounteagle (Ross), Cnoc na h-Iolaire. 'The eagle hill'.

Mountgerald (Ross), An Claon. The English name refers to a local notable, while the Gaelic name is 'the slope'.

Mountrich (Ross), Cill Chomhghain. The English name is a 19th century creation, replacing Kilchoan which is from the Gaelic name, 'St Comhghan's church'.

Moy (Inverness), A' Mhòigh; (Ross), A' Mhuaigh; (Sutherland), A' Mhuigh. 'The plain'.

Moy Bridge (Ross), Drochaid Mhuaigh. 'The bridge of Moy'.

Moy Lodge (Mull), Taigh na h-Abhainn. The Gaelic name is 'the house by the river'.

Moyle (Ross), Meile. This name is unclear but appears to be unrelated to the area in Ireland with the same anglicised name.

Moyness (Nairn), Muighnis. 'Meadow on the plain'.

Mualich (Perth), Muthalaich. This may be 'gentle green hill'. Mualaichbeg is *Muthalaich Beag*, 'small Mualich', and Mualichmore is *Muthalaich Mór*, 'big Mualich'.

Muasdale (Argyll), Muasdal. This Norse name may be 'moss valley'.

Muck (Inverness), Eilean nam Muc. Although this name appears to mean 'the island of the pigs', it is actually 'the island of the whales', from Gaelic *muc*, 'pig', a short form of *muc-mhara*, 'whale'. A native of the island is a *Mucanach*, also nicknamed a *piatan*, 'pet lamb'.

Muckairn (Argyll), Mucàrna. The meaning is unclear although the old form, *Bo-càrna*, suggests *both*, 'hut'. Muckairn churchyard is *Cladh an Easbaig Earaild*, 'the graveyard of Bishop Harold'. The strangeness of local people was referred to in the term *iongantas muinntir Mhucàrna*. Local people were known as *geàrra-ghobaich Mhucàrna* for their quick-wittedness.

Muckernich (Ross), A' Mhucarnaich. 'The swine place'.

Muckersie (Perth). This is a diminutive form of the name found in 'Muckross', as suggested by the old anglicised form, 'Mucrosin', possibly from *Mucrosan*, 'small swine wood'.

Muckovie (Inverness), Mucamhaigh. 'Swine plain'.

Muckrach (Inverness), Mucrach. 'Swine place'.

Muckraw (West Lothian). This may be 'swine fort', from *Mucrath*.

Muckross (Fife). 'Swine wood', from *Mucros*.

Mucomir (Inverness), Magh Comair. 'Plain of the confluence'.

Mudale (Sutherland), Modhudal. 'Valley of the muddy river', from Norse.

Mugeary (Skye), Mùigearraidh. 'Narrow field', from Norse.

Muie (Sutherland), A' Mhuigh. 'The plain'.

Muieblairie (Ross), Muigh Bhlàraigh. 'Dappled moor'.

Muir of Aird (Benbecula), Sliabh na h-Àirde. 'The moor of the headland'.

Muir of Fairburn (Ross), Blàr Fharabraoin. 'Moor of Fairburn'.

Muir of Ord (Ross), Am Blàr Dubh. 'Ord' is a rounded hill, from Gaelic *òrd*. The Gaelic name is 'the black moor'. The Ord Arms Hotel is on the site of *an Taigh Bhàn*, 'the white house'.

Muir of Tarradale (Ross), Blàr Tharradail. 'The moor of Tarradale'.

Muirshearlich (Inverness), Muir Sìorlaich. 'Plain of the broom rape'. Gaelic *muir* means 'sea', but the original name was *Magh Sìorlaich*, which became corrupted.

Muirtown (Inverness), Baile an Fhraoich; (Ross), Mórdun. While the English name is 'moor farm', the Gaelic name in Inverness is 'heather village', and in Ross may be 'great fort'.

Mulben (Banff), Am Muileann Bàn. 'The white mill'.

Muldoanich (Barra), Maol Dòmhnaich. 'The blunt headland of the Lord'.

Mulhagery (Lewis), Mol Chadha a' Ghàrraidh. 'The shingle beach at the pass by the enclosure'.

Mull, Muile. This name is pre-Gaelic, and has no connection with the names of headlands such as 'Mull of Kintyre'. Poetically Mull is known as *Muile nam Mór-bheann*, 'Mull of the great mountains'. The coastland of Mull opposite Morvern is *An Leathair Mhuileach*, 'the Mull slope', while Mull and Morvern are jointly known as *An Dreòllainn*. The place-names of Mull are mentioned in the saying *Ceithir busaichean fichead an Île's ceithir àrdacha fichead am Muile*, 'Twenty four *buses* in Islay and twenty four *ards* in Mull'. A native of Mull is a *Muileach*, but local people were also nicknamed *Doideagan* after a witch said to live in the island. The alleged nature of Mull people is referred to in a number of sayings, such as *Slìob am Muileach is sgròbaidh e thu, sgròb am Muileach is slìobaidh e thu*, 'Stroke the Mull person and he'll scratch you, scratch the Mull person and he'll stroke you' and *Muileach is Ìleach is deamhan, An triùir as miosa air an domhain. Is miosa am Muileach na an t-Ìleach, Is miosa an t-Ìleach na an deamhan*, 'A Mull person, an Islay person and the devil, The three worst in the world. The Mull one is worse than the Islay one, The Islay one is worse than the devil'.

Mullinloan (Inverness), Muileann an Lòine. 'The mill at the pond'.

Mull of Cara (Gigha), Maol Chara. 'The rounded headland of Cara'.

Mull of Galloway (Wigtown), Maol Ghall-ghàidheil or Maol nan Gall. 'The rounded headland of Galloway' or 'the rounded headland of the non-Gaels'.

Mull of Kintyre (Argyll), Maol Chinn Tìre. 'The rounded headland of Kintyre'.

Mull of Logan (Wigtown), Maol Logain. 'The rounded headland by the hollow'.

Mull of Oa (Islay), Maol na h-Obha. 'The rounded headland of the Oa'.

Multovie (Ross), Multabhaidh. 'Wedder plain'.

Mundurno (Aberdeen). This may be 'pebbly hill or moor', from *Mon(adh) Dòrnach*.

Mungasdale (Ross), Mùngasdal. 'Monk's valley', from Norse.

Munlochy (Ross), Poll Lòchaidh. The English form is 'the mouth of the dark water', from an older Gaelic name *Bun Lòchaidh*. The modern Gaelic name is 'the pool of the dark water'.

Murlaggan (Inverness), Mùrbhlagan or Mùrlagan. 'Rounded sea inlet'.

Murriel (Aberdeen). This was formerly 'Rathmurriel', from *Ràth Muirghil*, 'the round fort of Muriel'.

Murthly (Perth), Mórthlaich. 'Large green hill'.

Musall (Sutherland), Musal. 'Moss field', from Norse.

Musdale (Argyll), Mùsdal. This may be 'moss valley', from Norse.

Mussadie (Inverness), Musadaidh. 'Stale damp place'.

Muthil (Perth), Maothail. This may be 'gentle place'. The Roman camp at Ardoch was known as *Cathair Mhaothail*, 'Muthil fort'.

Naast (Ross), Nàst. This may be 'boat place', from Norse.

Nairn, Inbhir Narann. 'Mouth of the Nairn'. The town's nickname was *Baile Spealtaig*, 'splinter town'. Nairnshire is *Siorrachd Inbhir Narann*.

Narrachan (Argyll), An Arthar. These names are unclear.

Nask (Barra), An Nasg. If this name is of Gaelic origin, it means 'the link' or 'connection'.

Navar (Angus). 'The sacred lands of St Barr', from *Neimheadh Bharra*.

Nave Island (Islay), Eilean Néimh. 'St Ném's island'.

Navidale (Sutherland), Neimheadal. 'Valley of the sacred lands', from Gaelic/Norse.

Navitie (Fife). *See* Navity.

Navity (Ross), Neamhaididh. 'Place of sacred lands'.

Nedd (Sutherland), An Nead. 'The nest'. Local people were known as *eòin*, 'birds'.

Neist (Skye), An Éist. 'The horse' from Norse. A more full name is *An Éist Fhiadhaich*, 'wild Neist'. Neist Point is *Rubha na h-Éist* or *Gob na h-Éist*.

Ness (Lewis), Nis. 'Headland', from Norse. A native of Ness is a *Niseach*, nicknamed a *guga*, 'gannet'.

Nether Lorne (Argyll), Latharna Ìochdarach. 'Lower Lorne'.

Nethybridge (Inverness), Cinn Drochaid. The Gaelic name is 'bridge end'.

Nevie (Banff), Neimheadh Chrìosda. 'Sacred lands'. The Gaelic name is 'the sacred lands of Christ'.

New Aberdour (Aberdeen), Obar Dobhair. 'Mouth of the water'. 'New' in the English form distinguishes this place from its namesake in Fife.

Newbigging (Aberdeen, Angus, Lanark). 'New building'. The Gaelic name of Newbigging in Mar is Coire Laoigh, 'the corry on the Lui'.

Newburgh (Aberdeen), Baile Ùr Fobharain. The Gaelic name is 'the new village of Foveran'.

New Deer (Aberdeen), Achadh Reite. The English name distinguishes this place from Old Deer. The Gaelic name contains achadh, 'field', but the second part is unclear. It is found anglicised as 'Auchreddy'.

Newe (Aberdeen). 'Sacred lands', from Neimheadh.

New Kelso (Ross), Eadar Dhà Charrann, Cealsaidh or Cealso Ùr. The English name was given by a farmer who settled here from Kelso. The original name, Eadar Dhà Charrann, is 'between two Carrons'. Cealsaidh is a gaelicisation of 'Kelso', and Cealso Ùr is 'New Kelso'. The fair held here was known as Fèill Chealsaidh, 'Kelso Fair'.

New Luce (Wigtown), Baile Ùr Ghlinn Lus. The Gaelic name is 'the new village of Glen Luce'.

Newmills (Ross), Am Muileann Ùr. The Gaelic name is 'the new mill'.

Newmore (Ross), An Neo Mhór. 'The large sacred lands'.

Newpark (Lewis), Gearraidh Sgor. The English name is self-explanatory, while the Gaelic is 'fertile land by the wood', from Norse.

New Pitsligo (Aberdeen). 'Pitsligo'

contains Pictish pett, 'share' or 'lands', while the second element is Gaelic sligeach, 'shelly'.

New Street (Lewis), Am Poileagan. The Gaelic name is unclear.

Newton (several). 'New village or farm'. The are a variety of Gaelic names for the different Newtons throughout the country. Newton in Argyll is An Fhadhail Dhubh, 'the black ford'. Newton in Arran is Baile Nodha, 'new farm', which is sub-divided into North Newton or Cùl a' Bhaile, 'back of the farm', and South Newton which is simply Baile Nodha. Nearby Newton Point is Rubha a' Chùirn, 'the headland by the cairn'. In Lewis, Newton is Ionaicleit, 'brow cliff', from Norse, and the people were nick-named fithich dhubha, 'black ravens'. In North Uist, Newton is Baile MhicPhàil, 'MacPhail's farm'. In Ross and Tiree, Newton is Am Baile Nodha, 'the new farm or village'.

Newtonferry (North Uist), Port nan Long. The English name is 'the ferry at Newton', while the Gaelic one is 'harbour of the ships'. Local people are faoileagan, 'seagulls'.

Newtonmore (Inverness), Baile Ùr an t-Sléibh or An Sliabh. 'The new village of the moor'. Gaelic also has the shorter name, 'the moor'.

Newton Stewart (Wigtown), Baile Ùr nan Stiùbhartach. 'The new town of the Stewarts'.

New Valley (Lewis), An Gleann Ùr. 'The new valley'.

Nigg (Aberdeen); (Ross), An Neag or An Uig. 'The notch'. The second Gaelic name is that used locally in Easter Ross. The Sands of Nigg are An Oitir, 'the long low promontory'.

Nithsdale (Dunfries), Srath Nid. 'The valley of the Nith'. An older English name is 'Stranit', showing the con-nection to the Gaelic name.

Nonach (Ross), Nònach. 'Foam or spume place', the current Gaelic form having assimilated the definite article into the name which may originally have been similar to *Omhanaich* (Onich).

Nonakiln (Ross), Neo na Cille. 'The sacred lands of the church'.

Northbay (Barra), Am Bàgh a Tuath. 'The north bay'.

North Berwick (East Lothian), Bearaig a Tuath. 'North' distinguishes this place from Berwick in England, which for a time was termed South Berwick.

North Cuan (Seil), Cuan Saoil. The English name distinguishes this place from South Cuan. The Gaelic name is 'Cuan of Seil', *cuan* here meaning 'bay' rather than the normal meaning of 'ocean'.

North Kessock (Ross), Ceasag a Tuath. The older name is *Aiseag Cheasaig*, 'the ferry of Kessock'. *See* **Kessock**.

North Queensferry (Fife), Port na Banrighinn. The English name distinguishes this place from South Queensferry. The Gaelic name is 'the port of the queen' and does not contain 'north'.

North Rona (Lewis), Rònaigh. The English name distinguishes this island from the other Rona near Raasay. The name means 'rough island', from Norse. It is also known as *Rònaigh an Daimh* which appears to be 'Rona of the stag' but may in fact be *Rònaigh an Taibh*, 'Rona of the Atlantic', containing the old word *tabh*, 'ocean', from Norse.

Northton (Harris), An Taobh Tuath. The English name is 'north farm' while the Gaelic name is 'the north side'.

North Uist, Uibhist a Tuath. *See* **Uist**. North Uist is also known locally as *an Ceann a Tuath*, 'the north end', and is nicknamed *Tìr an Eòrna*, 'the land of barley'. A native of North Uist is a *Tuathach*, 'northerner'.

Noss Head (Caithness), Rubha Nòis.

'The headland of the river mouth', from Gaelic/Norse. This name was originally *Rubha an Òis* but became contracted.

Noster (Harris), Nostair. 'North farm', from Norse.

Nostie (Ross), Ceann na Mòna. The English form is from *Nòsdaidh* which in turn is from *òst-thaigh*, 'inn', but the current Gaelic name is 'the end of the peat bog'. Nostie Bridge is *Drochaid Nòsdaidh*, retaining the older Gaelic name.

Novar (Ross), Taigh an Fhuamhair. 'The house of the giant'.

Nuide (Inverness), Noid. 'Green place'.

Nunton (Benbecula), Baile nan Cailleach. 'The village of the nuns'. Nunton graveyard is *Cladh Mhoire*, 'graveyard of St Mary'.

Oa (Islay), An Obha. 'The headland'. Local people were nicknamed *cuthagan*, 'cuckoos'.

Oape (Ross), An t-Òb. 'The bay', from Norse.

Oban (Argyll), An t-Òban. 'The little bay'. The full name is *An t-Òban Latharnach*, 'little bay of Lorne'. A Gaelic equivalent of 'When in Rome...' is *Ma tha thu san Òban, dèan mar an t-Òban*, 'If you're in Oban, do as Oban does'.

Obsdale (Ross), Òbasdal. 'Bay valley', from Norse.

Ochtavullin (Argyll), Ochdamh a' Mhuilinn. 'The octave or eighth-land at the mill'.

Ochtermuthil (Perth). 'The top of Muthil', from *Uachdar Mhaothail*.

Ochtertyre (Perth), Uachdar Thìre. 'The top of the land'.

Ochtofad (Argyll), An t-Ochdamh Fada. 'The long octave or eighth-land'.

Ochtomore (Argyll), An t-Ochdamh Mór. 'The big octave or eighth-land'.

Ochtow (Sutherland), An t-Ochdamh. 'The octave or eighth-land'.

Ockle (Argyll), Ocal or Ochdal. This

Norse name is unclear but may contain either *dalr*, 'valley', or *vøllr*, 'field'.

Octofad (Islay), An t-Ochdamh Fada. *See* **Ochtofad**.

Octomore (Islay), An t-Ochdamh Mór. *See* **Ochtomore**.

Octovulin (Islay), Ochdamh a' Mhuilinn. 'The eighth-land of the mill'.

Oldany (Sutherland), Alltanaigh. 'Fruit island', from Norse. Oldany Island is *Eilean Alltanaigh*.

Old Croggan (Mull). There is no Gaelic equivalent of this name as Gaelic distinguishes between Old Croggan's two parts, *Baile Geamhraidh*, 'winter farm', and *Baile nan Seabhag*, 'the hawks' farm', considering them as two separate places.

Old Deer (Aberdeen), Déir. The English name uses 'Old' to distinguish this from New Deer. The Gaelic name was believed to be from *deur*, 'a tear', but this is unclear. The earliest examples of written Scottish Gaelic are in *Leabhar Dhéir*, 'the Book of Deer'.

Old Kilpatrick (Dunbarton). 'Old' is used to distinguish this place from New Kilpatrick at Bearsden. Kilpatrick itself is *Cill Phàdraig*, 'St Patrick's church'.

Oldshorebeg (Sutherland), Àisir Beag. 'Small path or pass', a Norse/Gaelic name.

Oldshoremore (Sutherland), Àisir Mór. 'Big path or pass', from Norse/Gaelic.

Ollach (Skye), An t-Òlach. This may be 'the rank grass'. Upper Ollach is *An t-Òlach Shuas*.

Onich (Inverness), Omhanaich. This is thought to mean 'froth place', possibly referring to a frothy beach.

Opinan (Ross), Na h-Òbaidhnean. 'The little bays'. There are two places with this name, the first near Gairloch also known as *Òbaidhnean Gheàrrloch* and the second near Laide known as *Òbaidhnean an Leothaid* or *Òbaidhnean an Uillt Bheithe*.

Orbost (Skye), Orabost. This Norse name may be 'Orri's farm' or 'seal farm'.

Orchill (Perth), Urchoill. 'Wood side'.

Ord (Skye), An t-Òrd. 'The rounded hill'.

Ordie (Aberdeen). 'Place of the rounded hill', from *Òrdaigh*.

Ord of Caithness (Caithness), An t-Òrd Gallach. 'The Caithness rounded hill'.

Orinsay (Lewis), Orasaigh. 'Ebb island', from Norse.

Orkie (Fife). 'Pig place', from *Orcaidh*, earlier *Orcan*.

Orkney, Arcaibh. 'Land of the swine or whale people', a tribal name. An Orcadian is an *Arcach*. The Pentland Firth is *An Caol Arcach*, 'Orcadian Sound'.

Ormaclete (South Uist), Ormacleit. 'Shale rock or hill'.

Ormidale (Argyll), Ormadal. 'Shale valley'.

Ormiscaig (Argyll), Ormasgaig. This may be 'shale strip of land' or 'Orm's strip of land', from Norse.

Ormsaigbeg (Argyll), Ormsaig Bheag. 'Shale bay' or 'Orm's bay', from Norse, with Gaelic *beag*, 'small'.

Ormsary (Argyll), Ormsaraidh. 'Orm's field' or 'shale field', from Norse.

Ormscaig (Ross), Ormasgaig. *See* **Ormiscaig**.

Oronsay (Colonsay), Orasa; (Skye), Orasaigh. *See* **Orinsay**.

Orosay (South Uist), Orasaigh. *See* **Orinsay**.

Orsay (Islay), Orasa or Orasaigh. *See* **Orinsay**.

Osdal (Skye), Òsdal. 'River mouth valley', from Norse.

Ose (Skye), Òs. 'River mouth', from Norse.

Osedale (Ross), Òsdal. *See* **Osdal**.

Oskaig (Raasay), Òsgaig. 'Strip of land at a river mouth', from Norse.

Oskamull (Mull), Osgamul. This may be 'ox island', from Norse.

Osmigarry (Skye), Osmaigearraidh. 'Asmund's field or pasture land', from Norse.

Osnaburgh (Fife). This appears to include the same first element as in Osnabrück in Germany. This place is also known as Dairsie, which is 'oak stance' from *dair* and *fasadh*.

Ostaig (Skye), Ostaig. 'East bay', from Norse.

Ostem (Harris), Ostam. 'East islet', from Norse.

Otter Ferry (Argyll), An Oitir or Port na h-Oitrich. 'The long low promontory' or 'the harbour at the long low promontory'.

Otternish (North Uist), Odarnais. 'Sharp point headland'.

Outend (Scalpay), An Ceann a-Muigh. 'The outside end'.

Overscaig (Sutherland), Ofarsgaig. 'Over strip of land'.

Ovie (Inverness), Ubhaidh. This is said to be from *uabhaidh*, 'terrible', but may actually refer to some oval-shaped feature, from Gaelic *ugh*, 'egg'.

Pabay (Harris), Pabaigh. 'Priest island', from Norse. A native of Pabay was a *Pabach* or *cathan*, 'sea bird'.

Pabbay (Barra, Skye), Pabaigh. *See* **Pabay**.

Paible (North Uist), Paibeil. 'Priest village', from Norse. A saying warns, *Na toir bó á Paibeil, 's na toir bean á Boighreigh*, 'Don't take a cow from Paible or a wife from Boreray'.

Paiblesgarry (North Uist), Paiblisgear-raidh. 'Fertile pasture land of Paible', from Norse.

Pairc (Lewis), A' Phàirc. 'The park'. The full name is *A' Phàirc Leódhasach*, 'the Lewis Park'.

Paisley (Renfrew), Pàislig. 'Basilica', from Latin.

Palascaig (Ross), Feallasgaig. 'Hilly strip of land', from Norse.

Palnure (Kirkcudbright). This may be 'the pool by the yew tree or trees', from *Poll an Iubhair* or *Poll nan Iubhar*, but *see* **Achanalt**.

Panbride (Angus). 'St Bridget's hollow', with Brythonic *pant*, 'hollow', or a gaelicised version giving *Pann Brìghde*.

Panmuir (Angus). 'Large hollow' or 'St Mary's hollow', from Brythonic *pant* or a gaelicised version such as *pann*, and Gaelic *mór* or *Moire*.

Pannanich (Aberdeen), Pananaich. 'Place of hollows', with a Brythonic origin. Pannanich Wells is *Fuaran Phananaich*.

Papadil (Rum), Pàpadal. 'Priest valley', from Norse.

Parkend (Lewis), Ceann nam Buail-tean. The Gaelic name is 'the end of the folds'.

Partick (Glasgow), Pearthaig or Partaig. 'Little copse', from Brythonic. The term *cho luath ri muileann Phearthaig* means 'as fast as Partick mill'. The Gaelic form *Partaig* has probably come into use under the influence of the English form.

Patt (Ross), A' Phait. 'The lump'. The full name is *A' Phait Mhonarach*, 'the Monar lump'.

Paulfield (Ross), Am Bàrd. It is unclear who is referred to in the English name. The Gaelic name is 'the meadow'.

Pearsie (Angus), Parsaidh. This may be 'copse place', from Brythonic or Pictish.

Peebles, Na Puballan. This may be 'pavilions', from Brythonic *pebyll* with English and Gaelic plurals. Peebles-shire is *Siorrachd nam Puballan*.

Peinchorran (Skye), Peighinn a' Chor-rain. 'The pennyland at the narrow headland'.

Peinlich (Skye), Peighinn an Lighiche. 'The pennyland of the doctor'.

Peinmore (Skye), Am Peighinn Mór. 'The large pennyland'.

Peinness (Skye), Peighinn an Easa. 'The pennyland by the waterfall or stream'.

Penbreck (Ayr). 'Speckled pennyland', from *Peighinn Breac*.

Penick (Nairn). This may be 'small pennyland', from *Peighinneag*.

Penifiler (Skye), Peighinn nam Fìdhleir. 'The pennyland of the fiddlers'.

Peninerine (South Uist), Peighinn nan Aoireann. 'The pennyland at the raised beaches'.

Pennycraig (Islay), Creagan na Peighinne. 'The small rock at the pennyland'.

Pennycross (Mull), Peighinn na Croise. 'The pennyland of the cross', the cross in question being *Crois an Ollaimh*, 'the doctor's cross', known as 'Beaton's Cross' in English.

Pennyfuir (Argyll), Peighinn a' Phùir. 'The pennyland of the pasture'.

Pennyghael (Mull), Peighinn a' Ghàidheil. 'The pennyland of the Gael'.

Penrioch (Arran), A' Pheighinn Riabhach. 'The brindled pennyland'.

Pensoraig (Skye), Peighinn Sòraig. 'Pennyland by the muddy bay', from Gaelic/Norse.

Pentaskill (Angus). 'Land of the gospel', from Pictish *pett* and Gaelic *soisgeul*.

Persie (Perth), Parasaidh or Parsaidh. *See* **Pearsie**.

Perth, Peairt. 'Copse', from Brythonic/Pictish. The term *bho Pheairt gu Hiort*, 'from Perth to St Kilda', was used to delineate the extent of the Gaelic speaking areas. According to another saying, *Tatha mhór nan tonn, bheir i sgrìob lom air Peairt*, 'Great Tay of the waves will cut a swathe through Perth'. The town is also mentioned in the saying *Trì iongantasan na h-Alba: drochaid Obar Pheallaidh, tobraichean Ghlinn Iucha is cluig Pheairt*, 'The three wonders of Scotland: Aberfeldy bridge, the wells of Linlithgow and the bells of Perth'. Perthshire is *Siorrachd Pheairt*, and a Perth person is a *Peairteach*.

Peterburn (Ross), Alltan Phàdraig. 'Peter's little stream'.

Peterculter (Aberdeen). 'Peter's Culter'.

Peterhead (Aberdeen), Ceann Phàdraig or Inbhir Ùigidh. 'Peter's headland'. The name *Ceann Phàdraig* is a fairly recent translation from English. The town was known as *Inbhir Ùigidh*, 'mouth of the Ugie' in the eastern Gaelic speaking areas. Inverugie itself is located nearby.

Petersport (Benbecula), Port Pheadair. 'Peter's port'.

Petley (Ross), Am Maol Buidhe. The English name comes from the surname of the wife of a previous proprietor. The Gaelic name is 'the yellow rounded hill'.

Pettensier (Moray). 'The farm of the joiners', with Pictish *pett* and Gaelic *saor*.

Petty (Inverness), Peitidh. 'Piece of land', from Pictish *pett* with a Gaelic locative ending.

Phantassie (East Lothian, Fife). This may mean ' damp gentle slope', from *Fàn Taise*.

Philiphaugh (Roxburgh), Filiopfach. 'Philip's haugh', from English.

Phoineas (Inverness, Ross), Foinnis. 'Under-meadow'. Phoineas in Ross is also known as *Fothairis*.

Phoness (Inverness), Fothairis. *See* **Phoineas**.

Pien (Arran), A' Pheighinn. 'The pennyland'.

Pinhannet (Ayr). This appears to be 'the pennyland of the mother church', from *Peighinn na h-Annaid*.

Pinmore (Ayr). This may be 'large pennyland', from *Peighinn Mòr*.

Pinwherrie (Ayr). This may be 'pennyland of the corrie', from *Peighinn a' Choire*.

Pirnmill (Arran), Am Muileann or A' Mhuilinn. 'Mill of the pirns'.

The Gaelic name is 'the mill', the full name being *Am Muileann Iteachan*, 'the pirn mill'. Another name, *Muileann nam Piùirneachan*, 'mill of the pirns', suggests that the English name came first and was later translated into Gaelic.

Pitagowan (Perth), Baile a' Ghobhainn. 'The smith's farm', from Pictish/Gaelic.

Pitarrick (Perth), Baile an Tarraig. 'Farm of the pulling', possibly referring to the steep hill road above it, from Pictish/Gaelic.

Pitcairn (Fife). 'Farm at the cairn', from *peit* and *càrn*.

Pitcalnie (Ross), Baile Chailnidh or Cuilt Eararaidh. 'Farm at the hard place', from Pictish/Gaelic. The second Gaelic name is 'secluded spot of the parching'. The Strath of Pitcalnie is *Srath Chuilt Eararaidh*.

Pitcalzean (Ross), Baile a' Choillein. 'Farm by the small wood', from Pictish/Gaelic.

Pitcaple (Aberdeen). 'Farm of the horse', from Pictish/Gaelic, *Peit/Baile nan Capall*.

Pitcarden (Moray). 'Farm by the thicket', from Pictish, *Peit Chàrdainn*.

Pitcarmick (Perth), Baile Charmaig. 'Cormac's farm', from Pictish/Gaelic.

Pitcastle (Perth), Baile a' Chaisteil. 'The farm at the castle', from Pictish/Gaelic.

Pitchaish (Banff). This may be 'steep farm', from Pictish/Gaelic, *Peit/Baile Chais*.

Pitchroy (Moray). 'Hard farm', from Pictish/Gaelic, *Peit/Baile Chruaidh*.

Pitconochie (Fife). 'Duncan's farm', from Pictish/Gaelic, *Peit/Baile Dhonnchaidh*.

Pitcorthie (Fife). 'The farm of the standing stone', from Pictish/Gaelic, *Peit/Baile Coirthe*.

Pitcorthy (Aberdeen). *See* **Pitcorthie**.

Pitcruive (Perth), Peit Chraoibh. 'The farm at the tree', from Pictish/Gaelic. Unusually, the Gaelic form of the

name has retained Pictish *pett* rather than amending it to Gaelic *baile*.

Pitfaed (Ross), Baile Phàididh. 'Paddy's farm', from Pictish/Gaelic.

Pitfichie (Aberdeen). This may be 'raven farm' or 'farm at the raven place', from Pictish/Gaelic, *Peit/Baile Fithichidh*.

Pitfodels (Aberdeen). 'The copse at the section of land', from *Bad Fodail*.

Pitfour (Perth, Ross), Baile Phùir. 'The farm at the pasture', from Pictish/Gaelic.

Pitfuir (Ross), Pit Fhùir. *See* **Pitfour**. Interestingly, Gaelic has retained *pit* rather than change it to *baile.*.

Pitfure (Sutherland), Baile Phùir. *See* **Pitfour**.

Pitgaveny (Moray). 'The farm of the stirk', from Pictish/Gaelic, *Peit/Baile a' Ghamhna*.

Pitglassie (Banff), Baile Glasaidh; (Ross), Baile a' Ghlasaich. 'The farm by the grassy land', from Pictish/Gaelic.

Pitgrudie (Sutherland), Baile Ghrùididh. 'The farm by the gravelly river', from Pictish/Gaelic.

Pithogarty (Ross), Baile Shogartaidh. 'Farm at the priest's place', from Pictish/Gaelic.

Pitkeathley (Perth). 'Cathalan's farm', from Pictish/Gaelic, *Peit/Baile Chathalain*.

Pitkennedy (Angus). 'Kennedy's farm', from Pictish/Gaelic, *Peit/Baile a' Cheanadaich*.

Pitkenny (Fife). 'Cainneach's farm', from Pictish/Gaelic, *Peit/Baile Chainnigh*.

Pitkerrald (Inverness), Baile Chaoraill. 'Caorall's farm', from Pictish/Gaelic.

Pitkerrie (Ross), Baile Chéirigh. This name may contain a form of *ciar*, 'dark', giving 'farm at the dark place', from Pictish/Gaelic.

Pitlochie (Fife). This farm name referred originally to a stone, *clach*, rather than a loch.

Pitlochrie (Angus), Baile Chloichrigh. 'The farm at the stony place', from Pictish/Gaelic.

Pitlochry (Perth), Baile Chloichrigh. *See* **Pitlochrie**. This used to be known as *Both Chloichrigh*, 'the hut at the stony place'. *See* **Atholl**.

Pitmachie (Aberdeen). This is said to be 'Maol Fheichin's farm', from Pictish/Gaelic, *Peit/Baile Mhaol Fheichin*.

Pitmaduthy (Ross), Baile MhicDhuibh or Peit MhicDhuibh. 'MacDuff's farm', from Pictish/Gaelic.

Pitmedden (Aberdeen). 'Middle farm', from Pictish/Gaelic, *Peit/Baile Meadhain*.

Pitmurchie (Aberdeen). 'Murchadh's farm', from Pictish/Gaelic, *Peit/Baile Mhurchaidh*.

Pitnacree (Perth), Baile na Craoibhe. 'The farm with the tree', from Pictish/Gaelic.

Pitnellie (Ross), Baile an Eunlaith. 'The farm of the poultry', from Pictish/Gaelic.

Pitourie (Inverness), Baile Odharaidh. 'The farm at the dun-coloured place', from Pictish/Gaelic.

Pittencrieff (Fife). 'Farm at the tree or trees', from Pictish/Gaelic *Peit/Baile na Craoibhe* or *Peit/Baile nan Craobh*.

Pittendreich (Moray, Perth), Baile an Dreich. 'The farm at the hill face', from Pictish/Gaelic.

Pittentaggart (Aberdeen). 'The farm of the priest', from Pictish/Gaelic *Peit/Baile an t-Sagairt*.

Pittentraill (Sutherland), Baile an Tràill. 'The farm of the serf', from Pictish/Gaelic. This is also known locally as *Bad an Tràill*, 'the spot of the serf'.

Pittenweem (Fife). 'The farm by the cave', from Pictish/Gaelic, *Peit/Baile na h-Uaimh*.

Pitteuchar (Fife). 'Farm at the river bank', using *eochair*, 'edge, bank', as found in 'Yoker'.

Pittyvaich (Banff). 'The farm with the byre', from Pictish/Gaelic, *Peit/Baile a' Bhàthaich*

Pityoulish (Inverness), Baile Gheollais. 'The farm at the bright place', from Pictish/Gaelic.

Pladda (Arran), Plada. 'Flat island', from Norse.

Plocrapol (Harris), Plocrapol. This Norse name contains *bólstaðr*, 'farm', but the first part is unclear.

Plockton (Ross), Am Ploc. 'The pimple'. The English name has 'town' attached. The full Gaelic name is *Ploc Loch Aillse*, 'the pimple of Lochalsh', nicknamed *baile nam bochd*, 'the village of the poor'.

Pluscarden (Moray). Although the first part of the name is unclear, the second is 'thicket', from Pictish *carden*.

Point (Lewis), An Rubha. 'The headland'. A native of Point is a *Rubhach*, also nicknamed a *sùlaire*, 'gannet', or *turnag*, 'duck', the last name imitating the Point accent.

Point of Sleat (Skye), An Rubha or Rubha Shléite. 'The headland' or 'headland of Sleat'.

Point of Stoer (Sutherland), Rubha an Stòir. 'The headland of Stoer'.

Polbain (Ross), Am Poll Bàn. 'The white pool'.

Poldrait (West Lothian). 'The pool at the bridge', from *Poll na Drochaid*.

Polglass (Ross), Am Poll Glas. 'The grey-green pool'.

Polin (Sutherland), Pòlain. 'The farm', from Norse.

Polkemmet (West Lothian). If this is a Gaelic name, it may be 'pool at the crooked place', from *Poll Camaid*.

Polla (Sutherland), Am Polladh. 'The pool' or 'pool river', from Norse.

Pollagharrie (Ross), Poll a' Ghearraidh. 'The pool of the cut', referring to a land feature.

Polloch (Argyll), Poll Loch. 'Mud loch'.

Pollochar (South Uist), Poll a' Charra. 'The pool by the standing stone'.

Pollosgan (Skye), Poll Losgann. 'Frog pond'.

Polmaddie (Argyll), Poll a' Mhadaidh. 'The pool of the wolf'.

Polmadie (Glasgow). This appears to be 'the pool of the son of God', from *Poll Mac Dé*.

Polmont (Stirling). This may be 'muddy moor' or 'pool moor', from *Poll-Mhon(adh)*, or a cognate Brythonic source.

Polnessan (Ayr). 'The pool of the stream or waterfall', from *Poll an Easain*.

Poniel (West Lothian). 'Neil's pool or stream', from *Poll Néill*.

Poolewe (Ross), Poll Iubh or Abhainn Iubh. 'The pool on the Ewe river'. The second Gaelic name is 'River Ewe'. The coast from Poolewe to Cove is known as *An Slios*, 'the side'.

Porin (Ross), Pòrainn. 'Pasture (place)'. Porin Churchyard is *Cladh Phòrainn* but used to be known as *Cladh Mèinn*, 'churchyard of Mid Strathconon'.

Port an Righ (Ross), Port an Draoidh. 'The druid's harbour'. The English name, which looks like 'the king's harbour', is from a mis-understanding of the Gaelic name.

Port Appin (Argyll), Port na h-Apann or Port na Croise. 'The port of Appin' or 'the port of the cross'. An older name is *Achadh a' Bhirlinn*, which appears to mean 'the field of the galley' although one would usually expect *Achadh na Birlinn*.

Port Askaig (Islay), Port Asgaig. 'The harbour at ash bay', from Gaelic/Norse.

Portavadie (Argyll), Port a' Mhadaidh. 'The harbour of the wolf'.

Portban (Tiree), Am Port Bàn. 'The white or fair harbour'.

Port Bannatyne (Bute), Port MhicEamailinn. 'Bannatyne's harbour'. The

old name is *Baile a' Chamais*, 'the village on the bay'.

Port Charlotte (Islay), Port Sgioba or Sgioba. The English name is from the mother of Frederick Campbell of Islay. The Gaelic names are 'harbour at the ship river' or simply 'ship river', from Norse.

Portclare (Inverness), Port Chlàir. 'The harbour at the plain'.

Port Dundas (Glasgow), Am Port. The English name commemorates the Dundas family, while the Gaelic name is simply 'the port'.

Port Ellen (Islay), Port Ìlein. This is named after the wife of Frederick Campbell of Islay. The old name is *Leòdamas*, 'Leòd's harbour', from Norse.

Portessie (Banff). This may be 'the harbour at the stream place', from *Port Easaidh*. The local name is 'the Sloch', from *sloc*, 'pit'.

Portfield (Mull), Achadh a' Phuirt. 'The field by the port'.

Port Glasgow (Renfrew), Port Ghlaschu. 'The port of Glasgow'.

Portgordon (Banff), Port Ghòrdain. 'The port of the Gordons'.

Port Henderson (Ross), Portaigil or Portaigin. The Gaelic names mean 'port ravine', from Norse. Locals are known as *cnùdanan*, 'gurnards'.

Portinisherrich (Argyll), Port Innis Sia Ràmhaich. 'The port of the island of the six-oar galley'.

Portknockie (Banff). 'Harbour at the hilly place', from *Port Chnocaidh*.

Portlethen (Kincardine). This may be 'broad harbour', from *Port Leathann*.

Port Logan (Wigtown), Port an Neasaig. The English name commemorates the Logan family, while the older Gaelic name is 'the port at the little isthmus'.

Portmahomack (Ross). Port Mo Cholmaig. 'St Colman's harbour'.

Portmoak (Kinross). 'St Mayota's village', from *Port M' Aodhaig*.

Portmoluag (Lismore), Port Mo Luaig. 'St Mo Luag's harbour'.

Port Mor (Tiree), Am Port Mór. 'The big harbour'.

Portmore (Peebles); (Muck), Am Port Mór. In Muck, the name means 'the big harbour', but in Peebles it is probably 'the big village'.

Portnacon (Sutherland), Port nan Con. 'The harbour of the hounds'.

Portnacraig (Perth), Port na Creige. 'The village at the rock'.

Portnacroish (Argyll). 'The harbour of the cross', from *Port na Croise*.

Portnadoran (Inverness), Port nan Dobhran. 'The port of the otters'.

Portnaguran (Lewis), Port nan Giùran. 'The harbour of the barnacles'.

Portnahaven (Islay), Port na h-Abhainne. 'Harbour at the river'. There is an argument that this may be a gaelicisation of a name originally including Norse *höfn* (harbour) rather than Gaelic *abhainn* (river). The Gaelic name of neighbouring Port Charlotte is of Norse origin.

Portnaheile (Ross), Port na h-Éile. The defining element of this name is unclear.

Portnalong (Skye), Port nan Long. 'The harbour of the ships'.

Port of Menteith (Perth), Port Loch Innis mo Cholmaig or Am Port. 'The port of the Lake of Menteith' or 'the port'.

Port of Ness (Lewis), Port Nis or Am Port. 'The harbour of Ness' (or simply 'the harbour' in Gaelic). The village's old name was *Calaigmhol*, from Norse.

Port Patrick (Wigtown), Port Phàdraig. 'Patrick's harbour'. This was earlier known as *Port Rìgh*, 'king's harbour'.

Port Ramsay (Lismore), Port Ramasa or Port Ramasaigh. The second part of this name is Norse for 'raven island', and the island in question, *Eilean Ramasa*, is just offshore.

Portree (Skye), Port Rìgh. 'King's harbour'. This is said originally to have been *Port Ruighe*, 'slope harbour'. An earlier name was Kiltaraglan, from *Cill Targhlain*, 'St Talorcan's church', also found in 'Kiltarlity'.

Portskerra (Sutherland), Port Sgeirea. 'Skerry harbour'.

Portsonachan (Argyll), Port Samhnachain. 'The port of the river trout' or 'the port at the sorrel place'.

Portsoy (Banff). This may be 'saithe harbour', from *Port Saoithe*.

Portuairk (Argyll), Port Uairce or Port Uaraig. This may be 'Ualraig's harbour'.

Portvasco (Sutherland), Port Faisgeach. Locally this is said to be 'sheltered harbour'.

Portvoller (Lewis), Port Mholair. This may be 'port by the field', from Norse.

Port Wemyss (Islay), Bun Othan. The Wemyss family are commemorated in the English name, but the Gaelic name means 'river mouth'.

Poulouriscaig (Sutherland), Poll Aoraisgeig or Poll Éirisgeig. This hybrid Gaelic/Norse name may be 'pool at the gravel beach strip of land' or even 'pool at Erik's bay'.

Poyntzfield (Ross), An Àrdach. A family name is used in the English name. The Gaelic name is 'the high place'.

Prabost (Skye), Pràbost. This name is said to have been *Bréabost* originally, which is 'broad farm', from Norse.

Prescaulton (Moray). 'Hazel thicket', from *Preas Calltainn*.

Presnerb (Angus), Preas na h-Earb. 'Thicket of the roe deer'.

Proncycroy (Sutherland), Prannsaidh Cruaidh. 'Hard tree place', including what appears to be a Brythonic or Pictish element for 'tree'.

Pubil (Perth), Puball. 'Pavilion' or 'tent'.

Purin (Fife). 'Pasture place', from *Pòran*.

Quaish (Tiree), Cu-dhéis *See* **Cuigeas**.

Quarryfield (Ross), Taigh an Rothaid. The Gaelic name means 'the road house'.

Quarryhill (Ross), Cnoc an t-Sabhail. The Gaelic name means 'the hill at the barn'.

Queebec (Ross), Muileann Luathaidh. The English name commemorates Quebec, while the Gaelic name means 'waulk mill'.

Quidinish (Harris), Cuidinis. 'Cattle fold headland', from Norse.

Quier (Lewis), Cuidhir. 'Cattle folds', from Norse.

Quinish (Mull), Cuidhinis. 'Cattle fold headland', from Norse.

Quothquan (Lanark). This may be 'common land', from *Coitcheann*.

Raarem (Harris), Ràiream. 'Islet with a nook', from Norse.

Raasay, Ratharsair or Ratharsaigh. 'Roe deer island', from Norse. The island also has the by-name of *Eilean nam Fear Móra*, 'the island of the great men'. Raasay House is *Taigh Mór a' Chlachain*, 'big house of Churchtown'. A Raasay person is a *Ratharsach*, nicknamed a *saoidhean*, 'saithe'. A saying lists the various wells of Raasay, *Tobar na Creachainn an Ósgaig, Tobar an Dòmhnaich sa Ghleann, Tobar an Fhìona aig Tobhtagan, Tobar nam Bioran an Glaic nan Curran, 's an Tobar Mór an Suidhisnis*.

Raddery (Ross), Radharaidh. 'Arable land not in use'.

Raemoir (Kincardine). This may be from *Ràth Mór*, 'large circular fort'.

Raffin (Sutherland), An Ràthan. 'The small circular fort'.

Rafford (Moray), Ràthard or Ràthfard. This may be 'high circular fort'.

Rahoy (Argyll), Rathuaidhe. This may be 'northern circular fort', from an earlier *Ràth Thuaidhe*.

Raigbeg (Inverness), (An) Ràthaig Bheag. 'Small place of the circular fort'.

Raigmore (Inverness), (An) Ràthaig Mhór. 'Large place of the circular fort'.

Raith (Fife). 'Circular fort', from *Ràth*.

Raitts (Inverness), Ràt or Ràta. 'Circular fort'. *See* **Atholl**.

Ralia (Inverness), An Ràth Liath. 'The grey circular fort'.

Ramasaig (Skye), Ramasaig. 'Raven bay', from Norse.

Ramorgan (Fife). This is said to be 'Morgan's circular fort', from *Ràth a' Mhorganaich*.

Ramornie (Fife). *See* **Ramorgan**.

Ranish (Lewis), Rànais or Radhairnis. 'Roe deer headland', from Norse.

Rannagulzion (Perth), Ruigh nan Cuileag. 'The sheiling of the flies'.

Rannoch (Perth), Raineach. 'Bracken'. Rannoch Moor is *Mòinteach Raineach* or *Madagan na Mòine* (locally *Madaigein na Mòin*). The north side of Loch Rannoch is *An Slios Mìn*, 'the smooth slope', while the south side is *An Slios Garbh*, 'the rough slope', and contains *An Giuthsach*, 'the Black Wood of Rannoch'. Rannoch was known poetically as *Raineach nam bó*, 'Rannoch of the cows', and appears in the saying, *Trì gearastain na h-Albann – Dùn Breatann, Dùn Chailleann is Madaigein na Mòin*, 'Three fortresses of Scotland – Dumbarton, Dunkeld and Rannoch Moor'.

Rarichie (Ross), Ràth Riachaidh. 'Circular fort at the scratching place'. Easter Rarichie is *Ràth Riachaidh Shìos*, 'lower Rarichie', Wester Rarichie is *Ràth Riachaidh Shuas*, 'upper Rarichie', and Lower Rarichie is *Baile a' Phuill*, 'farm by the pool'.

Rascarrel (Kirkcudbright). This may be 'Cearbhall's headland', from *Ros Chearbhaill*.

Ratagan (Ross), Ràtagan 'Small circular fort'.

Rathelpie (Fife). 'Alpin's circular fort', from *Ràth Ailpein*.

Rathillet (Fife). This may be 'circular fort of the Ulstermen', from *Ràth Uladh*.

Ratho (Midlothian). 'Circular fort place', from *Ràthach*.

Rattray (Perth), Raitear or Baile Raiteir. 'Fort place' or 'village of the fort place'.

Rayne (Aberdeen). 'Division', from *Rann*.

Reay (Caithness), Meaghrath or Ràth. 'Mid fort' or 'fort'. The poet Rob Donn MacKay spelled this name as *Mìodhrath* or *Mìodhradh*.

Reay Forest (Sutherland), Dùthaich MhicAoidh. This deer forest is 'MacKay's country' in Gaelic.

Rechullin (Ross), An Ruigh Chuilinn. 'The holly slope'.

Redburn (Inverness), An t-Allt Ruadh. 'The red-brown stream'.

Redcastle (Ross), An Caisteal Dearg or An Caisteal Ruadh. 'The red castle'. Gaelic has two words for 'red'; *dearg* is the bright crimson to scarlet colour while *ruadh* is more russet or red-brown. The old name of this place was *Eadar Dà Dhobhar*, 'between two waters' or Edradour.

Redcliff (Skye), An Uamh Ruadh. 'The red-brown cave', in Gaelic.

Redfield (Ross), An Raon Dearg. 'The red plain'.

Redgorton (Perth). 'The circular fort by the enclosed field', from *Ràth a' Ghoirtein*.

Redkirk Point (Dumfries), Rinn Phàdraig. 'Point of the red church'. The old form in English is Reynpatrick, from the Gaelic name for 'Patrick's headland'.

Redpoint (Ross), An Rubha Dearg. 'The red headland'. The north end of the village is *Am Baile Shìos* while the southern end is *Am Baile Shuas*. The old name of Redpoint is *An Rubha Lachdann*, 'the swarthy or dun-coloured headland'.

Reef (Lewis), An Riof; (Tiree), An Ruighe. In Lewis the name means 'the reef', from Norse, while in Tiree it appears to mean 'the slope', but may originally have been from Norse also.

Regoilachy (Ross), Ruigh Ghobhlachaidh. 'Slope at the forked field'.

Rehourie (Nairn), An Ruigh Shamhraidh. 'The summer sheiling'.

Reiff (Sutherland), An Rif. 'The reef', from Norse.

Reinakyllich (Perth), Raon nan Coileach. 'The field of the cockrels'.

Reisgill (Sutherland), Rìdhisgil. 'Brushwood gully', from Norse.

Relugas (Moray). 'Slug slope or sheiling', from *Ruigh Lùgais*.

Remony (Perth), An Réidh-Mhuin. 'The level hill'.

Renfrew, Rinn Friù. 'The headland of the current', from Brythonic. Renfrewshire is *Siorrachd Rinn Friù*.

Renish Point (Harris), Rubha Réinis. This may be 'reed headland', from Gaelic/Norse.

Reraig (Ross), Réaraig. 'Reed bay', from Norse.

Resaurie (Ross), Ruigh Samhraidh. 'Summer sheiling'.

Rescobie (Angus). This may be 'the wood of splinters or thorns', from *Ros Sgolban* as an old form of the anglicised name, Roscolbyn, suggests.

Resipol (Argyll), Réiseapol. This may mean 'brushwood farm', from Norse.

Resolis (Ross), Ruigh Solais or Ruigh Sholais. 'Bright slope'. Resolis parish is *Sgìre Ruigh Sholais* or *Sgìre Mhàrtainn*, the latter meaning 'St Martin's parish'.

Restenneth (Angus). This may be 'wood of fire', from Brythonic or Gaelic, *Ros Teine*.

Reudle (Mull), Raodal or Raoghadal. This may be the same name as **Rodel**.

Revack (Moray), Ruigh a' Bhaic. 'The sheiling at the hollow'.

Reyran (Argyll), Radharan. This may refer to a patch of arable land unused.

Rhegreannoch (Ross), An Ruigh Ghrianach. 'The sunny slope'.

Rheindown (Ross), Ruigh an Dùin. 'The slope of the fort'.

Rhelonie (Ross), Ruigh an Lòin. 'The slope of the wet meadow'.

Rhenetra (Skye), Réineatra. This may be 'rowan township', from Norse.

Rhenigadale (Harris), Réinigeadal. This may be 'rowan bay valley', from Norse.

Rhian (Sutherland), An Ruighean. 'The little slope'.

Rhianbreck (Sutherland), An Ruighean Breac. 'The speckled little slope'.

Rhicarn (Sutherland), Ruigh nan Càrn. 'The slope of the cairns'.

Rhiconich (Sutherland), An Ruigh Còinnich. 'The mossy slope'.

Rhicullen (Ross), Ruigh a' Chuilinn. 'The slope of the holly'.

Rhidorroch (Ross), An Ruigh Dhorch. 'The dark slope'.

Rhiedorroch (Perth). An Ruigh Dhorch. See **Rhidorroch**.

Rhifail (Sutherland), An Ruigh Fàil. 'The hedge or dyke slope'.

Rhigolter (Sutherland), Ruigh a' Ghalldfhir or Ruigh a' Ghalldair. This is said to be 'the slope of the lowland man', but the second element may be Norse.

Rhilochan (Sutherland), Ruigh an Lochain. 'The slope of the small loch'.

Rhiloisk (Sutherland), An Ruigh Loisgte. 'The burnt slope'.

Rhinns of Galloway (Wigtown), Ranna Ghall-ghàidheil or Na Rannaibh. 'The divisions of Galloway' or 'the divisions'.

Rhireavoch (Ross), An Ruigh Riabhach. 'The brindled slope'.

Rhitongue (Sutherland), Ruigh Thunga. 'The slope of Tongue'.

Rhives (Ross), Na Ruighean or Ruigheas (Black Isle), Na Ruigheanan (Easter Ross); (Sutherland), An Ruigheach. In the Black Isle, Rhives

is *Na Ruighean*, 'the slopes', or *Ruigheas*, 'slope place'; in Easter Ross, it is *Na Ruigheanan*, 'the slopes'; in Sutherland, it is *An Ruigheach*, 'the slope place'.

Rhu (Dunbarton, Inverness), An Rubha. 'The headland'.

Rhubain (Eriskay), An Rubha Bàn. 'The fair headland'.

Rhubodach (Bute), An Rubha Bódach. 'The Bute headland'.

Rhughasinish (South Uist), Rubha Ghaisinis. 'The headland of goose point', from Gaelic/Norse.

Rhunahaorine (Argyll), Rubha na h-Aoireann. 'The headland of the raised beach'.

Rhuvanish (Berneray), Rubha Mhànais. 'Magnus's headland'.

Rhynamarst (Banff), Ruigh nam Mart. 'The slope or sheiling of the cattle'.

Rhynd (Fife); (Perth), Rinn Dealgros. In Perth this is 'the point of the thorny wood'. The name in Fife is simply from *Rinn*, 'point'.

Rhynettan (Inverness), Ruigh an Aitinn. 'The sheiling of the juniper'.

Rhynie (Aberdeen), Roinnidh; (Ross), Ràthan. The Aberdeen name means 'division place', and the Ross name is 'small circular fort'.

Ribigill (Sutherland), Ribigil or Ruibigil. 'Lady's farm', from Norse. The old form in English was Regebol.

Rigg (Skye), Ruig. 'Ridge', from Norse.

Rimsdale (Sutherland), Rumasdal. 'Roaring stream valley', from Norse.

Rinavey (Perth), Rinn a' Bheithe. 'The point at the birch'.

Rinavie (Sutherland), Roinnimhigh. 'Point plain'.

Ringdoo Point (Kirkcudbright). 'Black point', from *Rinn Dubh*, with English 'point' added.

Rinloan (Aberdeen), Ruigh an Lòin. 'The sheiling at wet meadow'.

Rinns of Islay (Islay), Na Ranna, Na Roinn Ìleach or Roinn Ìle. 'The divisions' or 'the division of Islay'. A native of the Rhinns is a *Rannach*. There is a saying, *Nam b' eileanach mi, gum b' Ìleach mi; Nam b' Ìleach mi, bu Rannach mi*, 'If I were an islander, I'd want be from Islay; If I were from Islay, I'd want to be from the Rinns'.

Rintoul (Kinross). 'The slope or sheiling at the barn', from *Ruigh an t-Sabhail*.

Rispond (Sutherland), Ruspainn. 'Copse place'.

Roag (Skye), Ròdhag. This may be 'deer bay', from Norse. Roag people were known as *coilich*, 'cockrels', and their ability to make use of odds and ends is recorded in the saying, *Chan eil maide cam no dìreach nach fhaigh feum ann an Ròdhag*, 'There isn't a stick, bent or straight, that can't be made use of in Roag'. In Lewis, the name of *Loch Roag* is *Locha Ròg* and is said to derive from a Norse loanword for a shag.

Robertson (Skye), Robasdan. This is a personal name and it is unusual to find personal names used as place-names in Gaelic.

Rockall (Harris), Ròcal. This Norse name may contain *fjall*, 'mountain'. Rockall may have been the origin of the mythical *Ròcabarra*, as in the saying, *Nuair thig Ròcabarra ris, 's ann a thèid an saoghal sgrios*, 'When Rocabarra appears, the world will be destroyed'.

Rockfield (Ross), A' Chreag or Creag Tarail Bheag. The Gaelic names are 'the rock' and 'the small rock of Tarrel'.

Rodel (Harris), Ròdal or Roghadal. 'Rood valley', from Norse. Rodel Church is *Eaglais Chliamhain*, 'St Clement's Church'.

Rogart (Sutherland), Sgìre Raoghaird or Sgìr' Raoird. The *Raoghard* or 'Rogart' element is 'great enclosed field'. The Gaelic name contains *sgìre*, 'district', and the 'Rogart' element is never used on its own in Gaelic.

Rogie (Ross), Ròagaidh or Rothagaidh.

This may mean 'great hill face'. A local ditty describes the people from a number of nearby places, *Daoine beaga Ròagaidh 's crogaichean Thairbh-idh; Buic Srath Ghairbh, meanbhlaich Srath Bhrainn; Fithich dhubh Loch Carrann 's clamhanan Loch Bhraoin*, 'Little men from Rogie and crocks from Tarvie; Bucks from Strath Garve, runts from Strath Bran; Black ravens from Lochcarron hawks from Loch Broom'.

Rohallion (Perth), Ràth Chailleann. 'The circular fort of the Caledonians'.

Romanno (Peebles). This may be 'the circular fort of the monks', from *Ràth Manach* in earlier Gaelic, now *Ràth Mhanach*. Nearby Lamancha was previously known as Grange of Romanno.

Rome (Perth), Ruam. 'Graveyard', from Latin *Roma*, 'Rome', which became restricted in meaning to 'graveyard'.

Romesdale (Skye), Ròmasdal. 'Giant's valley', from Norse.

Rona Lodge (Raasay), Taigh Mór na h-Acarsaid. In Gaelic the name is 'the big house at the anchorage', referring to Acairseid Mhor on the island of South Rona.

Ronay (Grimsay), Rònaigh. 'Rough island', from Norse.

Rora (Aberdeen). This may be 'great circular fort', from *Ròrath*.

Roro (Perth), Ruadh-Shruth. 'Red-brown stream'.

Roroyeare (Perth), Ruadh-Shruth Gheàrr. 'Short red-brown stream'.

Roscobie (Fife). *See* **Rescobie**.

Rosebank (Ross), Cùil Choinnich. The Gaelic name is 'Kenneth's secluded spot'.

Rosehall (Sutherland), Innis nan Lìon. The English form is 'horse field', from Norse, while the Gaelic name is 'the flax meadow'.

Rosehaugh (Ross), Peit Dhonnchaidh. The Gaelic name is 'Duncan's land or farm' and is unusual in that it has retained Pictish *pett* rather than changing it to Gaelic *baile*.

Rosehearty (Aberdeen), Ros Àbhartaich. 'Àbhartach's headland'.

Rosemarkie (Ross), Ros Mhaircnidh. 'Headland of the horse stream'.

Roshven (Argyll), Roisbheinn. 'Horse mountain', from Norse/Gaelic.

Rosinish (Benbecula, Eriskay), Roisinis. 'Horse headland', from Norse.

Roskeen (Ross), Ros Cuithne. This may mean 'antler headland'.

Roskill (Ross), An Roisgeil; (Skye), Roisgil. 'Horse gully', from Norse.

Rosneath (Dunbarton), Ros Neimhidh. 'The headland of the sacred lands'. The old name was simply *Neimheadh*, 'sacred lands'.

Ross (Kirkcudbright, Ross), Ros. The Kirkcudbright name is 'headland', and would probably have been *An Ros* in Gaelic locally. The Ross-shire name is probably 'forest', but may be 'headland', referring either to the Black Isle or Tarbat Ness. The divisions of Ross are Easter Ross, *Ros an Ear* or commonly *Taobh Sear Rois*; Wester Ross, *Ros an Iar* or *Taobh Siar Rois*; and Mid Ross, *Ros Meadhanach*. North-east Ross is *Machair Rois*, 'the plain of Ross' and the Black Isle is *an t-Eilean Dubh*. The east side of Ross-shire and Inverness-shire was known as *a' Mhachair* to the inhabitants of the west coat. Ross-shire is *Siorrachd Rois* and Ross and Cromarty is *Ros is Cromba*. A native of Ross is a *Rosach*.

Rossal (Mull, Sutherland), Rosal. 'Horse field', from Norse.

Rossdhu (Dunbarton), Ros Dubh. 'Black headland'. Locally the definite article was not used in this name, although it would be expected.

Rossie (Perth), Ros nan Cléireach. 'The headland of the clerics' in Gaelic, while the English form is 'headland', possibly with a Gaelic locative attached, suggesting that locally the

place may have been called in Gaelic simply *Rosaidh*.

Ross of Mull (Mull), An Ros Mhuileach. 'The Mull headland'.

Rosyth (Fife), Ros Saidh. The current Gaelic name refers to a headland but the second element has been adapted from an original *Ros Fhìobha*, 'the headland of Fife'.

Rothes (Moray), Ràthais. 'Circular fort place'.

Rothesay (Bute), Baile Bhóid. The English form appears to be a Norse island name. The Gaelic name is 'the town of Bute'. Rothesay's old church was *Cille Bhruic*, 'St Broc's church' and the parish was known as *Sgìreachd Bhruic*, 'St Broc's parish'. The fair held here in May was *Féill Bhruic*.

Rothiemay (Aberdeen). This may be 'the circular fort on the plain', from *Ràth a' Mhaigh*.

Rothiemurchus (Inverness), Rata Mhurchais. 'Murchas's circular fort'.

Rothienorman (Aberdeen). This may be 'the Normans' circular fort'.

Rotmell (Perth), Rathad a' Bhile. 'The road by the rock edge'.

Rottearns (Perth), Ràth Éireann. 'The circular fort of the Earn'. The English name has a plural attached.

Rovie (Ross), Ròmhaigh. 'Great plain'.

Rowardennan (Stirling), Rubha Àird Eónain. 'Point on the headland of Adamnan'.

Roxburgh, Rosbrog. 'Roch's burgh', from English. Roxburghshire is *Siorrachd Rosbruig*.

Roybridge (Inverness), Drochaid Ruaidh. 'The bridge over the Roy'. The old name was *A' Cheapach*, 'the tillage plot'. The church is *Cille Choireil* or *Cille Choirill*, 'St Caireall's church'.

Ruaig (Tiree), Ruthaig. 'Clearing bay', from Norse.

Ruantallain (Jura), Rubha an t-Sàilein. 'The headland at the small inlet'.

Ruarach (Ross), An Ruadhrach. 'The red-brown place'.

Rubha Ardvule (South Uist), Rubha Àird a' Mhaoile. 'The point of the blunt headland'.

Rubha Bhoisinnis (Berneray), Rubha Bhoisinis. 'The headland of Bhoisinis', from Gaelic/Norse. *Bhoisinis* itself is 'current point'.

Rubha a' Chumhainn Bhig (Jura), Rubha a' Chumhaing Bhig. 'The headland at the small narrow place'.

Rubha Mhic 'ille mhaoil (Jura), Rubha MhicIlleMhaoil. 'MacMillan's headland'.

Rubha Reidh (Ross), Rubha Réidh. 'Level point'. The old and local name for this headland is *An t-Seann Sgeir*, 'the old skerry', and Rubha Reidh lighthouse is known as *Taigh-solais na Seann Sgeir*.

Rudhadubh (Grimsay), An Rubha Dubh. 'The black headland'.

Ru Hunish (Skye), Rubha Hùinis. This Gaelic/Norse name contains both languages' words for 'headland', but the first Norse element may be from a personal name based on *húna*, 'bear cub'. The related name of Hungladder, from *Hùnagladair*, is nearby.

Rum, Rùm. This is a pre-Gaelic name and unclear. A part of Rum is known as *Na Hearadh Rumach*, 'Rum division', using a term, *Na Hearadh*, also found in Harris and in Islay. The Cuillins of Rum are known as *An Cuiltheann Rumach*. A native of Rum is a *Rumach*, also nicknamed a *ròcas*, 'rook'.

Rummond (Fife). 'The circular fort of Manau', from *Ràth Mhanainn*.

Runroy (Perth), An Raon Ruadh. 'The red-brown field'.

Runtaleave (Angus). This may be 'the plain at two moorlands', from *Raon Dà Shliabh*.

Rushgarry (Berneray), Ruisigearraidh. 'Fertile pasture land of the horse', from Norse.

Ruskich (Perth), Rùsgaich. 'Marshy place'.

Russel (Ross), Riseail. 'Mare field', from Norse.

Ruthven (Aberdeen, Angus, Banff, Berwick, Inverness). In Aberdeen, Angus, Banff and Inverness this is Gaelic *Ruadhainn*, 'red-brown place'. The Berwick name may be of the same origin, or more likely have been planted there in commemoration of another Ruthven.

Ryefield (Ross), Ach an t-Seagail. 'The field of rye'.

Rynechtera (Inverness), Ruigh an Eachdra. It is unclear what this sheiling or croft name means.

Rynuie (Inverness), Ruigh an Naoimh. Although said locally to be 'sheiling or croft of the saint', the second part may have had a different origin.

Ryvoan (Inverness), Ruigh a' Bhothain. 'The sheiling or croft with the hut'.

Saddell (Argyll), Saghadal. 'Saw valley', from Norse.

St Andrews (Fife), Cill Rìmhinn. This is the place to which St Andrew's relics were said to have been brought. The Gaelic name was originally *Cinn Rìmhinn*, 'end of the royal moor', and the present form gave rise to the name Kilrymonth. The latter part of the name is a contraction of *rìgh-mhonadh*, 'king's moor', referring to a moor said to have been given by King Aonghas to St Andrew. Kingsmuir is in the area.

St Catherines (Argyll), Cill Chaitriona. 'St Catherine's church'.

St Cyrus (Angus), Eaglais Chiric. 'St Cyricius's church'. This place used to be known in English as Ecclesgreig.

St Fergus (Aberdeen), Peit Fhearghais. The English name commemorates the church of Fergus, whereas the Gaelic name is 'Fergus's farm', containing Pictish *pett*, 'lands or farm'.

St Fillans (Perth), Am Port Mór.

The Gaelic name is 'the big port or village'.

Salen (Argyll, Mull), An Sàilean. 'The small inlet'. The full name of Salen in Argyll is *an Sàilean Suaineartach*, 'Salen of Sunart', while in Mull it is *Sàilean Dubh Chaluim Chille*, 'black Salen of St Columba'.

Saligo (Islay), Sàiligeo. This Norse name may be 'sheep ravine'.

Saline (Fife). This appears to be 'small barn', from the old diminutive *sabhailín*.

Sallachy (Ross, Sutherland), Saileachaidh. 'Willow place' or 'willow wood'.

Saltburn (Ross), Alltan an t-Salainn. 'The little stream of salt'.

Saltcoats (Ayr), Baile an t-Salainn. The English name is 'salt cotts'. The Gaelic version is 'the salt town'.

Saltpans (Argyll), Na Coireacha Salainn. 'The salt pans', where salt was gathered.

Salum (Tiree), Sathalum. This Norse name may mean 'sheep islet'.

Samadalan (Inverness), Samh nan Dailichean. This appears to mean 'the tidal surge by the haughs'.

Samala (North Uist), Samhla. This Norse name may be 'sheep isle'.

Sand (Ross), Sannda. 'Sand river', from Norse. Sand in Gairloch is known in full as *Sannda Gheàrrloch* while Sand near Laide is *Sannda an Leothaid*. People from Sand in Gairloch are known as *eich*, 'horses'. Big Sand is *Sannda Mhór* while Little Sand is *Sannda Bheag*.

Sanda (Argyll), Àbhainn or Eabhainn. The English form is 'sand island', from Norse. The Gaelic form is pre-Gaelic.

Sandaig (Inverness), Sanndaig. 'Sand bay', from Norse.

Sandaveg (Eigg), Sannda Bheag. 'Little Sanda', from Norse/Gaelic, *Sannda* being 'sand river'.

Sandavore (Eigg), Sannda Mhór. 'Big Sanda', from Norse/Gaelic, *Sannda* being 'sand river.

Sanday (Canna), Sanndaigh. 'Sand island', from Norse.

Sandbank (Argyll), Taigh a' Chladaich; (Mull), An t-Aoineadh Beag. The Gaelic name of Sandbank in Argyll is 'the house by the shore'. An older English name was Claddyhouse, showing that the local Gaelic was *Taigh a' Chladaigh* with the older form of the genitive singular rather than the standard form given above. *See* **Acharanny**. In Mull the Gaelic name means 'the small steep promontory'.

Sandray (Barra), Sanndraigh. 'Sand island', from Norse.

Sandside (Sutherland), Sanndasaid. 'Sand dwelling', from Norse.

Sandwick (Lewis, South Uist), Sanndabhaig. 'Sand bay', from Norse. Lower Sandwick in Lewis is *Mol Shanndabhaig*, 'the shingle beach of Sandwick'.

Sandwood (Sutherland), Seannabhad or Sannabhad. Both the English and Gaelic names are misleading, in that the name's origin is Norse 'sand water'.

Sangobeg (Sutherland), Saingea Beag. 'Small sandy ravine', from Norse/Gaelic.

Sangomore (Sutherland), Saingea Mór. 'Large sandy ravine', from Norse/Gaelic.

Sanna (Argyll), Sanna. 'Sand river', from Norse. Sanna Point is *Rubha Shanna*.

Sannaig (Jura), Sannaig. 'Sand bay', from Norse.

Sannox (Arran), Sannaig. 'Sand bay', from Norse. The English version has a plural form.

Sanquhar (Ayr, Moray). 'Old stone fort', from *Seann Chathair*.

Sartle (Skye), Sartail. This may be 'muddy valley', from Norse.

Sasaig (Skye), Sàsaig. 'Cask bay', from Norse.

Satran (Skye), Sàtran. This name is unclear.

Sauchieburn (Stirling), Allt a' Phuill Sheilich. The English name is 'willow wood stream', and the Gaelic is 'stream of the willow pool'.

Saundaig (Tiree), Sanndaig. 'Sand bay', from Norse.

Savalbeg (Sutherland), Sàbhal Beag. This is from Norse for 'high mountain', with Gaelic for 'small' attached.

Savalmore (Sutherland), Sàbhal Mór. *See* **Savalbeg**, but in this case the Gaelic attachment is 'large'

Savary (Argyll), Samharaidh. This appears to be 'sorrel sheiling'.

Scadabay (Harris), Sgadabhagh. This Norse name may be 'tax bay'. Local people were nicknamed *cait*, 'cats'.

Scaladale (Harris), Sgaladal. 'Valley of soft rock', from Norse.

Scalan (Banff), An Sgàilean. 'The little shelter'.

Scalasaig (Colonsay, Inverness), Sgalasaig. 'Skali's bay', from Norse.

Scaliscro (Lewis), Sgealascro. This Norse name may mean 'Skali's river pit'.

Scallasdale (Argyll), Sgalasdal. 'Skali's valley', from Norse.

Scallastle (Mull), Sgalasdal. *See* **Scallasdale**.

Scalpay (Scalpay, Skye), Sgalpaigh. 'Ship island', from Norse. Scalpay by Harris is also *Sgalpaigh Na Hearadh* and Scalpay near Skye is *Sgalpaigh an t-Sratha*, Scalpay of Strath'. A Scalpay person is a *Sgalpach*.

Scamadale (Inverness), Sgamadal. This Norse name denotes a valley, but the first part of the name is unclear.

Scaniport (Inverness), Sganaphort. 'Ferry by the cleft'.

Scaravay (Harris), Sgarabhaigh. 'Cormorant island', from Norse.

Scarba (Jura), Sgarba. 'Cormorant island', from Norse.

Scardroy (Ross), Sgàrd Ruaidh. 'Red-brown swathe of land'.

Scarinish (Tiree), Sgairinis. 'Notch headland', from Norse.

Scarista (Harris), Sgarastadh. 'Township of the notch or cut', from Norse. Scaristavore is *Sgarastadh Mhór*, 'big Scarista'.

Scarp (Harris), An Sgarp. 'Barren', from Norse.

Scatwell (Ross), Sgatail. 'Tax field', from Norse.

Scolpaig (North Uist), Sgolpaig. 'Ship bay', from Norse.

Scone (Perth), Sgàin. This may mean 'cleft'.

Sconser (Skye), Sgonnsar. The meaning of this name is not clear.

Scoonie (Fife). 'Place of the lumpish hill', from *Sgonnaidh*, earlier *Sgonnan*.

Scoraig (Ross), Sgoraig. 'Rift bay', from Norse. An uncomplimentary saying about Scoraig claims, *Sgoraig sgreachach, 's dona beag i - àite gun dìon, gun fhasgadh, gun phreas no coille*, 'Repulsive Scoraig, small and no good - a place without protection, shelter, bush or wood'. Local people were known as *coin*, 'dogs'.

Scorguie (Inverness), Sgòr Gaoithe. 'Windy hill'.

Scotasay (Harris), Sgotasaigh. 'Scots' island', from Norse.

Scotsburn (Ross), Allt nan Albannach. 'Stream of the Scots'. An older name from Norse was *Uladal*, 'Ulli's valley'.

Scotscalder (Caithness), Caladal nan Gall or Cal nan Gall. The English name means 'Calder of the Scots', while the Gaelic name is 'Calder of the non-Gaels'.

Scottas (Inverness), Sgotas or Sgòiteas. The meaning of this name is unclear.

Scotven (Grimsay), Sgotbheinn. This name is unclear, but may be Norse/Gaelic for 'tax mountain' or 'Scots' mountain'.

Scourie (Sutherland), Sgobharaidh. 'Shed sheiling'. Scouriemore is *Sgobharaidh Mhór*, 'large Scourie'.

Scudiburgh (Skye), Sgudabrog. This

name contains Norse for 'castle', but the first part is dubious.

Scullamus (Skye), Sgùlamus. 'Skúli's moss or farm', from Norse.

Scurrival Point (Barra), Rubha Sgoire-abhail. 'Headland of the wooded hill', from Gaelic/Norse.

Seabeg (Kincardine, Stirling). 'The small seat', from *An Suidhe Beag*.

Seaboard Villages (Ross), Bailtean na Mara or Na Trì Port Mara. 'The villages by the sea' or 'the three sea ports', referring to Cadboll, Shandwick, Hilton, etc.

Seafield (Ross), Rubha Nòis. The English name is 'field by the sea'. The Gaelic name is 'the headland of the river mouth', from Gaelic/Norse. *See* **Noss Head**.

Seaforth Head (Lewis), Ceann Loch Shìophort. 'The head of Loch Seaforth'.

Seaforth Island (Harris, Lewis), Eilean Shìophort. 'The island of Seaforth'.

Seamore (Stirling). 'The large seat', from *An Suidhe Mór*.

Second Coast (Ross), An t-Eirtheaire Shuas. The Gaelic name is 'the upper coast'.

Seil, Saoil. This is probably a pre-Gaelic name. A Seil person is a *Saoileach*.

Seilebost (Harris), Seilebost. 'Shell farm', from Norse.

Selkirk (Selkirk), Sailcirc. This is a church name, from English. Selkirkshire is *Siorrachd Shailcirc*.

Severie (Perth), Suidhe Bhrith' 'The judge's seat', from *Suidhe a' Bhritheimh*.

Sgodachail (Ross), Sguit Chathail. 'Cathal's croft'.

Shader (Lewis), Siadar. 'Village', from Norse. Shader in Point, also known as Shulishader in English, is *Siadar an Rubha*. Lower Shader near Barvas is *Siadar Iarach* and Upper Shader is *Siadar Uarach*. Local pronunciation

collected by Oftedal suggest a preferable spelling of *Siadair*.

Shagarry (Skye), Seoigearraidh. The first element of this Norse name referring to pasture land may represent 'sea'.

Shandwick (Ross), Seannduaig. 'Sand bay', from Norse. Local people were known as *seanndlairean*, 'chandlers', and *slaiteirean*, a word related to *slat*, 'fishing rod' which also suggests a tall, thin person.

Shannochie (Arran), Sean Achaidh. 'Old field'.

Shanquhar (Aberdeen). 'Old stone fort', from *Seann Chathair*.

Shanrie (Banff), An t-Seann Ruighe. 'The old sheiling'.

Shantullich (Ross), An t-Sean Tulaich. 'The old green hill'.

Shanwell (Moray). 'Old village or farm', from *Seann Bhaile*.

Shawbost (Lewis), Siabost. 'Sea farm'. New Shawbost is *Pàirc Shiaboist* 'Shawbost park' or *A' Phàirc*, 'the park'. North Shawbost is *Siabost a Tuath* (*Siabost bho Thuath* on roadsigns) and South Shawbost is *Siabost a Deas* (*Siabost bho Dheas* on roadsigns).

Sheader (Skye), Siadar. 'Village', from Norse.

Shedog (Arran), Seideag. The meaning of this name is unclear.

Shegarton (Dunbarton), Sìth-Ghartan. 'Fairy field'.

Sheil Bridge (Ross), Drochaid Sheile. 'The bridge of the Sheil'. The old name was *An Taigh Bàn*, 'the white house'.

Sheildaig (Ross), Sìldeag. 'Herring bay', from Norse. People from Sheildaig by Applecross were known as *gathan dubha* which may refer to beards of oats or barley. Sheildaig in Gairloch is known in full as *Sìldeag Gheàrrloch*.

Sheildinish (Lewis), Sildinis. 'Herring headland', from Norse.

Sheilfoot (Argyll), Bun na h-Abhann.

The English name is 'mouth of the Sheil', but the Gaelic name is simply 'the mouth of the river'.

Shenval (Banff, Inverness), An Seann Bhaile. 'The old farm'.

Sheriffmuir (Perth), Sliabh an t-Siorraim or Monadh an t-Siorraim. 'The moor of the sheriff'. The Battle of Sheriffmuir is known as *Blàr Sliabh an t-Siorraim*.

Sheshader (Lewis), Seiseadar. 'Sea village', from Norse.

Shetland, Sealtainn. These names are an anglicisation and a gaelicisation of Norse *Hjaltland*. A Shetlander is a *Sealtainneach*. The old Gaelic name for Shetland was *Innse Cat*, 'islands of the Cat people'.

Shian (Argyll), An Sìthean. 'The fairy hill'. North and South Shian are *An Sìthean a Tuath* and *An Sìthean a Deas* respectively.

Shian Ferry (Argyll), Port an t-Sìthein. 'The harbour at the fairy hill'.

Shiant Islands (Lewis), Na h-Eileanan Móra. The Gaelic name is 'the big islands'. The English name comes from an older Gaelic one, *Na h-Eileanan Sianta*, 'the charmed or holy islands'.

Shillay (North Uist), Sileigh. 'Herring island', from Norse.

Shinagag (Perth), Sionagag. 'Old gap', one of the old roads from Atholl to Strathardle.

Shinness (Sutherland), Sìnnis. This may be 'old meadow' from *seann innis*. West Shinness is *Seann Sìnnis*, 'old Shinness'.

Shirrabeg (Inverness), Siorrath Beag. 'Little Shirra', an unclear name which may contain *ràth*, 'circular fort'.

Shirramore (Inverness), Siorrath Mór. 'Big Shirra'. *See* **Shirrabeg**.

Shiskine (Arran), An t-Seasgann. 'The boggy or sedgy place'.

Shona (Argyll), Eilean Seona. This may be 'sea island', from Norse. The Gaelic name also has 'island' attached.

The old Gaelic name for the island was *Arthràigh*, 'foreshore island', similar to that of **Erraid**.

Shoretown (Ross), Baile a' Chladaich. 'The village by the shore'.

Shulishader (Lewis, Skye), Siùiliseadar. 'Village at the sea slope', from Norse. The village in Lewis is more commonly known as *Siadar an Rubha*, 'Shader in Point'.

Shulista (Skye), Siùlasta. 'Place at the sea slope', from Norse.

Shuna (Argyll), Siùna. This may be 'sea island', from Norse.

Sidinish (North Uist), Saighdinis. This Norse name may be 'slope headland'.

Skallary (Sutherland), Sgalaraidh. 'Field of soft rock', from Norse.

Skeabost (Skye), Sgeubost. 'Skiði's farm', from Norse.

Skelbo (Sutherland), Sgeireabol. 'Rock farm', from Norse.

Skelpick (Sutherland), Sgeilpeach. This may be 'rock farm', from Norse.

Skelpie (Fife). Old forms of the name show this to derive from *Gasg Ailpein*, 'the projecting ridge of Ailpean'.

Skene (Aberdeen), Sgàin. This may mean 'cleft' and may be the same name as found in 'Scone'.

Skerinish (Skye), Sgeirinis. 'Skerry headland', from Norse.

Skerray (Sutherland), Sgeirea. This may be 'skerry river'.

Skerricha (Sutherland), Sgeir a' Chadha. 'The skerry at the pass'.

Skiag Bridge (Sutherland), Drochaid Sgiathaig. 'The bridge at the winged place or river'.

Skiary (Sutherland), Sgiatharaidh. This meaning of this name is unclear, but might be 'winged field or sheiling', from Norse.

Skiberscross (Sutherland), Sìobarsgaig. 'Syborg's piece of land', from Norse.

Skibo (Sutherland), Sgìobal. 'Shell farm', from Norse. This was known as *Sgìobal nan ùbhlan*, 'Skibo of the apples'.

Skigersta (Lewis), Sgiogarstaigh. 'Skeggi's place', from Norse.

Skillymarno (Aberdeen), Sgàilean Mearnaig. 'St Ernoc's or M' Ernoc's shelter'.

Skinidin (Skye), Sgianaidean. The meaning of this name which is a plural is unclear, but may derive from Norse *skjóna*, 'dappled horse'. *Sgianailt* in Lewis is 'rough hill ground of the dappled horses', and this may be related.

Skinnertown (Ross), Baile nan Sginnearach. 'The village of the Skinners'.

Skinnet (Sutherland), Sgianaid. *See* **Skinidin**.

Skipness (Argyll), Sgibinis. 'Ship headland'.

Skirinish (Skye), Sgeirinis. 'Skerry headland', from Norse.

Skye, An t-Eilean Sgitheanach. This may be 'the indented island'. An alternative form of the name is *an t-Eilean Sgiathanach*, which points to *sgiath*, 'wing', as the root of the name. A poetic name of the island is *Eilean a' Cheò*, 'island of the mist'. A Skye person is a *Sgitheanach*.

Skye of Curr (Inverness), Sgiath Churr. 'The wing (of land) at the pit'.

Slackbuie (Inverness), An Slag Buidhe. 'The yellow hollow'. Upper Slackbuie was known as *Cnoc na Circe*, 'hill of the hen', or Knocknakirk in English. *Slag* as opposed to *lag* was the usual term locally to denote a hollow.

Slaggan (Ross), An Slagan Odhar. The Gaelic name is 'the dun-coloured little hollow', whereas the English name is only 'hollow'.

Slamannan (Stirling). 'The moor of Manau', from *Sliabh Mhanainn*.

Slattadale (Ross), Sléiteadal. 'Smooth valley', from Norse.

Sleach (Aberdeen), An Sliabhach. 'The moor place', formerly Easter Sleach in English.

Sleat (Skye), Sléite or Sléibhte. This is from Norse *sléttr*, 'smooth'. A native

of Sleat is a *Sléiteach*, also nicknamed a *coileach*, 'cockerel'. At least three sayings exist concerning the women of Sleat - a visit that lasts too long is called *céilidh nam ban Sléiteach*, 'a visit from Sleat women'; Sleat was compared to neighbouring Strath in *Clachan an t-Sratha's mnathan Shléite*, 'the stones of Strath and the women of Sleat'; and the area is also known as *Sléite rìomhach nam ban bòidheach*, 'lovely Sleat of the beautiful women'.

Sletell (Sutherland), Sléiteil. 'Smooth field', from Norse.

Sliddery (Arran), Slaodraidh. This name has connotations of trailing or dragging.

Sligachan (Skye), Sligeachan. 'Small shell place'.

Sligo (Aberdeen). 'Shell place', from *Sligeach*.

Slockavullin (Argyll), Sloc a' Mhuilinn. 'The hollow by the mill'.

Sluggans (Skye), Na Sluganan. 'The hollows'.

Slumbay (Ross), Slumba. 'Slim bay', from Norse.

Sma' Glen (Perth), An Caol-Ghleann. 'The narrow glen'. The full name is *Caol-Ghleann Ghlinn Amain*, 'the narrow glen of Glen Almond'.

Small Isles (Inverness), Na h-Eileanan Tarsainn; (Jura), Na h-Eileanan Beaga. The Small Isles of Inverness-shire (Canna, Eigg, Muck and Rum) are called 'the cross islands', referring to their situation between Morar on the mainland and Uist in the west. In Jura, the Gaelic name is 'the small islands'.

Smaull (Islay), Smeidheal. This may be 'narrow field', from Norse.

Smerclete (South Uist), Smeircleit. This may be 'butter rock or hill', from Norse.

Smiorasair (Ross), Smiorasair. 'Butter sheiling', from Norse.

Smirasary (Inverness), Smiorasaraidh. *See* **Smiorasair**.

Smithstown (Ross), Baile a' Ghobhann. 'The village of the smith'.

Smithton (Inverness), Baile a' Ghobhainn. *See* **Smithstown**.

Smoo (Sutherland), Smudha. 'Cave', from Norse. This is the location of Smoo Cave.

Snishival (South Uist), Snaoiseabhal. This Norse name may mean 'snowy sea mountain'.

Snizort (Skye), Sniothasort. 'Snow firth', from Norse.

Soay (Skye, St Kilda), Sòaigh. 'Sheep island', from Norse.

Soilshan (Inverness), An Soillsean. 'The bright place'.

Soilzarie (Perth), Soillearaidh. 'Light place'. This is the opposite of 'Dollerie'.

Soletote (Skye), Sòlatobht. 'Toft of the solan goose', from Norse.

Sollas (North Uist), Solas. This name is unclear. *Solas* means 'light', but is unlikely to mean that here.

Sorisdale (Coll), Sórasdal. 'Mud valley', from Norse.

Sorn (Ayr). 'Kiln', from *Sorn*.

Soroba (Argyll), Sòroba. 'Muddy village', from Norse.

Soroby (Tiree), Sóiribidh. *See* **Soroba**.

South Cuan (Luing), Cuan Luinn. The English name distinguishes this place from North Cuan. The Gaelic name is 'Cuan of Luing'.

Southend (Argyll), Ceann mu Dheas. This is at the south end of Kintyre.

South Kessock (Inverness), Ceasag a Deas. The older name is *Port Cheasaig*, 'the port of Kessock'. *See* **Kessock**.

South Queensferry (West Lothian), Cas Chaolas or Cas Faoileas. The Gaelic name is 'steep strait'. 'South' in the English name distinguishes this from North Queensferry in Fife, and this was the royal crossing point as opposed to Earlsferry further east.

South Rona (Raasay), Rònaigh. The Gaelic name is 'rough island'. 'South' in the English name distinguishes

this island from North Rona, to the north of Lewis.

South Uist, Uibhist a Deas or Uidhist a Deas. *See* **Uist**. South Uist is also known as *an Ceann a Deas*, 'south end' and *Tìr a' Mhurain*, 'the land of marram grass'. A person from South Uist is a *Deasach*.

Soval (Lewis), Sóbhal. 'Sheep mountain', from Norse.

Soyal (Ross), Saoidheal. 'Sheep meadow', from Norse.

Spean Bridge (Inverness), Drochaid Aonachain. The English name refers to the River Spean. The Gaelic name is 'the bridge at the market place'. The old name was *Aonachan*, 'market place', which survives in 'Unachan'.

Speyside (Banff, Moray), Fàn Spé. The Gaelic name is 'the gentle slope of the Spey'. The river itself is mentioned in the saying, *Spé, Dé is Tatha, na trì uisge as motha fon adhar,* 'Spey, Dee and Tay, the three greatest rivers under the sun'.

Spinningdale (Sutherland), Spainnigeadal. This Norse name contains *dalr*, 'valley', but the first element is unclear.

Spittal of Glenshee (Perth), An Spideal or Spideal Ghlinn Sìth. 'The hospice' or 'the hospice of Glenshee'.

Sponish (North Uist), Spònais. This Norse name contains *nes*, 'headland', but the first element is unclear.

Springfield (Ross), Achadh an Fhuarain. 'The field of the spring'.

Spynie (Moray). This may be 'thorny place', and related to 'Spean'.

Sronphadruig (Perth), Sròn Phàdraig. 'Patrick's nose', referring to a nose-shaped topographical feature.

Stack Island (Eriskay), Eilean an Staca. 'Island of the pillar rock', from Gaelic/Norse.

Staffa (Mull), Stafa. 'Staff island', from Norse.

Staffin (Skye), An Taobh Sear or Stafainn. The English and second Gaelic names come from Norse and may contain the word for 'staff' or be based on *stamh*, a type of seaweed. The first Gaelic name means 'the east side'. Staffin Island is *Eilean Stafainn*.

Stair (Ayr). 'Stepping stones' or 'rough bridge', from *stair*.

Star (Fife). 'Stepping stones' or 'rough bridge', from *stair*.

Steall (Inverness), Steall. 'Waterfall'.

Stein (Skye), Steinn. 'Stone', from Norse.

Steinish (Lewis), Steinnis. 'Stone headland', from Norse.

Stenschol (Skye), Steinnseal. 'Stone hill or field', from Norse.

Stewarton (Ayr), Baile nan Stiùbhartach. 'Town of the Stewarts'.

Stewartry (Kirkcudbright), An Stiùbhartachd. 'Stewarded lands'. This is the old name for Kirkcudbrightshire.

Stilligarry (South Uist), Stadhlaigearraidh. 'Rocky fertile land', from Norse.

Stirkhill (Ross), Meallan a' Ghamhna. *See* **Mellongaun**.

Stirling, Sruighlea. This is said to be a Brythonic name meaning 'dwelling place of Melyn', which led to the older English form, Strivelin. Stirlingshire is *Siorrachd Shruighlea*.

Stix (Perth), Na Stuiceannan. 'The stumps'.

St Katherines (Aberdeen). An older name of the place, Raitt, is from *Rat*, 'circular fort'.

St Kilda, Hiort. Neither the English nor Gaelic names are clear, but the English form is thought to refer to a well, while the Gaelic name may contain an old word for 'death'. A number of sayings refer to St Kilda, such as *bho Pheairt gu Hiort* or *eadar Peairt is Hiort*, 'from Perth to St Kilda', which signifies the former extent of the Gaelic speaking areas. *B' fheàrr leam gun robh e ann an Hiort*, 'I wish he were in St Kilda', is said of someone one wishes to be rid of. A *pòsadh Hiortach*, 'a St Kilda wedding', means a wedding between close

relations. A threat to a badly behaved child is *Cuiridh mi a Hiort thu air muin mairt*, 'I'll send you to St Kilda on a cow's back'. A native of St Kilda was a *Hiortach*.

St Monans (Fife). 'St Maoineann's church'. The old name was Abercrombie, from *Obar Chrombaidh*, 'mouth of the crooked river'.

St Ninians (Inverness), Slios an Trinnein. The Gaelic name is 'St Ninian's slope', from an older *Slios Shant Rinnein*.

Stobo (Peebles). This may be 'stump place', from *Stobach*.

Stockay (North Uist), Stocaigh. 'Chasm island', from Norse.

Stockinish (Harris), Stocainis. 'Chasm headland', from Norse.

Stoer (Sutherland), An Stòr. 'Large', from Norse. A local saying is *'S fhada Dùn Éideann bhon fhear a tha ag éirigh san Stòr*, 'Edinburgh is far from the man who rises in Stoer'.

Stonefield (Argyll, Skye), Achadh na Cloiche. 'The field of the stone'.

Stoneybridge (South Uist), Staoinibrig. 'Stony slope', from Norse.

Stoneyfield (Inverness), Sgrìodan-Sgràd; (Lewis), Buaile na Cloich; (Ross), Féith nan Clach. In Inverness the name refers to a stony ravine, but the second element is unclear. In Lewis, the name is 'enclosure by the stone', while in Ross it is 'the stony bog channel'.

Stoneykirk (Wigtown). 'Stony field', from Norse.

Stormyhill (Skye), Cnoc na Gaoithe. The Gaelic name is 'the windy hill'.

Stormont (Perth). 'Moor with stepping stones', from *stair* and *monadh*, as is shown in an old form of the name, Starmunth.

Stornoway (Argyll, Lewis), Steòrnabhagh. 'Rudder bay' or 'steering bay', from Norse. The inhabitants of various parts of Stornoway in Lewis are mentioned in the rhyme,

Fithich dhubha Ionacleit, sliogairean shìos a' bhaile, daoine uasal Ceann a' Bhàigh, spàgairean Ghiùirseadair, 'Black ravens from Newton, sneaks from down the town, noble folk from Bayhead, clumsy folk from Guershader'.

Straad (Bute), An t-Sràid. 'Street'.

Strabane (Arran), Srath Bàn. 'Fair or white river haugh'.

Stracathro (Angus), Srath Chatara. The first part of this name is 'strath', but the second is unclear, although said to be 'mossy', from *càtharach*. However, it would be unusual for *th* to revert to *t*.

Strachur (Argyll), Srath Chura. 'Strath of the pit'.

Straloch (Aberdeen); (Perth), Srath Locha. The Perth name is 'strath of the loch', and the Aberdeen name may be of the same origin.

Stranraer (Wigtown), An t-Sròn Reamhar. 'The broad headland'.

Strath (Ross, Skye), An Srath. 'Strath'. The full name of Strath in Ross is *Srath Gheàrrloch*, 'strath of Gairloch', and in Skye *Srath MhicFhionghain*, 'MacKinnon's Strath', which is contrasted with Sleat in the saying, *Clachan an t-Sratha's mnathan Shléite*, 'the stones of Strath and the women of Sleat'. People from Strath in Skye are nicknamed *faochagan*, 'whelks'.

Strathaird (Skye), Srath na h-Àirde. 'The strath with the headland'.

Strathallan (Perth), Srath Alain. 'The strath of the Allan'.

Strathan (Sutherland), Srathan. 'Little strath'. Strathan West is *Srathan Shuas*.

Strathanmore (Sutherland), An Srathan Mór. 'The big little strath'.

Strathardle (Perth), Srath Àrdail. 'The strath of the Ardle'.

Strathaven (Lanark). This may be 'the strath of the river', from Gaelic *Srath Abhainne*.

Strath Aven (Banff), Srath Thàmhainn. 'The strath of the Aven'.

Strathbeg (Aberdeen). 'Small strath', from Gaelic *Srath Beag*.

Strathblane (Stirling), Srath Bhlàthain. 'St Blane's strath'.

Strathbogie (Aberdeen), Srath Bhalgaidh. 'The strath of the Bogie'. *See* **Huntly**.

Strathbraan (Perth), Srath Freamhainn. 'The strath of the Braan'. The name of the river is *Breamhainn*.

Strathbran (Ross), Srath Brain or Srath Brainn. 'The strath of the Bran'. People from the area were nicknamed *meanbhlaich*, 'runts'.

Strathbrora (Sutherland), Srath Bhrùra. 'The strath of the River Brora'. This strath contains seven churches, *Cill nam Bràthair, Cill Pheadair Bheag, Cill Pheadair Mhór, Cill Chaluim Chille, Cill Eathain, Cill Mearain* and *Cill Ach Breanaidh*.

Strathcarron (Ross), Srath Carrann. 'The strath of the Carron'. Local people are known as *Carrannaich*.

Strathclyde (Dunbarton, Lanark, Renfrew), Srath Chluaidh. 'The strath of the Clyde'.

Strathconon (Ross), Srath Chonainn. 'The strath of the Conon'. A rhyme shows that the names of the straths and rivers in this area do not always coincide, *Abhainn Mìg tre Srath Chonainn, Abhainn Chonainn tre Srath Bhrainn, Abhainn Dubh-chuileagach tre Srath Ghairbh, trì aibhnichean gun tairbh iad sin,* 'River Meig through Strathconan, River Conon through Strathbran, river of the black flies through Strathgarve, three unprofitable rivers.' Mid Strathconon is known as *Mèinn*.

Strathdearn (Inverness), Srath Éireann. 'The strath of the Findhorn'. There is a saying comparing the five divisions of Strathdearn (which means 'the strath of Ireland', referring to the Findhorn River) with those of Ireland, *Tha cóig cóigimh an Éirinn's tha cóig cóigimh an Srath Éireann, ach* *'s fheàrr aon chóigeamh na h-Éireann na cóig cóigimh Srath Éireann*, 'There are five fifths in Ireland and five fifths in the strath of Ireland, but one fifth of Ireland is better than five fifths of the strath of Ireland'. The divisions of Strathdearn are *Cóig na Feàrna, Cóig nan Sgàlan, Cóig na Sìthe, Cóig a' Mhuilinn* and *Cóig nam Fionndaraich*. The distinctiveness of Strathdearn's place-names is commented on in another saying, *Tha cóig bothan an Loch Abar, cóig gasgan ann am Bàideanach 's cóig cóigean ann an Srath Éireann*, 'There are five boths in Lochaber, five gasgs in Badenoch and five cóigs in Strathdearn'. *See* **Strathearn**.

Strathdee (Aberdeen, Kincardine), Srath Dhé. 'The strath of the Dee'. *See* **Deeside**.

Strath Dionard (Sutherland), Srath Dìonaird. 'The strath of the Dionard'.

Strathdon (Aberdeen), Srath Dheathain. 'The strath of the Don'.

Strathearn (Perth), Srath Éireann. 'The strath of the Earn'. *Éire*, the Gaelic original of 'Earn', is one of a group of names including *Eilg, Banbh* and *Fótla* which were poetic by-names for Ireland and were applied to places in Scotland.

Strathendrick (Stirling), Srath Eunaraig. 'The strath of the Endrick'.

Stratherrick (Inverness), Srath Fhairgeag or Srath Fharragaig. 'The strath of the Farigaig'.

Strathfillan (Perth), Na Sraithibh or Srath Chinn Fhaolain. The English name commemorates St Fillan. The first Gaelic name is 'the straths' and the second is 'the strath of the church of St Fillan', from an earlier *Srath Chill Fhaolain*. Strathfillan churchyard is *Clachan Shraithibh*, and to express the phrase 'in Strathfillan', Gaelic uses *air na Sraithibh*, 'on the straths'.

Strathfleet (Sutherland), Srath Fleòid. 'The strath of the Fleet'.

Strathgartney (Perth), Srath Ghartain. 'Gartan's river haugh'.

Strathgarve (Ross), Srath Ghairbh. 'The strath of Garve'. Local people were nicknamed *buic*, 'bucks'.

Strathgirnock (Aberdeen), Srath Goirneig. 'The strath of the Girnock'.

Strathgryfe (Renfrew). 'The strath of the Gryffe', probably from *Srath Ghrìobha*. This is the old name of Renfrewshire.

Strath Halladale (Sutherland), Srath Healadail. 'The strath of the Halladale'.

Strathisla (Banff), Srath Ìle. 'The strath of the Isla'.

Strathkanaird (Ross), Srath Chainneart. 'The strath of the can firth', from Gaelic/Norse.

Strathkyle (Ross, Sutherland), Srath a' Chaoil. 'The strath at the strait', referring to *an Caol Catach*, 'Kyle of Sutherland'. The old name was *Slios a' Chaolais*, 'the slope at the strait'.

Strathlachlan (Argyll), Srath Lachlainn. 'Lachlann's strath'.

Strathmartine (Angus). 'Martin's strath', from Gaelic *Srath Mhàrtainn*.

Strathmashie (Inverness), Srath Mhathaisidh. 'The strath of the good haugh'.

Strathmiglo (Fife). 'Boggy strath' or 'boggy river holm', from *Srath Mioglach*.

Strathmore (several), An Srath Mór. 'The big strath'. Strathmore in Angus and Perth was known as *A' Mhachair*, 'the plain', to speakers of Perthshire Gaelic.

Strathnairn (Inverness, Nairn), Srath Narann. 'The strath of the Nairn'.

Strathnaver (Sutherland), Srath Nabhair. 'The strath of the Naver'.

Strathnoon (Inverness), Srath Nìn. In this case *srath* is a river holm, but the second element is unclear.

Strath of Applecross (Ross), Srath Mhaol Chaluim. The large strath in Applecross is 'the strath of the devotee of St Columba' in Gaelic.

Strath of Kildonan (Sutherland), Srath Ilidh. The English name refers to Kildonan, but the Gaelic name is 'the strath of the Helmsdale River'. A local person is known an *Ileach*.

Strath of Pitcalnie (Ross), Srath Chuilt Eararaidh. *See* **Pitcalnie**.

Strathore (Fife). 'The strath of the River Ore'.

Strath Ossian (Inverness), Srath Oisein. 'The strath of Ossian'.

Strathoykel (Sutherland), Srath Òiceall. 'The strath of the Oykel'.

Strathpeffer (Ross), Srath Pheofhair. 'The strath of the bright river'.

Strathrannoch (Ross), Srath Raineach. 'Bracken strath'.

Strathrory (Ross), Srath Uaraidh. 'The strath of the Rory'.

Strathrusdale (Ross), Srath Rùsdail. 'The strath of Rusdale'.

Strathspey (Inverness, Moray), Srath Spé. 'The strath of the Spey'.

Strathtay (Perth), Srath Tatha. 'The strath of the Tay'.

Strath Tirry (Sutherland), Srath Tìridh. 'The strath of the Tirry'.

Strath Tongue (Sutherland), Srath Thunga. 'The strath of Tongue'.

Strathtummel (Perth), Srath Teimhil. 'The strath of the Tummel'.

Strath Vagastie (Sutherland), Srath Bhàgastaidh. The meaning of the second, Norse, part of this strath name is unclear, although it may be 'watching place'.

Strathwhillan (Arran), Srath Chuilinn. Although the current name is 'holly strath', this place was first called *Tìr Chuilinn*, 'holly land'.

Strathy (Ross), An t-Srathaidh; (Sutherland), Srathaidh. The Ross name is 'the little strath', while the Sutherland name either means the same or 'strath place'.

Strathyre (Perth), An t-Iomaire Riabhach or An t-Iomaire Fada. 'The brindled rigg' or 'the long rigg'. These names apply to the village only, the old English form of which was Immerioch. The valley of Strathyre is *Srath Eadhair*, 'the strath of the corn land'.

Streens of Findhorn (Nairn), Na Srianan. 'The restraints', referring to narrows in the River Findhorn.

Street of Kincardine (Inverness), An t-Sràid. The Gaelic name is simply 'the street'.

Strichen (Aberdeen). This may be a strath name. The old name of the village was Mormond, from Gaelic *Mór Mhon(adh)*, 'large hill'.

Stroanpatrick (Kirkcudbright). 'Patrick's point', from *Sròn Phàdraig*.

Strollamus (Skye), Stròlamus. 'Stúrli's moss or farm', from Norse.

Stroma (Caithness), Stròma. 'Current island', from Norse.

Stromay (North Uist), Sròmaigh. *See* **Stroma**.

Strombane (North Uist), An Sròm Bàn. 'The fair stream'.

Strome (Ross), An Sròm; (South Uist), An Sròm Dearg. The Ross name is 'the current', from Norse. In South Uist it is 'the red stream'.

Stromeferry (Ross), Port an t-Sròim. 'The port at the current', from Gaelic/Norse.

Stronachlachair (Perth), Sròn a' Chlachair. 'The mason's point'.

Stronachullin (Argyll), Sròn a' Chuilinn. 'The holly point'.

Stronafyne (Dunbarton), Sròn na Fine. 'Point of the clan', referring to the inner circle of the clan.

Stronchreggan (Argyll), Sròn a' Chritheagain. This may be 'the point of the little aspen'.

Stronchrubie (Sutherland), Sròn Chrùbaidh. 'The point at the bent place'.

Strond (Harris), Srannda. 'Beach', from Norse.

Strone (Argyll, Inverness, Jura), An

t-Sròn. 'The point'. Strone in Inverness-shire is in full *Sròn a' Chaisteil*, 'the point of the castle', referring to nearby Urquhart Castle which is known as *Caisteal na Sròine*, 'the castle at the point'. Strone Glen in Argyll is *Gleann na Sròine*, 'the glen of the headland'.

Stroneba (Inverness), Sròn na Bà. 'The point of the cow'.

Strone of Cally (Perth), Sròn Challaidh. 'The point at the hazel place'.

Strone Point (Argyll), Rubha Sroigheann; (Inverness), Sròn a' Chaisteil. The Argyll name is 'Striven Point', while the Inverness name is 'the point of the castle'. *See* **Strone**.

Stronlossit (Inverness), Sròn Losaid. 'The point on the Lossit'.

Stronmilchan (Argyll), Sròn Mhaolagain. 'Maolagan's point' or 'the point at the little rounded place'.

Strontian (Argyll), Sròn an t-Sìthein. 'The point at the fairy hill'.

Stronyre (Perth), Sròn Eadhair. 'The headland of the corn field'.

Struan (North Uist), An Sruthan Ruadh; (Perth), Srùthan; (Skye), An Sruthan. In North Uist this is 'the red-brown stream', while in Perth and Skye it is 'stream' or 'the stream'.

Struanmore (Skye), An Sruthan Mór. 'The big stream'.

Strumore (North Uist), An Sruth Mór. 'The big current'.

Struy (Inverness, Ross), An t-Srùigh. 'The current place'.

Stuartfield (Aberdeen). 'Stuart's field'. The old name was Crechie, probably from Gaelic *Creichidh*, 'shaking place'.

Stuckindroin (Dunbarton), Stùc an Droighinn. 'Thorn hill'.

Stylemouth (Perth), Cùil nan Cnàimh. The English name is 'mouth of the Style', while the Gaelic one is 'nook of the bones'.

Succoth (Argyll), An Socach. 'The sow place'.

Suddie (Ross), Suidhe. 'Seat'. Easter Suddie is also covered by the same Gaelic name.

Suie (Banff, Perth), An Suidhe. 'The seat'. The full name in Banff is *Suidhe Artair*, 'Arthur's seat', whilst in Perth it is *Suidhe Fhaolain*, 'St Fillan's seat'.

Suisgill (Sutherland), Sìdhisgil. 'Seething gully', from Norse.

Suishnish (Raasay, Skye), Suidhisnis. 'Seething headland', from Norse.

Suledale (Skye), Sùladal. 'Sea slope valley', from Norse.

Sulishader (Skye), Sùlaiseadar. 'Sea slope place', from Norse.

Summer Isles (Ross), Na h-Eileanan Samhraidh. 'The islands of summer'.

Sunart (Argyll), Suaineart. 'Svein's firth', from Norse, known poetically as *Suaineart Ghorm nan Darach*, 'verdant Sunart of the oaks'. The rivalry between Sunart and neighbouring Ardnamurchan is recorded in the saying, *Sùrd le Suaineart! Chaidh Àird nam Murchan a dholaidh!*, 'Let Sunart rejoice! Ardnamurchan has been ruined!'. Pre-Norse, Loch Sunart was called *A' Mhorbhairne*, 'the sea gap', which has been transferred to the district of Morvern.

Sunderland (Islay), Sionarlann. This may be an imported name with the Gaelic form merely representing local pronounciation.

Sunipol (Argyll), Suaineapol. 'Svein's farm', from Norse.

Sunisletter (Inverness), Suainisleitir. 'Svein's level land', from Norse.

Sutherland, Cataibh. The English name is 'southern land' from the point of view of the Norse, while the Gaelic name is 'Cat people's land', referring to the tribe also mentioned in the name of Caithness and in the old Gaelic name of Shetland. East Sutherland is *Machair Chat*, 'plain of Sutherland', and the hilly area behind it is *Bràigh Chat*, 'upland of Sutherland'. The central part of the county is *Dìthreabh Chat*, 'wilderness of

Sutherland', and north Sutherland or the Reay Forest is *Dùthaich MhicAoidh*, 'MacKay's country'. South-east Sutherland between Bonar Bridge and Dornoch is *Fearann Coscraigh*, 'Coscrach's land'. A Sutherland person is a *Catach*. Historically, Sutherland did not include *Dùthaich MhicAoidh* or Assynt.

Sutors of Cromarty (Ross), Na Sùdraichean. 'The tanners', two headlands facing each other across the mouth of the Cromarty Firth.

Swainbost (Lewis), Suaineabost. 'Svein's farm', from Norse.

Swordale (Lewis, Ross, Skye), Suardal. 'Grassy valley', from Norse.

Swordle (Argyll), Suardal. *See* **Swordale**.

Swordly (Sutherland), Suardailigh. 'Grassy slope', from Norse.

Sydera (Sutherland), Siara. *See* **Cyderhall**.

Syre (Sutherland), Saghair. This may stem from Norse *saurr*, 'marsh'.

Taagan (Ross), Na Tathagan. 'The in-fields', from Norse.

Tahay (North Uist), Tathaigh. 'High island', from Norse.

Tain (Ross), Baile Dhubhthaich. The English form is from the pre-Celtic river name. Tha Gaelic name is 'St Duthac's town' and the sanctuary here was *Comraich Bhaile Dhubhthaich*. Tain fair was *Fèill Dubhthaich*, 'St Duthac's fair', but the fair held at Lammas was *Fèill Bearchain* or *Fèill Bhearchain*, 'St Bearchan's fair'. The town is linked with places further north in the rhyme, *Baile Dhubhthaich bòidheach, Dòrnach na goirt; Sgìobal nan ùbhlan 's Bil an arain choirc'; Earabol nan coileagan, Dùn Robain a' chàil; Goillspidh nan sligean dubh 's Druim Muighe a' bhàrr,* 'Beautiful Tain, Dornoch of starvation; Skibo of the apples and Bil of the oatcakes; Embo of the cockles,

Dunrobin of the kail; Golspie of the mussels and Drumuie of the cream'.

Talisker (Skye), Talaisgeir. 'Sloping rock', from Norse.

Tallabheith (Perth), Tall a' Bheithe. 'The rock at the birch'.

Talladale (Ross), Tealldhadal. 'Ledge valley', from Norse. Loch Maree Hotel was known as *Taigh-òsta Thealldhadal*.

Talmine (Sutherland), Tealamainn. This Norse name appears to contain 'ledge', but the second part of the word is unclear. Upper Talmine is *Tealamainn Uthard* and Lower Talmine is *Tealamainn Stàn*.

Tamdhu (Moray), An Tom Dubh. 'The black hillock'.

Tamnavay (Lewis), Tamnabhaigh. 'Harbour bay', from Norse.

Tanera (Ross), Tannara. 'Harbour island', from Norse. Tanera Beg is *Tannara Bheag* and Tanera More is *Tannara Mhór*.

Tangusdale (Barra), Tangasdal. 'Valley of the sharp ridge', from Norse.

Tannach (Caithness). 'Green field', from Gaelic *Tamhnach*.

Tannadice (Angus), Tanachais. This may be from *tamhnach*, 'green field'. The church here was known as *Cill Earnain*, 'St Ernan's church'.

Tannochside (Lanark). This contains Gaelic *tamhnach*, 'green field', with English 'side' attached.

Tannock (West Lothian). *See* **Tannach**.

Taransay (Harris), Tarasaigh. 'Taran's island', from Norse.

Tarbat (Ross), Tairbeart. 'Isthmus'. Tarbat Church and Parish are respectively *Cill Mo Cholmaig* and *Sgìre Mo Cholmaig*, dedicated to St Colman. Nearby is *Port Mo Cholmaig* or 'Portmahomack'. Tarbat Ness is *Rubha Thairbeirt*.

Tarbert (several), An Tairbeart. 'The isthmus'. Some of the places named thus in English have more complete

Gaelic names. Tarbert on Loch Fyne is *Tairbeart Loch Fìne*, 'the isthmus of Loch Fyne', where locals were referred to by terms such as *fithich dhubha*, 'black ravens', *ducairean*, 'guillemots' and *gallachan*, 'bitches'. In Harris, Tarbert is *Tairbeart Na Hearadh*, 'the isthmus of Harris', where East Tarbert is simply *an Tairbeart* and West Tarbert is *an Taobh Siar*, 'the west side'. To express 'in Tarbert', Gaelic uses *air an Tairbeart*, 'on Tarbert'.

Tarbet (several), An Tairbeart. 'The isthmus'. The full name of Tarbet on Loch Lomond is *Tairbeart Loch Laomainn*, 'the isthmus of Loch Lomond', or *An Tairbeart Laomainneach*, 'the Lomond isthmus'. At Loch Nevis it is *Tairbeart Loch Nibheis*, 'the isthmus of Loch Nevis'.

Tarbrax (West Lothian). This may be 'speckled hill', from Gaelic *Tòrr Breac* with an English plural.

Tarbreakes (Fife). *See* **Tarbrax**.

Tarland (Aberdeen), Turlann. 'Bull field', from an older *Tarbhlann*. Tarland Church is *Cill Mo Luaig*, 'Mo Luag's church', and the fair here was *Féill Bhrìghd*, 'Bridget's Fair'.

Tarlogie (Ross), Tàrlagaidh. This is thought to be a Pictish name, meaning 'white brow'.

Tarradale (Ross), Tarradal. This Norse name may be 'peat valley'.

Tarrel (Ross), Tarail. 'Over-cliff'. A saying mentions *Tarail Mhór is Tarail Bheag is Tarail fon a' chreig*, 'Big Tarrel, Little Tarrel and Tarrel under the rock'.

Tarrnacraig (Arran), Tòrr na Creige. 'The hill of the rock'.

Tarskavaig (Skye), Tarsgabhaig. 'Cod bay', from Norse.

Tarves (Aberdeen). This may be 'bull place', from *Tarbhais*.

Tarvie (Ross), Tairbhidh. 'Bull place'. Local people were known as *crogaichean*, 'crocks'.

Tarvit (Fife). This may be 'bull place', from *Tarbhaid*.

Tavool (Mull), Tàbol. 'High farm', from Norse.

Taychreggan (Argyll), Taigh a' Chreagain. 'The house by the little rock'.

Tayinloan (Argyll, Skye), Taigh an Lòin. 'The house by the pond'.

Taymouth (Perth), Bealach. 'Pass'. The full name is *Bealach nan Laogh*, 'the pass of the calves'. Taymouth Castle is *Caisteal Bhealaich*.

Taynish (Argyll), Taighnis. This may be 'high headland', from Norse.

Taynuilt (Argyll), Taigh an Uillt. 'The house by the stream'.

Tayport (Fife). This harbour on the Tay used to be known as Portincraig, from Gaelic *Port na Creige*, 'the harbour at the rock'.

Tayside (Angus, Perth), Taobh Tatha. The river itself occurs in the saying, *Spé, Dé is Tatha, na trì uisge as motha fon adhar*, 'Spey, Dee and Tay, the three greatest rivers under the sun'. The north side of Loch Tay is *Deisear*, 'south-facing land', while the south side is *Tuathar*, 'north-facing land'.

Tayvallich (Argyll), Taigh a' Bhealaich. 'The house at the pass'.

Tayvullin (Islay), Taigh a' Mhuilinn. 'The house at the mill'.

Teanamachar (North Uist), An t-Seana Mhachair. 'The old machair'.

Teanassie (Ross), Taigh an Fhasaidh. 'The house at the stance'.

Teangue (Skye), An Teanga. 'The tongue' or 'spit of land'. Upper Teangue is *Bràigh na Teanga*, 'the upper part of Teangue'.

Teaninich (Ross), Taigh an Aonaich. 'The house on the moor'.

Teawig (Ross), Taigh a' Bhuic. 'The house of the buck'.

Teilesnish (Harris), Teilisnis. 'Cave headland', from Norse.

Temple (Midlothian), Baile nan Trodach. This name commemorates the Knights Templar. The old form in English was Ballentroddoch, 'the farm of the combatants'.

Tenandry (Perth), An t-Seanaontachd. 'The old leased land'.

Tenga (Mull), An Teanga. *See* **Teangue**.

Terreagles (Dumfries). 'Village with a church', from Brythonic.

Tersets (Aberdeen). This may be 'crossing path', from *Tarsaid*.

Texa (Islay), Teacsa. This Norse island name is unclear.

Thundergay (Arran), Tòrr a' Ghaoth. 'The windy hill'. North Thundergay, known also as Lenimore, is *Lèanaidh Mór* or *Lèanaidh Mhór*, 'big meadow'. South Thundergay is *Achadh Mór*, 'big field', also known as Auchamor in English.

Thurso (Caithness), Inbhir Theòrsa. The English name is the name of the river, while the Gaelic name is 'mouth of the Thurso'.

Tibbermore (Perth). 'Big well', from Gaelic *Tiobar Mór*.

Tigharry (North Uist), Taigh a' Ghearraidh. 'The house on the fertile land'.

Tighnabruaich (Argyll), Taigh na Bruaich. 'The house on the bank'. The Tighnabruaich area is known as Kerry or *An Ceathramh Comhalach*, 'the Cowal quarterland', and a native of the area is a *Ceathrach*.

Tighnafiline (Ross), Taigh na Faoilinn or Taigh na Fadhlainn. 'The house by the shore field'.

Tighphuirst (Argyll), Taigh a' Phuirt. 'The house at the port'.

Tillydrine (Aberdeen). 'The green hill of thorns', from *Tulach an Droighinn*.

Tillyfour (Aberdeen). 'The green hill of the pasture', from *Tulach Phùir*.

Tillyfourie (Aberdeen). 'The green hill at the pasture place', from *Tulach Phùiridh*.

Tillytarmont (Aberdeen). 'The green hill of the sanctuary', from *Tulach an Tèarmainn*.

Timsgarry (Lewis), Tuimisgearraidh. The first part of this Norse field name

may be a personal name.

Tipperty (Aberdeen). 'Place of wells', from *Tiobartaidh*.

Tirandrish (Inverness), Tìr an Dris. 'The land of the briars'.

Tirarragan (Mull), Tìr Fheargain. 'Feargan's land'.

Tirarthur (Perth), Tìr Artair. 'Arthur's land'.

Tiree, Tiriodh. 'Corn land'. The island is known as *Tiriodh ìosal an eòrna*, 'low Tiree of the barley'. East Tiree is known as *an Cinn t-Sear*, 'east end', and the west part is known as *an Cinn t-Siar*, 'west end'. A Tiree person is a *Tiristeach*.

Tirfuir (Lismore), Tìr a' Phùir. 'The land of the pasture'.

Tirghoil (Mull), Tìr a' Ghoill. 'The land of the non-Gael'.

Tirinie (Perth), Tìr Ìngnidh. 'The land of the claw place'. A saying maintains, *Cha bhi Tòiseach air Tìr Ìngnidh, 's cha bhi Tìr Ìngnidh gun Tòiseach*, 'Tirinie will never have a master, and Tirinie will never be without a master'. This saying depends on the ambiguity of *tòiseach* which means 'leader' or 'master', but also 'Macintosh'.

Tiroran (Mull), Tìr Odhrain. 'St Oran's land'.

Tiumpan Head (Lewis), Ceann an Tiùmpain or Rubha an Tiùmpain. 'The headland of the drumming'. A variant spelling, *Ceann an t-Siùmpain*, is also seen.

Tobermory (Mull), Tobar Mhoire. 'St Mary's well'. This was formerly known as *Tobar Maol Rubha*, 'St Maol Rubha's well'.

Toberonochy (Luing), Tobar Dhonnchaidh. 'Duncan's well'.

Tobson (Bernera), Tòpsann. 'Sound or head of the bay', from Norse.

Toe Head (Harris), Gob an Tobha. 'The peak at the grassy point', from Gaelic/Norse.

Tokavaig (Skye), Tòcabhaig. 'Tóki's bay', from Norse.

Toldunie (Perth), Tail Dùnaidh. This may be 'haugh of the fort place'.

Tollie (Ross), Tollaidh. 'Place of holes'.

Tolmachan (Harris), An Tolmachan. 'The little knoll'.

Tolsta (Lewis), Tolastadh. 'Tholf's place', from Norse. New Tolsta is *Am Baile Ùr*, 'the new village' and North Tolsta is *Tolastadh bho Thuath*. Tolsta Head is *Ceann Tholastaidh*

Tolstachaolais (Lewis), Tolastadh a' Chaolais. 'Tolsta at the narrows', from Norse/Gaelic

Tolvah (Inverness), Toll a' Bhàthaidh. 'The drowning hole'.

Tomatin (Inverness), Tom Aitinn. 'Juniper hillock'.

Tombae (Banff). 'The birch hillock', from *An Tom Beithe*.

Tombain (Moray). 'The fair hillock', from *An Tom Bàn*.

Tomchrasky (Inverness), Tom Chrasgaidh. 'The hillock at the crossing place'.

Tomcrail (Perth), Tom MhicRéill. 'MacNeil's hillock', the spelling showing the local pronunciation of *MacNéill* as *MacRéill*.

Tomdoun (Inverness), An Tom Donn. 'The brown hillock'.

Tomich (Inverness), Tomaich. 'Hillock place'.

Tomidhu (Aberdeen), Na Toman Dubh. 'The black hillocks'.

Tomintoul (Banff), Tom an t-Sabhail. 'The hillock with the barn'.

Tomnahurich (Inverness), Tom na h-Iubhraich. 'The hillock of the yew wood'.

Tomnamoon (Moray). 'The hillock of the peat', from *Tom na Mòna*.

Tomnavoulin (Banff), Tom Mhuilinn. 'The hillock at the mill'.

Tong (Lewis), Tunga. 'Tongue' or 'spit of land', from Norse. Under the influence of English, the locally accepted name in Gaelic is *Tong* or *Tòng*.

Tongadale (Skye), Tungadal. 'Tongue valley', from Norse.

Tongue (Sutherland), Ceann Tàile, Tunga or Circeabol. The English and second Gaelic names are 'tongue of land', from Norse. The first Gaelic name is 'bay head' and is an abbreviation of *Ceann Tàile MhicAoidh*, 'MacKay's Kintail'. The last Gaelic name is 'church farm' from Norse, and is known as Kirkiboll in English, now part of Tongue.

Torastan (Coll), Torathasdan. This may be 'Thorir's dwelling', from Norse.

Torastay (Lewis), Torastaigh. 'Torfi's farm', from Norse.

Toravaig (Skye), Tòrabhaig. 'Thorir's bay' or 'peat bay', from Norse.

Torbain (Fife). 'Fair hill', from *An Tòrr Bàn*.

Torbane (West Lothian). *See* **Torbaine**.

Torbeg (Arran), An Tòrr Beag. 'The small hill'.

Torcastle (Inverness), Tòrr a' Chaisteil. 'The hill of the castle'.

Tore (Ross), An Tòrr. 'The hill'. The name *An Todhar*, 'fertiliser', is now seen on roadsigns.

Torechastle (Moray). *See* **Torcastle** and **Dallas**.

Torgorm (Ross), An Tòrr Gorm. 'The green hill'. *See* **Glen Gorm**.

Torgyle (Inverness), Tòrr a' Ghoill. 'The hill of the non-Gael'. The settlement of Torgyle Bridge is *Ceann Drochaid*, 'bridge end'.

Torinturk (Argyll), Tòrr an Tuirc. 'The hill of the boar'.

Torloisk (Mull), Tòrrloisgt or An Tòrr Loisgte. 'Burnt hill'.

Torlum (Benbecula), Tòrlum. This may be 'Thorir's holm', from Norse.

Torlundy (Inverness), Tòrr Lunndaidh. 'The hill of Lundy'.

Tormore (Arran, Moray, Skye), An Tòrr Mór. 'The big hill'.

Tornapress (Ross), Treamhar nam Preas. 'The settlement of the thickets'.

Tornaveen (Aberdeen). This may be 'hill of the Fianna', from *Tòrr na bhFiann*, now written *Tòrr nam Fiann*.

Torness (East Lothian); (Inverness, Mull), Tòrr an Easa. In East Lothian the name is 'Thorir's or Thora's headland' or maybe 'peat headland', from Norse. In Inverness and Mull it is 'the hill at the waterfall'. The Gaelic name above applies only to the places in Inverness and Mull.

Torphichen (West Lothian). This may be 'Fechin's hill', from Gaelic or Brythonic.

Torphin (Midlothian). 'White hill', from *An Tòrr Fionn*.

Torphins (Aberdeen). *See* **Torphin**.

Torrachilty (Ross), Tòrr Àicheallaidh. 'The hill of Achilty'.

Torrance (Dunbarton). 'Hillocks', from *Torrain* or *Torranan* with an English plural.

Torridon (Ross), Toirbheartan. This denotes a place where boats were dragged overland, the word being related to *tairbeart*, 'isthmus'.

Torrin (Skye), Na Torranan or Na Torran. 'The hillocks'.

Torrisdale (Argyll), Tórasdail; (Sutherland), Tòrrasdal. 'Thorir's valley', from Norse.

Torrish (Sutherland), Torrais. 'Hill place'.

Torrobol (Sutherland), Torrobol. This may be 'peat farm' or 'Thorir's farm', from Norse.

Torry (Aberdeen, Fife). 'Hill place', from *Tòrraidh*, earlier *Tòrran*.

Torrylin (Arran), Tòrr an Linne. 'The hill by the pool'.

Torsa (Luing), Torsa. 'Thorir's island'.

Torvean (Inverness), Tòrr Bheathain. 'Bean's hill'.

Toscaig (Ross), Toghsgaig. 'Strip of land at the howe', from Norse.

Totachocaire (Skye), Tobhta a' Chò-caire. 'The cook's house site', from Norse/Gaelic.

Totaig (Ross), An Tobhtaig. 'The bay at the house site', from Norse.

Totamore (Coll), An Tobhta Mhór. 'The big house site', from Norse/Gaelic.

Totarder (Skye), Tobhta Àrdair. 'The house site on the high water', from Norse/Gaelic.

Totarol (Bernera), Tobhtarol. 'Hill of the house sites', from Norse.

Tote (Skye), An Tobhta. 'The house site', from Norse.

Toteronald (Skye), Tobhta Raghnaill. 'Ronald's house site'.

Totescore (Skye), Tobhta Sgoir. 'House site at the wood', from Norse.

Touch (Fife). 'Green hill', from *tulach*.

Tough (Aberdeen, Fife). *See* **Touch**.

Tougal (Inverness), An Taobh Geal. 'The white side or area', possibly referring to the white sandy beaches of Morar.

Toulvaddie (Ross), Toll a' Mhadaidh. 'The lair of the fox or wolf'.

Tournaig (Ross), Tùrnaig. 'Rounded hillock'.

Toward (Argyll), Tollard. This name appears to denote holes or caves. Toward Point is *Rubha Thollaird*.

Towie (Aberdeen). 'Hole place', from *Tollaigh*.

Tralligill (Sutherland), Tràiligil. 'Serf's gully', from Norse.

Tralee (Argyll), Trà Lì or Tràigh Lì. This may be 'beach at the slope', from Gaelic/Norse.

Trantlebeg (Sutherland), Tranntail Beag. 'Little Trantle', from Norse for 'Thrond's field', with Gaelic for 'small' added.

Trantlemore (Sutherland), Tranntail Mór. 'Big Trantle'. *See* **Trantlebeg**.

Treaslane (Skye), Triaslainn. The meaning of this name is unclear.

Treshnish (Mull), Treisinis. This Norse headland name is unclear.

Tressady (Sutherland), Treasaididh. 'Battle place'.

Trinafour (Perth), Trian a' Phùir. 'Third-land of the pasture'.

Trislaig (Argyll), Trìoslaig. This Norse name refers to a bay, but the first element of the name is unclear.

Trodday (Skye), Tròndaigh. 'Thrond's

headland', from Norse. The same personal name appears in 'Trotternish'.

Troon (Ayr), An Truthail or An t-Sròn. 'The nose-shaped headland', from Brythonic *trwyn*. The second Gaelic name is cognate with the Brythonic original. The first Gaelic name, 'the stream or current', was used in Arran Gaelic and is a corruption of the original name.

Trossary (South Uist), Trosaraidh. 'Thrasi's fertile land', from Norse.

Trotternish (Skye), Tròndairnis. 'Thrond's headland', a personal name also found in 'Trodday'. Trotternish people were nicknamed *coin*, 'dogs', and known as *stapagaich*, 'stapag people', by their neighbours in Duirinish. Trotternish itself was known as *Dùthaich nan Stapag* or *am Fearann Stapagach*, 'the stapag land', *stapag* being an oatmeal-based dish. The northern part of Trotternish is *Ìochdar Thròndairnis*, 'lower Trotternish', while Braes is *Bràighe Thròndairnis*, 'upper Trotternish', as well as *Bràighe Phort Rìgh*, 'upper Portree'.

Troup Head (Aberdeen), Ros Cuisne. This headland is 'cold headland' in Gaelic.

Trumisgarry (North Uist), Truimisgearraidh. 'Thrum's fertile land', from Norse.

Trumpan (Skye), Trumpan. The meaning of this name is obscure.

Tubeg (Sutherland), An Taobh Beag. 'The small area'.

Tulchan (Angus, Moray), Tulachan. 'Little green hill'.

Tulliallan (Fife). This *tulach* name may contain the elements found in **Alloa** and **Alva**.

Tullich (Aberdeen), An Tulach; (Ross), An Tulaich. 'The green hill'. Tullich Church in Aberdeen is *Cill Nachlain*, 'St Nathalan's church'. Tullich Muir in Ross is *Blàr na Tulaich*.

Tullichewen (Dunbarton), Tulach Eóghainn. 'Ewen's green hill'.

Tullimet (Perth), Tulach Mhait or Tulach a' Mhaid. The second part of the name is unclear, but *tulach* is 'green hill'.

Tulloch (several), An Tulach. 'The green hill'.

Tullochbeg (Aberdeen). 'Small green hill', from *An Tulach Bheag*.

Tullybanchor (Perth), Tulaich Bheannchair. 'The green hill at the horn place'.

Tullybardine (Perth), Tulach Bhàirdne. 'The green hill of the poet's land'.

Tullybelton (Perth), Tulach Bhealltainn. 'The green hill of Beltane'.

Tullybreck (Fife). 'Speckled green hill', from *Tulach Bhreac*.

Tullyfergus (Perth), Tulach Fhearghais. 'Fergus's green hill'.

Tullygreig (Aberdeen). This may be 'Ciric's or Giric's green hill', from *Tulach Chiric* or *Tulach Ghiric*.

Tullymurdoch (Perth), Tulach Mhuirich. 'Muireach's green hill'.

Tummel Bridge (Perth), Drochaid Dubhaig or Drochaid Choinneachain. 'The bridge over the black stream' or 'bridge at the junction' in Gaelic.

Tumore (Sutherland), An Taobh Mór. 'The large area'.

Turriff (Aberdeen), Baile Thurra or Torraibh. This may be 'hill place', also 'the village of the hill place' in Gaelic. An older form *Turbhruadh* is found in the Book of Deer, but is unclear.

Tweedale (Berwick, Peebles, Selkirk), Srath Thuaidh. 'Strath of the Tweed'.

Tynayere (Perth), Taigh Neimh Gheàrr. 'The house at the short sacred land'.

Tyndrum (Perth), Taigh an Droma. 'The house on the ridge'.

Tynribbie (Argyll), Taigh an Ribe or Taigh an Ribidh. The first part of the name means 'house', but the final element is unclear.

Tyrie (Aberdeen, Fife). 'Land place', from *Tìridh*.

Uachdar (Benbecula), An t-Uachdar. 'The top'.

Uags (Ross), Na h-Uamhagan. 'The little caves'.

Udale (Ross), Uadal. 'Yew valley', from Norse.

Uidh (Vatersay), An Ùidh. 'The isthmus', from Norse.

Uig (Coll, Lewis), Ùig; (Ross), An Ùig; (Skye), Ùige. 'Bay', from Norse. A native of Uig in Lewis is an *Ùigeach*, and the people here were known as *daoine uaisle Ùig*, 'the noble folk of Uig'

Uigean (Lewis), Na h-Ùigean. 'The bays', from Norse.

Uiginish (Skye), Ùiginis. 'Bay headland', from Norse.

Uigshader (Skye), Ùigiseadar. 'Bay township', from Norse.

Uiskevagh (Benbecula), Uisgeabhagh. This may be 'ox bay', from Norse.

Uist, Uibhist or Uidhist. This may be 'corn island'. North Uist is *Uibhist a Tuath*. It is also known as *an Ceann a Tuath*, 'the north end', and *Tìr an Eòrna*, 'the land of barley'. South Uist is *Uibhist a Deas*, also known as *an Ceann a Deas*, 'the south end', and *Tìr a' Mhurain*, 'the land of marram grass'. A Uist person is an *Uibhisteach*.

Ulladale (Ross), Uladal. 'Wolf valley', from Norse.

Ullapool (Ross), Ulapul. 'Wolf farm' or 'Ulli's farm', from Norse. Local people were known as *sùlairean*, 'gannets', and *crodh*, 'cattle'.

Ullinish (Skye), Uilinis or Uilbhinis. 'Wolf headland', from Norse.

Ulva (Mull), Ulbha. 'Wolf island', from Norse.

Umachan (Raasay), Iumachan. This name appears to be of Gaelic origin, but is unclear.

Unachan (Inverness), Aonachan. 'Market place'.

Unakille (Skye), Baile Ung na Cille. The Gaelic name has *baile*, 'village', attached to 'ounce-land of the church'.

Unapool (Sutherland), Ùnabol. This Norse farm name may contain 'ounceland' as its first element.

Ungeshader (Lewis), Ungaiseadar. This may be 'ounce-land township', from Norse. Local pronunciation collected by Oftedal suggests a preferable spelling of *Ungaiseadair*.

Uphall (West Lothian). 'Up haugh', from English. Uphall parish used to be known as Wester Strathbroc, from *Srath Broc*, 'strath of badgers', now *Srath Bhroc*. Easter Strathbrock is the old name for the parish of Broxburn.

Uppat (Sutherland), Upaid. This name is unclear.

Uragaig (Colonsay), Uragaig. This is 'small rubble mound' or 'bay at the small rubble mound', from Norse.

Urchany (Ross), Urchanaidh. This is said to mean 'place beside the bog cotton'.

Urgha (Harris), Urgha. 'Rubble mound', from Norse.

Urinbeg (Arran), Uaran Beag. 'Small spring'. As is seen in several Arran place-names comprising noun and adjective, the definite article is not used, although the norm elsewhere as well as in Arran itself.

Uroch (Wigtown). This is 'yew place', from *Iubhrach*.

Urquhart (Fife); (Inverness), Urchadan; (Moray), Urchard. 'Woodside', from Pictish. Urquhart Parish in Inverness is *Urchadan Mo Chrostain*, 'St Drostan's Urquhart'. Urquhart Castle in Inverness is *Caisteal na Sròine*, 'castle at the point'. Nether Urquhart in Moray was formerly known as *Ìochdar Urchaird*. The name in Fife is most likely the same as that in Moray.

Urrard (Perth), Urrard. 'Prominent landmark'.

Urray (Ross), Urrath. 'Prominent fort'.

Urvaig (Tiree), An Urbhaig. 'Bay at the rubble place', from Norse.

Ushinish (South Uist), Ùisinis. The first part of this Norse headland name is unclear.

Vaitem (Harris), Bhéiteam. 'Wet island', from Norse.

Valamus (Lewis), Bhalamus. 'Whale farm', from Norse.

Valasay (Bernera), Bhàlasaigh. 'Whale island', from Norse.

Vale of Leven (Dunbarton), Magh Leamhna or Srath Leamhna. 'Elm plain' or 'elm strath'. The Vale of Leven is part of the area of Lennox which is *Leamhnachd* in Gaelic. A native of Lennox is a *Leamhnach*.

Vallay (North Uist), Bhàlaigh. 'Whale island' or 'shallow water island', from Norse, the latter being appropriate here.

Valtos (Lewis, Skye), Bhaltos. 'River mouth', from Norse.

Varkasaig (Skye), Bharcasaig. 'Castle bay', from Norse.

Vaternish (Skye), Bhatairnis. 'Water headland'. Local people were nicknamed *cait*, 'cats'. Vaternish Point is *Rubha Bhatairnis*.

Vatersay, Bhatarsaigh. 'Water island'. Vatersay village is *Baile Bhatarsaigh*. A native of Vatersay is a *Bhatarsach*.

Vatisker (Lewis), Bhatasgair. 'Water skerry', from Norse.

Vatten (Skye), Bhatan. 'Water', from Norse.

Vaul (Tiree), Bhalla. 'Hill', from Norse. Upper Vaul is *Bràigh Bhalla*, 'the upper part of Vaul'.

Viewfield (Skye), Goirtean na Creige. The English name is 'field with a view', while the Gaelic is 'the enclosed field by the rock'.

Village (Scalpay), Am Baile. 'The village'.

Votersay (North Uist), Bhoitearsaigh. *See* **Vatersay**.

Vuia Mor (Bernera), Bhuia Mór. 'Large Vuia', or 'house island', from Norse.

Wards (Harris), An Rubha Àrd. 'The high headland'.

Waterloo (Ayr, Perth); (Skye), Achadh a' Chùirn. In Perth, houses were built especially for veterans of the battle of Waterloo. In Skye, the area was settled by returning soldiers from Waterloo. The Gaelic name only applies to Waterloo in Skye and is 'the field at the cairn'.

Waternish (Skye), Bhatairnis. *See* **Vaternish**.

Waterstein (Skye), Bhatairsteinn. 'Water stone', from Norse.

Waterton (Ross), Baile nam Fuaran. This is 'water farm' in English, but 'the farm of the springs' in Gaelic.

Weavers Point (North Uist), Rubha an Fhigheadair. 'Headland of the knitter/weaver'.

Weem (Perth), Baile a' Chlachain. The English form is a corruption of Gaelic *uamh*, 'cave', while the Gaelic name is 'the village with the churchyard'.

Wemyss (Fife). This may be 'cave place', from *Uamhais*.

Wemyss Bay (Renfrew). *See* **Wemyss**, but this name may stem from the Wemyss family.

Westerdale (Caithness), An Dail Shuas. 'The upper or wester dale'.

Wester Ross (Ross), Ros an Iar. This is also known in Gaelic as *Taobh Siar Rois*, 'the west side of Ross', although this is not used locally.

Westertown of Duntelchaig (Inverness), Bail Shuas. 'Upper or wester farm' at Duntelchaig.

West Kilbride (Ayr, South Uist). In the Ayr name, 'West' is used to distinguish this place from East Kilbride in Lanarkshire. In South Uist the Gaelic name is simply *Cille Bhrìghde*, 'St Bridget's church', 'West' being used in English to differentiate it from neighbouring East Kilbride which is *Taobh a' Chaolais*, 'beside the sound', in Gaelic.

West Lothian, Labhdaidh an Iar or Lodainn an Iar. *See* **Lothian**.

West Side (Lewis), An Taobh Siar.

'West side'. A native of the area is a *Siarach*.

Whitebridge (Inverness), An Drochaid Bhàn. 'The white bridge'.

Whitefarland (Arran), An Aoirinn. 'White headland' is the English name, but the Gaelic name is 'the raised beach'. Whitefarland Point is *Rubha na h-Aoireann*.

Whitefield (Arran), Srath Bhàn; (Inverness), An t-Achadh Bàn. In Arran, the name is 'white river-holm', but in Inverness it is 'the white or fallow field'.

Whitehouse (Argyll), An Taigh Bàn. 'The fair or white house'.

Whiteness (Ross), Rubha na h-Innse Móire. The English form is 'white headland', from Norse, and the Gaelic name is 'the headland at the big meadow'.

Whithorn (Wigtown), Taigh Mhàrtainn. The English name is 'white house', from English, and the Gaelic name is 'Martin's house'. Earlier Gaelic names for this place were *Rosnat*, 'small promontory' and *Futarna*, a gaelicised version of the Latin form of the English name. This was the site of *Candida Casa* of St Ninian.

Whiting Bay (Arran), Am Bàigh or Eadar Dhà Rubha. The Gaelic name are 'the bay' and 'between two headlands'.

Wiay (Benbecula), Bhuia or Fùidheigh.

'House island', from Norse.

Wick (Caithness), Inbhir Ùige. The English form is 'bay', from Norse, and the Gaelic is 'the mouth of the Wick river', from Gaelic/Norse. The fair held at Wick was called *Féill Fhearghais*, 'St Fergus's Fair'.

Wigtown, Baile na h-Ùige. 'Town on the bay', from Norse/English. The Gaelic version is a translation. Wigtownshire is *Siorrachd Bhaile na h-Ùige*.

Wilkhaven (Ross), Port nam Faochag. 'The harbour of the whelks'.

Windhill (Ross), Cnoc na Gaoithe. 'The hill of the wind'.

Woodend (Argyll, Skye), Ceann na Coille. 'End of the wood'.

Woodlands (Ross), An Claon Uachdrach. 'Land of the wood', in English, but this is 'the upper slope' in Gaelic.

Woodside (Ross), Ceann na Coille. The Gaelic name is 'the end of the wood'.

Wyvis (Ross), Coire Bhacaidh. The English name comes from the mountain name, *Beinn Uais*, 'mountain of terror' or Ben Wyvis. The Gaelic name is 'corrie of the ghost'. Wyvis Forest is *Frìth Uais*.

Yellow Wells (Ross), Am Fuaran Buidhe. The Gaelic is 'the yellow spring'.

Yoker (Glasgow). 'River bank', from obsolete Gaelic *eochair*.

Lochs and Sea Areas

Alness Bay (Ross), Camas Alanais. The Gaelic and English names both mean the same.

Annat Bay (Ross), Am Poll Mór or Linne na h-Annaid. The first Gaelic name is 'the big pond', the local name of the bay. The second Gaelic name is 'the firth of Annat'.

Atlantic Ocean, An Cuan Siar. The Gaelic name is 'Western Ocean'. In Argyll and islands this is known as *An Cuan Mór*, 'the Great Ocean'. In poetry the Atlantic was known as *An Tabh*, from Norse.

Avoch Bay (Ross), Camas Abhach. The Gaelic and English names both mean the same.

Beauly Firth (Inverness, Ross), Linne Fharair or Poll an Ròid. This arm of the Moray Firth is known in Gaelic as 'the firth of the Farrar' and as 'the pool of the rood', referring to a cross erected on a small island in the 13th century.

Broad Bay (Lewis), An Loch a Tuath. The 'broad bay' may originally have been named by the Norse, as there is a village on the bay named *Bréibhig*, from the Norse for 'Broad Bay'. The Gaelic name is 'the North Loch'.

Cambuscurrie Bay (Ross), Camas Curaidh. The Gaelic name is 'inlet of the coracles'. The English form has duplicated *camas* by adding 'bay' to the Gaelic original.

Campbeltown Loch (Argyll), Loch Chille Chiarain. The Gaelic name is 'the loch at St Ciaran's church'. This loch was known in English by an anglicised form of the Gaelic name until that was superceded by the present English name following the foundation of the planned town of Campbeltown.

Corryvreckan (Argyll), Coire Bhreacain. 'Breacan's cauldron', referring to the whirlpool here. A saying has it, *Ge b' e nach stiùir coire a' bhrochain, cha stiùir Coire Bhreacain*, 'He who cannot manage the porridge cauldron, will never manage Breacan's cauldron'.

Craig Bay (Ross), Lùb na Creige. 'The bay of Craig'.

Cromarty Bay (Ross), Camas Chrombaigh. The Gaelic and English names both mean the same.

Cromarty Firth (Ross), Caolas Chrombaigh. Although the English name mentions a firth, the Gaelic name is 'the strait of Cromarty'.

Crom Loch (Ross), An Crom Loch. 'The crooked loch'.

Crowlin Sound (Ross, Skye), An Linne Chròlaigeach or An Linne Chròlainneach. The Gaelic name is the 'the Crowlin Firth'.

Cuillin Sound (Rum, Skye), An Linne Sgitheanach. The Gaelic name is the 'the Skye Firth'.

Dornoch Firth (Ross, Sutherland), Caolas Dhòrnaich. The Gaelic name is 'the strait of Dornoch'.

Dorus Mor (Argyll), An Doras Mór. 'The great gate', leading out into the Atlantic from the shelter of the Argyll islands.

East Kyle of Bute (Argyll, Bute), An Caol an Ear. The Gaelic name is 'the east sound'.

Eilean Tigh Sound (Raasay), Caolas Eilean Taighe. The Gaelic and English names both mean the same.

Firth of Clyde (Argyll, Arran, Ayr), An Linne Ghlas, (Argyll, Bute, Renfrew), Linne Chluaidh. The Firth of Clyde south of Arran is known as *An Linne Ghlas*, 'the grey-blue firth'. *Linne Chluaidh*, 'the firth of the Clyde', extends from Arran up to Inverclyde. In the Gaelic of Arran, the Firth of Clyde between Arran and Ayrshire was called *Caol an Eilein*, 'the island strait'.

Firth of Forth (Fife, East Lothian, West Lothian, Midlothian), Linn Giùdain. The English name refers to the River Forth. The Gaelic name is not entirely clear, although *linn* or *linne* is used to denote a firth or sea loch. *Giùdain* may be related to Gododdyn, the Brythonic people who inhabited the Lothians prior to the arrival of the Scots and Angles.

Firth of Lorne (Argyll), An Linne Latharnach. 'The Lorne firth', in Gaelic.

Firth of Tay (Angus, Fife, Perth), Linne Tatha or Loch Tatha. The Gaelic names are 'the firth of the Tay' and 'the loch of the Tay'. The latter name was used in Perthshire Gaelic, but is also the name applied to Loch Tay.

Flowerdale Bay (Ross), Ceann an t-Sàil or Òb Cheann an t-Sàil. The English name refers to the settlement name of Flowerdale, while the Gaelic names are 'the head of the inlet' and 'the bay at the head of the inlet'.

Gairloch (Ross), Geàrrloch. 'Short loch'.

Gareloch (Argyll, Dunbarton), An Geàrr Loch. 'The short loch'.

Gunna Sound (Coll, Tiree), Am Bun Dubh. This sound which surrounds the islet of Gunna between Coll and Tiree is known as 'the black mouth' in Gaelic.

Holy Loch (Argyll), An Loch Sianta. 'The sacred or holy loch'.

Horseshoe Bay (Ross), Crudh an Eich. The Gaelic name is simply 'the horseshoe'.

Inner Sound (Raasay, Ross), An Caolas Ratharsach or An Linne Ratharsach. The English name uses 'inner' to signify that this sound links Raasay to the mainland. The Gaelic name of the Inner Sound is the 'the Raasay strait or firth'. The Sound of Raasay is another sea area, linking Raasay with Skye, but with the same Gaelic name.

Kerry Bay (Ross), Inbhir Chearraidh. The English name refers to the bay into which the Kerry River flows, while the Gaelic name is 'the mouth of the Kerry'.

Kilbrannan Sound (Argyll, Arran), An Caolas Brandanach, An Caolas Srandanach or Caol a' Bhrannaidh. This may be 'St Brendan's strait'.

Kilchoan Bay (Argyll), Bàgh Chille Chomhghain. The Gaelic and English both mean the same.

Kyle Akin (Skye), Caol Àcain. 'Haakon's narrows', referring to a Norse king.

Kyle More (Raasay, Skye), An Caol Mór. 'The big narrows'.

Kyle of Lochalsh (Ross, Skye), Caol Loch Aillse. 'The narrows of Lochalsh'.

Kyle Rhea (Inverness, Skye), Caol Reatha. 'The narrows at the current'. *See* **Kylerhea**.

Kyle Rona (Raasay), An Caol Rònach. 'The Rona narrows', referring to the island of South Rona.

Kyles Flodday (Benbecula), Caolas Fhlodaidh. 'The strait of Flodday'.

Kyles Knoydart (Inverness), Caolas Chnòideart. 'The strait of Knoydart'.

Kylesku (Sutherland), An Caolas Cumhang. 'The narrow strait'.

Kyles Morar (Inverness), Caolas Mhórair. 'The strait of Morar'.

Kyles of Bute (Argyll, Bute), Na Caoil Bhódach. 'The Bute narrows'. The East Kyle is *An Caol an Ear* while the West Kyle is *An Caol an Iar* or *An Caol Ceathrach*, 'the Kerry sound'.

Kyles Scalpay (Harris, Scalpay), Caolas Sgalpaigh. 'The strait of Scalpay'.

Kyles Stockinish (Harris), Caolas Stocainis. 'The strait of Stockinish'.

Lake of Menteith (Perth), Loch Innis Mo Cholmaig or Loch a' Phuirt. The Gaelic names do not refer to the district of Menteith, but to the island and 'the port', meaning Port of Menteith. The island is *Innis Mo Cholmaig*, 'St. Colman's island'.

Linn of Morvern (Argyll), An Linne Mhorbhairneach. 'The Morvern firth'.

Little Loch Broom (Ross), An Locha Beag. This arm of Loch Broom is known as 'the small loch' in Gaelic.

Little Minch (Benbecula, North Uist, Skye), An Cuan Sgìth. This is an extension of the main Minch. The Gaelic name is 'the Skye ocean'.

Loch Achilty (Ross), Loch Àicheallaidh. 'The loch of Achilty'.

Loch Achonchie (Ross), Loch Achadh Dhònnchaidh. 'The loch at Duncan's field'.

Loch Affric (Inverness), Loch Afraic. 'The loch of the Affric'.

Loch Ailort (Inverness), Loch Ailleart. *See* **Lochailort**.

Loch Ainort (Skye, South Uist), Loch Aoineart. *See* **Lochainort**.

Loch Aline (Argyll), Loch Àlainn. *See* **Lochaline**.

Loch Alsh (Ross), Loch Aillse. *See* **Lochalsh**.

Loch Ard (Perth), Loch na h-Àirde. 'The loch with the headland'.

Loch Arkaig (Inverness), Loch Airceig. 'Loch of the difficult river'.

Loch Arklet (Stirling), Loch Aircleid. 'Loch at the difficult slope'.

Loch Ashie (Inverness), Loch Athaisidh. 'Loch at the bare meadow'.

Loch Assynt (Sutherland), Loch Asainn or Loch Asainte. 'The loch of Assynt'.

Loch Avich (Argyll), Loch Abhaich. 'The loch at the water place'.

Loch Awe (Argyll), Loch Obha. 'The loch of fresh water'. *See* **Lochawe**.

Loch Bee (South Uist), Loch Bì. The meaning of the second, Norse, element of this name is unclear.

Loch Beneveian (Inverness), Loch Beinn a' Mheadhain. 'The loch of the middle mountain'.

Loch Bervie (Sutherland), Loch Biorbhaigh. This might be 'loch of boiling water', but in its location a Norse derivation might be likely, such as 'the head of the loch of the rock river'.

Loch Boisdale (South Uist), Loch Baghasdail. *See* **Lochboisdale**.

Loch Bracadale (Skye), Loch Bhràcadail. 'The loch of Bracadale'.

Loch Brittle (Skye), Loch Breadail. 'The loch at the broad valley', from Gaelic/Norse.

Loch Broom, Loch a' Bhraoin (Perth), Loch Bhraoin (Ross). 'The loch of water'.

Loch Buie (Mull), Locha Buidhe. 'Yellow loch'.

Loch Carron (Ross), Loch Carrann. 'Loch of the rough water'. *See* **Lochcarron**.

Loch Cluanie (Ross), Loch Chluainidh. 'The loch of Cluanie'.

Loch Coruisk (Skye), Loch a' Choir' Uisge. 'The loch at the fresh water corrie'.

Loch Coulter (Inverness), Loch Caoldair. 'The loch of the narrow water'.

Loch Creran (Argyll), Loch Creurain. The meaning of this name is unclear.

Loch Dochfour (Inverness), An Eadarloch. 'The between-loch', between Loch and River Ness.

Loch Duich (Ross), Loch Dubhthaich. 'St. Duthac's loch'.

Loch Duntelchaig (Inverness), Loch

Dhùn Deilcheig. 'The loch of Duntelchaig'.

Loch Dunvegan (Skye), Loch Dhùn Bheagain. 'The loch of Dunvegan'.

Loch Earn (Perth), Loch Éireann or Loch Éir. 'The loch of the Earn'. The second Gaelic name reflects local pronunciation.

Loch Eck (Argyll), Loch Aic. The meaning of this name is unclear. It is alleged to mean 'the loch of the notch', but this seems unlikely.

Loch Eil (Argyll, Inverness), Loch Iall. 'Thong loch', referring to its long thin shape.

Loch Eilt (Inverness), Loch Aoillt. The meaning of this name is unclear.

Loch Eishort (Skye), Loch Eiseort. This is a Norse name.

Loch Eport (North Uist), Loch Euphort. 'Isthmus loch', from Norse.

Loch Ericht (Perth), Loch Eireachd. 'Assembly loch'.

Loch Erisort (Lewis), Loch Eireasort. 'Harris firth' from Norse.

Loch Errochty (Perth), Loch Eireach-daidh. 'Loch at the assembly place'.

Loch Etchachan (Aberdeen), Loch Éiteachain. This may be 'loch of the little foul one'.

Loch Etive (Argyll), Loch Éite. 'Loch of the foul one', referring to Éiteag, a spirit said to live in the waters.

Loch Ewe (Ross), Loch Iubh. 'Yew loch'.

Loch Eynort (Skye), Loch Aoineart. 'Isthmus loch', from Norse.

Loch Fad (Bute), An Loch Fada. 'Long loch'.

Loch Fannich (Ross), Loch Fainich. This is of pre-Gaelic origin and may refer to surging waves.

Loch Farraline (Inverness), Loch Farralainn. The meaning of this name is unclear.

Loch Finlaggan (Islay), Loch an Eilein. The English form appears to come from Gaelic Fionn Lagan, 'white or fair hollow', which became

corrupted to Loch Bhìollagain, a name by which the loch used to be known in Gaelic. The present Gaelic name is 'the loch with the island', referring to Eilean na Comhairle where Comhairle nan Eilean, comprising the main clan chiefs, used to gather.

Loch Fleet (Sutherland), Loch Fleòid. 'Loch of the current', from Gaelic/Norse. This is one of the few instances on the east coast of loch being used to designate a firth or sea loch rather than a freshwater inland loch.

Loch Frisa (Mull), Loch Phrìosa. The Norse element of this name contains á, 'river', but the rest is unclear.

Loch Fyne (Argyll), Loch Fìne. 'Loch of wine'. People from the surrounding area were nicknamed mucan biorach, 'porpoises'.

Loch Garve (Ross), Loch Maol Fhinn. This loch near Garve is known in Gaelic as 'the loch of Fionn's devotee'.

Loch Garry (Inverness), Loch Garadh. 'Copse loch'.

Loch Gelly (Fife), Loch Gheallaidh. 'Loch of the white water'.

Loch Gilp (Argyll), Loch Gilb. 'Chisel loch', referring to its shape.

Loch Glass (Ross), Loch Ghlais. 'Loch of the stream'.

Loch Goil (Argyll), Loch Goibhle. 'The loch of the fork'. See **Lochgoilhead**.

Loch Hope (Sutherland), Loch Hòb. 'Loch of the bay', from Gaelic/Norse.

Loch Hourn (Inverness), Loch Shùirn or Loch Shubhairne. 'Loch of the berry gap'.

Loch Inchard (Sutherland), Loch Uinnseort. 'Loch of the meadow firth'.

Lochindorb (Moray), Loch nan Doirb. 'Loch of the minnows'.

Loch Katrine (Perth), Loch Caiteirein. This may refer to a dark or gloomy location.

Loch Killisport (Argyll), Loch

Caolasport. This is a Norse firth name, but the Norse specifier is unclear.

Loch Laggan (Inverness), Loch an Lagain. 'Loch of Laggan'.

Loch Lamlash (Arran), Loch an Eilein. The Gaelic name is 'loch with the island', referring to Holy Island. *See* **Holy Island** and **Lamlash**.

Loch Langavat (Lewis), Loch Langabhat. 'Long fresh water loch', from Norse.

Loch Lee (Angus), Loch Lìgh. It is unclear what this name means.

Loch Leven (Argyll, Inverness, Kinross), Loch Liobhann. 'Loch of the smooth water'.

Loch Linnhe (Argyll, Inverness), An Linne Dhubh and An Linne Sheileach. The English name has used Gaelic *linne*, 'firth', as a specific element here. The first Gaelic name is 'black firth' and refers to the upper part of Loch Linnhe inside the narrows at Corran. The second name is 'brackish firth' and is applied to the part of Loch Linnhe beyond Corran towards the open sea.

Loch Loch (Perth), Loch Lòch. 'Dark loch'. Locally it is said that this loch is so called because it was so big it was named twice.

Loch Lochay (Perth), Loch Lòchaidh. 'Loch of the dark river'.

Loch Lochy (Inverness), Loch Lòchaidh. 'Loch of the dark river'.

Loch Lomond (Dunbarton, Stirling), Loch Laomainn. This pre-Gaelic name is thought to mean 'beacon', referring in some way to Ben Lomond.

Loch Long (Argyll, Ross), Loch Long. 'Loch of ships'.

Loch Loyal (Sutherland), Loch Laghail. This name of Norse origin is said to be 'law mountain', applied in the first instance to Ben Loyal, then transferred to the loch.

Loch Lubnaig (Perth), Loch Lùdnaig. This may mean 'finger-shaped loch'.

Loch Liuchart (Ross), Loch Luinncheirt. 'Encampment loch'.

Loch Lyon (Perth), Loch Lìomhann. 'Loch of the smooth water'.

Loch Maddy (North Uist), Loch nam Madadh. 'Loch of the wolves', referring to rocks named *na Madaidhean*, 'the wolves'.

Loch Mahaick (Perth), Loch Mo Thathaig. 'St Mo Thatha's loch'.

Loch Maree (Ross), Loch Ma Ruibhe. 'St Maol Rubha's loch'. This loch had two older names, *Loch Feadhail Feas* and *Loch Iubh*.

Loch Moidart (Inverness), Loch Mhùideart. 'Narrow firth', from Norse.

Loch Monar (Ross), Loch Mhonair. 'Loch at the upland place'.

Loch Morar (Inverness), Loch Mhórair. 'Loch of the great water'.

Loch More (Inverness), An Loch Mór; (Sutherland), Loch an Reidhinidh. The English form is from the Gaelic for 'big loch'. In Sutherland the name is unclear but may contain *reidhneach* which is applied to a cow yielding no milk.

Loch Morie (Ross), Loch Mhoire. 'St Mary's loch', a northern equivalent of 'St Mary's Loch' in Roxburghshire.

Loch Morlich (Inverness), Loch Mhùrlaig. 'Loch with the small inlet'.

Loch Moy (Inverness), Loch na Mòighe. 'Loch on the plain'.

Loch Mullardoch (Inverness), Loch Maol Àrdaich. 'Loch at the blunt high place'.

Loch na Caoidhe (Sutherland), Loch na Cuinge. The English form is from a misreading or mispronunciation of the Gaelic name which means 'loch of the yoke'.

Lochnagar (Aberdeen), Loch na Gàire. 'Loch of the loud noise'.

Loch na Keal (Mull), Loch nan Ceall. 'Loch of the cells'.

Loch Naver (Sutherland), Loch Nabhair. This pre-Gaelic name has connotations of swimming.

Loch Nell (Argyll), Loch nan Eala. 'Loch of swans'.

Loch Ness (Inverness), Loch Nis. This name is most likely pre-Gaelic, denotes a river and is unrelated to Norse *nes*, 'headland'.

Loch Nevis (Inverness), Loch Nibheis. This name was believed to stem from *uabhas*, 'terror', but the basis of the name is that of the river Nevis which comes from an Indo-European root with connotations of wetness.

Loch of Lintrathen (Angus), Linn Tréithean. *See* **Lintrathen**.

Loch of Strathbeg (Aberdeen). 'Loch at the small strath'.

Loch Oich (Inverness), Loch Obhaich. 'Loch of fresh water'. This name was earlier *Loch Abha* with the same meaning.

Loch Ouirn (Lewis), Loch Odhairn. The meaning of this name is unclear.

Loch Portan (North Uist), Loch Portain. 'Loch with a little harbour'.

Loch Quoich (Inverness), Loch Chuaich. 'Loch at the hollow'.

Loch Rannoch (Perth), Loch Raineach. 'Loch of Rannoch'.

Loch Riddon (Argyll), Loch Ruadhail. This is said to be 'loch at the red place', but *see* **Glendaruel**.

Loch Roag (Bernera, Lewis), Locha Ròg. See **Kinlochroag**.

Loch Rosque (Sutherland), Loch a' Chroisg. 'Loch at the crossing place'.

Loch Ruthven (Inverness), Loch Ruadhainn. 'Loch at the red-brown place'.

Loch Ryan (Ayr, Wigtown), Loch Rìoghaine. This may be 'loch of Rian', containing a personal name.

Loch Scavaig (Skye), Loch Sgàbhaig. 'Loch at the shaw bay'.

Loch Scridain (Mull), Loch Sgrìodain. This appears to be 'scree loch'.

Loch Seaforth (Harris, Lewis), Loch Shìophort. 'Loch of the sea firth', from Gaelic/Norse.

Loch Sheil (Argyll, Inverness), Loch Seile. This may be 'brackish loch'.

Loch Shell (Lewis), Loch Sealg. This name is unclear.

Loch Shin (Sutherland), Loch Sin. This is said to be 'loch of the old river', but may be of a pre-Gaelic origin.

Loch Skiport (South Uist), Loch Sgioport. 'Ship firth', from Norse.

Loch Slapin (Skye), Loch Shlaopainn. The meaning of this name is unclear. A saying applied to someone very thirsty or keen on drink is, *Dhòladh e Loch Shlaopainn*, 'He would drink Loch Slapin.'

Loch Slin (Ross), Loch Slinn. 'Loch of the weaver's sleye'. This loch has since been drained.

Loch Snizort (Skye), Loch Snìothasort. 'Snow firth', from Norse.

Loch Spallander (Argyll), Loch Spealadair. 'Scytheman's loch'.

Loch Spelve (Mull), Loch Spéilbhidh. The meaning of this name is unclear.

Loch Striven (Argyll), Loch Sroigheann. The meaning of this name is unclear.

Loch Sween (Argyll), Loch Suain. 'Svein's loch', from Gaelic but containing a Norse personal name.

Loch Tarbert (Argyll, Harris), Loch an Tairbeirt. 'Loch at the isthmus'.

Loch Tay (Perth), Loch Tatha. This is a pre-Gaelic river name. The same Gaelic name is applied in Perthshire Gaelic to the Firth of Tay.

Loch Teachuis (Argyll), Loch Tiacais. The meaning of this name is unclear.

Loch Treig (Inverness), Loch Tréig. This is said to be 'loch of death'.

Loch Trool (Ayr), Loch an t-Sruthail. 'Loch of the current or stream'.

Loch Tulla (Argyll), Loch Toilbhe. This name is pre-Gaelic and unclear.

Loch Tummel (Perth), Loch Teimhil. 'Loch of the dark river'.

Loch Uiskevagh (Benbecula), Loch Uisgeabhagh. 'Ox bay', from Norse.

Loch Ussie (Ross), Loch Ùsaidh.

The name is obscure and may be pre-Pictish.

Loch Varkasaig (Skye), Loch Bharcasaig. 'Loch at castle bay', from Gaelic/Norse.

Loch Vatandip (Lewis), Loch Bhatandìob. 'Loch of deep fresh water', from Gaelic/Norse.

Loch Venacher (Perth), Loch Bheann-chair. 'Loch at the horned place'.

Loch Voil (Perth), Loch Bheothail. This is said to mean 'lively loch', but the name may have been corrupted through time.

Machrie Bay (Arran), Bàgh a' Mhach-aire. 'Bay of Machrie'.

Minch, A' Mhaoil and An Cuan Sgìth. The English name is similar to *Man-che*, the French term for the English Channel. The first Gaelic name refers to the sea area between Lewis and the mainland, and is related to the 'Moyle' between Scotland and Ireland. In Wester Ross, this sea area is called *An Cuan Leódhasach*, 'the Lewis ocean'. The second Gaelic name, 'the Skye ocean', is applied to the sea between Skye and the Western Isles. The saying, *Tha dà thaobh air a' Mhaoil*, 'there are two sides to the Minch', is used to mean that there are two ways to seeing things.

Moray Firth, An Cuan Moireach, Geòb Mhoireibh and Linne Mhoireibh. The first Gaelic name is 'the Moray ocean', the second is 'bight of Moray' and the third is 'firth of Moray'.

Munlochy Bay (Ross), Òb Poll Lòchaidh. 'Bay of Munlochy'.

Narrows of Raasay (Raasay, Skye), Caol na h-Àirde. The Gaelic name is 'sound at the headland'.

Nechtansmere (Angus), Linn Garan. The English name is 'Nechtan's loch' while the Gaelic is 'Garan's pool'.

Nigg Bay (Ross), Camas Neig. 'Inlet of Nigg'.

North Channel, Sruth na Maoile.

The Gaelic name is 'Moyle channel', referring to the Mull of Galloway or of Kintyre.

North Ford (Benbecula), An Fhadhail a Tuath. 'North sea ford'. The old name was *Fadhail na Comraich*, 'ford of the sanctuary'.

North Sea, An Cuan a Tuath or Muir Lochlainn. The Gaelic names are 'north ocean' and 'sea of Scandanavia'. The seas around Orkney are known as *An Cuan Arcach*, 'the Orcadian ocean'.

Oban Bay (Argyll), Bàgh an Òbain. 'Bay of Oban'. Oban itself is 'small bay'.

Pentland Firth (Caithness, Orkney), An Caol Arcach. The English form is from Norse for 'Pictland firth', while the Gaelic name is 'Orcadian narrows'.

Port Henderson Bay (Ross), Lùb Phortaigil. 'The bay of Port Hend-erson'.

Portree Loch (Skye), Loch Chaluim Chille. The Gaelic name is 'St Columba's loch'.

Redpoint Bay (Ross), Lùb an Rubha. 'The bay of the point', in Gaelic.

Salen Bay (Argyll), Bàgh an t-Sàilein. 'Bay of Salen', which itself means 'small inlet'.

Sand Bay (Ross), Lùb Shannd. 'The bay of Sand'.

Sea of the Hebrides (Barra, Canna, South Uist), An Cuan Barrach and Cuan Uibhist. The Gaelic names are 'the Barra ocean' and 'ocean of Uist'.

Solway Firth, Linne Shalmhaigh. This name may originally be of Nordic origin.

Sound of Barra (Barra, South Uist), Caolas Bharraigh. 'Strait of Barra'.

Sound of Bernera (Bernera, Lewis), Sruth Iorseadair. The Gaelic name is 'current of Earshader'.

Sound of Berneray (Berneray, North Uist), Caolas Bheàrnaraigh. 'Strait of Berneray'.

Sound of Boreray (North Uist), Caolas a' Mhòrain. The name of this strait is unclear, although it may be related to *Àird a' Bhorrain*, 'Ardvorran'.

Sound of Canna (Canna, Rum), An Caol Canach. 'The Canna sound'.

Sound of Carna (Argyll), Caol Chàrna. Both names mean the same.

Sound of Eriskay (Eriskay, South Uist), Caolas Éirisgeigh. 'Strait of Eriskay'.

Sound of Harris (Berneray, Harris), Caolas Na Hearadh. 'Strait of Harris'.

Sound of Iona (Iona, Mull), Caol Idhe. 'Sound of Iona'.

Sound of Islay (Islay, Jura), An Caol Ìleach or Caol Ìle. 'The Islay sound'.

Sound of Jura (Argyll, Jura), An Linne Dhiùrach or An Linne Rosach. The Gaelic names are 'the Jura firth' and 'the Ross firth', which refers to a headland.

Sound of Longa (Ross), An Caol Beag. The Gaelic name is 'small sound'.

Sound of Mull (Argyll, Mull), Caol Muile. 'Sound of Mull'.

Sound of Pabbay (Barra), Caolas Phabaigh. 'Strait of Pabay'.

Sound of Raasay (Raasay, Skye), An Caolas Ratharsach or an Linne Ratharsach. The Gaelic name is 'the Raasay sound or firth', and is also applied to the Inner Sound.

Sound of Sandray (Barra), Caolas Shanndraigh. 'Strait of Sandray'.

Sound of Scalpay (Harris, Scalpay), Caolas Sgalpaigh. 'Strait of Scalpay'.

Sound of Scarba (Jura), Bealach a' Choin Ghlais. The Gaelic name is 'Pass of the grey dog'.

Sound of Shiant (Lewis), Sruth nam Fear Gorm. The Gaelic name is 'current of the blue men'.

Sound of Sleat (Inverness, Skye), An Linne Shléiteach. The Gaelic name is 'the Sleat firth'.

Sound of Vatersay (Barra, Vatersay), An Caolas Cumhang. The Gaelic name is 'the narrow strait'.

South Ford (Benbecula, South Uist), An Fhadhail a Deas. 'The south sea ford'.

Strait of Corryvreckan (Jura), Coire Bhreacain. 'Breacan's cauldron', referring to the whirlpool here. A saying has it, *Ge b' e nach stiùir coire a' bhrochain, cha stiùir Coire Bhreacain*, 'He who cannot manage the porridge cauldron, will never manage Breacan's cauldron'.

Udale Bay (Ross), Camas Uadail. 'Inlet of Udale'.

Uig Bay (Lewis), Camas Ùig. 'Inlet of Uig'.

Vatersay Bay (Vatersay), Bàgh Bhatarsaigh. 'Bay of Vatersay'.

West Kyle of Bute (Argyll, Bute), An Caol an Iar or An Caol Ceathrach. The Gaelic names are 'the west sound' and 'the Kerry sound'.

Rivers

Add, Abhainn Àd or An Abhainn Fhada. The meaning of this name is unclear. The second Gaelic name is 'long river', but this is not the original, rather a rationalising attempt to give the name meaning.

Adder This pre-Celtic Indo-European name comes from a root meaning 'watercourse'.

Affrick, Afraic or Abhainn Afraic. 'Dappled river'.

Albany Burn, Allt an Albannaigh. 'The Scotsman's stream'.

Alder, Eallar or Abhainn Eallair. This may be from a Gaelic source meaning 'rock'.

Aldie Water, Allt Àthaigh. The English name suggests a Gaelic origin from *allt*, 'stream', while the Gaelic name is 'Eathie stream'.

Aldourie Burn, Dobhrag or Allt Dobhraig. 'Little water'.

Ale This is from a pre-Celtic source meaning 'flow', and from the same origin as 'Allan'.

Allan, Alan or Abhainn Alain. *See* **Ale**.

Allander, Alandar. This appears to be the river name 'Allan' or 'Alan' with *dobhar*, 'water', added.

Almond, Aman or Abhainn Amain. This is from a Celtic origin meaning 'river'.

Alness, Abhainn Alanais. 'River of the Alan place'. This name contains 'Alan' with a suffix denoting 'place'. The river might originally have been called simply 'Alan'.

Annan, Anainn or Abhainn Anann. This name is said to commemorate the water goddess Anu.

Annaty Burn, Allt na h-Annaide. 'Stream of Annat', which itself means 'mother church'.

Aray, Aora. It is unclear what the meaning of this name is, but it may be from a pre-Gaelic source meaning 'watercourse'.

Arder, Àrdar or Abhainn Àrdair. 'High water'.

Ardle, Àrdail or Abhainn Àrdail. 'River of the high place'.

Arkaig, Airceig or Abhainn Airceig. 'Difficult river'.

Aven, Athfhinn. 'Very bright river'. This was formerly known as *an t-Uisge Bàn*, 'the white river'.

Averon, Abharan or Abhainn Abharain. This comes from Celtic *abh* denoting a river.

Avon, Abhann. *See* **Averon**.

Awe, Abha or Uisge Abha. *See* **Averon**.

Ayr, Àr or Abhainn Àir. This may be pre-Celtic Indo-European and mean 'watercourse'.

Balgy, Abhainn Bhalgaidh. 'River of Balgy', which in turn means 'bag-shaped place'.

Balnagowan, Uaraidh or Abhainn Uaraidh. The English form is that of a place through which this river, also known as 'Strathrory' flows. The Gaelic name has its origins in *uar*, 'landslip'.

Banavie, Banbhaidh. 'Pig river'.

Banvie, Banbhaidh. *See* **Banavie**.

Beauly, Farar or Abhainn nam Manach. The English name is from the town of Beauly, while the first Gaelic form is from a pre-Celtic root conveying 'wetness'. The second

Gaelic name is 'river of the monks', referring to the monastery at Beauly known as *Manachainn Mhic Shimidh*.

Bervie, Biorbhaigh. 'Boiling river'.

Blackadder This is the same as **Adder**, but with 'Black' attached to distinguish it from the 'Whiteadder'.

Black Cart This is the same as **Cart**, but with 'Black' attached to distinguish it from the 'White Cart'.

Black Devon, Duibhe. The basic name means 'black one', i.e. 'black river'.

Bogie, Balgaidh or Abhainn Bhalgaidh. 'Bag river', referring to bag-shaped pools.

Boyne, Bòinn or Abhainn Bhòinn. Like its counterpart in Ireland, this name may be pre-Gaelic.

Boyndie This name stems from 'eternal goddess'. *See* **Boyndie**, p. 32.

Braan, Breamhainn or Abhainn Bhreamhainn. 'Bellowing river'.

Bran, Bran/Brann or Abhainn Bhrain/Bhrainn. 'Raven river'.

Brannie, Branaidh or Abhainn Bhranaidh. 'Raven river'.

Brerachan, Briathrachan or Abhainn Bhriathrachain. 'Small talkative river'.

Brora, Brùra or Abhainn Bhrùra. 'Bridge river', from Norse.

Brothock Burn, Brothag or Abhainn Bhrothaig. 'River of heat'.

Bruar, Bruthar or Abhainn Bhruthair. 'Bridge river', referring to natural rock formations.

Burn of Brown, Allt Bhruthainn. 'Stream of heat'.

Burn of Vat, Allt na Dabhaich. 'Stream of the vat or davoch'.

Caddon, Cadan or Abhainn Chadain. 'Warlike river'.

Calder, Caladar or Abhainn Chaladair. 'Hard water'.

Callater, Caladar or Abhainn Chaladair. *See* **Calder**.

Calvie, Cailbhidh or Abhainn Chailbhidh. 'Stalk river', possibly referring to reeds.

Cander 'Fair water', from Brythonic.

Carron, Carrann or Abhainn Charrann. 'Rough water'.

Cart This is said to come from a Gaelic root meaning 'to clean', but may be pre-Celtic.

Cassley, Carsla or Abhainn Charsla. 'River of the castle place'.

Cattie, Cataidh or Abhainn Chataidh. 'Cat river'.

Clova, Clàbha or Abhainn Chlàbha. The meaning of this name is unclear.

Clyde, Cluaidh or Uisge Chluaidh. This is an unclear pre-Gaelic name.

Coe, Comhan or Abhainn Chomhan. This may be a tribal name attached to the river.

Cona, Cona or Abhainn Chona. This may be 'dog river'.

Conan, Conann or Abhainn Chonainn. 'Dog river'.

Conglass, Conghlais or Abhainn Chonghlais. 'Dog stream'.

Connie, Conaidh or Abhainn Chonaidh. 'Dog river'.

Conon, Conann or Abhainn Chonainn (Ross), Connan or Abhainn Chonnain (Skye). The river in Ross is 'dog river', but in Skye is based on *Connan*, the name of a saint.

Cowie, Collaidh or Abhainn Chollaidh. 'Hazel river'.

Craig, Abhainn na Creige or Abhainn Bhràigh Thaithisgeail. This is named after 'Craig' through which the river passes. The alternative Gaelic name is 'river of the upper part of Taithisgeail', which in turn is a Norse name.

Creed, Abhainn Ghrìde. 'Grit or shingle river', from Norse.

Creran, Creuran or Abhainn Chreurain. This name is obscure.

Crombie, Crombaidh or Abhainn Chrombaidh. 'Bent river'.

Daer, This Brythonic name is possibly related to the Dare or *Dâr* in Wales.

Dee, Dé or Uisge Dé. This Celtic name has connotations of divinity and is based on the same root as *dia*, 'god'.

Deveron, Dubh-Éireann. This name

is basically the same as that of the 'Earn', namely a commemoration of Ireland from the term *Éire*. The 'Deveron' has Gaelic *dubh*, 'black' attached to give 'Black Earn', perhaps to distinguish it from the Findhorn, or 'White Earn', which although now known in Gaelic simply as *Éireann* appears from the English form to have formerly been preceded by *fionn*, 'white'

Devon, Duibhe or Abhainn Duibhe. This Gaelic name connotes blackness.

Dionard, Dìonard or Abhainn Dìonaird. This is probably from Norse *dyn* and *fjórðr*, giving 'noisy sea loch'.

Divie, Dubhaidh or Duibhidh (Banff), Duibhe or Abhainn Duibhe (Inverness). *See* **Devon**.

Dochart, Dochard or Abhainn Dochaird. This name may be related to 'Cart' although with negative connotations as implied by the prefix *do-*.

Doe, Dotha or Abhainn Dotha. This is said to be named after *Dotha* or *Dogha*, a water sprite drowned in the River Barrow in Ireland. However, the name may simply mean 'bad water'.

Don, Deathain or Abhainn Deathain. Like its sister river, the Dee, this name implies divinity although from a different root. The English form of the name appears to have by-passed Gaelic and come directly from Pictish.

Doon Although believed to represent *Dubh*-abhainn (Black river), this is from the same source as *Don*.

Dorback, Dorbag or Uisge Dhorbaig. 'Minnow river'.

Douglas, Dùghlas or Abhainn Dùghlais. 'Black river'.

Dubh Lighe, Dubhailigh or Abhainn Dubhailigh. 'River of the black rocky place'.

Dulnain, Tuilnean or Abhainn Tuilnein. 'Flood river'.

Dye Water, Uisge Dhàidh. It is unclear

what this name means. Cairn Dye is known as *Càrn an Tàilleir*, 'the tailor's cairn', but if this is the original name of the mountain, it is unlikely to be that of this river.

Earn, Uisge Éireann or Uisge Éir. This is a commemoration of Ireland, from the term *Éire*.

Easter Fearn Burn, Allt Fheàrna Àrd. 'The stream of Easter Fearn'.

Eathie Burn, Allt Àthaigh. 'Stream of Eathie'. This is also known as the 'Aldie Water'.

Echaig, Eachag or Abhainn Eachaig. 'Little horse river'.

Edderton Burn, Allt Eadardain. 'Stream of Edderton'.

Elchaig, Eilcheag or Abhainn Eilcheig. This river is said to have been named after a water sprite living in it, however it is likely that the sprite was named after the river. The name may be related to **Ellachie**.

Ellachie, Eileachaidh or Abhainn Eileachaidh. 'River at the rocky place'.

Elvan This name may denote 'stony' from a Gaelic or other Celtic root.

Endrick, Eunarag or Abhainn Eunaraig. 'Snipe river'.

Ericht, Eireachd or Abhainn Eireachd. 'River of assemblies'.

Errochty, Eireachdaidh or Abhainn Eireachdaidh. *See* **Ericht**.

Esk, Uisge Easg. This is a Celtic term for river found in the Brythonic speaking areas. The North Esk is *Easg Thuath* and the South Esk is *Easg Dheas* in Aberdeenshire and Perthshire Gaelic.

Esragan, Easragan. 'The little river of the waterfalls'.

Etive, Éite or Abhainn Éite. This name carries implications of foulness and was the abode of *Éiteag*, a water sprite.

Ettrick The meaning and origin of this name are unclear.

Farrar, Farar or Uisge Farair and

Abhainnn nam Manach. This name appears to be pre-Celtic and from an Indo-European root meaning 'wet'. The alternative Gaelic name is 'river of the monks', referring to the monastery at Beauly. In English this is also known as 'Beauly River'.

Fender, Fionndar or Abhainn Fhionn-dair. 'White water'.

Fernate, Feàrnaid or Abhainn Fheàrnaid. 'Alder river'.

Feshie, Féisidh or Abhainn Fhéisidh. 'River of the boggy haugh'.

Fiddich, Fiodhach or Abhainn Fhiodh-aich. 'River of the wood place'.

Findhorn, Uisge Éire or Uisge Éireann. This name is based on *Éire* in commemoration of Ireland. The English form suggests the name once contained *fionn*, 'white', perhaps to distinguish it from *Dubh Éireann*, 'black Earn', or 'Deveron'.

Finglas, Fionnghlais or Abhainn Fhionnghlais. 'White river'.

Finlas, Fionnghlais or Abhainn Fhionnghlais. *See* **Finglas**.

Fintaig, Abhainn Fhionntaig. 'Little white river'.

Fionn Lighe, Fionnailigh or Abhainn Fhionnailigh. 'River at the white rocky place'.

Forth, Foirthe or Abhainn Foirthe, For or Uisge For. This is an unclear name although it may be from a Brythonic source as the form *Gwerid* is found which is equivalent to *Foirthe*. The upper stretches of the Forth are known in Gaelic as *an Abhainn Dubh*, 'the black river'.

Fowlis, Foghlais or Uisge Foghlais. 'Lower river'.

Fruin, Freòin or Abhainn Freòin. This name may be based on Gaelic *freòine*, 'rage'.

Fyne, Fìne or Uisge Fìne. 'Wine', a name occasionally applied to good-tasting water.

Gadie, Gadaidh or Abhainn Ghadaidh. 'Twig river'.

Gairn, Garthan or Abhainn Gharthain. 'Calling river'.

Garnock, Gairneag 'Crying river', the same as 'Girnaig' and 'Girnock'.

Garry, Garadh or Abhainn Gharadh (Inverness), Gar or Abhainn Ghar (Perth). 'Copse river'.

Garve, Abhainn Ghairbh. 'River of Garve', which in turn is 'rough place'.

Gaur, Gamhair or Uisge Ghamhair. This name carries implications of winter.

Gelder, Gealdar or Abhainn Ghealdair. 'White water'.

Geldie, Geallaidh or Abhainn Gheallaidh. 'White river'.

Girnaig, Goirneag or Abhainn Ghoirneig. *See* **Garnock**.

Girnock, Goirneag or Allt Ghoirneig. *See* **Garnock**.

Girvan, Garbhan or Abhainn Gharbhain. 'Rough river'.

Glass, Abhainn Ghlais. 'River'. Gaelic has attached the more commonly used *abhainn*, 'river'.

Glaster, Glasdar or Abhainn Ghlasdair. 'Grey river'.

Glen Lochsie Burn, Allt Lòchsaidh. The English form has added 'burn' to the name of the glen through which the river flows. The Gaelic name is 'stream of the dark river'.

Glorat, Glòraid or Abhainn Ghlòraid. 'Babbling river'.

Gloy, Glaoidh or Abhainn Ghlaoidh. 'Viscous or gluey river'.

Golly, Gollaidh or Abhainn Ghollaidh. 'Blind river', perhaps implying that it is overgrown.

Gormack, Gormag or Allt Ghormaig. 'Blue river'.

Gowrie, Gobharaidh or Allt Ghobharaidh. 'Goat river'.

Grudie, Grùididh or Abhainn Ghrùididh. 'Gravelly river'.

Halladale, Abhainn Healadail. This river takes its name from the Norse, 'hallowed valley', through which it flows.

Helmsdale, Ilidh or Abhainn Ilidh. The English name is that of the town at the mouth of the river. The Gaelic name is unclear, but is also applied, as *Srath Ilidh*, to the Strath of Kildonan through which it flows.

Irvine This name, with counterparts in Wales, is unclear.

Isla, Ìle or Ìl. This name is unclear. The Gaelic form is the same as that of the name of the island of Islay, but it is unclear whether they are from the same origin.

Jed The origin of this name is unclear.

Kale, Calan. 'Calling river'.

Keltney Burn, Allt Chailtnidh. 'Stream of the hard river'.

Kelty, Cailtidh. 'Hard river'.

Kerry, Abhainn Chearraidh. 'Copse river', from Norse.

Kingie, Cingidh or Abhainn Chingidh. 'Hero river'.

Kymah Burn, Uisge Chìoma. This name is unclear.

Lavern, Labharan or Abhainn Labharain. 'Loud or talkative river'.

Lawers, Labhar or Uisge Labhair. 'Loud river'.

Laxford, Lusard or Abhainn Lusaird. This Norse name is 'salmon firth'.

Lednock, Liadnag or Abhainn Liadnaig. This name is unclear but may be of Gaelic origin.

Leithen Water, Leitheann or Abhainn Leitheinn. This Brythonic name has connotations of wetness.

Leven, Leamhan or Uisge Leamhain (Dunbarton), Lìobhann or Abhainn Lìobhann (Argyll, Fife, Kinross). The Dunbarton name is 'elm river' and has given rise to the name *Leamhnachd*, 'Lennox'. The other Levens are 'smooth river'.

Levern, Labharan. 'Loud or talkative river'.

Linhouse Water, Caladar or Uisge Chaladair. The English name is that of a place while the Gaelic is 'hard water'.

Linn O'Dee, Eas Dhé or An Linne. The English form is 'pool on the Dee', while the Gaelic names are 'Dee waterfall' and 'the pool'.

Liver, Lìbhir. This may be 'smooth river'.

Livet, Lìobhaid or Uisge Lìobhaid. 'Smooth river'.

Lochay, Lòcha or Uisge Lòcha. 'Dark or black river'. The river which flows into Loch Tay is also known as *Lòcha Albannach*, 'Lochay of Alba', to distinguish it from *Lòcha Urchaidh*, 'Lochay of Orchy', which flows into the Orchy.

Lochty, Lòchaidh or Abhainn Lòchaidh. *See* **Lochay**.

Lochy, Lòchaidh or Abhainn Lòchaidh. 'Dark or black river'. The short River Lochy which flows into Loch Linnhe is the subject of a sarcastic saying, *Is mòid a' mhuir Lòchaidh*, 'The sea is the bigger for the Lochy'.

Lossie, Losaidh or Uisge Losaidh. 'Herb or vegetation river'.

Loy, Abhainn Laoigh. 'Calf river'.

Lugar Water 'Bright river', from a Celtic origin.

Lui, Abhainn Laoigh. *See* **Loy**.

Luthnot, Luthnait or Abhainn Luathnait. 'Swift river'.

Lyon, Lìomhann or Uisge Lìomhainn. 'Smooth river'.

Mallie, Màilidh or Abhainn Mhàilidh. This is said to be the name of saint. *See* **Dalmally** and **Kilmallie**.

Markie, Marcaidh or Abhainn Mharcaidh. 'Horse river'.

Mashie, Mathaisidh or Abhainn Mhathaisidh. 'River of the good haugh'.

May Water, Uisge Méidh. The meaning of this name is unclear.

Meig, Mìg or Abhainn Mìg. This may be 'boggy river' if a Gaelic name, but its origins may be older.

Milk This Celtic name has connotations of rotting or putrefaction.

Morar, Mórar or Abhainn Mhórair. 'Great water'.

Moriston, Abhainn Mhoireasdan. Whilst this name is said to mean 'great river', it is from a different origin.

Mossat, Abhainn Mhusaid. 'Stale river'.

Mussadie, Abhainn Mhusaididh. *See* **Mossat**.

Nairn, Narann or Abhainn Narann. This pre-Gaelic name carries connotations of swimming or flowing.

Nant, Abhainn Neannta. 'Nettle river'.

Naver, Nabhar or Abhainn Nabhair. This pre-Gaelic name implies moistness.

Ness, Nis or Uisge Nis. This Indo-European name denotes a stream or river.

Nethan, Neitheann or Abhainn Neitheinn. 'Pure river'.

Nethy, Neithich or Abhainn Neithich. 'Pure river'. The Inverness Nethy was said to be inhabited by spirits called *na Neithichean* and when in spate it was said, *Tha na Neithichean a' tighinn*, 'The Nethy spirits are coming'.

Nevis, Nibheis or Abhainn Nibheis. This is commonly said to derive from *uabhas*, 'terror', but the source is pre-Gaelic with connotations of moistness.

Nith, Nid or Abhainn Nid. This may be from Brythonic, meaning 'new'.

Nochty Water, Uisge Nochda. 'Naked water'.

Noe, Abhainn Nodha. 'New river'.

North Esk, Easg Thuath. 'Esk' is a Celtic term for 'river' found widely in the Brythonic speaking areas.

Oich, Obhaich or Abhainn Obhaich. This is based on Celtic *abh*, 'river', and was previously *Abha*.

Orchy, Urchaidh or Abhainn Urchaidh. 'Wood river'.

Orrin, Oirrinn or Abhainn Oirrinn and Orthainn or Abhainn Orthainn. 'Offering', a religious term. This river

was said to be haunted by *Cailleach na h-Abhann*, 'hag of the river'.

Oykel, Òiceall or Abhainn Òiceill. This is pre-Gaelic for 'high river'.

Pattack, Patag or Abhainn Phataig. 'Pot river'. Because this river does not follow the expected course eastwards into the Spey it is called *Patag dhubh bhalgach an aghaidh uisge Alba*, 'Black, bag-like Pattack against the waters of Scotland'.

Pean, Peathan or Abhainn Pheathain. This pre-Gaelic name is unclear.

Peffery, Peofhar or Abhainn Pheofhair. This pre-Gaelic name means 'bright'.

Peffray *See* **Peffery**.

Polly, Pollaidh or Abhainn Phollaidh. 'Pool river'.

Pools of Dee, Lochan Dubh na Làirige. These pools are called 'black lochs at the pass' in Gaelic.

Prosen, Pràsag or Uisge Phràsaig, Pràsan or Uisge Phràsain. This may be a personal name of pre-Gaelic origin.

Roy, Uisge Ruaidh. 'Red-brown river'.

Ruchill, Abhainn Rùchaill. This was said locally to stem from *ruadh thuil*, 'red-brown flood', but appears to contain *coille*, 'forest'.

Ruthven, Abhainn Ruadhainn. 'River at the red-brown place'.

Scaddle, Sgadal or Abhainn Sgadail. This name comes from a Norse valley name.

Scotsburn, Allt nan Albannach. 'Stream of the Scots'.

Shee, Sìdh or Uisge Sìdh. 'Fairy river'.

Sheil, Seile or Abhainn Seile. This Indo-European name denotes a stream.

Shin, Sin or Abhainn Sin. This may derive from Gaelic *sean*, 'old', or be a pre-Celtic Indo-European term for 'river'.

Shira, Siara or Abhainn Siara. 'Eternal river'.

Silverburn This name previously contained the Pictish or Brythonic element *pefr*, 'bright', as found in names such as 'Peffray'. The English name may reflect this brightness by the use of the term 'silver'.

Skiach, Allt na Sgitheach. 'Thorn stream'.

South Esk, Easg Dheas. 'Esk' is a Celtic term for 'river' widely found in the Brythonic speaking areas.

Spey, Spé or Uisge Spé. This is said to be 'thorn river', but may be of a pre-Gaelic origin. This river is mentioned in *Spé, Dé agus Tatha - trì uisgeachan as motha fon adhar*, 'Spey, Dee and Tay - the three greatest rivers under the sun'.

Spean, Spiothan or Abhainn Spiothain. This appears to be 'small thorn river', a diminutive form of the root of 'Spey', but may be pre-Gaelic.

Strathrory, Uaraidh or Abhainn Uaraidh. The English form comes from the name of the strath through which this river, also known as 'Balnagowan River', flows. The Gaelic name comes from *uar*, 'landslip'.

Strathrusdale, An Abhainn Dubh. The English form is that of the strath through which the river flows. The Gaelic name is 'black river'.

Strathy, Abhainn Shrathaidh. This name refers to the place through which the river flows.

Tain This comes from an Indo-European root meaning 'flow'.

Tanar, Tanar or Uisge Thanair. This is said to come from *torann*, 'thunder'.

Tanner Water *See* **Tanar**.

Tarf Water, Uisge Thairbh. 'Bull river'.

Tarff, Abhainn Thairbh. *See* **Tarf Water**.

Tay, Tatha or Uisge Tatha. This may be from the same Indo-European root meaning 'flow' as *Tain*. The might of the river is mentioned in the saying, *Tatha mhór nan tonn, bheir i sgrìob lom air Peairt*, 'Great Tay of the waves will cut a swathe through Perth'.

Teatle, Teatall or Abhainn Teataill. This pre-Gaelic name is obscure.

Teith, Uisge Tèadhaich. This obscure name mentions *Tèadhaich*, the Gaelic name of the Vale of Menteith.

Teviot This appears to be from an Indo-European root meaning 'flow'.

Thurso, Abhainn Theòrsa. This Norse name is possibly 'Thori's river'.

Tilt, Teilt or Abhainn Teilt. The meaning of this name is unclear.

Treig, Tréig or Abhainn Tréig. This is said to be 'river of death'.

Tromie, Tromaidh or Abhainn Tromaidh. 'Elder tree river'.

Truim, Abhainn Truim. *See* **Tromie**.

Tummel, Teimhil or Abhainn Teimhil. 'River of darkness'.

Turret, Turraid or Uisge Thurraid. 'Dry river', meaning one which reduces in size in summer.

Tweed, Tuaidh or Uisge Thuaidh. This pre-Gaelic name is unclear, as is an earlier Gaelic form, *Tumaid*.

Tyne This seems to be from an Indo-European root meaning 'flow'.

Ugie, Uigidh. The meaning of this name is unclear.

Urie, Uaraidh or Ùraidh. This may stem from *uar*, 'landslip', or may mean 'fresh river'.

Water of Allachy, Uisge Aileachaidh. 'River at the stony place'.

Water of Leith, Uisge Lìte. This pre-Gaelic name has connotations of moistness.

Water of Lus, Uisge Lus. 'Herb or vegetation river'.

Wells of Dee, Fuaran Dhé. 'Spring of the Dee' in Gaelic.

Wester Fearn Burn, Allt Grùgaig. The English name contrasts this stream with the Easter Fearn Burn, while in Gaelic the name appears to contain Norse *vík*, 'bay'.

Whiteadder, This is the same as **Adder**, but with 'White' attached to distinguish it from the 'Blackadder'.

White Cart This is the same as **Cart**, but with 'White' attached to distinguish it from the 'Black Cart'.

White Water, An t-Uisge Bàn. 'White river'.

Wick, Abhainn Ùige. The English form is the name of the town which is of Norse origin. The Gaelic form is a gaelicisation of the same Norse word, *vík*, 'bay'.

Ythan This is from a Celtic root for 'talk'.

Mountain Passes

Am Bealach Buidhe 'Ballochbuie' or 'the yellow pass', near Crathie in Aberdeenshire.

Am Bealach Maol 'Ballochmyle' or 'the blunt pass', in Ayrshire.

Am Bealach Mór 'The large pass', between Loch Awe and Loch Craignish.

Am Bealach Ruadh 'The red-brown pass', between Meall Reamhar and Beinn Fuath in Perthshire.

An Crasg 'Crask' or 'the crossing', between Lairg and Tongue in Sutherland.

An Làirig 'The pass', between Boath and Glenglass in Ross-shire.

An Làirig Leacach 'The slabbed pass', between Lianachan and the head of Loch Treig in Lochaber.

An Sloc 'The Slochd' or 'the pit', between Tomatin and Carrbridge in Inverness-shire.

Bealach a' Bhràigh Bhig 'Pass at the small upland', betweel Orval and Glen Shellesdar in Rum.

Bealach a' Chaolais 'Pass at the strait', leading inland from Kyles Stuley in South Uist.

Bealach a' Chonnaidh 'Pass of the fuel', between Glen Buckie and Gleann Dubh in Perthshire.

Bealach a' Ghlinne 'Pass at the glen', north of Fiunary in Argyll.

Bealach a' Mhorghain 'Shingle pass', at the foot of Ben Edra in Skye.

Bealach an Dubh-bhràighe 'Pass at the black upland', between Orval and a' Bhrìdeanach in Rum.

Bealach an Fhuarain 'Pass at the spring', between Ainshval and Trallaval in Rum.

Bealach an Òir 'Pass of gold', between Askival and Trallaval in Rum.

Bealach an t-Suidhe 'Bellochantuy' or 'pass of the seat', in Kintyre.

Bealach a' Phosta 'Postman's pass', between Sunart and Kingairloch.

Bealach Àrnabhal 'Pass of Arnaval', between Arnaval and Trinival in South Uist.

Bealach Baircmheall, Bealach Barcabhal. 'Pass of Barkeval', between Barkeval and Hallival in Rum.

Bealach Carragh Dhòmhnaill Ghuirm 'Pass at the rock of blue Donald', between Benmore and Maola Breac in South Uist.

Bealach Collaigh 'Pass at the hazel river or place', west of Ben Wyvis in Ross.

Bealach Crosgard 'Pass of Crosgard', between Benmore and Glen Liadale in South Uist.

Bealach Heileasdail 'Hellisdale pass', between Benmore and Ben Corodale in South Uist.

Bealach MhicNéill 'MacNeil's pass', inland from Kinloch in Rum.

Bealach na Ba, Bealach nam Bó. *See* **Bealach nam Bó**.

Bealach na Gaoithe 'Windy pass', in Argyll.

Bealach na h-Imriche 'Migration pass', near Dunoon in Cowal. Also between Strathbeg and Loch Dionard in Sutherland.

Bealach nam Bó 'Pass of the cattle', between Applecross and Kishorn in Wester Ross. Also the pass south of Loch Katrine below Ben Venue in Perthshire.

Bealach nam Bròg 'Pass of the shoes',

between Wyvis Forest and Loch-broom.

Bealach nam Mèirleach 'Pass of the thieves', between Strathmore and Loch Merkland in Sutherland.

Bealach nan Cabar 'Pass of the antlers', between Strathyre and Glen Artney in Perthshire.

Bealach nan Cabrach 'Pass of the antler places', in Glen Orchy.

Bealach nan Corr 'Pass of the cranes', south of Knockfarrel in Ross.

Bealach nan Laogh 'Pass of the calves', at Taymouth in Perthshire.

Bealach na Sgàirde 'Scree pass', through Glamaig in Skye.

Bealach Sgrìodain 'Scree pass', between Conaglen and Glen Hurich in Argyll.

Bealach Sheubhal 'Sheaval pass', between Sheaval and Trinival in South Uist.

Bealach Sloc an Eich 'Pass at the horse's pit', between Glen Cribesdale and Kinlochteacuis in Argyll.

Cadha Fionndain 'Fintan's path', between Tolly and the Averon in Ross.

Creagach Bhealadair 'Pass of Ballater' or 'rocky place of Ballater', in Deeside.

Cumhang a' Bhrannraidh 'Pass of Brander' or 'pass at the obstruction', in Argyll.

Cumhang Dhùghlais 'Pass of Lyon' or 'pass at the black river', at the mouth of Glen Lyon.

Cumhang Lànaigh 'Pass of Leny', between Callander and Strathyre.

Féith Bhealach 'Boggy channel pass', between Bealach Heileasdail and Ben Corodale in South Uist.

Fionn-Làirig 'White pass', at Killin in Perthshire.

Làirig Àirnein 'Àirnean's pass', between Inveraray and the foot of Glen Falloch.

Làirig an Lochain 'Pass at the little loch', between Bridge of Balgy and

Loch Tay. Also between Strathrus-dale and Dibidale in Ross.

Làirig an Tùir 'The tower pass', on the south side of Strath Nairn.

Làirig Bhaile Dhubhthaich 'Lairgs of Tain' or 'pass of Tain', between Tain and Edderton.

Làirig Bhreislich 'Pass of confusion', between Bridge of Balgy and Glen Lochay in Perthshire.

Làirig Chalabha This name is unclear, but the route lies between Rannoch and Inverwick.

Lairig Ghru, Làirig Dhrù. 'Pass of the Druie'. In Braemar this was known as *an Làirig Shuas*, 'the upper pass'.

Làirig Ghartain 'Gartan's pass', in Glen Etive.

Làirig Ìlidh 'Pass of Isla', between Lochearnhead and the north side of Glen Dochart.

Làirig Luaidhe 'The lead pass', between Glen Lyon and Glen Lochay in Perthshire.

Lairig Lui, Làirig an Laoigh. 'Pass at the Lui'. In Braemar this was called *an Làirig Shìos*, 'the lower pass'.

Làirig Mheachdainn This name is unclear but the pass runs between Loch Tay and Loch Rannoch.

Làirig Mìle Marcachd 'Pass of a mile of riding', between Kenmore and Glen Quaich in Perthshire. This was formerly known as *Làirig Monadh Marcachd*, 'pass at the riding hills'.

Làirig Mhuice 'Pass of the pig river', between Inverwick and Rannoch.

Làirig nan Lunn 'Pass of the staves', between Pubil and Kenknock in Perthshire.

Làirig Nodha 'Pass of Noe', between Glen Noe and Glen Strae in Argyll.

Làirig Phrasgain 'Pass of the troop', in Glen Almond.

Làirig Thurraid 'Pass of Turret' or 'pass of the dry river', at the head of Glen Roy in Lochaber.

Màm a' Choire Uidhir 'Gap at the dun-coloured corrie', in Mull.

Màm Beathaig 'Beathag's gap', in Ardgour.

Màm Lìrein 'Lìrean's gap', in Mull.

Màm na Céire 'The wax gap', in Morvern.

Màm Ràtagain 'The Ratagan gap', between Kintail and Glenelg.

The Slochd, An Sloc. 'The Slochd' or 'the pit', between Tomatin and Carrbridge in Inverness-shire.

Hills and Mountains

Although many hill and mountain names are spelled in an approximate Gaelic form, the spelling is often divergent from accepted modern norms. In such cases below, the generally used form is in bold followed by the form which adheres to Gaelic orthography where there is a difference between the two.

A' Bhuidheanach Bheag. 'The little yellow hill'.

A' Chailleach. 'The old woman'.

A' Chaoirnich. This name is unclear but may be connected with rowan-berries.

A' Chioch, A' Chìoch. 'The breast'.

An Coileachan. 'The little cockrel'.

A' Choinneach, A' Chòinneach. 'The moss'.

A' Chralaig, A' Chràlaig. The meaning of this name is unclear.

A' Ghlas-beinn. 'The grey-green mountain'.

Ainshval, Ainseabhal. 'Hill of the rocky ridge'.

Airgiod Bheinn, Airgead Bheinn. 'Silver mountain'.

Am Basteir, Am Baisteir. 'The baptist' or 'the executioner' depending on the name's original form.

Am Bathach, Am Bàthach. 'The byre'.

Am Bodach. 'The old man'.

Am Faochagach. 'The whelk-like mountain'.

A' Mhaighdean. 'The maiden'.

A' Mharconich, A' Mharcanaich. 'The horse mountain'.

Am Màm 'The gap', in Glenorchy.

Am Màm Mór 'The large gap', in the Mamore Forest.

An Caisteal. 'The castle'.

An Cruachan. 'The conical hill'.

An Dun, An Dùn. 'The (hill)fort'.

An Gearanach. 'The complainer'.

Angel's Peak, Sgòr an Lochain Uaine. In Gaelic this is 'the peak of the green lochan', and is also known as **Sgor an Lochain Uaine**.

An Riabhachan. 'The brindled one'.

An Ruadh-mheallan. 'The small red-brown lumpish hill'.

An Sgarsoch, An Sgairseach. 'The knotty or fissured hill'.

An Sgorr, An Sgòr. 'The pinnacle'.

An Sidhean, An Sìthean. 'The fairy mound'.

An Socach. 'The sow'.

An Stac. 'The stack'.

An Stuc, An Stùc. 'The exposed rocky steep hill'.

An Tudair, An Tughadair. 'The thatcher'.

Aodann Chleireig, Aodann Chléireig. The second element in this name is unclear, but *aodann* refers to a hill-face.

Aonach air Chrith. 'Shaking steep hill'.

Aonach Beag, An t-Aonach Beag. 'The small steep hill'.

Aonach Buidhe, An t-Aonach Buidhe. 'The yellow steep hill'.

Aonach Eagach, An t-Aonach Eagach. 'The notched steep hill'.

Aonach Meadhoin, An t-Aonach Meadhain. 'The middle steep hill'.

Aonach Mor, An t-Aonach Mór. 'The great steep hill'.

Aonach Shasuinn, Aonach Shasainn. 'The steep hill of the English'.

Argyll Hills, Am Monadh Leacanach. 'The slabbed hills', north of Inveraray.

Arkle, Airceil or Arcail. The first part of this Norse mountain name is unclear.

Askerven, Àisgeirbheinn. This may be 'ash field mountain', from Norse/Gaelic.

Askival, Aisgeabhal or Asgabhal. 'Ash wood hill', from Norse.

Auchnafree Hill. *Achadh na Frìthe* is 'field of the deer forest'.

Bac an Eich. 'Hollow of the horse'.

Badandun Hill. *Bad an Dùin* is 'place of the hill(fort)'.

Baosbheinn, Badhais-bheinn or Baoghais-bheinn. This may be 'drenched mountain'.

Beinn a' Bha'ach Ard, Beinn a' Bhàthaich Àrd. 'High mountain of the byre'.

Beinn a' Bhuird, Beinn a' Bhùird. 'Table mountain'.

Beinn a' Bhuiridh, Beinn a' Bhùiridh. 'Mountain of bellowing'.

Beinn a' Chaisgein Beag. 'Small mountain of the impediment'.

Beinn a' Chaisgein Mor, Beinn a' Chaisgein Mhór. 'Large mountain of the impediment'.

Beinn a' Chaisteal, Beinn a' Chaisteil. 'Castle mountain'.

Beinn a' Chaolais. 'Mountain of the narrows'.

Beinn a' Chaorainn, Beinn a' Chaorthainn. 'Rowan mountain'.

Beinn a' Chapuill, Beinn a' Chapaill. 'Mountain of the horse'.

Beinn a' Chearcaill. 'Mountain of the circle'.

Beinn a' Chlachain. 'Mountain of the kirkton or churchyard'.

Beinn a' Chlachair. 'The stonemason's mountain'.

Beinn a' Chlaidheimh. 'Mountain of the sword'.

Beinn a' Chleibh, Beinn a' Chléibh. 'Creel mountain'.

Beinn a' Chochuill, Beinn a' Chochaill. 'Husk mountain'.

Beinn a' Choin. 'Mountain of the dog'.

Beinn a' Chreachain, Beinn a' Chreachainn. 'Mountain with a bare rocky surface'.

Beinn a' Chroin, This may be 'mountain of the cloven hoof'.

Beinn a' Chrulaiste, Beinn a' Chrùlaiste. 'Mountain with a rocky hill'.

Beinn a' Chuallaich. 'Mountain of the cattle (herding)'.

Beinn a' Chuirn, Beinn a' Chùirn. 'Horn mountain'.

Beinn a' Ghlo, Beinn a' Ghlò or na Beinnichean Glotha. The meaning of the second part of this name is unclear. The second Gaelic name was used locally.

Beinn a' Mhanaich. 'Mountain of the monk'.

Beinn a' Mheadhoin, Beinn a' Mheadhain, 'Mountain of the middle'.

Beinn a' Mhuinidh or Beinn a' Mhunaidh. 'Mountain of the hill range'.

Beinn Achaladair, Beinn Ach Chaladair. 'Mountain of Achallater'.

Beinn Airigh Charr, Beinn Àirigh a' Charr. 'Mountain with the sheiling at the rock ledge'.

Beinn an Dothaidh, Beinn an Dòthaidh. 'Mountain of singeing'.

Beinn an Eoin, Beinn an Eòin. 'Bird mountain'.

Beinn an Lochain. 'Mountain of the little loch'.

Beinn an Oir, Beinn an Òir. 'Gold mountain'.

Beinn Bhalgairean. 'Mountain of foxes'.

Beinn Bhan, A' Bheinn Bhàn. 'The white or fair mountain'.

Beinn Bharrain, Beinn a' Bharrain. 'Mountain of the crest'.

Beinn Bheag, A' Bheinn Bheag. 'The small mountain'.

Beinn Bheoil, Beinn a' Bheòil. 'Mouth mountain'.

Beinn Bheula. This name is unclear.

Beinn Bhreac, A' Bheinn Bhreac. 'The speckled mountain'.

Beinn Bhreac-liath, A' Bheinn Bhreac Liath. 'The speckled grey-blue mountain'.

Beinn Bhrotain, Beinn a' Bhrodain. 'The mountain of the bog'.

Beinn Bhuidhe, A' Bheinn Bhuidhe. 'The yellow mountain'.

Beinn Chabhair, Beinn a' Chabhair. This is said to mean 'mountain of the hawk'.

Beinn Challum, Beinn Chaluim. 'Calum's mountain'.

Beinn Chaorach. 'Sheep mountain'.

Beinn Chuirn, Beinn a' Chùirn. 'The mountain of the cairn'.

Beinn Clachach, A' Bheinn Chlachach. 'The stony mountain'.

Beinn Damh. 'Mountain of stags'.

Beinn Damhain. 'Mountain of the spider or little stag'.

Beinn Dearg, A' Bheinn Dearg. 'The red mountain'.

Beinn Dearg Bheag, A' Bheinn Dearg Bheag. 'The small red mountain'.

Beinn Dearg Mhor, A' Bheinn Dearg Mhór. 'The large red mountain'.

Beinn Dearg Mor, A' Bheinn Dearg Mhór. 'The large red mountain'.

Beinn Dhorain, Beinn Dobhrain. 'Mountain of the river'.

Beinn Direach, A' Bheinn Direach. 'The straight mountain'.

Beinn Donachain, Beinn Donnchain. 'Duncan's mountain'.

Beinn Dorain, Beinn Dobhrain. 'Mountain of the river'.

Beinn Dronaig, Beinn Dronnaig. 'Mountain with a small ridge'.

Beinn Dubh, A' Bheinn Dubh. 'The black mountain'.

Beinn Dubhchraig, Beinn Dubh-chreig. 'Mountain of the black rock'.

Beinn Each. 'Mountain of horses'.

Beinn Eibhinn, Beinn Éibhinn. This is either 'pleasant mountain' or 'Éibhinn's mountain', a personal name.

Beinn Eich. 'Horse mountain'.

Beinn Enaglair, Beinn Eunacleit. 'Brow cliff mountain', from Gaelic/Norse.

Beinn Eunaich. This may be 'hunting or fowling mountain'.

Beinn Fhada, A' Bheinn Fhada. 'The long mountain'.

Beinn Fhionnlaidh, Beinn Fhionnlaigh. 'Finlay's mountain'.

Beinn Gaire, Beinn Gàire. 'Mountain of the loud noise'.

Beinn Ghlas, A' Bheinn Ghlas. 'The grey mountain'.

Beinn Ghobhlach, A' Bheinn Ghobhlach. 'The forked mountain'.

Beinn Heasgarnich, Beinn Sheasgar-naich. This may be 'mountain of the barren place'.

Beinn Iaruinn, Beinn Iarainn. 'Iron mountain'.

Beinn Ime. 'Butter mountain'.

Beinn Iutharn Bheag, Beinn Iuthairn Bheag. 'Small mountain of hell'.

Beinn Iutharn Mhor, Beinn Iuthairn Mhór. 'Large mountain of hell'.

Beinn Lair, Beinn Làir. 'The mare mountain'.

Beinn Leoid, Beinn Leòid. 'Ljót's mountain', a Norse personal name.

Beinn Liath Mhor, A' Bheinn Liath Mhór. 'The large grey-blue mountain'.

Beinn Liath Mhor a'Ghiubhais Li, Beinn Liath Mhór a' Ghiuthais Léith. 'The large grey-blue mountain of the grey-blue pine tree'.

Beinn Liath Mhor Fannich, Beinn Liath Mhór Fainich. 'The large grey-blue mountain of Fannich'.

Beinn Lochain, Beinn an Lochain. 'Mountain of the small loch'.

Beinn Luibhean. 'Mountain of small plants'.

Beinn Maol Chaluim, Beinn Mhaol Chaluim. 'Calum's bare mountain'.

Beinn Mhanach. 'Mountain of monks'.

Beinn Mheadhoin, A' Beinn Mheadh-ain. 'The middle mountain'.

Beinn Mheadhonach, A' Bheinn

Mheadhanach. 'The middle mountain'.

Beinn Mhic Chasgaig, Beinn Mhic-Casgaig. 'MacCaskaig's mountain'.

Beinn Mhic Mhonaidh. 'Mountain of the son of the moor'.

Beinn MhicCedidh, Beinn Mhic-Céididh. 'MacKeady's mountain'.

Beinn Mholach, A' Bheinn Mholach. 'The grizzled mountain'.

Beinn Mhor, A' Bheinn Mhór. 'The large mountain'.

Beinn na Caillich. 'Mountain of the old woman'.

Beinn na Cille. 'Mountain of the church'.

Beinn na Cloiche. 'Mountain of the stone'.

Beinn na Doire Leithe, Beinn na Doire Léithe. 'Mountain of the grey-blue oak-grove'.

Beinn na Feusaige. 'Mountain of the beard'.

Beinn na Gainimh. 'Mountain of the sand'.

Beinn na Gucaig. 'Mountain of the acorn'.

Beinn na h-Eaglaise. 'Mountain of the church'.

Beinn na h-Uamha. 'Mountain of the cave'.

Beinn na Lap, Beinn nan Lap. 'Mountain of the spots or dapples'.

Beinn nam Fuaran. 'Mountain of the springs'.

Beinn na Muice. 'Mountain of the pig'.

Beinn nan Aighenan, Beinn nan Aigheanan. 'Mountain of the stags'.

Beinn nan Caorach. 'Mountain of the sheep'.

Beinn nan Eun. 'Mountain of the birds'.

Beinn nan Imirean or Beinn nan Iomairean. 'Mountain of the riggs'.

Beinn nan Lus. 'Mountain of the plants or herbs'.

Beinn nan Oighreag. 'Mountain of the cloudberries'.

Beinn nan Ramh, Beinn nan Ràmh. 'Mountain of the oars'.

Beinn Narnain. This name is unclear.

Beinn na Sroine, Beinn na Sròine. 'Mountain of the nose'.

Beinn Odhar, A' Bheinn Odhar. 'The dun-coloured mountain'.

Beinn Odhar Bheag, A' Bheinn Odhar Bheag. 'The small dun-coloured mountain'.

Beinn Resipol, Beinn Réiseapuil. 'Mountain of Resipol'.

Beinn Ruadh, A' Bheinn Ruadh. 'The red-bron mountain'.

Beinn Sgaillinish, Beinn Sgàilinis. 'Mountain of Sgaillinish', from Gaelic/Norse.

Beinn Sgritheall. 'Scree mountain'.

Beinn Sgulaird. This name is unclear.

Beinn Shiantaidh. This may be 'holy mountain'.

Beinn Spionnaidh. 'Mountain of strength or might'.

Beinn Suidhe. 'Sitting mountain'.

Beinn Talaidh, Beinn Tàlaidh. 'Enticing mountain'.

Beinn Tarsuinn, Beinn Tarsainn. 'Cross mountain'.

Beinn Teallach. This appear to be 'mountain of the hearths'.

Beinn Tharsuinn, A' Bheinn Tarsainn. 'The cross mountain'.

Beinn Trilleachan, Beinn Trilleachan. 'Mountain of grey plovers'.

Beinn Tulaichean. 'Mountain of green hills'.

Beinn Udlaidh, A' Bheinn Ùdlaidh. 'The gloomy mountain'.

Beinn Udlamain, Beinn Ùdlamain. 'Mountain of the swivel'.

Belig, Beilg. This name is unclear.

Ben A'an, Am Binnein. 'The pinnacle'.

Ben Aden, Beinn Aodainn. 'Mountain of the hill face'.

Ben Aigan, Beinn Éiginn. 'Mountain of extremity'.

Ben Alder, Beinn Eallair. 'Mountain of the rocky river'.

Ben Alligin, Beinn Àiliginn. 'Alligin mountain'.

Ben Armine, Beinn Armainn. 'Mountain of the steward or commander'.

Ben Arthur, Beinn Artair. This appears to be 'Arthur's mountain', but the derivation may lie elsewhere with an element linked to the name of Arrochar. This mountain is also known as 'The Cobbler' and *An Greusaiche Crom*, 'the hunched cobbler'.

Ben Aslak, Beinn Aslag. This contains a Norse element, possibly a personal name.

Ben Attow, A' Bheinn Fhada. 'The long mountain'.

Ben Aven, Beinn Athfhinn. 'Mountain of the bright river'.

Ben Bhraggie, Beinn Bhragaidh. It is unclear what the second element here means, although *brag* can denote a sharp sound.

Ben Buie, A' Bheinn Bhuidhe. 'The yellow mountain'.

Ben Challum, Beinn Chaluim. 'Calum's mountain'.

Ben Chonzie, Beinn Chomhainn. This name may be related to that found in 'Glencoe', in which case it may be a tribal name.

Ben Cleuch. 'Cleuch' is a Lowland Scots for denoting a ravine or gully.

Ben Cruachan, Cruachan or Cruachan Bheann. 'Roughly conical hill' or 'roughly conical hill of the mountains'. It is said of this mountain, *Teirgidh Cruachan Bheann gun dad a dhol ri cheann*, 'Ben Cruachan will wear away if there's nothing put on top of it'.

Ben Damph, Beinn Damh. 'Mountain of stags'.

Ben Donich, Beinn Dòmhnaich. 'Mountain of the Lord'.

Ben Edra, Beinn Eadarra. The second part of this may be a river name.

Beneveian, Beinn a' Mheadhain. 'Mountain in the middle'.

Ben Ever, Beinn Eimhir. 'Eimhir's mountain'.

Ben Gulabin, Beinn Ghulbain. 'Beak mountain'.

Ben Hee, A' Bheinn Shìth. 'The magic mountain'.

Ben Hope, Beinn Hòb. 'The mountain of Hope', referring to the place called *Hòb* or 'Hope' in Sutherland.

Ben Ketland, Beinn Ceiteilein. This name may contain a Brythonic element for 'wood'.

Ben Klibreck, Beinn Cleithbrig. 'Klibreck mountain'.

Ben Lawers, Beinn Labhair. 'Lawers mountain'.

Ben Ledi, Beinn Lididh. This name is unclear.

Ben Lomond, Beinn Laomainn. This name may have its origin in a Brythonic term for 'beacon'.

Ben Loyal, Beinn Laghail. This is 'law mountain' from Norse.

Ben Lui, Beinn Laoigh. 'Calf mountain'.

Ben Macdui, Beinn Mac Duibh. 'Mountain of Dubh's son'.

Ben More, A' Bheinn Mhór. 'The large mountain'.

Ben More Assynt, Beinn Mhór Asainte. 'Large mountain of Assynt'.

Ben More Coigach, Beinn Mhór na Cóigich. 'Large mountain of Coigach'.

Ben More Mull, Beinn Mhór Mhuile or A' Bheinn Mhór Mhuileach. 'The large Mull mountain'.

Ben Nevis, Beinn Nibheis. This name appears to have been applied in the first instance to the river and has an Indo-European root meaning 'wet'. It was commonly believed to stem from *uabhas*, 'terror', and the area has a forbidding reputation. However Ben Nevis is rather dismissed in a saying, *Beinn Nibheis mhór a' glaodhaich na laighe-siubhla's cha tàinig aiste ach an luchag-fheòir*, 'Great Ben Nevis howling with its birth pains and all that come out of it was a field mouse'.

Ben Oss, Beinn Òis. 'Mountain at the river mouth', from Gaelic/Norse.

Ben Rinnes, Beinn Ruaidhneis. 'Mountain at the red-brown haugh'.

Ben Stack, Beinn Stac. 'Stack mountain', from Gaelic/Norse.

Ben Starav, Beinn Starabh. This may contain a personal name but is unclear.

Ben Tee, Beinn an t-Sithidh. 'Mountain of the blast'.

Ben Tirran. This name is unclear.

Ben Vair, Beinn a' Bheithir. 'Serpent mountain'.

Ben Vane, A' Bheinn Mheadhain. 'The middle mountain'.

Ben Venue, A' Bheinn Mheanbh. 'The tiny mountain'.

Ben Vorlich, Beinn Mhùrlaig. 'Mountain at the inlet'.

Ben Vrackie, Beinn a' Bhreacaidh. 'Mountain of the speckled stream'.

Ben Vuirich, Beinn a' Bhùraich or Beinn Bhùraich nam Madadh Móra. 'Mountain of bellowing' or 'mountain of the bellowing of the great wolves or hounds'.

Ben Wyvis, Beinn Uais. This may stem from *uabhas*, 'terror'.

Benyellary, Beinn na h-Iolaire. 'Eagle mountain'.

Ben y Hone, Beinn a' Chòinnich. 'Moss mountain'.

Bidean a' Ghlas-Thuill, Bidean a' Ghlas-thuill. 'Pinnacle of the grey hole'.

Bidean an Eoin Deirg, Bidean an Eòin Deirg. 'Pinnacle of the red bird'.

Bidean nam Bian. 'Pinnacle of the hides'.

Bidein a' Chabair, Bidean a' Chabair. 'Pinnacle of the antler'.

Bidein a' Choire Sheasgaich, Bidean a' Choire Sheasgaich. 'Pinnacle of the barren or reedy corrie'.

Binnein an Fhidhleir, Binnein an Fhìdhleir. 'Fiddler's pinnacle'.

Binnein Beag, Am Binnein Beag. 'The small pinnacle'.

Binnein Mor, Am Binnein Mór. 'The large pinnacle'.

Binnein Shios, Am Binnein Shìos. 'Easter pinnacle'.

Binnein Shuas, Am Binnein Shuas. 'Wester pinnacle'.

Biod an Fhithich or Bioda an Fhithich. 'Hill top of the raven'.

Black Mount, Am Monadh Dubh. 'The black mount or range of hills'.

Blath Bhalg, Blàth-Bhalg. This may be 'bag-shaped place of blossom'. *See* **Blebo**, p. 30.

Blaven, Blàbheinn. 'Blue mountain', from Norse/Gaelic.

Boar of Badenoch, An Torc. 'The boar'. Nearby is the **Sow of Atholl**.

Brack, The. 'Speckled'.

Braeriach, Am Bràigh Riabhach. 'The brindled upland'.

Braes of Greenock, Bràigh Ghrianaig. 'Upper part of Greenock'.

Braid Hills 'Braid' here either means 'broad' or comes from *bràigh*, 'upper part', as found in 'Breadalbane'. These are thought to be the hills recorded as *Monadh Éideann*, 'upland area of Eidyn'.

Braigh Coire Chruinn-bhalgain, Bràigh Coire a' Chruinn-bhalgain. 'Upper part of the corrie of the round bag'.

Braigh nan Uamhachan, Bràigh nan Uamhachan. 'Upland of the caves'.

Breabag. If this name is Norse it is 'broad bank'; if Gaelic it is unclear.

Broad Cairn, Càrn Bràghaid. 'Upland cairn'.

Brown Cow Hill, A' Bhó Dhonn. 'The brown cow'.

Bruach na Frithe, Bruthach na Frìthe. 'Brae of the deer forest'.

Buachaille Etive Beag, Buachaille Éite Beag. 'The small shepherd of Etive'.

Buachaille Etive Mor, Buachaille Éite Mór. 'The large shepherd of Etive'.

Buck, The, Am Boc. 'The buck'.

Buidheanach Bheag, A' Bhuidheanach Bheag. 'The small yellow hill'.

Bynack Beg, A' Bheithneag Bheag. 'The small little mountain'.

Bynack More, A' Bheithneag Mhór or

Beinn Bheithneag. 'The large little mountain'.

Cac Carn Beag, Cadha a' Chàirn Beag. 'Small pass at the cairn'.

Cac Carn Mor, Cadha a' Chàirn Mór. 'Large pass at the cairn'.

Caenlochan, Cadha an Lochain. 'Path at the small loch'.

Cairn Bannoch, An Càrn Beannach. 'The pointed cairn or hill'.

Cairn Dye, Càrn an Tàilleir. This appears to be 'tailor's hill', but the origin of the name may be older and obscure.

Cairngorm, An Càrn Gorm. 'The blue hill'.

Cairngorms, Am Monadh Ruadh. 'The red-brown mountain range'. This contrasts with *am Monadh Liath*, 'the grey-blue mountain range', nearby.

Cairn Lochan, Càrn an Lochain. 'Cairn or hill at the small loch'.

Cairn of Claise, Càrn na Claise. 'Cairn or hill with a furrow'.

Cairn of Gowal, Càrn a' Ghobhail. 'The forked cairn or hill'.

Cairn O'Mount, Càrn Mhon. 'Cairn at the hill range'.

Cairnsgarroch, An Càrn Sgarach. 'The fissured cairn or hill'.

Cairntoul, Càrn an t-Sabhail. 'Hill or cairn of the barn'.

Cairnwell, Càrn a' Bhalg or An Càrn Bhailg. 'Bag-shaped hill or cairn'.

Caisteal Abhail, Caisteal Ghabhail. 'Forked castle'.

Cam Chreag, Cam-chreag. 'Bent or distorted rock'.

Campsie Fells These hills in the Campsie area are thought to be those referred to as *am Monadh Beannach*, 'the peaked range of hills'.

Canisp, Canasp. This name is unclear.

Carlownie Hill This is thought to be 'elm fort', from *Cathair Leamhnach*.

Carn a' Chaochain, Càrn a' Chaochain. 'Hill or cairn of the small stream'.

Carn a' Chlamhain, Càrn a' Chlamhain. 'Hawk hill or cairn'.

Carn a' Choin Deirg, Càrn a' Choin Deirg. 'Hill or cairn of the red dog'.

Carn a' Choire Bhoidheach, Càrn a' Choire Bhòidhich. 'Hill or cairn at the beautiful corrie'.

Carn a' Choire Ghairbh, Càrn a' Choire Ghairbh. 'Hill or cairn at the rough corrie'.

Carn a' Chuilinn, Càrn a' Chuilinn. 'Holly hill or cairn'.

Carn a' Gheoidh, Càrn a' Gheòidh. 'Goose hill or cairn'.

Carn a' Ghille Chearr, Càrn a' Ghille Cheàrr. This appears to be 'hill or cairn of the wrong boy', but *ceàrr* can also mean left-handed.

Carn a' Ghlas-uillt, Càrn a' Ghlas-uillt. 'Hill or cairn of the grey stream'.

Carn a' Mhaim, Càrn a' Mhàim. 'Hill or cairn at the pass'.

Carnan Cruithneachd, Càrnan Cruithneachd. This seems in its current form to mean 'small hill or cairn of wheat', but originally may have been *Càrn nan Cruithneach*, 'hill or cairn of the Picts'.

Carn an Fhreiceadain, Càrn an Fhreiceadain. 'Hill or cairn of the guard'.

Carn an Righ, Càrn an Rìgh. 'King's hill or cairn'.

Carn an Tionail, Càrn an Tionail. 'Hill or cairn of the gathering'.

Carn an t-Sagairt Beag, Càrn an t-Sagairt Beag. 'Priest's small hill or cairn'.

Carn an t-Sagairt Mor, Càrn an t-Sagairt Mór. 'Priest's large hill or cairn'.

Carn an Tuirc, Càrn an Tuirc. 'Boar's hill or cairn'.

Carn Aosda, An Càrn Aosta. 'The old hill or cairn'.

Carn Ballach, An Càrn Ballach. 'The ragged hill or cairn'.

Carn Ban, An Càrn Bàn. 'The white hill or cairn'.

Carn Ban Mor, An Càrn Bàn Mór. 'The large white hill or cairn'.

Carn Bhac, Càrn a' Bhac. 'Hill or cairn

at the hollow'.

Carn Bhinnein, Càrn a' Bhinnein. 'Hill or cairn of the pinnacle'.

Carn Breac, An Càrn Breac. 'The speckled hill or cairn'.

Carn Bhren, Càrn Bhrein. 'Hill or cairn of rotten-ness'.

Carn Chuinneag, Càrn Chuinneag. 'Hill of cairn of the milking pails'.

Carn Dearg, An Càrn Dearg. 'The red hill or cairn'.

Carn Dearg Meadhonach, An Càrn Dearg Meadhanach. 'The middle red hill or cairn'.

Carn Dearg Mor, An Càrn Dearg Mór. 'The large red hill or cairn'.

Carn Ealar, Càrn an Fhìdhleir. 'Fiddler's hill or cairn'.

Carn Ealasaid, Càrn Ealasaid. 'Elizabeth's hill or cairn'.

Carn Eas, Càrn an Eas. 'Hill or cairn at the waterfall'.

Carn Easgann Bana, Càrn nan Easgann Bàna. 'Hill or cairn of the white eels'.

Carn Eighe, Càrn Eighe. This may be 'icy hill or cairn'.

Carn Etchachan, Càrn Éiteachain. This may be 'hill or cairn of the little foul one', including an element found in the river name *Éite* or 'Etive'.

Carn Ghluasaid, Càrn a' Ghluasaid. 'Hill or cairn of movement'.

Carn Glas-choire, Carn Ghlas-choire 'Hill or cairn of the grey-green corrie'.

Carn Gorm, An Càrn Gorm. 'The blue hill or cairn'.

Carn Liath, An Càrn Liath. 'The grey-blue hill or cairn'.

Carn Loch nan Amhaichean, Càrn Loch nan Amhaichean. 'Hill or cairn of the loch of the necks'.

Carn Mairg, Càrn Mairg. 'Merk cairn'.

Carn Mhic an Toisich, Càrn Mhic an Tòisich. 'Macintosh's hill or cairn'.

Carn Mor, An Càrn Mór. 'The large hill or cairn'.

Carn Mor Dearg, An Càrn Mór Dearg. 'The large red hill or cairn'.

Carn na Baintighearna, Càrn na Baintighearna. 'The lady's hill or cairn'.

Carn na Breabaig, Càrn na Breabaig. This appears to be 'hill or cairn of the little kick'.

Carn na Caim, Càrn na Caim. 'Hill or cairn with the bend'.

Carn na Coinnich, Càrn na Còinnich. 'Hill or cairn of the moss'.

Carn na Coire Mheadhoin, Càrn na Coire Meadhain. 'Hill or cairn at the middle corrie'.

Carn na Con Dhu, Càrn nan Con Dubh. 'Hill or cairn of the black dogs'.

Carn na Criche, Càrn na Crìche. 'Hill or cairn at the boundary'.

Carn na Drochaide, Càrn na Drochaide. 'Hill or cairn at the bridge'.

Carn na h-Easgainn, Càrn na h-Easgainn. 'Hill or cairn of the eel'.

Carn nam Fiaclan, Càrn nam Fiaclan. 'Toothed hill or cairn'.

Carn na Nathrach, Càrn na Nathrach. 'Hill or cairn of the snake'.

Carn nan Gabhar, Càrn nan Gobhar. 'Hill or cairn of the goats'.

Carn nan Gobhar, Càrn nan Gobhar. 'Hill or cairn of the goats'.

Carn nan Tri-tighearnan, Càrn nan Trì Tighearnan. 'Hill or cairn of the three lords'.

Carn na Saobhaidhe, Càrn na Saobhaidhe. 'Hill or cairn at the lair'.

Carn Salachaidh, Càrn Shalachaidh. 'Hill or cairn of Sallachy'.

Carn Sgulain, Càrn Sgùlain. 'Basket-shaped hill or cairn'.

Ceann na Baintighearna. 'The lady's head'.

Chno Dearg, A' Chnò Dhearg. This appears to be 'the red nut', but the name may have an earlier different form.

Cir Mhor, A' Chìr Mhór. 'The large comb'.

Ciste Dhubh, A' Chiste Dhubh. 'The black chest'.

Clisham, An Cliseam. The meaning of this name is unclear.

Cnap a'Chleirich, Cnap a' Chléirich. 'The cleric's lumpish hill'.

Cnap Chaochan Aitinn. 'Lumpish hill of the juniper stream'.

Cnap Coire na Spreidhe, Cnap Coire na Spréidhe. 'Lumpish hill at the cattle corrie'.

Cnap Cruinn, An Cnap Cruinn. 'The round lumpish hill'.

Cnoc Coinnich, Cnoc Còinnich. 'Hill of moss'.

Cobbler, An Greusaiche Crom. The Gaelic name is 'the hunched cobbler'. This is also known as **Ben Arthur**.

Coinneach Mhor, A' Chòinneach Mhór. 'The large moss'.

Conachraig, Conachreag. 'Hound rock'.

Conival, Conamheall or Conabhal. The spelling of the first Gaelic form looks as though the name means 'hound hill'. However, the name is Norse and contains *fjall*, 'mountain', but the first part is unclear and may be related to that which appears in the village name **Connista**.

Cook's Cairn, Càrn MhicCùga. 'Mac-Cook's hill'.

Corra-bheinn. 'Uneven mountain'.

Corrag Bhuidhe, A' Chorrag Bhuidhe. 'The yellow finger'.

Corryhabbie Hill. Although of Gaelic origin, the second element of this name is unclear.

Corwharn. This may be *Corr-chàrn*, 'uneven hill or cairn', or *Coire a' Chàirn*, 'corrie of the cairn or hill'.

Craig a' Chaorainn, Creag a' Chaorthainn. 'Rowan rock'.

Craig an Loch, Creag an Locha. 'Rock by the loch'.

Craig Coire na Fiar Bhealaich, Creag Coire na Fiar-bhealaich. 'Rock at the corrie by the crooked pass'.

Craig Dubh, A' Chreag Dhubh. 'The black rock'.

Craig Leek, Creag Lic. 'Slab rock'.

Craignaw. 'Rock of the waters', from *Creag n-Abha*, or 'rock of the water', from *Creag an Abha*.

Craig of Gowal, Creag a' Ghobhail. 'The forked or split rock'.

Cranstackie, Cranstacaidh. This is said to mean 'rugged stack', but the first element of the name is unclear.

Creach Beinn, Creach-bheinn. 'Hill of plunder'.

Creach Bheinn, Creach-bheinn. 'Hill of plunder'.

Creag a' Mhadaidh. 'Rock of the wolf'.

Creag a' Mhaim, Creag a' Mhàim. 'Rock at the pass'.

Creagan a' Chaise. 'Little rock of the steepness'.

Creagan a' Choire Etchachan, Creagan Choire Éiteachain. This may be 'little rock of the corrie of the foul one'. *See* **Carn Eiteachan**.

Creagan na Beinne. 'Rocks of the mountain'.

Creag Bhalg. 'Rock of the bag shapes'.

Creag Dhubh, A' Chreag Dhubh. 'The black rock'.

Creag Dhubh Mhor, A' Chreag Dhubh Mhór. 'The big black rock'.

Creag Each. 'Rock of horses'.

Creag Gharbh, A' Chreag Gharbh. 'The rough rock'.

Creag Ghuanach, A' Chreag Ghua-nach. 'The unsteady rock'.

Creag Leacach, A' Chreag Leacach. 'The slabbed rock'.

Creag Liath, A' Chreag Liath. 'The grey-blue rock'.

Creag MacRanaich, Creag MhicRànaich. 'MacRanaich's rock'. This surname is unclear.

Creag Meagaidh. 'The rock at the boggy place'.

Creag Mhor, A' Chreag Mhór. 'The large rock'.

Creag nan Damh. 'Rock of the stags'.

Creag nan Gabhar, Creag nan Gobhar. 'Rock of the goats'.

Creag Pitridh. 'Petrie's rock'.

Creag Rainich. 'Bracken rock'.

Creag Ruadh, A' Chreag Ruadh. 'The red-brown rock'.

Creag Tharsuinn, Creag Tharsainn. 'Cross or over rock'.

Creag Uanach. *See* **Creag Ghuanach.**

Creag Uchdag. 'Rock of small slopes'.

Creise, Clach Leathad. The Gaelic name is 'stone slope', while the more common name is from Gaelic for 'grease/fat'.

Croit Bheinn, Croit-bheinn. 'Hump mountain'.

Cruach an t-Sidhein, Cruach an t-Sìthein. 'Conical hill of the fairy mound'.

Cruach Ardrain, Cruach Àrdrain. 'Conical hill of the Ardran', as in Inverardran.

Cruach Coireadail. 'Conical hill of Coireadal'.

Cruach Innse. 'Conical hill of Inch'.

Cruach nam Mult. 'Conical hill of the wedders'.

Cruach nan Capull, Cruach nan Capall. 'Conical hill of the horses'.

Cruinn a' Bheinn, Cruinne-bheinn. 'Rounded mountain'.

Cuidhe Crom, An Cuidhe Crom. 'The bent fold'.

Cuillins, An Cuiltheann. There have been many attempts at interpreting this name, but none have proved satisfactory.

Cuillins of Rum, An Cuiltheann Rumach. *See* **Cuillins.**

Culardoch, Cùl Àrdaich. 'Back of the high place'. *Cùl* was used poetically to refer to long flowing hair, and perhaps that sense is intended here.

Cul Beag, An Cùl Beag. 'The small back'. *See* **Culardoch.**

Cùl Mhàm 'The back gap', in Morvern.

Cul Mor, An Cùl Mór. 'The large back'. *See* **Culardoch.**

Dagrum, An Dà Dhruim. 'The two ridges'.

Dechmont This is said to be *Deagh Mhonadh*, 'good hill', *See* **Dechmont** above.

Derry Cairngorm, Càrn Gorm an Doire. 'The blue hill or cairn of the oak-grove'.

Devil's Point, Bod an Deamhain. 'The devil's penis' in Gaelic.

Doune Hill. 'Hill of the hillfort', from *An Dùn.*

Driesh, Drìs. This is said to be 'thorn', but the long vowel in the Gaelic name goes against this.

Druim Fada, An Druim Fada. 'The long ridge'.

Druim nan Cnamh, Druim nan Cnàmh. 'Ridge of the bones'.

Druim na Sgriodain, Druim na Sgrìodain. 'Ridge of the scree'.

Druim Shionnach. 'Ridge of foxes'.

Druim Tarsuinn, Druim Tarsainn. 'Cross ridge'.

Drumalban, Druim Albann. 'The ridge of Scotland'.

Duchray Hill, Meall nan Leitir. The names in the two languages are different, the Gaelic name being 'Lumpish hill of the broad slopes'.

Dumbarton Rock, Ail Chluaidh. The Gaelic name is 'rock of the Clyde', and this was the capital of the Brythonic people of Strathclyde.

Dun Caan, Dùn Càna. This is said to be 'white hill'.

Dun da Ghaoidhe, Dùn Dà Ghaoithe. 'Hill of the two winds'.

Eididh nan Clach Geala, Éididh nan Clach Geala. This appears to be 'web of the white stones'.

Fafernie, Féith Feàrnaidh. 'Boggy channel at the alder place' or 'boggy channel of the alder stream'.

Faochagach, Am Faochagach. 'The whelk-like one'.

Faochaig. This name may be connected to *faochag*, 'whelk'.

Fara, Am Faradh. 'The ladder'.

Farragon Hill, Cnoc Fheargain. 'Feargan's hill'.

Fashven, Faisbheinn. This may be 'mountain of the stance'.

Fiarach, Feurach. 'Grassy place'.

Fionn Bheinn, Fionn-bheinn. 'White mountain'.

Firmounth, Am Monadh Giuthais. 'The pine upland'.

Five Sisters of Kintail, Beanntan Chinn Tàile or Peathraichean Chinn Tàile. The first Gaelic name is simply 'the Kintail mountains', while the second is 'the sisters of Kintail' and may have been influenced by the English name.

Foinaven, Foinne-bheinn. 'Wart mountain'.

Fonab Hill, An Suidhe. The English form takes its name from Fonab nearby. The Gaelic name is 'the seat'.

Fourman Hill, Fuar-mhon or Fuar-mhonadh. 'Cold hill'.

Fraochaidh. 'Heather place'.

Fraoch Bheinn, Fraoch-bheinn. 'Heather mountain'.

Fuar Tholl, Fuar-tholl. 'Cold crevice'.

Gairbeinn, Garbh-bheinn. 'Rough mountain'.

Gairich, Gàirich. 'Howling or roaring'.

Garbhanach, An Garbhanach. 'The rough little one'.

Garbh Bheinn, Garbh-bheinn. 'Rough mountain'.

Garbh Chioch Mhor, Garbh-chìoch Mhór. 'Great rough breast'.

Garelet Hill, Geàrr-leathad. 'Short slope'.

Geal-charn, Geal-chàrn. 'White hill or cairn'.

Geal-charn Mor, Geal-chàrn Mór. 'Large white hill or cairn'.

Gearanach, An Gearanach. This may be 'the moaning one'

Glamaig, Glàmaig. This is said to be 'deep gorge'.

Glas Bheinn, Glas-bheinn. 'Grey-green mountain'.

Glas Bheinn Mhor, Glas-bheinn Mhór. 'Large grey-green mountain'.

Glas-charn, Glas-chàrn. 'Grey-green hill or cairn'.

Glas Maol, Glas-mheall. 'Grey-green lumpish hill'.

Glas Tulaichean, Glas-thulaichean. 'Grey-green low hills'.

Gleouraich, Gleadhraich. The Gaelic name suggests 'great noise'.

Goat Fell, Gaoda-bheinn. This is said to be 'windy mountain', but the first element may be Norse.

Grampians, Am Monadh. The English name comes from a misreading of Latin *Mons Graupius*, while the Gaelic name is 'the mountain range'. East of Drumochter the hills are called *Monadh Miongaig*, 'the Minigaig range', and to the west they are *Monadh Dhruim Uachdair*, 'the Drumochter range'.

Great Knock, An Cnoc Mór. 'The large hill'.

Groban, An Gnoban. 'Little hillock'.

Gulvain, Gaor-bheinn. The meaning of this name is unclear.

Hartaval, Hartabhal. 'Hart hill', from Norse.

Inaccessible Pinnacle, An Stac. The modern English name has largely replaced the Gaelic name meaning 'the stack'.

Kelman Hill, Caol-mhon or Caol-mhonadh. 'Slender hill'.

Knockmore Hill, An Cnoc Mór. 'The large hill'.

Knock of Alves, Cnoc na h-Àbhais. 'The hill of Alves'.

Ladder Hills, Monadh an Fhàraidh. The English name is a translation from Gaelic.

Ladhar Bheinn, Ladhar-bheinn. 'Hoof mountain'.

Ladylea Hill. This may be 'the grey-blue slope', from *An Leathad Liath*.

Largo Law Old forms of the name show this to be from *Cnoc Leargach*, 'the hill of Largo'.

Lamentation Hill, Creag a' Chòin-neachain. The Gaelic name is 'the rock of moss' and the English is a mistranslation, replacing *còinneach*, 'moss', with *caoineadh*, 'lamenting'.

Leana Mhor, An Lèana Mhór. 'The big meadow'.

Leathad an Taobhain. 'Slope of the rib or rafter'.

Leum Uilleim. 'William's leap'.

Liathach, An Liaghaich. This may stem from *liath*, 'grey-blue'.

Lochnagar, Beinn Chìochain. The English name is from the loch in the mountain and is said to be from *Loch na Gàire*, 'loch of the loud noise'. The Gaelic name is 'mountain of the little breast'.

Lomond Hills, Cuspairean Ualais. The English form may be related to the element found in 'Ben Lomond', meaning 'beacon'. The Gaelic name looks as though it means 'Wallace's objects', but *ualais* may be a metathesis of *uasal* and may ultimately be related to 'Ochil'.

Luinne Bheinn, Luinne-bheinn. This may be 'angry or unpredictable mountain'.

Lurg Mhor, An Lurg Mhór. 'The large ridge gradually extending to a plain'.

Mam na Gualainn. 'Gap of the shoulder/ridge'.

Mamore, Am Màm Mór. 'The large gap', referring to a pass.

Mam Sodhail, Màm Sabhail. 'Gap of the barn'.

Mannoch Hill, Cnoc nam Manach. 'Monks' hill'.

Maoile Lunndaidh. 'Bare hill of Lundy', which in turn describes a marshy place.

Maol Chean-dearg, Maol Cheann-dearg. 'Blunt red head'.

Maovally, Maobhalaidh. This name is unclear.

Marsco, Marsgo. This seems to be 'sea wood', from Norse.

Mayar. This name and its origins are obscure.

Meall a' Bhuachaille. 'Lumpish hill of the herdsman'.

Meall a' Bhuiridh, Meall a' Bhùiridh. 'Lumpish hill of the bellowing'.

Meall a' Chaorainn, Meall a' Chaorthainn. 'Lumpish hill of the rowan'.

Meall a' Choire Leith, Meall a' Choire Léith. 'Lumpish hill of the grey-blue corrie'.

Meall a' Chrasgaidh. 'Lumpish hill of the crossing place'.

Meall a' Chrathaich. This appears to be 'lumpish hill of the shaking'.

Meall a' Churain, Meall a' Churrain. 'Lumpish hill of the carrot'.

Meall a' Ghiubhais, Meall a' Ghiuthais. 'Lumpish hill of the fir or pine'.

Meall a' Mhuic, Mealla Mhuice. 'Lumpish hill of the pig river'. *See* **Inverwick** (Perth).

Meall a' Phubuill, Meall a' Phubaill. 'Lumpish hill of the pavilion or tent'.

Meall an Fheur Loch, Meall an Fheur-loch. 'Lumpish hill of the grassy loch'.

Meall an Fhudair, Meall an Fhùdair. 'Lumpish hill of the powder'.

Meall an t-Seallaidh. 'Lumpish hill of the view'.

Meallan a' Chuail. 'Small lumpish hill of the bundle (of sticks)'.

Meallan Liath Coire Mhic Dhughaill, Meallan Liath Coire MhicDhùghaill. 'Grey-blue lumpish hill of MacDougall's corrie'.

Meallan nan Uan. 'Small lumpish hill of the lambs'.

Meall Blair, Meall a' Bhlàir. 'Lumpish hill of the plain'.

Meall Buidhe, Am Meall Buidhe. 'The yellow lumpish hill'

Meall Chuaich. 'Lumpish hill of the hollow'.

Meall Corranaich. It is unclear what the second element of this name means.

Meall Dearg, Am Meall Dearg. 'The red lumpish hill'.

Meall Doire Faid, Meall Doire Fàid. 'Lumpish hill of the furrowed oak grove'.

Meall Dubh, Am Meall Dubh. 'The black lumpish hill'.

Meall Dubhag, Meall Dubhaig. 'The lumpish hill at the black stream'.

Meall Fuarvonie, Meall Fuar-mhonaidh. 'Lumpish hill of the cold range of hills'.

Meall Garbh, Am Meall Garbh. 'The rough lumpish hill'.

Meall Ghaordie, Meall Ghaoirdidh. The second part of this name is unclear.

Meall Glas, Am Meall Glas. 'The grey-green lumpish hill'.

Meall Glas-Choire, Meall Ghlas-choire. 'The lumpish hill at the grey-green corrie'.

Meall Gorm, Am Meall Gorm. 'The blue lumpish hill'.

Meall Greigh, Meall Greighe. 'Lumpish hill of the herd or flock'.

Meall Horn. 'Lumpish hill of the horn', from Gaelic/Norse. A more purely Norse form can be seen in Hornabhal/Horneval in Skye.

Meall Lighiche. 'Lumpish hill of the doctor'.

Meall Mor, Am Meall Mór. 'The large lumpish hill'.

Meall na Faochaig. 'Lumpish hill of the whelk'.

Meall na Fearna, Meall na Feàrna. 'Lumpish hill of the alder'.

Meall na h-Aisre. 'Lumpish hill of the path'.

Meall na h-Eilde, Meall na h-Éilde. 'Lumpish hill of the hind'.

Meall na Leitreach. 'Lumpish hill of the broad slope'.

Meall na Meoig, Meall na Meòig. 'Lumpish hill of the whey'.

Meall nam Maigheach. 'Lumpish hill of the hares'.

Meall nan Aighean. 'Lumpish hill of the stags'.

Meall nan Caorach. 'Lumpish hill of the sheep'.

Meall nan Ceapraichean. 'Lumpish hill of the stumpy hillocks'.

Meall nan Damh. 'Lumpish hill of the stags'.

Meallan nan Eagan. 'Lumpish hill of the notches'.

Meall nan Eun. 'Lumpish hill of the birds'.

Meall nan Gabhar, Meall nan Gobhar. 'Lumpish hill of the goats'.

Meall nan Subh. 'Lumpish hill of the berries'.

Meall Odhar, Am Meall Odhar. 'The dun-coloured lumpish hill'.

Meall Onfhaidh. 'Blustery lumpish hill'.

Meall Reamhar, Am Meall Reamhar. 'The fat lumpish hill'.

Meall nan Tarmachan. 'Lumpish hill of the ptarmigans'.

Meall na Teanga. 'Lumpish hill of the tongue'.

Meall Tairbh. 'Lumpish hill of the bull'.

Meall Tairneachan. This name may be connected with thunder.

Meaul, Am Meall. 'The lumpish hill'.

Meikle Pap, A' Chìoch Mhór. 'The large breast'.

Meith Bheinn, Mèith-bheinn. 'Fat mountain'.

Merrick. This may stem from *meur* (finger), but is unclear.

Millfore. This is probably 'cold lumpish hill', from *Am Meall Fuar*.

Monadh Fergie, Monadh Fheargaidh. 'Hill of the angry river'.

Monadh Mor, Am Monadh Mór. 'The big hill'.

Mona Gowan. 'Stirk hill', from *Mon(adh) a' Ghamhainn*.

Monamenach, Am Monadh Meadha-nach. 'The middle hill'.

Monega, Mon Agha. The second part of this name is unclear.

Mormond Hill, Mór-mhonadh. 'Large hill'.

Morrone, Mór-bheinn. 'Large mountain'.

Moruisg, Mórusg. This name is unclear.

Morven, Mór-bheinn. 'Large mountain'.

Mount Battock. This may be 'hill of

the small tufts of heather', from *Mon Badag*.

Mount Blair. 'Hill of the plain', from *Mon(adh) a' Bhlàir*.

Mount Eagle, Cnoc na h-Iolaire. 'Hill of the eagle'.

Mounth, Am Monadh. 'The mountain range'. This is an alternative name for the Grampians.

Mount Keen, Mon Caoin. 'Gentle hill'.

Mullach an Rathain, Mullach an Ràthain. 'Summit of the small circular fort'.

Mullach Clach a' Bhlair, Mullach Clach a' Bhlàir. 'Summit of the stone of the field or battle'

Mullach Coire Mhic Fhearchair, Mullach Coire MhicFhearchair. 'Summit of Farquharson's corrie'.

Mullach Coire nan Geur-oirean. 'Summit of the corrie of the sharp edges'.

Mullach Fraoch-choire. 'Summit of heather corrie'.

Mullach na Dheiragain, Mullach nan Dearganan. 'Summit of the kestrels'.

Mullach nan Coirean. 'Summit of the corries'.

Mullwharchar. This Gaelic name is obscure although there are several derivations equally probable.

Na Gruagaichean. 'The maidens'.

Ochil Hills, Sliabh Ochaill. 'Ochil' and *Ochaill* are from Brythonic *uchel*, 'high', which is related to *uasal*, 'noble'. *Sliabh* is not commonly used to refer to a hill in Scotland, although this is its common meaning in Ireland.

Old Man of Storr, Bodach an Stòrr. The English form is a translation from Gaelic which itself is a euphemism for *Bod an Stòrr*, 'the penis of Storr'.

Ord Hill, An t-Òrd. 'The rounded hill'.

Oreval, Oireabhal. This may be 'Orri's hill', from Norse.

Ormond Hill, Cnoc Mhoire. The English form may contain *monadh* or its pre-Gaelic equivalent for 'hill'. The Gaelic name is 'St. Mary's hill'.

Pap of Glencoe, Sgùrr na Cìche. In Gaelic this is 'peak of the breast'.

Paps of Jura, Beanntan Dhiùra. These breast-shaped hills are called 'the Jura mountains' in Gaelic.

Parallel Roads, Casan a' Ghlinne or Na Casan. This natural feature is referred to as 'paths of the glen' or 'the paths' in Gaelic.

Pressendye. Although of Gaelic origin, this name is unclear but may derive from *Preas an Taighe*, 'bush of the house'. There may be other more plausible derivations.

Pulpit Hill, Crannag a' Mhinisteir. The Gaelic name is 'the minister's pulpit'.

Quinag, A' Chuinneag. 'The milk pail'.

Quirang, A' Chuith-raing. This name is unclear. This range is known as *A' Bheinne Mhóir*, 'the big mountain' in Wester Ross Gaelic.

Roineaval, Ròineabhal. 'Rough hill', from Norse.

Roshven, Roisbheinn. 'Horse mountain', from Norse/Gaelic.

Ruadh-stac Beag. 'Small red-brown stack'.

Ruadh-stac Mor, Ruadh-stac Mór. 'Large red-brown stack'.

Sabhal Beag, Sàbhal Beag. 'Small saw mountain'.

Saddle, An Dìollaid. The English name is a translation from Gaelic.

Sail Chaorainn, Sàil a' Chaorthainn. 'The rowan heel'.

Saileag, An t-Sàileag. 'The small heel'.

Sail Gharbh, An t-Sàil Gharbh. 'The rough heel'.

Sail Gorm, An t-Sàil Ghorm. 'The blue heel'.

Sail Liath, An t-Sàil Liath. 'The grey-blue heel'.

Sail Mhor, An t-Sàil Mhór. 'The large heel'.

Saval, Sàbhal. 'Saw mountain', from Norse.

Scaraben, Sgaire-bheinn. 'Notched mountain', from Norse/Gaelic.

Schiehallion, Sìth Chailleann. 'Fairy hill of the Caledonians'.

Scour Ouran, Sgùrr Odhrain. 'Odhran's peak'.

Seana Bhraigh, Seana Bhràigh. 'Old upland'.

Sgairneach Mhor, An Sgàirneach Mhór. 'The large hill of loose stones'.

Sgiath a' Chaise. 'Wing of steepness'.

Sgiath Chuil, Sgiath a' Chùil. 'Wing of the back'.

Sgoran Dubh Mor, An Sgòran Dubh Mór. 'The large black pinnacle'.

Sgor an Lochain Uaine, Sgòr an Lochain Uaine. 'The pinnacle at the green lochan', also known as **Angel's Peak**.

Sgor Gaibhre, Sgòr Goibhre. 'Goat pinnacle'.

Sgor Gaoith, Sgòr Gaoithe. 'Windy pinnacle'.

Sgor Iutharn, Sgòr Iuthairn. 'Pinnacle of hell'.

Sgor Mor, An Sgòr Mór. 'The great pinnacle'.

Sgor na h-Ulaidh, Sgòr na h-Ulaidh. 'Pinnacle of the treasure'.

Sgorr a' Choise, Sgòr a' Choise. This may be 'pinnacle of the cavern' or 'steep pinnacle'.

Sgorr Bhan, An Sgòr Bàn. 'The white pinnacle'.

Sgorr Craobh a' Chaorainn, Sgòr Craobh a' Chaorthainn. 'Pinnacle of the rowan tree'.

Sgorr Dhearg, An Sgòr Dearg. 'The red pinnacle'.

Sgorr Dhonuill, Sgòr Dhòmhnaill. 'Donald's pinnacle'.

Sgorr Mhic Eacharna, Sgòr Mhic-Eacharna. 'MacEachern's pinnacle'.

Sgorr na Diollaid, Sgòr na Dìollaid. 'The saddle pinnacle'.

Sgorr nam Fiannaidh, Sgòr nam Fiannaidh. 'Pinnacle of the Fianna warrior band'.

Sgorr nan Lochan Uaine, Sgòr nan Lochan Uaine. 'Pinnacle of the small green lochs'.

Sgor Ruadh, An Sgòr Ruadh. 'The red-brown pinnacle'.

Sguman Coinntich, Sgùman Còinntich. 'Mound or stack of moss'.

Sgurr a' Bhac Chaolais, Sgùrr a' Bhac Chaolais. 'Peak of the hollow at the narrows'.

Sgurr a' Bhealaich Dheirg, Sgùrr a' Bhealaich Dheirg. 'Peak of the red pass'.

Sgurr a' Chaorachain, Sgùrr a' Chaorthachain. This may be 'peak of the rowan-berry place'.

Sgurr a' Chaorainn, Sgùrr a' Chaorthainn. 'Peak of the rowan'.

Sgurr a' Choire-bheithe, Sgùrr a' Choire Bheithe. 'Peak of the birch corrie'.

Sgurr a' Choire Ghlais, Sgùrr a' Choire Ghlais. 'Peak of the grey corrie'.

Sgurr a' Dubh Doire, Sgùrr an Dubh-dhoire. 'Peak of the black oak-grove'.

Sgurr a' Fionn Choire, Sgùrr an Fhionn-choire. 'Peak of the white corrie'.

Sgurr a' Gharaidh, Sgùrr a' Ghàraidh. 'Peak of the dyke'.

Sgurr a' Ghreadaidh, Sgùrr a' Ghreadaidh. This may be 'peak of the tormenting or hardship'.

Sgurr Alasdair, Sgùrr Alasdair. 'Alasdair's peak'. This name commemorates Sheriff Alexander Nicolson, the first man known to have reached the summit. Prior to this, the mountain was known as *An Sgùrr Biorach*, 'the sharp peak'.

Sgurr a' Mhadaidh, Sgùrr a' Mhadaidh. 'Peak of the wolf or fox'.

Sgurr a' Mhaim, Sgùrr a' Mhàim. 'Peak of the gap'.

Sgurr a' Mhaoraich, Sgùrr a' Mhaoraich. 'Peak of the shellfish'.

Sgurr a' Mhuilinn, Sgùrr a' Mhuilinn. 'Peak of the mill'.

Sgurr an Airgid, Sgùrr an Airgid. 'Peak of silver'.

Sgurr an Doire Leathain, Sgùrr an Doire Leathainn. 'Peak of the wide grove'.

Sgurr an Fhidhleir, Sgùrr an Fhìdhleir. 'Peak of the fiddler'.

Sgurr an Fhuarain. *See* **Scour Ouran**.

Sgurr an Lochain, Sgùrr an Lochain. 'Peak of the small loch'.

Sgurr an Utha, Sgùrr an Ùtha. 'Peak of the udder'.

Sgurr Ban, An Sgùrr Bàn 'The fair-coloured peak'.

Sgurr Breac, An Sgùrr Breac. 'The speckled peak'.

Sgurr Choinnich, Sgùrr Choinnich. 'Kenneth's peak'.

Sgurr Choinnich Mor, Sgùrr Choinnich Mór. ' Kenneth's big peak'.

Sgurr Coire Choinnichean, Sgùrr Coire Chòinnichean. 'Peak of the corrie of mosses'

Sgurr Cos na Breachd-laoigh, Sgùrr Còs nam Breac-laogh. 'Peak at the den of the speckled calves'.

Sgurr Dearg, An Sgùrr Dearg. 'The red peak'.

Sgurr Dhomhnuill, Sgùrr Dhòmhnaill. 'Donald's peak'.

Sgurr Dubh, An Sgùrr Dubh. 'The black peak'.

Sgurr Dubh Mor, An Sgùrr Dubh Mór. 'The large black peak'.

Sgurr Eilde Mor, Sgùrr Eilde Mór. 'Great peak of the hind'.

Sgurr Fhuaran. *See* **Scour Ouran**.

Sgurr Fhuar-thuill, Sgùrr Fhuar-thuill. 'Peak of the cold hole'.

Sgurr Fiona, Sgùrr Fìona. 'Wine peak'.

Sgurr Gaorsaic, Sgùrr Ghaorsaig. This name is unclear.

Sgurr Ghiubhsachain, Sgùrr a' Ghiuthsachain. 'Peak at the small pine wood'.

Sgurr Innse, Sgùrr Innse. 'The peak of Inch'.

Sgurr Mhic Bharraich, Sgùrr Mhic-Bharraich. 'MacVarich's peak'.

Sgurr Mhic Choinnich, Sgùrr Mhic-Choinnich. 'MacKenzie's peak'.

Sgurr Mhor, An Sgùrr Mór. 'The large peak'.

Sgurr Mhurlagain, Sgùrr Mhùrlagain or Sgùrr Mhùrbhlagain. 'The peak of Murlaggan'.

Sgurr Mor, An Sgùrr Mór. 'The large peak'.

Sgurr na Ba Glaise, Sgùrr na Bà Glaise. 'Peak of the grey cow'.

Sgurr na Banachdich, Sgùrr na Banachdaich. 'The milkmaid's peak'.

Sgurr na Carnach, Sgùrr na Càrnaich. 'Peak of the rocky place'.

Sgurr na Ciste Duibhe, Sgùrr na Ciste Duibhe. 'Peak of the black chest'.

Sgurr na Coinnich, Sgùrr na Còinnich. 'Peak of the moss'.

Sgurr na Fearstaig, Sgùrr na Feartaig. 'Sea-pink peak'.

Sgurr na Ciche, Sgùrr na Cìche. 'Peak of the breast'.

Sgurr na Lapaich, Sgùrr na Làpaich. 'Peak of the bog'.

Sgurr nan Ceannaichean, Sgùrr nan Ceannaichean. 'Peak of the merchants'.

Sgurr nan Ceathreamhnan, Sgùrr nan Ceathramhnan. 'Peak of the quarters'.

Sgurr nan Clach Geala, Sgùrr nan Clach Geala. 'Peak of the white stones'.

Sgurr nan Cnamh, Sgùrr nan Cnàmh. 'Peak of the bones'.

Sgurr nan Coireachan, Sgùrr nan Coireachan. 'Peak of the corries'.

Sgurr nan Conbhairean, Sgùrr nan Conbhairean. 'Peak at the confluences'.

Sgurr nan Each, Sgùrr nan Each. 'Peak of the horses'.

Sgurr nan Eag, Sgùrr nan Eag. 'Peak of the notches'.

Sgurr nan Eugallt, Sgùrr nan Eugallt. This is said to be either 'peak of the deathly streams' or 'peak of the precipices'.

Sgurr nan Fhir Duibhe, Sgùrr an Fhir

Dhuibh. 'The black(-haired) man's peak'.

Sgurr nan Gillean, Sgùrr nan Gillean. 'Peak of the lads'.

Sgurr na Ruaidhe, Sgùrr na Ruaidhe. 'Peak of red-brown-ness'.

Sgurr na Sgine, Sgùrr na Sgine. 'Peak of the knife'.

Sgurr Ruadh, An Sgùrr Ruadh. 'The red-brown peak'.

Sgurr Thuilm, Sgùrr Thuilm. 'Peak of Holm'.

Shalloch on Minnoch. This may be 'middle willow place', from *Seileachan Meadhanach*.

Sheaval, Seubhal. 'Sea hill'.

Shee of Ardtalnaig, Sìth Àird Talanaig. 'Fairy hill of Ardtalnaig'.

Slat Bheinn, Slat-bheinn. 'Rod mountain'.

Slioch, Sleaghach. 'Spear-like mountain'.

Sow of Atholl, An Socach. 'The sow'. Nearby is the **Boar of Badenoch**.

Spidean a' Choire Leith, Spidean a' Choire Léith. 'Pinnacle of the grey-blue corrie'.

Spidean Coinich, Spidean Còinnich. 'Mossy pinnacle'.

Spidean Coire nan Clach. 'Pinnacle of the stony corrie'.

Spidean Mealach, An Spidean Mialach. 'The lousy pinnacle'.

Sron a' Choire Chnapanich, Sròn a' Choire Chnapanaich. 'Nose of the hillocky corrie'.

Sron a' Choire Ghairbh, Sròn a' Choire Ghairbh. 'Nose of the rough corrie'.

Sron Garbh, An t-Sròn Gharbh. 'The rough nose-shaped hill'.

Sron nan Giubhas, Sròn nan Giuthas. 'Nose-shaped hill of the pine trees'.

Sron Riach, An t-Sròn Riabhach. 'The brindled nose-shaped hill'.

Stack Polly, Stac Pollaidh. 'Stack at the pool river'.

Stob, The, An Stob. 'The stump'.

Stob a' Bhruaich Leith, Stob a'

Bhruthaich Léith. 'Stump of the grey-blue slope'.

Stob a' Choin. 'Stump of the dog'.

Stob a' Choire Mheadhoin, Stob a' Choire Mheadhain. 'Stump of the middle corrie'.

Stob a' Choire Odhair. 'Stump of the dun-coloured corrie'.

Stob an Aonaich Mhoir, Stob an Aonaich Mhóir. 'The stump of Aonach Mór'.

Stob an Cul Choire, Stob a' Chùl-choire. 'Stump of the back corrie'.

Stob Ban, An Stob Bàn. 'The fair-coloured stump'.

Stob Choire Claurigh, Stob Choire Clamhraidh. 'Stump of the bellowing corrie'.

Stob Coir' an Albannaich, Stob Coire an Albannaich. 'Stump of the Scotsman's corrie'.

Stob Coire a' Chairn, Stob Coire a' Chàirn. 'Stump of the corrie of the cairn'.

Stob Coire a' Chearcaill. 'Stump of the corrie of the circle'.

Stob Coire an Laoigh. 'Stump of the corrie of the calf'.

Stob Coire Creagach, Stob a' Choire Chreagaich. 'Stump of the rocky corrie'.

Stob Coire Dheirg, Stob a' Choire Dheirg. 'Stump at the red corrie'.

Stob Coire Dubh, Stob a' Choire Dhuibh. 'Stump at the black corrie'.

Stob Coire Easain. 'Stump of waterfall corrie'.

Stob Coire Etchachan, Stob Coire Éiteachain. 'Stump at the corrie of the foul one'. *See* **Carn Etchachan**.

Stob Coire Leith, Stob a' Choire Léith. 'Stump at the grey-blue corrie'.

Stob Corrie Lochan, Stob Coire an Lochain. 'Stump at the corrie by the small loch'.

Stob Coire na Gaibhre, Stob Coire na Goibhre. 'Stump at the goat's corrie'.

Stob Coire nam Beith, Stob Coire

nam Beithe. 'Stump at the corrie of the birches'.

Stob Coire Raineach. 'Stump of the corrie of Rannoch'.

Stob Coire Sgreamhach, Stob a' Choire Sgreamhaich. 'Stump of the dreadful corrie'.

Stob Coire Sgriodain, Stob Coire Sgriodain. 'Stump of the corrie of Sgridain', a name referring to scree.

Stob Daimh. 'Stump of the stag'.

Stob Dearg, An Stob Dearg. 'The red stump'.

Stob Dubh, An Stob Dubh. 'The black stump'.

Stob Ghabhar, Stob Ghobhar. 'Goats' stump'.

Stobinian, Stob Binnein. 'Pinnacle stump'.

Stob na Broige, Stob na Bròige. 'Stump of the shoe'.

Stob na Cruaiche. 'Stump of the conical hill'.

Stob Poite Coire Ardair, Stob Poite Coire Àrdair. 'Stump of the pot of corrie of the high river'.

Storr, The, An Stòrr. 'The great one', from Norse.

Streap, An Streap. 'The climbing'.

Stuc a' Chroin, Stùc a' Chròthain. 'Stump of the small sheep fold'.

Stuc Beag, An Stùc Beag. 'The small hill'.

Stuchd an Lochain, Stùc an Lochain. 'Hill by the small loch'.

Stuc Mor, An Stùc Mór. 'The large hill'.

Suilven, Sula-bheinn. 'Pillar mountain', from Norse/Gaelic.

Teilesval, Teileasabhal. 'Cave hill', from Norse.

Tigh Mor na Seilge, Taigh Mór na Seilge. 'The large hunting house'.

Tinto. This name may be Gaelic or Brythonic and related to Gaelic *teine* or Brythonic *tân*, 'fire'. A possible source is Gaelic *teinnteach*, 'fiery, hot, fierce'.

Tirga Mor, Tiorga Mór. 'Great Tiorga'. It is unclear what the derivation of *Tiorga/Tirga* is.

Toll Creagach, An Toll Creagach. 'The rocky hole'.

Tolmount, An Tulmon. 'Naked hill' or 'brow hill'.

Tom a' Choinich, Tom a' Chòinnich. 'Mossy knoll'.

Toman Coinich, Toman Còinnich. 'Mossy hillock'.

Tom Buidhe, An Tom Buidhe. 'The yellow knoll'.

Tom Dubh, An Tom Dubh. 'The black knoll'.

Tom Meadhoin, Tom Meadhain. 'Middle knoll'.

Tom na Gruagaich. 'Knock of the maiden'.

Trallaval, Trallabhal or Trollabhal. 'Troll hill', from Norse.

Traprain Law, Dùn Peilleir. The English form has English *hláw*, 'hill' attached to a settlement name of Brythonic origin. The Gaelic form is from Brythonic 'fort of the spear shafts'.

Trossachs, Na Tròisichean or Na Tròsaichean. 'The crossing place hills'.

Trostan Hill, Cnoc Trostain. 'St Drostan's hill', the name of a Pictish saint.

Tullich Hill, An Tulach. 'The green hill'.

Uamh Bheag, An Uamh Bheag. 'The small cave'.

Uisgnaval Mor, Uisgneabhal Mór. This may be 'ox hill', from Norse.

White Mounth, Am Monadh Geal. 'The white hill or range of hills'.

Comhairlean

Councils

Aberdeen City Cathair Obar Dheathain; Baile Mór Obar Dheathain
Aberdeenshire Siorrachd Obar Dheathain
Angus Siorrachd Aonghais
Argyll and Bute Earra-Ghàidheal agus Bòid
City of Edinburgh Cathair Dhùn Éideann; Baile Mór Dhùn Éideann
City of Glasgow Cathair Ghlaschu; Baile Mór Ghlaschu
Clackmannan Clach Mhanainn
Dumfries and Galloway Dùn Phris agus Gall-ghàidheil
Dundee City Cathair Dhùn Deagh; Baile Mór Dhùn Deagh
East Ayrshire Siorrachd Inbhir Àir an Ear
East Dunbartonshire Siorrachd Dhùn Breatann an Ear
East Lothian Labhdaidh an Ear; Lodainn an Ear
East Renfrewshire Siorrachd Rinn Friù an Ear
Falkirk An Eaglais Bhreac
Fife Fìobh
Highland A' Ghàidhealtachd

Inverclyde Inbhir Chluaidh
Inverness City Cathair Inbhir Nis; Baile Mór Inbhir Nis
Midlothian Meadhan Labhdaidh; Meadhan Lodainn
Moray Moireibh
North Ayrshire Siorrachd Inbhir Àir a Tuath
North Lanarkshire Siorrachd Lannraig a Tuath
Orkney Islands Arcaibh
Perth and Kinross Peairt agus Cinn Rois
Renfrewshire Siorrachd Rinn Friù
Scottish Borders Criochan na h-Alba; Na Crìochan
Shetland Islands Sealtainn
South Ayrshire Siorrachd Inbhir Àir a Deas
South Lanarkshire Siorrachd Lannraig a Deas
Stirling Sruighlea
West Dunbartonshire Siorrachd Dhùn Breatann an Iar
Western Isles Na h-Eileanan Siar
West Lothian Labhdaidh an Iar; Lodainn an Iar

Maps

The maps on the following pages show the distribution of tribes, language groups and place-name elements according to the list below.

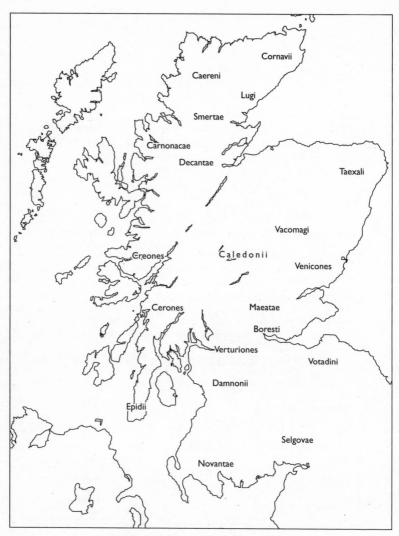

Map 1: Tribes known to the Romans

Map 1 shows the approximate locations of the tribes of *Albania*, as this country was known to the Romans.

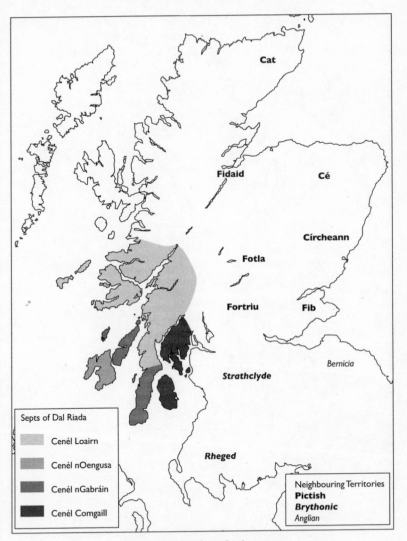

Map 2: Dal Riada and other areas

Map 2 shows the location of the different linguistic groupings in relation to the Scots of Dal Riada before the Scots had begun to expand into Pictish territory. Dal Riada itself was divided into the groups shown on the map on the basis of dynastic succession.

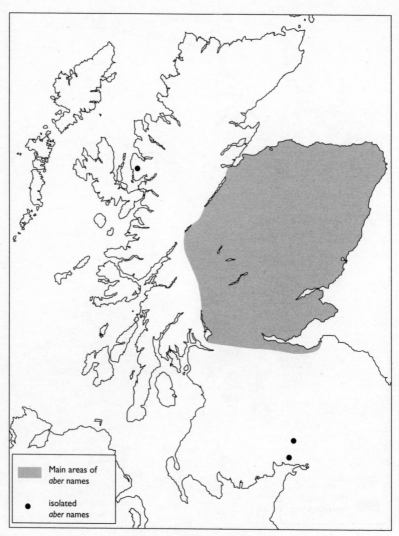

Map 3: Distribution of *aber*

Map 3 shows the area in which Pictish/Brythonic *aber*, 'river mouth', is widely found as a place-name element in names such as Aberlady and Obar Dheathain, together with isolated instances in Applecross and Dumfries-shire.

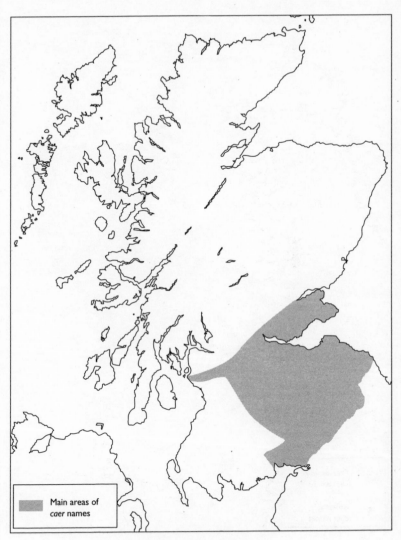

Map 4: Distribution of *caer*

Map 4 shows the area over which Brythonic *caer*, 'fort', is commonly found as a place-name element in such names as Caerlaverock and Carfrae.

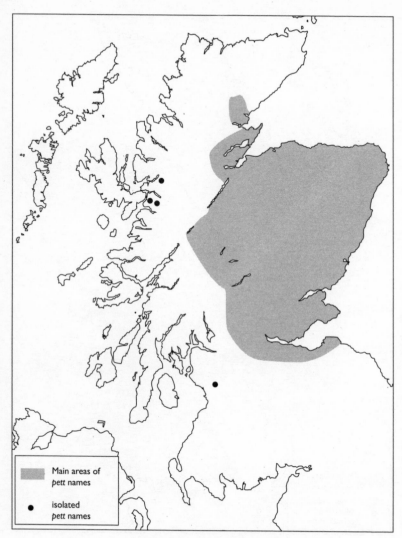

Map 5: Distribution of *pett*

Map 5 shows the distribution area of Pictish *pett* together with isolated examples. This generally becomes 'Pit-' as in Pitlochry and Pittenweem, but remains as 'Pet-' in Petty and is disguised as *Baile* in names in Gaelic such as Baile Chloichrigh where the English form retains the original *pett*.

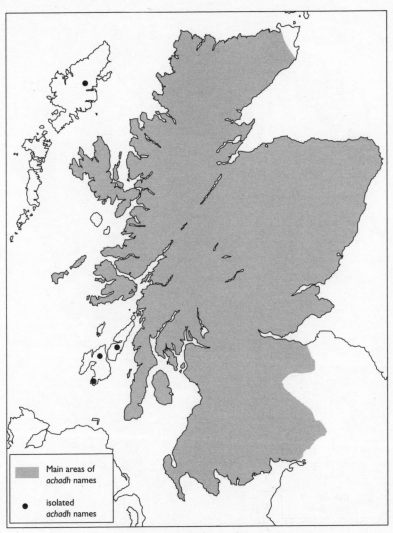

Map 6: Distribution of *achadh*

Map 6 illustrates the area in which Gaelic *achadh*, 'field', is commonly found as an element in place-names such as Achnasheen and Auchenrivock.

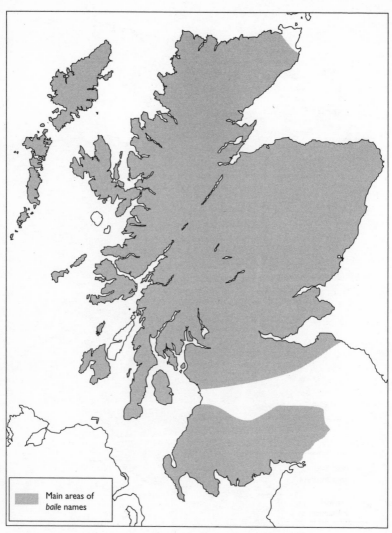

Map 7: Distribution of *baile*

Map 7 shows where the Scots were long enough settled to have begun farms and named them. This map shows that these names are not as widely distributed as the *achadh* field names on Map 6.

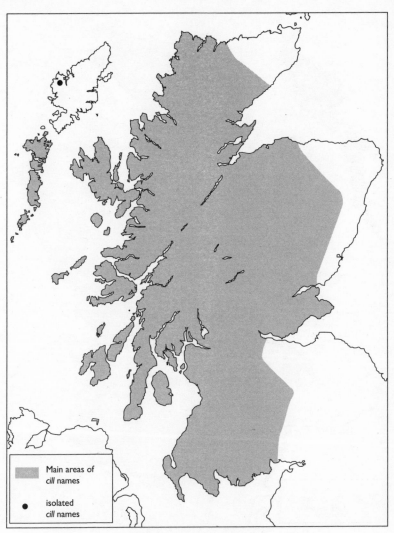

Map 8: Distribution of *cill*

Map 8 shows the area over which Gaelic *cill*, 'cell, church', is found as an element in place-names such as Kilmarnock and Kilbrare. Whilst most *cill* names are followed by the name of a holy person or saint, several are descriptive, such as *Cill Duinn* or Kildun, 'brown church'.

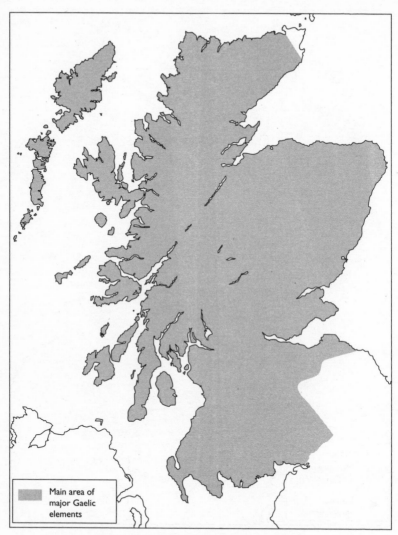

Map 9: Distribution of *achadh*, *baile* and *cill*

The combined distribution of the Gaelic elements, *achadh*, *baile* and *cill*, as shown on Map 9 give an indication of the maximum extent of the Gaelic speaking areas of the country. Although place-names in the unshaded south-eastern area contain personal names of a Gaelic origin, it is probable that Gaelic speakers formed only the upper strata of a society, the majority and lower ranks of which would have spoken English.

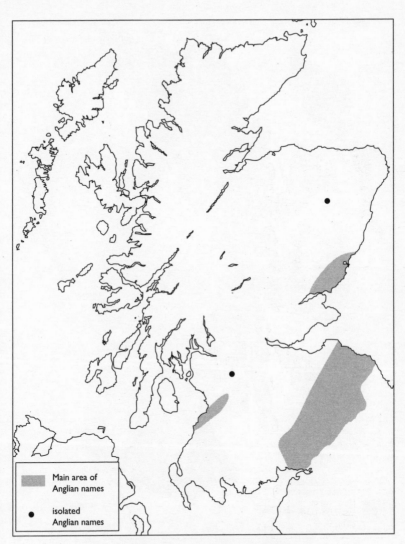

Map 10: Distribution of Oldest Anglian Names

Map 10 shows the areas containing the oldest Anglian names, those including elements such as *wíc* (village), *hám* (farm), *bótl* (house), *tún* (farm) and *-ing-* (people) which indicate human habitation.

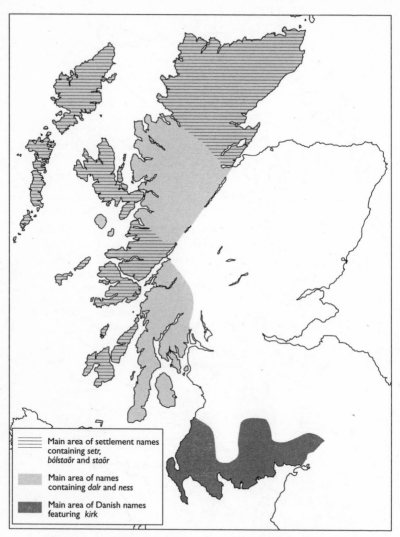

Map 11: Distribution of selected Norse names (including Danish)

Map 11 shows the extent of Norse and Danish penetration of Scotland, although only the area indicated by vertical lines features Norse settlement elements.

Map 12: Areas of Scotland (in English)

Map 13: Sgìrean na h-Alba (sa Ghàidhlig)

Bibliography

Alexander, W M. (1952) *Place-Names of Aberdeenshire*. Aberdeen:
Third Spalding Club

An tSuirbhéireacht Ordanáis. (1989) *Gasaitéar na hÉireann*. Dublin:
Rialtas na hÉireann

Atkinson, T. (1997) *South West Scotland*. Edinburgh: Luath Press

Black, G F. (1993) *Surnames of Scotland*. Edinburgh: Birlinn

Brownlie, N M. (1995) *Bailtean is Ath-Ghairmean a Tiriodh*.
Glendaruel:Argyll Publishing

Cox, R A V. (2002) *Place-names of Carloway, Isle of Lewis*. Dublin:
Dublin Institute for Advanced Studies

Diack, F. (1944) *The Inscriptions of Pictland*. Aberdeen: Third Spalding
Club

Dwelly, E. (1973) *Illustrated Gaelic - English Dictionary*. Glasgow:
Gairm

Ellice, E C. (1999) *Place Names of Glengarry and Glenquoich*. Exeter:
Ashley House Printing

Ferguson, J. (1985) *The Placenames of Berneray*. Inverness: Gaelic
Society of Inverness

Ferguson, K & Perrons, M. (1990) *Placenames of Islay*. Islay: Islay
Museums Trust

Flanagan, D & Flanagan, L. (1994) *Irish Place Names*. Dublin: Gill
and MacMillan

Forbes, A R. (1923) *Place-names of Skye*. Paisley: A. Gardner

Fraser, I. (1988) *The Placenames of Argyll*. Inverness: Gaelic Society of
Inverness

Fraser, I. (undated) *The Settlement Names of Gairloch Parish*. Gairloch:
Ross and Cromarty Heritage Society

Fraser, I. (1999) *The Place-names of Arran*. Glasgow: Arran Society of
Glasgow

Gillies, W. (1989) *Gaelic and Scotland/Alba agus a' Ghàidhlig*.
Edinburgh: Edinburgh University Press

Holmer, N. (1942) *The Irish Language in Rathlin Island, Co. Antrim*. Dublin: Royal Irish Academy

Holmer, N. (1957) *The Gaelic of Arran*. Dublin: Dublin Institute for Advanced Studies

Holmer, N. (1962) *The Gaelic of Kintyre*. Dublin: Dublin Institute for Advanced Studies

Johnston, J B. (1987) *Place-Names of Stirling District*. Stirling: Stirling District Libraries

Kerr, J. (1981) *Old Roads to Strathardle*. Kettering: John Kerr

McArthur, C. (undated) *The Placenames of Jura*. Jura: s.n.

MacBain, A. (1922) *Place Names, Highlands and Islands*. Stirling: Eneas MacKay

McCaffray, C. (1992) *Greens Guide to Sheriff Court Districts*. Edinburgh: W Green

MacDhòmhnaill, M M. (1997) *Ainmean Àite Sgìr' a' Bhac, Eilean Leòdhais*. Back: M M MacDhòmhnaill

MacDonald, A. (1941) *The Placenames of West Lothian*. Edinburgh: Oliver and Boyd

MacDonald, J. (undated) *The Place Names of Skye*. Duntulm: J MacDonald

MacDonald, M. (1985) *Fort William and Nether Lochaber*. Oban: West Highland Publications

MacKillop, D. (undated) *Sea Names of Berneray*. Inverness: Gaelic Society of Inverness

MacKinnon, L. (1973) *Placenames of Lochaber*. Fort William: Saltire Society

MacLean, R. (2004) *The Gaelic Place Names and Heritage of Inverness*. Inverness: Culcabock Publishing

MacLennan, J. (2001) *Place-names of Scarp*. s.n.

MacLeod, F. (1989) *Togail Tìr*. Stornoway: Acair

MacNeill, P & Nicholson, R. (1975) *Historical Atlas of Scotland c.400-c.1600*. St Andrews: Conference of Scottish Mediaevalists

McNeir, C L (ed.) (2001) *Faclair na Pàrlamaid, Dictionary of Terms*. Edinburgh: Scottish Parliament

Maxwell, H. (1894) *Scottish Land-names*. Edinburgh: William Blackwood and Sons

Maxwell, H. (1930) *The Place-names of Galloway*. Glasgow: Jackson, Wylie and Co.

Morgan, P. (1999) *Ainmean Àite Rùim, The Place-Names of Rùm.*
Rum: Dualchas Nàdair na h-Alba

Newton, M. (2010). *Bho Chluaidh gu Calasraid/From the Clyde to Callander.* Glasgow: The Grimsay Press

NicIain, C M. (1999) *Ainmean-Àiteachan Sgìre Sholais.* An Ceathramh Meadhanach: C M NicIain

Nicolaisen, W F H. (1986) *Scottish Placenames.* London: Batsford

Oftedal, M. (1954) 'The Village Names of Lewis'. Norsk Tidskift for Sprogvidenskap

Oileanaich Colaiste Inbhir Nis, (2004) *Roghainn an Raoin Rèidh.* Inverness: Inverness College

Ó Murchú, M. (1989) *East Perthshire Gaelic.* Dublin: Dublin Institute for Advanced Studies

Redford, M. (1988) 'Commemorations of Saints of the Celtic Church in Scotland' (unpublished MLitt Thesis). University of Edinburgh

Room, A. (1988) *Dictionary of Irish Placenames.* Belfast: Appletree Press

Scottish Qualifications Authority. (2009) *Gaelic Orthographic Conventions.* Glasgow: SQA

Skene, W F. (1887) *Celtic Scotland.* Edinburgh: David Douglas

Taylor, S. (1998) *The Uses of Place-Names.* Edinburgh: Scottish Cultural Press

Taylor, S. with Márkus, G. (2006-2008) *The Place-names of Fife, Volumes One - Three.* Donington: Shaun Tyas

Watson, A. & Allan, E. (1984) *Placenames of Upper Deeside.* Aberdeen: Aberdeen University Press

Watson, A & Clement, D. (1983) *Aberdeenshire Gaelic.* Inverness: Gaelic Society of Inverness

Watson, S. (ed.) (2007) *Saoghal Bana-mharaiche.* Ceann Drochaid: Clann Tuirc

Watson, W J. (1993) *The History of the Celtic Placenames of Scotland.* Dublin: Irish Academic Press

Watson, W J. (1976) *The Placenames of Ross and Cromarty.* Dingwall: Ross and Cromarty Heritage Society

Watson, W J. (2002) *Scottish Place-name Papers.* London: Steve Savage

Wentworth, R. (2006) *Gaelic Words and Phrases from Wester Ross.* Daviot: Clàr

In addition to the above, the publications of the Scottish Gaelic Texts Society, of local Comainn Eachdraidh, the newsletter of the Scottish Place-Name Society and the periodicals below contain much valuable information and sources on place-names.

Celtic Review
Celtic Studies
Cothrom
Gairm
Gath
Journal of Scottish Name Studies
Norsk Tidskrift for Sprogvidenskap
Revue Celtique
Scottish Gaelic Studies
Scottish History Society
Scottish Studies
Tocher
Transactions of the Gaelic Society of Inverness

The following websites are a valuable source of information:

Scottish Place-Name Society - www.spns.org.uk
Ainmean Àite na h-Alba - www.gaelicnames.org